The Spanish and the Portuguese Present Perfect in Discourse

Linguistik Aktuell/Linguistics Today (LA)
ISSN 0166-0829

Linguistik Aktuell/Linguistics Today (LA) provides a platform for original monograph studies into synchronic and diachronic linguistics. Studies in LA confront empirical and theoretical problems as these are currently discussed in syntax, semantics, morphology, phonology, and systematic pragmatics with the aim to establish robust empirical generalizations within a universalistic perspective.

For an overview of all books published in this series, please see
benjamins.com/catalog/la

General Editor
Elly van Gelderen
Arizona State University

Founding Editor
Werner Abraham
University of Vienna / University of Munich

Advisory Editorial Board

Josef Bayer
University of Konstanz

Cedric Boeckx
ICREA/UB

Guglielmo Cinque
University of Venice

Amy Rose Deal
University of California, Berkeley

Susann Fischer
University of Hamburg

Liliane Haegeman
Ghent University

Heejeong Ko
Seoul National University

Terje Lohndal
Norwegian University of Science and Technology

Will Oxford
University of Manitoba

Ian Roberts
Cambridge University

Florian Schäfer
Humboldt University

Carola Trips
University of Mannheim

C. Jan-Wouter Zwart
University of Groningen

Volume 279

The Spanish and the Portuguese Present Perfect in Discourse
by Lukas Müller

The Spanish and the Portuguese Present Perfect in Discourse

Lukas Müller
University of Cologne

John Benjamins Publishing Company
Amsterdam / Philadelphia

The paper used in this publication meets the minimum requirements of the American National Standard for Information Sciences – Permanence of Paper for Printed Library Materials, ANSI z39.48-1984.

DOI 10.1075/la.279

Cataloging-in-Publication Data available from Library of Congress:
LCCN 2022053188

ISBN 978 90 272 1314 3 (HB)
ISBN 978 90 272 5448 1 (E-BOOK)

© 2023 – John Benjamins B.V.
No part of this book may be reproduced in any form, by print, photoprint, microfilm, or any other means, without written permission from the publisher.

John Benjamins Publishing Company · https://benjamins.com

*A linguagem fez-se para que nos sirvamos dela,
não para que a sirvamos a ela.*
(Fernando Pessoa)

Table of contents

List of figures	XI
List of tables	XIII
List of abbreviations	XV
Acknowledgements	XVII

CHAPTER 1
Introduction 1
1.1 A cross-linguistic perspective on the PPC$_{PT}$ and the PPC$_{SP}$ 2
1.2 The discursive approach 5
1.3 Goals of the study 8
1.4 Overview of the chapters 10

CHAPTER 2
Fundamentals 13
2.1 Tense 14
   2.1.1 The ingredients of tense 14
   2.1.2 Quantificational vs. referential tense 23
2.2 Aspect 30
   2.2.1 Situation aspect 30
   2.2.2 Viewpoint aspect 33
2.3 Adverbials 35
2.4 Tense and aspect in discourse 40
   2.4.1 The macro-structure: Modes of discourse 41
   2.4.2 The micro-structure: Syntagmatic relations 45
2.5 The Present Perfect as a cross-linguistic category 52
   2.5.1 Diachrony and grammaticalization 52
   2.5.2 Synchrony 59
2.6 Conclusion 67

CHAPTER 3
The Portuguese *Pretérito Perfeito Composto* 69
3.1 General meaning and meaning effects 70
3.2 A note on diatopic variation 77

3.3   Quantificational readings   79
    3.3.1   I<small>PEX</small> readings   79
    3.3.2   Universal reading   83
    3.3.3   Characterizing readings   89
    3.3.4   Overview   93
3.4   Adverbials   96
3.5   Discourse   99
    3.5.1   PPC$_{PT}$ + PPC$_{PT}$ 99
    3.5.2   PPC$_{PT}$ + *Pretérito Perfeito Simples*   101
    3.5.3   PPC$_{PT}$ + Present Tense   103
    3.5.4   The macro-structure of discourse   105
3.6   Conclusion   107

CHAPTER 4
The Spanish *Pretérito Perfecto Compuesto*   111
4.1   General meaning and meaning effects   112
4.2   A note on diatopic variation   116
4.3   Quantificational readings   119
    4.3.1   Experiential reading   120
    4.3.2   Resultative reading   122
    4.3.3   Hot news reading   126
    4.3.4   Universal reading   127
    4.3.5   Overview   130
4.4   Is there a referential reading?   131
4.5   Adverbials   136
4.6   Discourse   139
    4.6.1   PPC$_{SP}$ + PPC$_{SP}$ 142
    4.6.2   PPC$_{SP}$ + *Indefinido*   144
    4.6.3   PPC$_{SP}$ + *Pluscuamperfecto/Imperfecto*   149
    4.6.4   The macro-structure of discourse   152
4.7   Conclusion   154

CHAPTER 5
Corpus study   157
5.1   Introduction   158
    5.1.1   Composition of the corpus   158
    5.1.2   Analysis of the data   163
    5.1.3   Overall frequencies   164

5.2 Adverbials   167
    5.2.1 Expectations   167
    5.2.2 Portuguese   167
    5.2.3 Spanish   169
    5.2.4 Discussion   175
5.3 The micro-structure of discourse   176
    5.3.1 Expectations   177
    5.3.2 Portuguese   178
    5.3.3 Spanish   189
    5.3.4 Discussion   198
5.4 Conclusion   203

CHAPTER 6
The PPC$_{SP}$'s referential drift   209
6.1 The PPC$_{SP}$ between quantification and reference   210
6.2 The attached *Imperfecto* as a test case for the PPC$_{SP}$'s cataphoric potential   217
6.3 Prominence and the PPC$_{SP}$ 219
    6.3.1 General remarks on prominence in discourse   219
    6.3.2 Prominent event domain vs. prominent post-state domain   220
6.4 Experiment: Acceptability judgements of PPC$_{SP}$ + *Imperfecto*   224
    6.4.1 Methodology   226
    6.4.2 Statistical analysis and results   232
    6.4.3 Discussion   238
6.5 Conclusion   245

CHAPTER 7
Conclusions   249
7.1 PPC$_{PT}$ and PPC$_{SP}$ as quantificational tense forms   250
7.2 Similarities and differences on the level of discourse   253
7.3 Outlook   256

Bibliography   259

List of items included in the experiment   271

Index   275

List of figures

Figure 2.1	Reichenbach's (1947) entries for tense (Mani et al. 2005: 72)	15
Figure 2.2	Time-spheres and zones (Declerck et al. 2006: 149)	19
Figure 2.3	Cognitive worlds with three perspectives on time (Botne and Kershner 2008: 153)	19
Figure 2.4	The 4 pillars of tense	22
Figure 2.5	Perfective vs. imperfective aspect (Gvozdanović 2012: 789)	34
Figure 2.6	Time-spheres and zones (Declerck et al. 2006: 149)	39
Figure 2.7	DRT box (Kamp et al. 2011: 204)	47
Figure 2.8	The pushing account of t_R (Becker and Egetenmeyer 2018: 34)	48
Figure 2.9	The pulling account of t_R (Becker and Egetenmeyer 2018: 34)	48
Figure 2.10	Stage II-Present Perfect	55
Figure 2.11	Aoristic drift of the Romance CP (Bertinetto and Squartini 2000: 422)	59
Figure 2.12	The PP as a quantificational tense form	62
Figure 2.13	Cognitive worlds with three perspectives on time (Botne and Kershner 2008: 153)	66
Figure 3.1	An XN analysis of (4) (Becker 2020a: 5)	73
Figure 3.2	PPC_{PT} allowing for event-internal definite quantification	81
Figure 3.3	PPC_{PT} impeding event-external definite quantification	81
Figure 3.4	*Duratividade absoluta* vs. *duratividade intermitente* (Ilari 2001: 144)	83
Figure 3.5	The quantificational readings of the PPC_{PT}	93
Figure 3.6	The episodic vs. characterizing readings of the PPC_{PT}	94
Figure 4.1	The PPC_{SP} as a purely quantificational tense form (preliminary)	114
Figure 4.2	Functional load of the PPC_{SP} according to diatopic variation (Azpiazu Torres 2019: 204)	117
Figure 4.3	Simplified syntactic structures of PPC_{SP-RES} and resultative construction	124
Figure 4.4	Updated typology of the PPC_{SP}'s readings	136
Figure 4.5	Perspectival shift in Example (34a)	148
Figure 4.6	Perspectival bridging in Example (35b)	149
Figure 4.7	Perspectival clash in Example (36)	150

Figure 5.1	Distribution of verbs: PPC$_{PT}$ vs. general	164
Figure 5.2	Distribution of verbs: PPC$_{SP}$ vs. general	165
Figure 5.3	Tempo-aspectual adverbials combined with PPC$_{PT}$: Yes vs. no	168
Figure 5.4	Types of adverbials combined with PPC$_{PT}$	169
Figure 5.5	Lexical types of adverbials combined with PPC$_{PT}$	170
Figure 5.6	Tempo-aspectual adverbials combined with PPC$_{SP}$: Yes vs. no	171
Figure 5.7	Typs of adverbials combined with PPC$_{SP}$	171
Figure 5.8	Lexical types of adverbials combined with PPC$_{SP}$	172
Figure 5.9	Micro-structural discursive factors complementing truth conditions in tense form choice	203
Figure 5.10	Discourse functions of PPC$_{PT}$ and PPC$_{SP}$	205
Figure 5.11	Grammaticalization path of the PPC$_{PT}$ and PPC$_{SP}$ as suggested by our analysis	206
Figure 6.1	Cognitive worlds with three perspectives on time (Botne and Kershner 2008: 153)	216
Figure 6.2	The PPC$_{SP}$ feat. prominent post-state domain vs. prominent event domain	221
Figure 6.3	Prominence and the access to the PPC$_{SP}$'s event domain	223
Figure 6.4	Map of Spain	233
Figure 6.5	Participants' answers to "My dialect belongs to …"	233
Figure 6.6	Acceptability scores per condition	235
Figure 6.7	Remoteness per tense	236
Figure 6.8	Acceptability scores per region	241
Figure 6.9	Group A vs. Group B	243
Figure 6.10	Acceptability scores per age	244
Figure 7.1	Integrating the account into the stage model	252
Figure 7.2	Micro-structural discourse functions and the stage model	256

List of tables

Table 2.1	Quantificational vs. Referential Tense	29
Table 2.2	Terminology in aspect theory	30
Table 2.3	Binary classification of the lexical classes (inspired by Filip 2012: 727)	31
Table 2.4	Tempo-aspectual adverbials	40
Table 2.5	The identifiability critieria for definiteness and specificity (von Heusinger 2002: 249)	50
Table 2.6	Cross-classification of definiteness and specificity (von Heusinger 2002: 253)	50
Table 2.7	Diachronic path of the PP (Bertinetto and Squartini 2000: 406, inspired by Harris 1982)	53
Table 2.8	The PP readings forming an implicational scale	59
Table 2.9	Tempo-aspectual adverbials combined with the quantificational PP	66
Table 3.1	Tempo-aspectual adverbials and the PPC_{PT}	98
Table 4.1	*tener* vs. *haber* (inpired by Detges 2000: 349)	125
Table 4.2	Tempo-aspectual adverbials and the PPC_{SP}	139
Table 4.3	Temporal relations between PPC_{SP} and Indefinido according to Moreno-Torres Sánchez (1999: 245)	141
Table 5.1	The Peninsular Spanish Corpus	159
Table 5.2	Poor PPC_{PT} frequencies in Brazilian series/movies	161
Table 5.3	The Brazilian Portuguese Corpus	162
Table 5.4	Expected discourse functions for PPC_{PT} and PPC_{SP}	178
Table 6.1	The grammaticalization path of the PPC_{SP} in Alicante Spanish from anterior to perfective (Schwenter 1994a: 99)	213
Table 6.2	The PPC_{SP} between quantification and reference	216
Table 6.3	A discursive approach to the PPC_{SP}'s referential drift	224
Table 6.4	The PPC_{SP}'s values in Peninsular Spanish according to Azpiazu Torres (2019: 204)	231
Table 6.5	12/65 participants with non-uniform diatopic background	234
Table 6.6	Linear mixed effect model for the main effect of tense	235
Table 6.7	Pairwise testing of tense interacting with remoteness	236
Table 6.8	Contrasts between the PPC_{SP} scores across the three major dialectal groups	237

List of abbreviations

CR	Current Relevance
BP	Brazilian Portuguese
EP	European Portuguese
GEN	Generic quantifier
IPEX	Indefinite pluractional existential
PP	Present Perfect
PPC_{SP}	Pretérito Perfecto Compuesto
PPC_{PT}	Pretérito Perfeito Composto
t_E	Event time
t_{LOC}	Location time
t_P	Perspective time
t_R	Reference time
t_S	Speech time
XN	Extended-Now

Acknowledgements

This book is a slightly revised version of my doctoral dissertation, which was accepted by the Faculty of Arts and Humanities of the University of Cologne *(Philosophische Fakultät der Universität zu Köln)* in May 2021. It would not have been possible to write it without the support of many people. In the following, I name some of them.

First of all, I thank Prof. Dr. Martin Becker, who had the idea of a comparative study of the Spanish and the Portuguese Present Perfect, supported me and invited me to join the *Tense and Aspect in Discourse* project, where I had the opportunity to develop my work as a contribution to collaborative research.

I thank Prof. Dr. Benjamin Meisnitzer, for introducing me to the fascinating field of Romance linguistics at the Johannes Gutenberg-Universität Mainz in 2014 and for very early on pushing my academic career by integrating me into academic networks that I would not have been part of without him.

I am grateful to Prof. Dr. Marco García García. Together with Prof. Dr. Petra Schumacher, Prof. Dr. Christiane Bongartz and apl. Prof. Dr. Doris Mücke, he led the a.r.t.e.s. class 8 Prominence in Language, which has been a great platform of academic exchange and a great source of motivation, especially in times of the pandemic, which the writing process of this book fell in.

This work was supported financially by the Deutsche Forschungsgemeinschaft (German Research Foundation), CRC 1252 *Prominence in Language* (Project-ID 281511265). The project was led by Prof. Dr. Klaus von Heusinger and equipped with an inspiring scientific spirit. Being part of a group of 19 doctoral candidates, I had the chance to receive training in data management and statistical analysis in R, outstandingly taught by Dr. Bodo Winter, which provided me with a range of new perspectives.

I am obliged to my colleagues Jakob Egetenmeyer for his help and advice, Paul Compensis for advice and discussion regarding the study design of the experiment, Maximilian Hörl for statistical consultancy, Nuria Martínez García and Diego Romero Heredero for help with the Spanish items included in the experiment, as well as Frank Zickenheiner for introducing me to the art of typesetting in Latex. Furthermore, I am very thankful to Thomas Batchelor for proofreading.

Last but not least, I am grateful to the John Benjamins Publishing Company for publishing this book, i.e. to Prof. Dr. Elly van Gelderen, who accepted it for the Linguistik Aktuell/Linguistics Today series, two anonymous reviewers for their feedback, as well as Kees Vaes, who managed the publishing process.

Bonn, August 2022

CHAPTER 1

Introduction

Portuguese and Spanish represent two closely related Ibero-Romance languages featuring linguistic similarities on many levels. This also concerns the semantic domains of tense and aspect. Consistently, they dispose of a Present Perfect featuring an almost equivalent formal side, as illustrated in (1).

(1) The Portuguese PPC$_{PT}$ and the Spanish PPC$_{SP}$
    a. *Este ano <u>tem sido</u> atípico.*
       this year has been atypical
       'This year has been (being) atypical.'
    b. *Este año <u>ha sido</u> atípico.*
       this year has been atypical
       'This year has been atypical.'

This formal similarity coheres with an almost identical label in the grammatical tradition, where the two are referred to as *Pretérito Perfeito Composto* (Portuguese) and *Pretérito Perfecto Compuesto* (Spanish). In contradiction to these parallels though, their meanings and functions are commonly described as significantly diverging from one another. Most prominently, this is aspectually manifested in their different readings, as suggested by the English translations provided in (1). While the Portuguese PPC$_{PT}$ in (1a) presents the situation as ongoing, the Spanish PPC$_{SP}$ in (1b) preferably presents it as completed.[1] This (simplified) picture of an antithetical relationship between the PPC$_{PT}$'s and PPC$_{SP}$'s meaning on the one hand, and form on the other hand, demands for a detailed study of the question of where the dividing lines between the two are exactly to be drawn.

This book presents a synchronic account of the two tense forms. In its theoretical part, it mainly builds on two pillars. First, it develops a cross-linguistic perspective on the PPC$_{PT}$ and the PPC$_{SP}$ in order to compare them in the context of a general framework of tense, aspect and the interplay between tense forms and tempo-aspectual adverbials (cf. Chapter 2). Below, in Section 1.1, this approach is

---

1. While (1a) applies to both European and Brazilian Portuguese (cf. also Section 3.2), diatopic variation needs to be thoroughly taken into account concerning the Spanish data. In most general terms, the preference of a bounded reading in (1b) applies to Peninsular Spanish (cf. also Section 4.2).

introduced and motivated in detail. Second, the study explicitly shifts the focus on the functions that the PPC$_{PT}$ and PPC$_{SP}$ typically fulfill on the level of discourse. This endeavour is based on the assumption that a discourse-based perspective is indispensable for an integral account of the question of which kind of meaning the PPC$_{PT}$ and PPC$_{SP}$ actually contribute, as well as to what extent they differ or take after each other in this regard. Discourse functions are thus argued to significantly complement the truth-conditional meaning component of tense forms. In Section 1.2, the discourse-based approach is motivated in detail.

The subsequent sections, introducing the comparative and discursive approach to the PPC$_{PT}$ and PPC$_{SP}$, are furthermore followed by an overview of the research goals of the study in Section 1.3, as well as an overview of the individual chapters in Section 1.4.

1.1 A cross-linguistic perspective on the PPC$_{PT}$ and the PPC$_{SP}$

There is a tradition of considering the Present Perfect an abstract, cross-linguistic semantic category. Accordingly, there are typical readings that are assumed to pertain to this category, as illustrated in (2).

(2) Typical Present Perfect readings   (Portner 2012: 1219)
    a. Resultative reading
       Mary has read Middlemarch.
    b. Continuative reading
       Mary has lived in London for five years.
    c. Existential reading
       The earth has been hit by giant asteroids before (and probably will be again).
    d. Hot news reading
       The Orioles have won!

Within a general theory of tense, these readings turn out to share the property of featuring quantificational temporal semantics. This is expressed in that each of them is derived either based on existential quantification, as in the experiential, resultative and hot news reading, or universal quantification, as in the continuative (or universal) reading. This characterization of the Present Perfect as a quantificational tense form particularly becomes crucial in the context of the fundamental opposition of quantificational vs. referential tense (cf. e.g. Grønn and Stechow 2016). In most general terms, quantificational tense forms are supposed to denote indefinite eventualities, while referential tense forms are supposed to denote definite eventualities. Applied to the distinction of the quantificational Present Perfect (conceived of as an abstract semantic category) and the referential Simple Past (conceived of as an abstract semantic category), the former serves to express the mere existence of a past eventuality, while the latter may determine the temporal location of a past eventuality. For example, (2c) may be paraphrased as "there is at least one past eventuality of `the earth be hit by giant asteroids` that temporally precedes the speech time."[2] By contrast, referential tense, as e.g. in "Last year, the earth was hit by giant asteroids", may be paraphrased as "there is a past eventuality of `the earth be hit by giant asteroids` that temporally precedes the speech time and that is referentially assigned to the adverbially provided location time *last year*" (cf. Section 2.1 for a detailed introduction of the quantificational vs. referential tense opposition).

As attested in particular with respect to the Romance languages, the semantic category of the Present Perfect is oftentimes morphosyntactically realized by the combination of a present tense auxiliary of *have* and a participle. Consistently, this morphosyntactic expression is most typically labelled as Present Perfect, as well. That is, in many languages and varieties, there tends to be a congruence between the Present Perfect as conceived of as a semantic category and the Present Perfect as a morphosyntactic form. Apparently though, there is counterevidence to this tendency, as tense-aspect systems are highly diverse and flexible and permanently suffer from ongoing changes and grammaticalization processes. In e.g. Portuguese, the typical perfectal readings listed in (2) pertain to the functional load of the formal Simple Past. Also, the Spanish PPC_{SP} is expected to acquire referential semantics at some point, as triggered by the "aoristic drift" (in our terms: "referential drift"), a tendency that has been cross-linguistically attested for the French *Passé Composé*. Put differently, the Spanish PPC_{SP} is supposed to abandon its purely quantificational semantics at some point (cf. Section 4.4 and Chapter 6).

However, the Spanish PPC_{SP}, as exemplified in (1b), is still classified as a typical representative of the Present Perfect giving rise to the typical perfectal readings. In this sense, the PPC_{SP} has been labelled a "well-behaved" Present Perfect (cf. Laca 2008), since it is based on a quantificational core meaning evoking existential and universal readings.

On the other hand, the Portuguese PPC_{PT} has been characterized as giving rise to highly idiosyncratic readings and meaning effects that clearly diverge from the ones indicated in (2). From a cross-linguistic perspective, this suggests a status of a rather "badly-behaved" Present Perfect. Conspicuously, this also correlates with its etymologically diverging auxiliary on the formal side. This has even led some scholars to consider the PPC_{PT} an aspectual periphrasis instead of an actual representative of the cross-linguistic Present Perfect:

---

2. The typewriter font is used for predicates lacking tempo-aspectual information, i.e. for predicates outside the scope of a tense form.

> In BP [*Brazilian Portuguese*], there is a consensus among linguists of semantic area studies about the inadequacy of the nomenclature "Pretérito Perfeito Composto", attributed to such periphrasis by the grammatical tradition. (Rocha 2017: 280)

By contrast, Bertinetto and Squartini 2000) have categorized the PPC$_{PT}$ as a Present Perfect, that, however, has dismissed common evolutionary trends (cf. Section 2.5).

PPC$_{PT}$ and PPC$_{SP}$ as quantificational tense forms

One of the central claims of this book is that PPC$_{PT}$ and PPC$_{SP}$ share the property of being based on quantificational semantics. In other words, it is claimed that the PPC$_{PT}$ and PPC$_{SP}$ are, on an abstract semantic level, more similar than they might appear from their readings. Accordingly, they resemble one another in that their inherently quantificational meaning contrasts with referential tense forms (both syntagmatically and paradigmatically). In most general terms, that means that both PPC$_{PT}$ and PPC$_{SP}$ most typically *quantify* over *indefinite* past eventualities instead of *referring* to *definite* past eventualities (cf. Section 2.1 for a detailed account). However, the comparison of the two reveals that temporal quantification may be spelled out quite differently: while the Spanish PPC$_{SP}$'s readings are mostly derived based on universal or existential quantification (exemplified by (2), cf. also Chapter 4), the Portuguese PPC$_{PT}$'s quantificational readings are derived based on universal quantification, as well as the two peculiar quantificational variants of "indefinite pluractional existential" (IPEX) quantification and characterizing quantification (cf. Chapter 3).

Furthermore, these different instantiations of temporal quantification lead to opposing trends already attestable in synchrony. On the one hand, the "badly-behaved" Portuguese PPC$_{PT}$ seems to specialize in its characterizing reading, a tendency that, in fact, matches the PPC$_{PT}$'s highly restrictive functional load and its very low ratios in terms of its general frequencies. On the other hand, the "well-behaved" Spanish PPC$_{SP}$ is affected by a referential drift, which means that it is on its way to undergoing a significant semantic update that results in an abandonment of its purely quantificational semantics in favor of adding referential readings to its repertoire. This evolutionary dynamic is particularly dealt with in Chapter 6. The results of this chapter's empirical part suggest that the innovative referential update has already been initiated but not yet accomplished.

In sum, the comparative study aims at exposing the PPC$_{PT}$'s and PPC$_{SP}$'s common quantificational, temporally indefinite core meaning, with particular emphasis on their diverging instantiations of this shared meaning component. In a more general research context, this approach is furthermore supposed to provide a new look on the general evolution of the Present Perfect in the Romance languages, as it suggests a reevaluation of the cross-linguistically attested typical grammaticalization path in the context of the temporal-semantic opposition of quantificational and referential tense.

In what follows, the explicit focus on the level of discourse is discussed.

1.2 The discursive approach

The truth-conditional meaning component of tense forms

Tense forms provide grammaticalized means to anchor eventualities in time. In most general terms, eventualities receiving a temporal index may be temporally anchored based on the tripartite distinction of past, present and future (3a)–(3c). Furthermore, they may be aspectually marked as bounded or unbounded (3d).

(3) a. *They wrote a lot.*
    b. *They write a lot.*
    c. *They will write a lot.*
    d. *They wrote / were writing a lot.*

Within a realistic, correspondance theory of meaning, "they wrote/write/will write" is true iff the eventuality of writing took place before/at/after the speech time that the utterance gets uttered at in the extra-linguistic world. Similarly, "they wrote/were writing a lot" is true iff the past eventuality of writing has been concluded or not.

However, it is particularly the usage of tense forms that suggests that "the nature of reality does not dictate the way that reality is represented in people's mind" (Pinker 2007: 4). In other words, in addition to the truth conditions imposed by a tense form, tense form choice is also influenced by the co-existence of inner-linguistic alternatives of how to present and configure situations and links between those situations. Alternatives provide different ways "to frame a situation" (ibid), which may be illustrated with (4). The depicted Spanish minimal pair contrasts *Indefinido* (Simple Past) and PPC$_{SP}$ combined with the verb *morir* ('(to) die'). In varieties of Spanish disposing of a productive *Indefinido* and a productive PPC$_{SP}$, both alternatives presented in (4) are fine, particularly when observed in isolation. While both expressions may be evaluated as true when applied to the same situation holding in the extra-linguistic world, the minimal pair emphasizes the idea of different ways of perspectivizing the grandfather's demise and of integrating it into the discourse.[3]

---

3. This functional division may not apply to varieties where one of the two tense forms is ousted by the other one, cf. Section 4.2.

(4) *Indefinido* vs. PPC$_{SP}$[4]
   a. Mi abuelo   (se) murió.
       my grandfather REFL died
       'My grandfather died.'
   b. Mi abuelo   ha muerto.
       my grandfather has died
       'My grandfather has died.'

The perspectival structure in discourse

In the tradition of Reichenbach (1947), the difference between (4a) and (4b) has been accounted for in terms of different configurations of the event time, speech time and reference time, which tense forms are supposed to denote by default. This is illustrated in (5). In order to maintain terminological consistency, we already apply our terminology featuring t_E (event time), t_S (speech time) and t_P (perspective time).[5]

(5) a. Simple Past: $t_E, t_P \prec t_S$
      b. Present Perfect: $t_E \prec t_S, t_P$

Accordingly, (4a) denotes the demise as preceding the speech time t_S and, crucially, as being perspectivized. By contrast, (4b) denotes the demise as preceding the speech time t_S while the perspective time t_P is set to equal the speech time. Put differently, the Present Perfect may be described, in most general terms, as asserting on the present, while the Simple Past asserts on the past. It follows that concatenating Present Perfect and Simple Past may create a perspectival shift from the present time-sphere towards the past time-sphere (or vice versa).[6] Accordingly, one of the two configurations of t_E, t_S and t_P indicated in (4) may be chosen in order to shift, or also to maintain the perspective time as it is set at a given stage of discourse. In the same vein, (5a) as linguistically realized in (4a) may represent the more convenient alternative when telling a story. By contrast, (5b) as linguistically realized in (4b) may represent the more convenient alternative in a report or an argument. In other

---

[4]. Some speakers report that (4a) requires *se*, while others accept (4a) without *se*. Independently of the semantic contribution of *se* and its status in terms of diasystematic variation, the minimal pair aims for emphasizing the contrast established by the opposition of *Indefinido* vs. PPC$_{SP}$.

[5]. In Reichenbach's (1947) terminology, these are labelled as E, S and R (reference time), i.e. Reichenbach's (1947) reference time R complies to our framework's perspective time t_P (cf. Section 2.1)

[6]. The terms present time-sphere and past time-sphere are taken from Declerck et al. (2006), cf. also Section 2.1.

words, different discourse modes and scenarios featuring different perspectival structures may impact tense form choice (cf. Section 2.4).

Related to that aspect, the configuration of t_P equalling t_S creates a meaning effect that is typically associated with the Present Perfect, namely that the underlying past eventuality is of particular relevance at the speech time t_S. Depending on whether the grandfather's demise is supposed to be linguistically presented as currently relevant or not, either of the two may provide the more adequate alternative. Again, this aspect supports the claim that "the nature of reality does not dictate the way that reality is represented in people's mind" (Pinker 2007: 4). After all, the demise of a person necessarily bears the ontological potential to affect the speaker's speech time in a highly relevant way, i.e. to be of current relevance. Conceiving of current relevance as a linguistically constructed configuration though, a speaker may still deliberately choose between highlighting or demoting the current relevance effect of the underlying past eventuality by perspectivizing the past time-sphere ($t_P \prec t_S$) or the present time-sphere (t_P, t_S).

The event-referential structure in discourse

There is further evidence suggesting that choice of tense form underlies inner-linguistic, discursive factors, as exemplified by the English data presented (6).

(6) Simple Past and Present Perfect in discourse
   a. <u>Has</u> anybody <u>seen</u> the murderer? – It <u>was</u> the gardener!
   b. <u>Has</u> anybody <u>seen</u> the murderer? – ?It <u>has been</u> the gardener!
   c. <u>Did</u> anybody <u>see</u> the murderer? – It <u>was</u> the gardener!
   d. <u>Did</u> anybody <u>see</u> the murderer? – ?It <u>has been</u> the gardener!

Strikingly, employing the Simple Past in the second sentence in each of the four versions of this fictive dialogue during an interrogation appears to be fine, while a Present Perfect in the second sentence appears to be less felicitous, if not odd. Again, an analysis based on truth conditions alone would fail to account for the observed effect. Instead, it is the preceding Simple Past that seems to block the use of the succeeding Present Perfect which might be, in most general terms, explained as follows. The Present Perfect's quantificational temporal semantics keep the denoted past eventualities indefinite. Thus, having introduced a past eventuality e to the discourse universe blocks elaborating on e by means of an indefinite tense form but favors a definite tense form (cf. Section 2.4). Put differently, the dynamic management of the event-referential structure in discourse parallels typical patterns and discourse functions known from definiteness in the nominal domain. This structural analogy has been studied in the tradition of Partee (1973, 1984) and is discussed in Section 2.1.

In sum, we assume that the study of the Portuguese PPC$_{PT}$ and the Spanish PPC$_{SP}$ necessarily imposes the need to take into account the inner-linguistic dimension of discourse, conceived of as their most natural setting, where they evolve semantics that complement their truth conditions and that may be missed when observing them in isolation:

> It is a ubiquitous feature of natural languages that utterances are interpretable only when the interpreter takes account of the contexts in which they are made – utterance meaning depends on context. Moreover, the interaction between context and utterance is reciprocal. Each utterance contributes (via the interpretation which it is given) to the context in which it is made. It modifies the context into a new context, in which this contribution is reflected; and it is this new context which then informs the interpretation of whatever utterance comes next.
>
> (Kamp et al. 2011: 125)

1.3 Goals of the study

Having motivated the need for a general framework to account for the PPC$_{PT}$ and PPC$_{SP}$ within a comparative perspective, as well as the particular focus on the discursive dimension related to the use and functions of the two tense forms, we formulate the following research goals.

(i) Develop a comparative and general framework for the PPC$_{PT}$ and PPC$_{SP}$ (Chapters 2–4)

The first goal is to develop a cross-linguistic framework enabling a comparative investigation of the similarities and differences of the PPC$_{PT}$ and PPC$_{SP}$. This particularly concerns the levels of tense, aspect and the interaction with tempo-aspectual adverbials. The framework is mainly based on the concepts discussed in the Anglo-Saxon literature on tense and aspect, since these, to a great extent, have not been applied yet to the study of the PPC$_{PT}$ and PPC$_{SP}$ to our knowledge. In this sense, we assume the framework to provide new insights to typical problems associated with the study of the PPC$_{SP}$ and PPC$_{PT}$. Most crucially, it is the fundamental semantic division of quantificational vs. referential tense which serves as a leitmotif throughout the whole book. It is supposed to help identify and, in particular, theoretically motivate the typical functions that the PPC$_{PT}$ and PPC$_{SP}$ fulfill in discourse (cf. goal (ii) below). Moreover, it provides new ways of approaching the PPC$_{SP}$'s referential drift, which has been labelled as the "aoristic drift" in the literature (cf. Section 4.4 and Chapter 6).

The study aims for a general approach in the sense that it does not investigate finegrained variational differences. However, the framework's cross-linguistic approach is assumed to be applicable (or extendable to) the study of particular varieties. For methodological reasons, there *are* coarse-grained variational restrictions. The discussed data are, on the one hand, restricted to European and Brazilian Portuguese, based on the working hypothesis that the PPC$_{PT}$ draws on the same semantics in the two varieties, although it is slightly more frequently used in European Portuguese (cf. Section 3.2). On the other hand, there is a restriction to Peninsular Spanish (cf. Section 4.2). Without a doubt, the Spanish PPC$_{SP}$ is significantly affected by diatopic variation, which mainly pertains to its diverging degree of grammaticalization, as shown by numerous studies. Still, the goal remains to account for the most important general trends of the Peninsular PPC$_{SP}$ in order to compare them to the PPC$_{PT}$'s.

(ii) Derive typical discourse functions based on (i) (Chapters 2–4).

Based on (i), the second goal is to explicitly add the focus on the discursive level by investigating the functions that are typically evoked by (or associated with) the two tense forms. This is in order to reach for an integral account of the question of what kind of meaning PPC$_{PT}$ and PPC$_{SP}$ contribute. The discursive dimension pertains to the macrostructural level of discourse (modes of discourse in the sense of Smith 2003) on the one hand, and to the micro-structural level of discourse on the other hand, which aims at the co-textual interplay of tense forms on the syntagmatic axis. Particular attention is paid to the latter level, since its relevance to the study of the PPC$_{PT}$ and PPC$_{SP}$ still represents an understudied field.

(iii) Test the hypotheses generated in Chapters 2–4 based on new data (Chapters 5–6).

The third goal is to apply the hypotheses generated in Chapters 2–4 to new data to test if they prove as valid. This empirical part is carried out by means of a corpus study on both PPC$_{PT}$ and PPC$_{SP}$ and an acceptability study that exclusively focusses on the PPC$_{SP}$'s referential drift. The corpus study's primary goal is to qualitatively investigate the micro-structural discourse functions discussed in the Chapters 2–4. The quantitative experiment's goal is twofold. On the one hand, it aims for determining the status of the Peninsular Spanish with respect to the referential drift, i.e. the PPC$_{SP}$'s status between quantification and reference. On the other hand, it aims for exploring if the measuring of acceptability judgements should be regarded, with respect to future studies, as a fruitful methodological extension of the common methods of testing for combinations with certain adverbials, measuring frequencies of the PPC$_{SP}$ vs. *Indefinido* in competing zones or performing forced choice tasks where participants are asked to choose from PPC$_{SP}$ vs. *Indefinido* in competing zones.

1.4 Overview of the chapters

In the following, a brief overview of the individual chapters is provided, outlining their contribution to the general structure of this book. More detailed overviews are furthermore provided at the beginning of each chapter.

Chapter 2 discusses the framework that is going to be applied in the study in detail. It is based on a review of the most important trends within the theory of tense, aspect, tempo-aspectual adverbials, the study of tense and aspect in discourse, as well as the diachronic and synchronic study of the Romance Present Perfect. This is to determine the point of departure of our study and which questions it necessarily has to address. The working hypothesis is developed that the Present Perfect is a quantificational tense form that does not take a location time t_{LOC} as an argument. This turns it indefinite and i.a. accounts for (i) that it most widely impedes combining with positional adverbials, (ii) that it typically blocks the discourse mode of narration and, related to that aspect, (iii) that it blocks the discourse-semantic encoding of temporal relations (such as temporal precedence or inclusion) with adjacent tense forms, i.e. with tense forms that are co-textually present (the pragmatic inferring of these relations based on e.g. world knowledge is not blocked though).

Chapter 3 applies the framework developed in Chapter 2 to a detailed account of the Portuguese PPC_{PT}. Crucially, different "universalized" readings, tracing back to an underlying temporal quantifier, are identified. These are "indefinite pluractional existential" (IPEX), universal and characterizing readings. With regard to the PPC_{PT}'s interplay with adjacent tense forms, the PPC_{PT} is i.a. argued to serve as a means to shape the perspectival structure in discourse. In particular, the characterizing reading is extrapolated as a sophisticated rhetorical means to contrast genericity (as expressed by the characterizing PPC_{PT}) with episodicity (as expressed e.g. by a Simple Past) for argumentative purposes in the discourse mode of argument.

Chapter 4 applies the framework developed in Chapter 2 to a detailed account of the Spanish PPC_{SP}. Crucially, existential readings (resultative, experiential and hot news), as well as universal readings are identified as tracing back to the PPC_{SP}'s underlying temporal quantification. Regarding the interplay with adjacent tense forms, the quantificational PPC_{SP} is argued to serve as means to shape the perspectival structure, as well as the event-referential structure via so-called "actualization effects" that discursively exploit the contrast of referential (definite) and quantificational (indefinite) tense forms. Furthermore, the chapter discusses the question of whether the PPC_{SP} already disposes of a referential reading in addition to its quantificational core meaning. On the discourse level, temporal anaphora and cataphora – which are predicted to be blocked by the quantificational PPC_{SP} – are discussed as potential test cases for detecting referential uses of the PPC_{SP}.

Chapter 5 presents a corpus study based on a manually created corpus consisting of movie and series subtitles, political speech, as well as transcripts of a political talkshow. The data turn out to widely match the assumptions and hypotheses derived in the previous chapters. Accordingly, the PPC_{PT} and PPC_{SP} do show diverging discourse functions in the data. The low-frequent PPC_{PT} suggests a specialization in shaping the rhetorical structure of arguments as discussed in Chapter 3. In particular, it is the characterizing reading that is suggested to systematically contribute to quasi-logical reasoning in the sense of Perelman and Olbrechts-Tyteca (1971), an argumentation technique that draws on the "prestige of logical thought". However, the universal and IPEX readings turn out to assume micro-structural discourse functions that overlap with the ones that the PPC_{SP} crucially fulfills. These pertain to the discursive management of the perspectival structure, as well as the event-referential structure by means of actualization effects established by the interplay with referential tense forms. Additionally, the Spanish data show a small number of cataphoric uses, i.e. examples where anaphoric tense forms get attached to the PPC_{SP}. These turn out to represent an interesting case from a theoretical perspective as they seem to be intertwined with the PPC_{SP}'s referential drift. Therefore, the PPC_{SP}'s cataphoric potential is discussed and experimentally investigated in detail in Chapter 6.

Chapter 6 is dedicated to the case study of the PPC_{SP}'s referential drift (which has been labelled the "aoristic drift" in the literature), i.e. the PPC_{SP}'s tendency to gradually abandon its purely quantificational core meaning in favor of additionally acquiring referential semantics. In particular, prominence – conceived of as a "basic underlying organizational principle of linguistic structuring" (Himmelmann and Primus 2015: 52) – is argued to account for the referential drift. The central claim is that the highlighting of the PPC_{SP}'s event domain as a prominent structural attractor licenses its cataphoric discourse function, i.e. the attaching of an anaphoric tense form. This, in turn, is argued to catalyze the referential drift. Put differently, highlighting the PPC_{SP}'s indefinite event domain as prominent is expected to turn it definite in the long run. Thus, the restructuring of a prominence-based asymmetry is argued to diachronically bridge the semantic gap between the quantificational and referential PPC_{SP}. Furthermore, an experiment of measuring acceptability judgements is reported. It suggests that PPC_{SP} uses that dispose of a prominent event domain (anchoring an anaphoric *Imperfecto*) indeed hint at an ongoing change. The results, interpreted on the basis of our framework, thus suggest that the PPC_{SP} already disposes of a reading that is situated right in between the two pillars of quantificational and referential tense. However, this reading is not yet referential, as it has not yet fully invaded the functional domain of the definite Simple Past.

Chapter 7 summarizes the main findings in light of the research goals formulated in Section 1.3. It puts in a nutshell the main results concerning the similarities and differences between the PPC$_{PT}$ and PPC$_{SP}$ on the several investigated levels, which pertain to their common quantificational semantics, their interplay with tempo-aspectual adverbials, as well as to the discourse functions that they most typically assume. Emphasis is furthermore put on a relation of the findings to the cross-linguistic stage model of the Romance Present Perfect, which is discussed on several occasions throughout the book, in order to reevaluate the insights in a more general research context. Finally, it outlines questions that still require further research. This prominently refers to the need of a finer-grained account of variational factors affecting the usage of the PPC$_{PT}$ and the PPC$_{SP}$, to which the present study's framework may contribute. Also, this refers to new questions that have emerged. In particular, the study of the micro-structural discourse functions typically assumed by the PPC$_{PT}$ and PPC$_{SP}$ opens up a range of desiderata requiring further research in the future.

CHAPTER 2

Fundamentals

This chapter is dedicated to the theoretic fundamentals needed for a detailed analysis of the Spanish and the Portuguese Present Perfect in discourse. As it turns out, there are several aspects of semantic theory involved in the study of temporal interpretation and the study of a particular tense form. Among those are the study of tense, aspect and discourse (cf. Klein 1994: 15ff.). Since there is no clear consensus in the rich literature on the referred topics – which is due to a range of traditions, as well as to language-specific needs for proper accounts of particular tense forms – we discuss the relevant literature and expose the view that we are going to apply in our study. Such an overview will help identify (i) the point of departure of our study, (ii) which questions our study necessarily has to address and (iii) to what extent we consider it to be a meaningful extension of previous work.

Section 2.1 introduces the semantic category of tense and its semantic "ingredients", mainly in the tradition of Reichenbach (1947) and the common extensions of his theory. We are going to develop a view on tense as an ordering function. Additionally, we discuss the opposition of quantificational vs. referential tense, a fundamental semantic distinction of two operations. While this distinction is a (more or less) established conception in the Anglo-Saxon literature on the semantics of tense, it has, to our knowledge, not yet been applied to the PPC_{SP} and PPC_{PT}. In particular, it helps account for different discourse functions of tense forms that are discussed in Section 2.4.

Section 2.2 provides an overview on the theory of aspect. Following a terminology that traces back to Smith (1991), the section is structured into two parts. The first part introduces the concept of situation aspect which, in most general terms, pertains to the question of *lexically* coded presence or absence of temporal boundaries of situations, i.e. of verbal predicates. The second part introduces the concept of viewpoint aspect, which may be pinned down to the question of *grammatically* coded presence or absence of temporal boundaries of situations.

Section 2.3 briefly discusses common classifications of adverbials that are related to the study of tense forms. We separate and analyze four tempo-aspectual adverbials that we are going to include in our study: positional adverbials, quantificational adverbials, durative adverbials and XN-adverbials (Extended-Now). Furthermore, we discuss their function of specifying one of the semantic ingredients of tense discussed in Section 2.1.

Section 2.4 introduces the discourse-based study of tense and aspect based on a distinction between the layers of (i) the macro-structure of discourse and (ii) the microstructure of discourse. While (i) refers to the modes of discourse in the tradition of Smith (2003), including categories such as narration or report, (ii) zooms in on the syntagmatic axis within a piece of discourse and encompasses, a.o. aspects, temporal anaphora and so-called actualization effects.

Section 2.5 provides an overview on the most important trends in the cross-linguistic research on the Present Perfect. The Romance PP is traditionally analyzed as following a grammaticalization path that makes it gradually lose its perfectal value in favor of an aoristic value. Accordingly, a PP in a given language can be synchronically classified as disposing of a rather innovative or a rather conservative meaning. Discussing common meaning effects, such as the famous PP puzzle and the concept of current relevance, we argue for an analysis of the PP as an inherently quantificational tense form that gives rise to existential or universal readings and that, crucially, lacks a location time.

2.1 Tense

2.1.1 The ingredients of tense

This section introduces the semantics of tense. More precisely, it treats tense as referring to the temporal meaning that is denoted by a verbal predicate which is located in time. The semantic category of tense differs from what we want to call tense form, a morphosyntactic category that is semantically composed of tense, aspect and modality. In other words, tense is one of the three ingredients of the so-called TAM-complex. In English, Simple Past (1a–i) and Simple Present (1b–i) represent instances of tense forms, while Past, Present and Future represent instances of the category tense.

(1) Tense vs. tense form
    a. Past tense
        i. *I saw John.*
        ii. *I had seen John.*
    b. Present Tense
        i. *I see John.*
        ii. *I am seeing John.*
    c. Future Tense
        i. *I shall/will see John.*
        ii. *I shall/will have seen John.*

Despite this distinction, the analysis of tense necessarily goes hand in hand with the analysis of tense forms due to their intertwinement. Reichenbach (1947) and his pioneering analysis of English tense forms has been one of the most influential approaches to tense and tense forms. Reichenbach's (1947) account features an accessible formalism that, at the same time, is very intuitive. The famous "Reichenbach-entries" are supposed to provide a classification of the tense forms by classifying them based on the configuration of three primitives: event time (E), reference time (R) and speech time (S). Additionally, the system assumes two basic relations between E, R and S, namely sequence and simultaneity. Simple Past is defined as denoting an eventuality that precedes speech time.[7] Moreover, the Simple Past refers to the past time that the eventuality has taken place (indicated by the constellation of R preceding S). The Present Perfect, on the contrary, denotes the same constellation except from the role of R: it is defined to equal S, i.e. to succeed E.

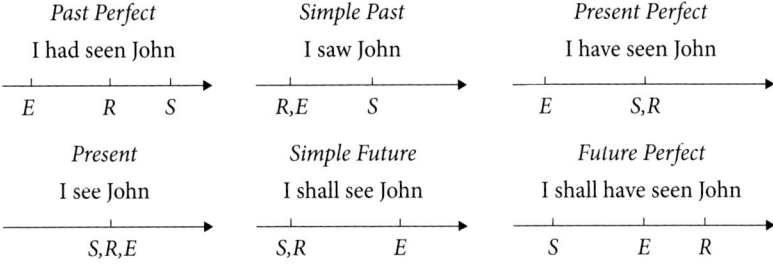

Figure 2.1 Reichenbach's (1947) entries for tense (Mani et al. 2005: 72)

Given that Reichenbach's proposal turned out to provide a useful cross-linguistic tool for the analysis of tense and the related grammaticalized tense forms, his seminal approach has had a huge influence on subsequent theories, at least for European languages. In this vein, the idea that the temporal domain consists of an architecture constituted by variables that change their configuration according to tense forms has become a consensus among semanticists. There is, however, a lot of discussion on the question of how many kinds of these variables one has to assume and how they should be defined properly. It turned out that Reichenbach's original model needed some refinements which has given rise to several updates and new proposals.

In the following, we will expound an analysis in the tradition of discourse-based perspectives on tense by assuming 4+1 ingredients: speech time t_s, eventuality

---

7. In line with Kamp et al. (2011: 199), "[w]e follow the widely adopted practice within the formal semantics of tense and aspect to use Bach's (1981) term "eventuality" as a common term for the events, states, processes etc. which verbs can be used to describe."

time t_E, location time t_{LOC}, perspective time t_P and, though discursively restricted (cf. below), reference time t_R. This architecture mainly follows the tradition of the Discourse Representation Theory (DRT, cf. e.g. Kamp 2013 and its applications to the temporal domain and Becker and Egetenmeyer 2018).

Speech time (t_S)
The concept of speech time can be considered to be the most uncontroversial one of Reichenbach's, as it has remained conceptually unchanged and thus entered the canonical view on tense.[8] It may be defined as "the time when a sentence is uttered or, in written texts, may be supposed to be uttered" (Becker and Egetenmeyer 2018: 36). The crucial point is that a proposition that gets a temporal index needs a deictic center. While past tense denotes an eventuality that takes place *before* t_S, future intends to refer to an eventuality that is encoded as occurring *after* t_S. Further, eventualities may also be expressed as occuring *simultaneous to* t_S. That is, t_S functions as a deictic center that an eventuality gets relatively anchored to.

Event time (t_E)
Reichenbach intended to define t_E as representing the interval that an eventuality is said to hold at, as can be intuitively deduced from Figure 2.1.[9] In a truth-conditional system, that would mean that t_E is the actual interval i for which it is said that the predicate yields a truth value of 1 or 0. In (1a–i), t_E equals the interval for which the proposition I see John yields a truth value.

Becker and Egetenmeyer (2018: 36) define t_E as representing "[t]he time the whole eventuality is supposed to take from its beginning (left boundary) to its completion (right boundary)". The authors add that t_E

> [...] is rarely specified in actual language use and generally remains undetermined. An example with explicit specification would be "John played tennis from 2 p.m. to 2.30 p.m." (Becker and Egetenmeyer 2018: 36)

---

8. However, scholars have used different terms to refer to the concept of speech time, such as "time of utterance" (Klein 1994), "t_0" (Kamp and Rohrer 1983) or "n", standing for "now" (Kamp and Reyle 1993; Becker and Egetenmeyer 2018).

9. Reichenbach (1947: 287) provides an informal definition, based on the example "Peter had gone": "[...] the point of the event is the time when Peter went; [...]. While Reichenbach speaks of time points, we adhere to the interval-based approach based on the assumption that a" dimensionless point is a mathematical construct that is not encountered in everyday life, and it seems almost counterintuitive to treat the continuum of temporal duration by using durationless points. [...] Even punctual expressions [...] do not single out the dimensionless entities of point logics but seem to refer, rather, to some more extended period [as in] *At 6 o'clock sharp, Harry left the office*." (Moens 1987: 40f.).

Further, the authors hint at the observation that lots of adverbs actually do not specify t_E. This can be illustrated with (2).

(2) a. *Yesterday, she bought a new car.*
     b. *At 4:30, I was hungry.*

While in (2a), it does not make sense to assume that the purchase of the car lasted all day, it is not plausible to assume that the speaker's hunger in (2b) lasted for 60 seconds. Instead, one should assume that in (2a), the purchase of the car is temporally included in *yesterday* ($t_E \subseteq$ *yesterday*), while the time 4:30 in (2b) is included in the state of being hungry ($4{:}30 \subseteq t_E$). This observation suggests the necessity of an additional concept that is relevant for temporal interpretation and that Reichenbach's account lacks: the location time.

Location time (t_{LOC})
Kamp et al. (2011) define t_{LOC} in the following way:

> Informally, the "location time" of an event is to be seen as the time when the event is said to occur and the location time of a state as the time at which the state is said to hold.[10] (Kamp et al. 2011: 200)

While t_E is the time that the denoted eventuality actually holds, t_{LOC} is supposed to provide the time at which t_E is *said* to hold, as exemplified in (2). According to the speaker's intentions at a given discourse stage, the granularity of t_{LOC} may vary, depending on what the speaker considers to be adequate, as illustrated in (3).

(3) Granularity of t_{LOC}
     a. *Last year, they bought a house.*
         t_E included in t_{LOC}
     b. *On Monday, they were at home.*
         t_{LOC} included in t_E
     c. *At 4:56:45 am, they signed the contract to complete the purchase of the house.*
         t_E included in (or equals?) t_{LOC}

Another concept that has been discussed in the literature is the topic time as proposed by Klein (1994, 2009). We consider Klein's topic time to comply with t_{LOC}. The term topic is a (not uncontroversial) term in the theory of information structure. With Krifka (2008: 265), it may be defined as "the entity or set of entities under which the information expressed in the comment constituent should be stored in the CG content" or as "the entity that a speaker identifies, about which then

---

10. Underlining added.

information, the comment, is given."[11] Applied to the study of tense and aspect, Klein's topic time is supposed to refer to the interval that the speaker asserts on. Yet, the reason for choosing the term t_{LOC} over topic time is that we prefer not to import this term from information structure to avoid terminological inconsistencies. In fact, we assume the semantics of tense not to be designed in a fashion that parallels the dimensions that are commonly assumed in information structure. These are topic–comment and focus–background. Following Klein, Gvozdanović (2012: 799) defines the topic time as being "confined to the deictic region of the narrator's focal concern." Here, focus ("focal concern") and topic, two concepts of different information-structural dimensions, seem to be conjoined but not consistently distinguished. Nevertheless, there is a crucial insight that Klein's approach and the discussion of his terminology contribute to our study: being the time that the speaker asserts on, t_{LOC} needs not be explicitly defined via an adverbial but may remain morphosyntactically covert. That is, t_{LOC} may co-exist with t_E independently of whether there is adverbial modification, as illustrated in (4).[12]

(4) Overt vs. covert t_{LOC}
 a. *Last year, they bought a house.*
 b. *It was raining.*

Perspective time (t_P)
Following Kamp (2013: 116), t_P may be defined as the "time from which the given information is viewed". Metaphorically, t_P provides a "vantage point" (cf. Kamp 2013: 119) on the timeline that creates a particular temporal perspective on an eventuality. This conception of the perspective time is quite similar to Reichenbach's reference time. In Figure 2.1, the Present Perfect is depicted as denoting E to precede R. The same constellation can be found for the Past Perfect and for the Future Perfect. This constellation is typical for morphological complex tense forms, i.e. for tense forms consisting of an auxiliary and a participle denoting some kind of anteriority. They create a perspective on an eventuality that is prior to a perspectival vantage point t_P.

We assume that there is not an infinite number of potential intervals that could serve as t_P although this mighht be intuititively suggested by the fact that the virtual timeline can be divided into an infinite number of intervals that could possibly

---

11. CG stands for Common Ground, a pragmatic theory that assumes a list of propositions that speakers jointly work on and presuppose in communication. The term traces back to Stalnaker's (1978) seminal work on assertion, a speech act that serves as a means to update the CG.

12. Within our framework, we assume that there is a location time (covert or overt) with referential tense and no location time with quantificational tense (cf. below).

serve as t_P – just as we assume it for t_E or t_{LOC}. We stick to the assumption that there is a restricted set of potential intervals following Declerck et al. (2006) who discuss the notion of "temporal focus" that obviously bears parallels with our t_P:

> The 'temporal focus' of a speaker is the time on which, through a particular tense choice, he focuses in the use of any given clause. [...] temporal focus can be defined as the phenomenon that the speaker draws attention to a particular kind of time – past, pre-present, present or post-present, [...] the corresponding 'absolute time zone'. (Declerck et al. 2006: 576)

The authors subsume these zones under two so-called time-spheres, namely the past time-sphere and the present time-sphere, as illustrated in Figure 2.2.

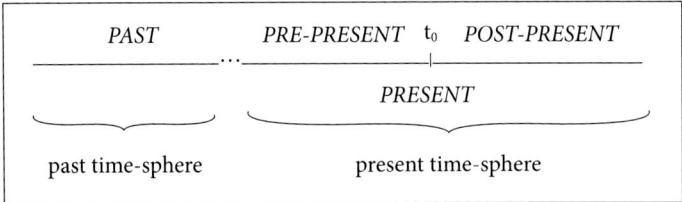

Figure 2.2 Time-spheres and zones (Declerck et al. 2006: 149)

It follows that, from a tempo-perspectival point of view, an assertion can be made about "then" and "now" (cf. Declerck et al. 2006: 200). A similar account is proposed by Botne and Kershner (2008) who study the tense and aspect systems in Bantu languages within their cognitive approach. The authors propose a two-dimensional segmentation consisting of a P-domain and a D-domain, as illustrated in Figure 2.3.

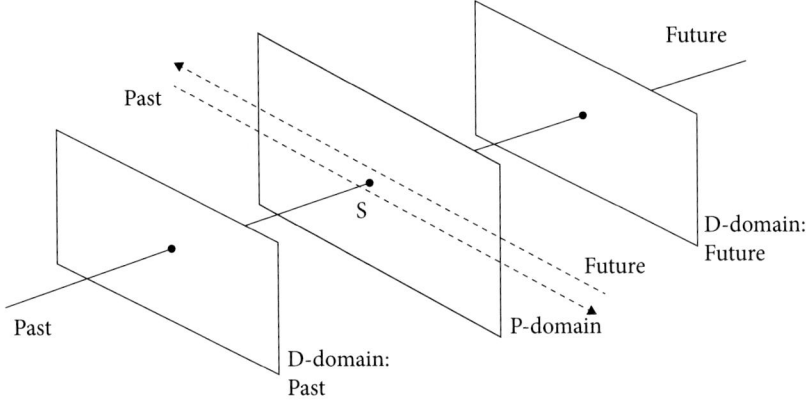

Figure 2.3 Cognitive worlds with three perspectives on time (Botne and Kershner 2008: 153)

First of all, the authors explicitly differentiate between the D-domains of Present and Future, which are merged in the present time-sphere in Declerck et al.'s (2006) approach. We will not discuss whether the present and future time-sphere should be distinguished or not given that we are exclusively interested in the separation of the past and present time-sphere (past D-domain and present D-domain), which are conceived as separate units in both accounts. The crucial assumption illustrated in Figure 2.3 is that both domains represent "different cognitive worlds" on different axes that can be navigated through.

While the temporal relations of anteriority and posteriority are associated with the P-domain, past and future pertain to the D-domain. A similar distinction was proposed by Weinrich (1964) within his famous distinction between *Besprochene Welt* ('discussed world') vs. *Erzählte Welt* ('narrated world'):

> Die Sprache kennt zweierlei Art Vergangenheit: eine, die unmittelbar zu mir gehört und die ich bespreche genau wie die Dinge, die mir in meiner Sprechsituation leiblich begegnen – und eine andere, die durch den Filter der Erzählung von mir distanziert ist. […] Wenn somit nicht alle Vergangenheit erzählt wird, so teilt umgekehrt nicht jede Erzählung Vergangenes mit.[13] (Weinrich 1964: 87)

Assuming anteriority operates on a different axis than past reference will become a crucial assumption for the analysis of the PPC$_{SP}$ in the Chapters 4–6. In sum, we assume that t_P is constituted by a time-sphere. We adhere to a bipartite partition featuring the past time-sphere and the present time-sphere that forms the set of potential intervals to constitute t_P. Accordingly, we update our preliminary definition of the Present Perfect: instead of defining t_S as equal to t_P (as proposed by Reichenbach), we define t_S to be included in t_P ($t_S \subseteq t_P$).

Referencetime (t_R)
The fifth ingredient is the reference time t_R. It is restricted by particular discursive conditions (cf. Section 2.4). Reichenbach's (1947) reference time R has been criticized as a too coarse-grained notion. This observation culminated in the Split-Reference-Time-Hypothesis, as noted by Rothstein (2008):

> [The] "split-reference-time-hypothesis" [is] much in the spirit of Kamp and Rohrer (1985) by saying that Reichenbach's reference time (r) must be split into a semantic part and a part that operates on the discourse level. (Rothstein 2008: 156)

---

13. 'Language knows two kinds of past: one that belongs directly to me and which I discuss just like the things that I encounter physically in my speech situation – and another that is distanced from me through the filter of the narrative. […] Thus, if not all the past is told, then conversely, not every narrative communicates the past.'

In line with the DRT (e.g. Kamp et al. 2011), as well as Becker and Egetenmeyer (2018), R splits up into t_P (as introduced above) and t_R. The concept of t_R is supposed to account for the dynamic update of temporal reference in discourse, i.e. for temporal anaphora.[14] Based on ideas on structural analogies between anaphora in the nominal and temporal domain in Partee (1973), scholars have developed theories of the use of tense forms in texts, in particular in stories or narrative passages, in order to account for the question of how temporal coherence is established in discourse. Now, the concept of t_R may be defined with Kamp et al. (2011) as the

> reference point […] (here as in many other cases: the time or event to which the story has so far advanced) with which the tense of the new sentence establishes a certain anaphoric relation. (Kamp et al. 2011: 199)

That is, t_R is a fundamental tool for the discourse-semantic encoding of narrative progression as it allows the location of an event in a narrative chain without the explicit use of adverbial modifiers. In this regard, it has a similar function as the location time t_{LOC}. It contributes the information of when an "event is said to occur" or a "state is said to hold". Kamp and Rohrer's (1983) classic French example in (5) illustrates how t_R may be updated or retained.

(5) Update vs. retention of t_R (Kamp and Rohrer 1983: 253)
    a. *Pierre entra, Marie téléphona.*
       Pierre entered Marie called
       'Pierre came in, Marie called someone.'
    b. *Pierre entra, Marie téléphonait.*
       Pierre entered Marie called
       'Pierre came in, Marie was on the phone.'

While in (30a), the *Passé Simple téléphona* causes an update in terms of a shift of t_R, it is maintained with the *Imparfait téléphonait* in (30b). In other words, (30a) denotes e_1 `Pierre enter` to precede e_2 `Mary call` ($e_1 \prec e_2$). On the other hand, (30b) denotes e_1 to be included in e_2 ($e_1 \subseteq e_2$). The related concept of viewpoint aspect and the licensing of t_R by the discourse mode of narration will be discussed in more detail in the Sections 2.2 and 2.4. For now, it is crucial to point out that t_R is the temporal ingredient that serves as a means to maintain temporal coherence by establishing chronological effects of temporal succession (shifted t_R) or temporal simultaneity (retained t_R) without the use of adverbial modifiers.

---

14. It seems that Reichenbach was actually aware of both components of R (cf. Kamp 2013: 113).

Integrating the ingredients
Putting these ingredients together, we characterize tense to be composed of t_S, t_E, t_{LOC} and t_P.[15] Figure 2.4 depicts an illustration of how these ingredients are arranged on a virtual timeline for the sentence "Yesterday I played soccer".

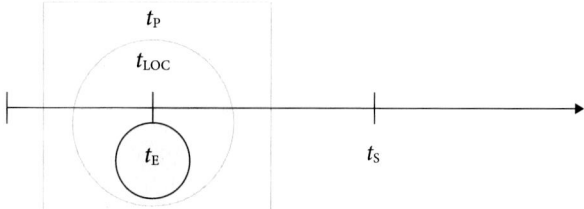

Figure 2.4 The 4 pillars of tense
Sentence "Yesterday I played soccer"; t_E: I play soccer; t_{LOC}: "yesterday"; t_P: Past time-sphere

Put in a formal language, we yield the picture of tense as an ordering function that takes t_S, t_P, t_E and t_{LOC} as its arguments in order to output different constellations of these based on the primitive relations of precedence ($\prec$) and inclusion ($\subseteq$). Applying this to e.g. the Simple Past, we face the interim problem of the need to account for aspect, as well. In this vein, the function indicated in (6) leaves open the relationship between t_{LOC} and t_E. The choice between the two options is driven by viewpoint aspect and will be discussed in Section 2.2.[16]

(6) Simple Past as an ordering function[17]

⟦SIMPLE PAST⟧: $\lambda t_S \lambda t_E \lambda t_P \lambda t_{LOC}$. $(t_E \left[\begin{smallmatrix}\subseteq\\\supseteq\end{smallmatrix}\right] t_{LOC}) \subseteq t_P \prec t_S$

Reads as:
The Simple Past is a function that takes t_S, t_E, t_P and t_{LOC} as its arguments and outputs t_E [to be a subset of/to be a superset of] t_{LOC}. The complex containing t_E and t_{LOC} is, in turn, a subset of t_P which covers the past time-sphere and which, in turn, precedes t_S.

---

15. Since t_R is restricted by additional discursive factors, we exclude t_R in the non-discursive characterization of tense forms for now.

16. Figure 2.4 depicts a perfective viewpoint for "Yesterday I played soccer" denoting t_E to be included in t_{LOC}.

17. In model theoretic semantics, the meaning of an expression is understood as a function that takes arguments and delivers an output. The formula indicates the arguments that the Simple Past takes (expressed by the items introduced by lambda) and the truth conditions that these arguments are mapped onto in order to yield a truth value.

2.1.2 Quantificational vs. referential tense

In the previous section, we have introduced the ingredients that compose the semantics of tense. In this section, we move the focus to t_E to discuss the problem of how t_E actually retrieves its temporal value. As it turns out, the basic semantic operations of reference and quantification – known from from the semantics of definiteness in the nominal domain – play a crucial role in this regard. A denoted past eventuality can either be attributed to a particular t_{LOC} (referential tense) or introduced to the discourse via quantification. This distinction is an outcome of a discussion that has been conducted over the past decades in formal semantics on the question of how to treat tense properly in a model-theoretic system and which has led to two positions:

i. Tense as an existential quantification over timepoints and intervals (in the tradition of Prior 1967; Montague (1973); Parsons 1990), also labelled indefinite tense,
ii. Tense as a referential expression to discourse-given or somehow available entities (in the tradition of Partee 1973, 1984), also labelled definite tense.

We follow Song (2005) and Grønn and Stechow (2016) in assuming that we need both accounts:

> The difficulty the two approaches are faced with is that neither takes an appropriate account of the variability of tense. [...] [I]n some context, the eventuality [...] is interpreted as being true at any time denoted by that tense, and in other context, [...] the eventuality [...] is interpreted as being true at a particular time supplied by the context.[18]   (Song 2005: 829f.)

In the following, we discuss the two types in detail.

Quantificational tense
Historically, the quantificational theory of tense was the first dominating approach in formal frameworks. It is often attributed to Prior (1967) and Montague (1973) (cf. Grønn and Stechow 2016: 318). According to this analysis, tense existentially quantifies over an interval (in our terms: tense existentially quantifies over t_E), which may be paraphrased as "there is a t_e". Or as Parsons (1990) puts it:

---

18. Song argues for choice functions that deliver, in the case of a referential reading, an interval needed for the interpretation.

> The default form of a simple sentence contains a quantifier that contributes a period of time. Tenses are elements that constrain this period to the past, the present, or the future. (Parsons 1990: 209)

This view is illustrated in (7), where we already apply our terminology introduced in the previous section. Given that quantification vs. reference refers to t_E and t_{LOC}, we omit t_P for now.

(7) The quantificational view on tense
   a. Simple Past
      I played soccer.
      $\exists t_E$ & $t_E \prec t_S$ & I play soccer at t_E
      There is an interval t_E & t_E is before t_S & I play soccer is true at t_E
   b. Will-Future
      I will play soccer.
      $\exists t_E$ & $t_E \succ t_S$ & I play soccer at t_E
      There is an interval t_E & t_S is before t_E & I play soccer is true at t_e

The quantificational account felicitously captures the vagueness of the exact temporal location of t_E in (7a) and (7b): all we can say is that there is an eventuality temporally restricted to the past or the future, whose exact temporal location on the virtual timeline remains indefinite (which is why quantificational tense also gets labelled indefinite tense). In his monograph on the semantics of events in English, Parsons (1990) extends the quantificational framework, applying it to adverbial modification. He assumes the same semantic operation, also when t_E gets adverbially modified, as illustrated in (8).

(8) Tense, temporal adverbials and quantification in   Parsons (1990: 209)
   a. *Yesterday, Brutus stabbed Caesar.*
      $\exists I$ [$I \prec now$ & $I \subset$ *Yesterday*] & Brutus stab Caesar at I
      Applying our terminology:
      $\exists t_E$ [$t_E \prec t_S$ & $t_E \subset t_{LOC}$ (*Yesterday*)] & Brutus stab Caesar at t_E
   b. *Yesterday at noon, Brutus stabbed Caesar.*
      $\exists I$ [$I \prec now$ & $I \subset$ *Yesterday* & $I \subset$ *Noons* & $\exists e \exists t$ [$t \in I$ & Stabbing(e) & Agent(e, Brutus) & Theme(e, Caesar) & Cul(e, t)]]
      Applying our terminology:
      $\exists t_E$ [$t_E \prec t_S$ & $t_E \subset t_{LOC-1}$ (*Yesterday*) & $t_E \subset t_{LOC-2}$ (*Noons*) & $\exists e \exists t$ [$t \in t_E$ & Stabbing(e) & Agent(e, Brutus) & Theme(e, Caesar) & Cul(e, t)]]

These examples illustrate how the location time t_{LOC} adds temporal information to the eventuality of Brutus stabbing Caesar. While (8a) temporally restricts the stabbing to yesterday, (8b) restricts it to yesterday at noon. The crucial point is that within a strict quantificational approach, the actual temporal location of t_E remains indefinite even though the location time t_{LOC} may be adverbially specified. In other words, it seems that the function of t_{LOC} is at most to minimize t_E's indefiniteness – and not to root it out. However, Parsons (1990) notes:

> Discourse can provide additional constraints on I [t_E]. For example, in a narrative, each event sentence describes an event that occurs after the preceding one. When occurring in a narrative, I will be a subject to a condition that it be after the time of the preceding event (if the sentence is an event sentence). There are many aspects of this sort affecting I; they are not discussed in this book. (Parsons 1990: 214)

Also, Parsons (1990) explicitly refers to Partee (1973, 1984) who challenged the quantificational view on tense, claiming that past tense may refer to

> [...] certain relevant parts of the past. This is an important phenomenon in the pragmatics of language use, but it affects the interpretation of our logical forms, not the forms themselves. The 'PAST' operator should be read 'for some relevant time in the past.' (Parsons 1990: 29)

As already pointed out, we adhere to the view that a referential theory tense – which explicitly captures that there are cases where "the past operator should be read for some relevant time in the past" – needs to be taken into account as a counterpart of the quantificational account.

Referential Tense
Several scholars have argued that a mere quantificational account for tense faces some serious problems, especially when it comes to the analysis of tense in discourse (cf. e.g. Enç 1986; Song 2005; Grønn and Stechow 2016, cf. also Section 2.4). The division between the quantificational and referential view on tense has been influenced by a famous conceptual analogy between the temporal and the nominal domain. It mainly draws back to the work of Partee (1973, 1984) and applies to the semantic operations of reference and anaphora.

(9) Analogy between nominal and temporal anaphora   (Partee 1973: 605)
   a. *Sam took the car yesterday and Sheila took it today.*
   b. *Sheila had a party last Friday and Sam got drunk.*

Both examples in (9) exhibit two propositions p_1 and p_2 that together form a small piece of discourse. They share the property that p_2 exhibits a referring expression that traces back to an antecedent introduced in p_1: In (9a), "it" refers back to "the car", in (9b), the temporal location of Sam getting drunk is resolved by reference to the party that Sheila had the Friday before. It follows that tense apparently may also retrieve its temporal reference by means of an anaphoric relation to its preceding discourse. After all, it seems unlikely that a hearer in (9b) would derive a reading of

"Sheila had a party last Friday and there is an interval t_E prior to t_S, such that Sam get drunk at t_E." Obviously, one could still come up with a context that would favor a quantificational reading for p₂. However, due to pragmatic conversational principles as proposed by Grice (1975), such as the maxim of manner ("be orderly, brief, avoid ambiguities"), we can assume that the speaker wants the hearer to derive the referential reading. This is not predicted by a strict quantificational theory which denies reference to a given interval in favor of an existential quantification that introduces a new interval.

In the same vein, Partee's famous example indicated in (10) motivates the need of a referential account of tense, as well.

(10) Quantificational readings and wrong interpretations (Partee 1973: 602)[19]
 a. *I didn't turn off the stove.*
    *($\exists t_E \prec t_S$) ¬ I turn off the stove at t_E
 b. *I didn't turn off the stove.*
    *¬ ($\exists t_E \prec t_S$) I turn off the stove at t_E

The two indicated quantificational readings for (10) can be paraphrased as follows: either there is a t_E in the past for which I turn off the stove is false (10a), or there is no t_E in the past (ever) for which I turn off the stove is true (10b). In fact, both interpretations probably do not cover the intended meaning. In the given context, it seems to be unlikely to existentially quantify over having turned off the stove before.[20] As pointed out by Partee, it rather seems that the speaker has a particular interval in mind. A possible scenario could be *"Today in the morning, I was in a hurry. I prepared some lunch, finished my presentation for today and then caught the bus. Oh wait a minute – I didn't turn off the stove!"* In other words, the Simple Past in (10) does not existentially quantify over an interval via introducing it, but rather refers to a given or inferable interval provided by the discourse.

In model-theoretic semantics, the cotextual retrieval of a referent needed for a referential expression has been accounted for by assignment functions for variables:

> A (variable) assignment is a partial function from *N* (the set of numbers) into D.
> (Heim and Kratzer 1998: 111)

Applied to the pronouns in "She likes him", the assignment could look like this:

---

[19]. Annotation adapted from Grønn and Stechow (2016: 322) and updated with our terminology.

[20]. A more adequate morphosyntactic output for a quantificational reading of (10) would actually choose the Present Perfect.

(11) *She likes him.*

$$[\![She_1]\!]^g, [\![him_2]\!]^g : \begin{bmatrix} 1 \to Mary \\ 2 \to Peter \\ 3 \to Paul \end{bmatrix}$$

The brackets demonstrate that an interpretation of the referential pronouns *she* and *him* is resolved relative to an indexed assignment function g. The function takes a referential form as its argument and outputs a referent. For now, we ignore the question of how this referent is actually retrieved, i.e. how the function outputs the right referent. Applying this to referential tense, we can derive an assignment function that takes a location time as its argument and outputs a value, i.e. an interval for t_{LOC}. While the index g is reserved for the assignment of nominal referents, we follow Song (2005) who introduces the index i to represent an assignment of temporal referents.[21] For Example (10), such an assignment function could look like this.

(12) *I didn't turn off the stove.*

$$[\![t_{LOC}]\!]^i : \begin{bmatrix} 1 \to while\ leaving\ the\ house\ today \\ 2 \to \quad at\ three\ o'clock \\ 3 \to \quad \ldots \end{bmatrix}$$

(12) illustrates a temporal interpretation of "I didn't turn off the stove" relative to an indexed assignment. Now, given that t_E is attributed to t_{LOC}, the eventuality's temporal location is definite. This index-driven model takes the dynamicity of cotextual and contextual meaning into account (which the quantificational approach lacks). Just as in the nominal domain, where referents of pronouns change as discourse unfolds, referred intervals are dynamically updated, as well.

A note on definiteness

As already pointed out, the analysis of quantificational vs. referential past bears parallels with the semantics of definiteness in the nominal domain, as argued by Partee (1973, 1984). Consequently, this led some scholars to consider referential tense as definite tense and quantificational tense as indefinite tense, accounting for the definite vs. indefinite temporal location of t_E (cf. Song 2005; Grønn and Stechow 2016). Obviously, it is beyond the scope of our study to discuss definiteness in the nominal domain, which is "one of the main research topics in formal semantics and analytic philosophy" (Brocher and Von Heusinger 2018: 3). We draw on the consensus that "most researchers agree that the semantics of the indefinite article comes with an existential entailment, such that it signals to the comprehender that

---

21. In addition to g and i, w would be a third index commonly assumed; w is supposed to indicate the interpretation of an expression relative to a world.

a referent exists without introducing an individual referent" (ibid). On the other hand, definite expressions "[contribute] a uniqueness presupposition" (Brocher and Von Heusinger 2018: 3). In this tradition, the definite article may be defined with Heim and Kratzer (1998):

$\llbracket \text{the} \rrbracket = \lambda f\colon f \in D_{\langle e, t \rangle}$, and there is exactly one x such that $f(x) = 1$.

(Heim and Kratzer 1998: 75)

This definition reads as "the smallest function that takes an entity of the type $\langle e, t \rangle$ and there is exactly one x such that $f(x)n = 1$."[22] Accordingly, the definite article triggers two presuppositions:

i. An existential presupposition, which requires that the referent of the definite NP must exist.[23] For instance, "the car" in (9a) has to exist in order that the whole expression can be interpreted. A famous example violating that principle traces back to Russell (1905: 483): "The king of France is bald". Since there is no king of France, there is a presupposition failure which causes that the expression becomes uninterpretable.
ii. A presupposition that the referent be uniquely identifiable. The mini-discourse "Two men came into a room. Suddenly, the man left". provides two possible referents for "the man". However, neither of the two men introduced in the first sentence is uniquely identifiable. Hence, this results in a presupposition failure of unique identifiability which explains the oddity.

Applying these criteria to the temporal domain and Partee's Example (10), we can derive the following presuppositions:

i. Existential presupposition: The definite reading presupposes that the referred interval exists.
ii. Unique identifiability: An interval is uniquely identifiable at a given stage of discourse such that it may serve as t_{LOC}. As it is the case in (10), this interval may also be inferred (e.g. "I didn't turn off the stove (while leaving the house today)") such that it does not necessarily have to be mentioned explicitly in the

---

22. In type theory, e and t are basic types which stand for "entity" and "truth value". Type $\langle e, t \rangle$ designates a function from an entity to a truth value. For instance, an intransitive verb like *smoke* is of the type $\langle e, t \rangle$. It is a function that takes an entity e (e.g. *Peter*) and maps it onto a truth value t (1 for *true* if *Peter smokes* is true; 0 for *false* if *Peter smokes* is false), cf. e.g. Heim and Kratzer (1998).

23. The existential presupposition seems to face problems when it comes to the analysis of fiction and fictional characters. It follows that the referred concept of existence is not necessarily tied to the extra-linguistic world.

preceding discourse. The assignment function felicitously outputs a value. If not, we encounter a presupposition failure that causes the meaning of (10) to be undefined in the definite (referential) reading. The hearer's solution to this puzzle might be to derive a quantificational reading.

Integrating the two accounts
Having introduced the distinction between quantificational (indefinite) tense on the one hand and referential (definite) tense on the other hand, we can now update our preliminary definition of the Simple Past in (6) by assuming a referential and quantificational version. The referential (definite) Simple Past stays the same: t_E is referentially assigned to t_{LOC}. Whenever t_{LOC} is adverbially specified by a positional adverbial, like "yesterday, in 1999 or at three", t_E becomes temporally definite, independently of t_{LOC}'s granularity (cf. Section 2.3 for the interplay between tense and adverbials). On the other hand, we define the quantificational Simple Past to lack t_{LOC} in its logical form. As a result, t_E becomes indefinite. In other words, we assume that the quantificational vs. referential distinction correlates with the absence vs. presence of t_{LOC}.

(13) Quantificational and referential Simple Past as ordering functions
   a. ⟦SIMPLE PAST$_{REF}$⟧: $\lambda t_S \lambda t_E \lambda t_P \lambda t_{LOC}. (t_E \left[\substack{\subseteq \\ \supseteq}\right] t_{LOC}) \subseteq t_P \prec t_S$
      i. *[Oh wait!] I didn't turn off the stove.*
      ii. *Yesterday, I played soccer.*
      iii. *In 1989, he was a farmer.*
   b. ⟦SIMPLE PAST$_{QUANT}$⟧: $\lambda t_S \lambda t_E \lambda t_P. t_E \subseteq t_P \prec t_S$
      i. *She wrote several books on the topic.*
      ii. *Knicks owner James Dolan recovered from coronavirus.*[24]

Distinguishing quantificational and referential tense will turn out to be crucial for our approach to the Portuguese PPC$_{PT}$, the Spanish PPC$_{SP}$, as well as our discourse-based account of the functions of the two tense forms. This first glance into the different functions taken over by definite and indefinite tense in discourse is summarized in Table 2.1.

Table 2.1 Quantificational vs. Referential Tense

	t_{LOC}	Presupposition	Discourse function
Quantificational tense	✗	✗	introduction of indefinite t_E
Referential tense	✓	uniquely identifiable interval	identification of t_{LOC}

24. *Washington Post* (04/22/20), https://www.washingtonpost.com/sports/2020/04/22/knicks-owner-james-dolan-recovered-coronavirus-set-donate-plasma/, 04/23/2020.

2.2 Aspect

This section introduces the semantic layer of aspect. As a first approximation, we may follow Comrie (1976: 3), who defines "aspects [to be] different ways of viewing the internal temporal constituency of a situation." This broad definition aims at a conception of aspect as a kind of schedule of an eventuality. As it turns out, this schedule is encoded on, and thus has to be interpreted at, two distinct levels that are commonly identified in aspect theory. In most general terms, one of them is lexically coded, while the other one is grammatically coded, which led to the influential terminology of lexical vs. grammatical aspect. Although researchers have mostly agreed on the theoretic conception of that bipartite structure, there is no consensus with regard to a standardized terminology. The (non-exhaustive) Table 2.2 provides an overview of the rich inventory of terminologies proposed in the literature.

Table 2.2 Terminology in aspect theory

Authors	The two layers of aspect	
de Swart (2012); Filip (2012)	Lexical Aspect	Grammatical Aspect
Vendler (1957)	Verb Schemata	?
Comrie (1976)	Situation	Aspect
Dowty (1979)	Aspectual Class	Aspectual Form
Smith (1991)	Situation Aspect	Viewpoint Aspect
Klein (1994); Dessì Schmid (2014)	Aktionsart	Aspect
Verkuyl (2005)	Inner Aspect	Outer Aspect

We adhere to Smith's (1991) terminology distinguishing situation aspect and viewpoint aspect because we particularly consider "viewpoint" to capture best the viewpoint aspect's function of encoding the relationship between t_E and t_{LOC} (cf. below).

2.2.1 Situation aspect

The analysis of the semantics of situation aspect traces back to Vendler (1957) and his observations concerning the temporal constitution of situations, i.e. verbal predicates including the verb-internal arguments. Vendler shows that some situations felicitously combine with particular adverbials, while others do not:

(14) "Verb schemata" and their meaning effects (Vendler 1957)
    a. What are you doing?
        i. *I am running (or writing, working)*.
        ii. **I am knowing (or loving, recognizing)*.
        iii. *I am writing the letter (or running a mile)*.
        iv. **I am reaching the top (or spotting the plane)*.

b. For how long...?
   i. *For how long did he push the cart?*
   ii. **For how long did he draw the circle?*
c. How long...?
   i. **How long did it take to push the cart?*
   ii. *How long did it take to draw the circle?*

In most general terms, the observed effects can be reduced to "the presence of some end, limit, or boundary" of certain situations (cf. Filip 2012: 721). As it turns out, there are three semantic traces contained in predicates whose presence or absence predicts the effects observed in (14): change, telicity and temporal extent/durativity (cf. Filip 2012: 727). Based on these three pillars, verbal predicates are typically divided into four groups, traditionally labelled as state, activity, accomplishment and achievement. Table 2.3 illustrates a common cross-classification of these four basic types.[25]

Table 2.3 Binary classification of the lexical classes (inspired by Filip 2012: 727)

Aktionsart	Predicate	[± CHANGE]	[± BOUNDARY]	[± TEMPORAL EXTENT]
State	*love, know*	−	−	+
Activity	*walk, run*	+	−	+
Accomplishment	*run a mile, draw a circle*	+	+	+
Achievement	*reach, win*	+	+	−

Based on that classification, we can account for the observations presented in (14): the Present Progressive in (14a) presupposes a predicate that fulfills the conditions of [+ CHANGE], [± BOUNDARY] and [+ TEMPORAL EXTENT], i.e. the Present Progressive combines with activities and achievements. The question of "For how long...?" (14b) presupposes a predicate that fulfills the conditions of [± CHANGE], [− BOUNDARY] and [+ TEMPORAL EXTENT], i.e. it combines with states and activities (an example for a state would be "For how long did (s)he live in New York?)". Furthermore, the question of "How long did it take...?" in (14c) presupposes a predicate that fulfills the conditions of [+ CHANGE], [+ BOUNDARY] and [+ TEMPORAL EXTENT], i.e. it combines with accomplishments (achievements may be coerced (converted) into accomplishments and become, as a consequence, felicitous as for instance in "How long did it take to reach the" top?)[26]

---

25. The [± BOUNDARY]-property is meant to capture the [± TELICITY]-property.

26. Cf. de Swart (1998) for coercion.

A rather formalized definition is proposed by Lohnstein (2011).

(15) Aktionsarten in Lohnstein (2011: 268ff.)[27]
   a. State [− DURATIVE, − RESULT] :
      $P_{STATE}(x)$ is true in an interval i, iff $P_{STATE}(x)$ is true for every $t \subset i$ of length 0.[28]
      Reads as:
      If a state-predicate P_{STATE} (e.g. know the answer) *takes an argument x* (e.g. Peter), *than P* (Peter know the answer) *is true at i, if and only if P is true at every time point t of length 0 that is part of the interval i.*
   b. Activity [+ DURATIVE, − RESULT]:
      If $P_{ACTIVITY}$ is true in an interval i, then $P_{ACTIVITY}(x)$ is true for every $(t \subset i)$ of length > 0
      Reads as:
      If an activity-predicate $P_{ACTIVITY}$ (e.g. push the cart) *takes an argument x* (e.g. Peter), *then P* (Peter push the cart) *is true at i, if and only if P is true at every time point t of length > 0 that is part of the interval i.*
   c. Accomplishment [+ DURATIVE], [+ RESULT]:
      If $P_{ACCOMPLISHMENT}(x)$ is true in an interval i, then $P_{ACCOMPLISHMENT}(x)$ is false for all $(t \subset i)$
      Reads as:
      If an accomplishment-predicate $P_{ACCOMPLISHMENT}$ (e.g. draw a circle) *takes an argument x* (e.g. Peter), *then P* (Peter draw a circle) *is true at i, if and only if P is false at every time point t that is part of i.*
   d. Achievement [− DURATIVE, + RESULT]:
      If $P_{ACHIEVEMENT}(x)$ is true in an interval i, then $P_{ACCOMPLISHMENT}(x)$ is false for all $(t \subset i)$

The state-definition (15a) is supposed to capture the perfectly homogeneous nature of a state interval. If Peter know the answer is true at i, then it is true for each atomic (i.e. $t = 0$) time t which is part of i. The notion of atomicity is supposed to account for the lack of any change going on with a state despite the temporal extent. This marks the crucial distinction between states and acitivities. The definition of activities captures the *almost* perfectly homogeneous nature of an activity interval. The idea is that activity predicates denote a temporal extension of P (durativity) such that they are true at any t which is part of i, as long as $t > 0$. This definition captures the condition that an accomplishment requires the evaluation of its culmination point in order to be rated true. In other words, $P_{ACCOMPLISHMENT}$ is necessarily

---

27. The definitions are translated from German; verbalizations of the definitions added.

28. 0 should be conceived of as infinitesimally 0. Otherwise, there would be no result.

false for each $t \subset i$. The definition of achievements actually equals the one for accomplishments. As Lohnstein (2011: 270) points out, the difference between the two lies in the criterion of durativity.

Having introduced the semantic properties characterizing situation aspect, it should be finally noted that situation aspect is sensitive to several factors, as illustrated in the non-exhaustive list in (16).

(16) Factors that may impact situation aspect
    a. Singular vs. Plural VP-internal argument   (cf. Verkuyl 2005)
       i. ✓*(to) build a house in two years*
      ii. **(to) build houses in two years*
     iii. **(to) build a house for two years*
     iv. ✓*(to) build houses for two years*
    b. Adverbial modification   (cf. "coercion", e.g. de Swart 1998)
       i. **(to) build a house repeatedly in two years*
      ii. **(to) build houses repeatedly in two years*
     iii. ✓*(to) build a house repeatedly for two years*
     iv. ✓*(to) build houses repeatedly for two years*

In (16a), the number of the verb-internal argument (house vs. houses) impacts the situation's telicity: while the plural number atelicizes the expression (by substracting a boundary), which results in felicitous combinations with "for two years", the singular number telicizes the expression (by adding a boundary), which results in felicitous combinations with "in two years". Adding an adverbial like "repeatedly" in (16b) though, atelicizes the expression independently of the argument's number.

2.2.2 Viewpoint aspect

We restrict our discussion of the viewpoint aspect to the most discussed phenomenon, namely the perfective-imperfective distinction. "Situations may be conceptualized either as total, indivisible wholes, or by envisaging their internal constituency" (Gvozdanović 2012: 781). In the Romance languages, this distinction is prominently encoded in the two past tense forms of Simple Past and Imperfect, as for instance in Portuguese:

(17) *Pretérito Perfeito Simples* vs. *Imperfeito* in Portuguese
                                                               (Ilari and Basso 2008: 293)
    a. *João começou a beber um copo de chope, quando teve início o*
       João started.SP to drink a   glass of beer   when   had start the
      tiroteio no   bar.
      shooting in the bar.
      'João started drinking a glass of beer when the shooting started in the bar.'

b. João começava   a beber um copo de chope, quando teve início o
   João started.IMP to drink a   glass of beer when   had start the
   tiroteio no   bar.
   shooting in the bar.
   'João was starting/about to drink a glass of beer when the shooting started in the bar.'

While the perfective past (17a) denotes the temporal boundaries of the denoted eventuality (i.e. start and end of e), the imperfective past (17b) zooms in, which blocks the perspectivization of the temporal boundaries of e. This idea of an "external vs. internal view" (cf. Kamp 2013: 128) on eventualities is also illustrated in Figure 2.5.

In the tradition of the DRT-framework (Discourse Representation Theory), we define viewpoint aspect as a grammaticalized means to express the relationship between the event time te and the location time t_{LOC} (cf. Kamp et al. 2011: 200, cf. also Becker and Egetenmeyer 2018: 9): the perfective viewpoint denotes t_E to be a subset of t_{LOC} ($t_E \subseteq t_{LOC}$). Conversely, the imperfective viewpoint denotes t_E to be a superset of t_{LOC} ($t_E \supseteq t_{LOC}$). These formalizations are able to account for why the perfective vs. imperfective viewpoint aspect creates an effect of (not) including the temporal boundaries of an eventuality. If these lay outside of t_{LOC}, they consequently cannot be "seen". On the other hand, if the eventuality is included in t_{LOC}, its whole dimension becomes visible.[29]

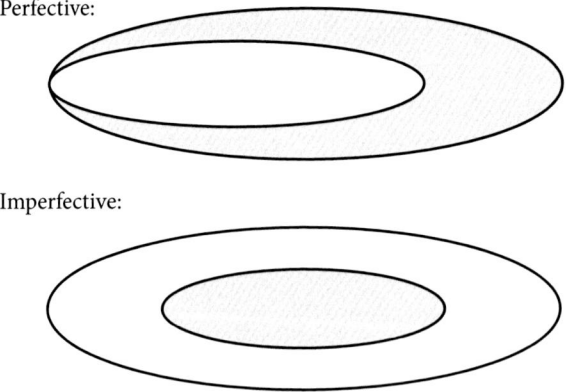

Figure 2.5 Perfective vs. imperfective aspect (Gvozdanović 2012: 789)

White circle: event

---

29. Klein (1994: 99f.) and Gvozdanović (2012: 789) define the viewpoint aspect as expressing the relationship between the eventuality and the topic time.

Again, we can update our conception of the semantics of the Simple Past as an ordering function by integrating the notion of viewpoint aspect. Given that we defined quantificational past not to call for a location time (cf. Section 2.1), it is not affected by the perfective-imperfective distinction and stays the same.

(18) Quantificational and referential Simple Past as ordering functions incl. viewpoint aspect
   a. ⟦SIMPLE PAST$_{REF\text{-}PERFECTIVE}$⟧ : $\lambda t_S \, \lambda t_E \, \lambda t_P \, \lambda t_{LOC}. \, (t_E \subseteq t_{LOC}) \subseteq t_P \prec t_S$
      i. *[Oh wait!] I didn't turn off the stove.*
      ii. *Yesterday, I played soccer*
   b. ⟦SIMPLE PAST$_{REF\text{-}IMPERFECTIVE}$⟧ : $\lambda t_S \, \lambda t_E \, \lambda t_P \, \lambda t_{LOC}. \, (t_E \supseteq t_{LOC}) \subseteq t_P \prec t_S$
      i. *When I came home, I was hungry.*
      ii. *In 1989, he was a farmer.*
   c. ⟦SIMPLE PAST$_{QUANT}$⟧: $\lambda t_S \, \lambda t_E \, \lambda t_P. \, t_E \subseteq t_P \prec t_S$
      i. *She wrote several books on the topic.*
      ii. *Knicks owner James Dolan recovered from coronavirus.*[30]

2.3 Adverbials

This section introduces tempo-aspectual adverbials. Tempo-aspectual adverbials have always played a crucial role in the analysis of problems and phenomena related to tense and aspect, as well as in the study of the Present Perfect. They are traditionally supposed to help in revealing the covert semantics of expressions based on the felicity or infelicity of particular combinations. In this section, we focus on the questions of which types of adverbials are relevant to the study of tempo-aspectual phenomena, how we may account for their semantics and the operations that they license, and how they fit into our general framework.

The term adverb traditionally refers to a morphosyntactic category forming the head of an adverbial phrase, such as "often" or "carefully". On the other hand, the term adverbial denotes a syntactic function, as well as a semantic category, that may be composed of a variety of morphosyntactic candidates. According to Rathert (2012: 237), these can be nominal phrases ("every year, last year"), nominal phrases combined with adpositions ("before X-mas, 3 weeks ago"), sentential adverbials ("before he left"), adverbs ("now, then") or adjectival adverbs ("earlier, later"). Leaving the form side and shifting to the meaning side, what qualifies tempo-aspectual adverbials is their particular interaction with the semantic ingredients of tense and aspect. Thus, we need to focus on those adverbials that interact in some

---

30. https://www.washingtonpost.com/sports/2020/04/22/knicks-owner-james-dolan-recovered-coronavirus-set-donate-plasma/, 04/23/2020.

relevant way with t_E, t_{LOC}, t_S, t_R and t_P. Put differently, these adverbials should answer questions like "when" (e.g. "yesterday, at three o'clock"), "how long" ("for three years, ever since") or "how often" ("six times, often") an eventuality is said to occur.

A distinction between modifying and quantifying adverbials is discussed in de Swart (1991).

(19) Modifying vs. quantifying adverbials (de Swart 1991)[31]
    a. Modifying adverbial
        [At *three/At ten/Tomorrow*], *I will go to the movies.*
    b. Quantifying adverbial
        I have [already/never/several times] been to this bar.

Applying our terminology, we are able divide the two in a straightforward way by grouping them into scoping over t_{LOC} vs. scoping over t_E. Following Kamp et al. (2011: 200), we defined the location time as "the time when the event is said to occur [...] [or] the time at which the state is said to hold" (cf. Section 2.1). Modifying adverbials explicitly aim at specifying t_{LOC}, be it rather fine-grained (e.g. "at 7.34 am") or rather course-grained (e.g. "last year"). On the other hand, we defined t_E with Becker and Egetenmeyer (2018: 36) as the "time the whole eventuality is supposed to take from its beginning (left boundary) to its completion (right boundary) [...]". In other words, t_E represents the actual "runtime" (cf. Altshuler 2016) of the eventuality itself. Now, we assume quantificational adverbials to quantify over t_E such that they may express (i) if there is an eventuality at all (mere existence of t_E, e.g. expressed by "already"), (ii) if there is no t_E ("not (yet)"), (iii) if there are several instances of t_E ("often, always, lots of times"), (iv) if there are only a few instances of t_E ("sometimes"), or (v) if there is an exact number of instances of t_E ("three times"). These questions can be answered without referring to temporal locations, i.e. without referring to t_{LOC}. Obviously, combinations of quantificational and positional adverbs are possible, such as in ("Last year, I have been to London several times".).

The distinction between modifying and quantifying adverbials furthermore correlates with the referential vs. quantificational tense opposition discussed in Section 2.1: while referential tense qualifies to combine with modifying adverbials, quantificational tense does so with quantificational adverbials. As a consequence, tempo-aspectual adverbials can serve as means to emphasize one of the two readings readings, as illustrated in (20). Both referential and quantificational readings in (20b) can be evoked with and without adverbial modification. However, the indicated adverbial expressions may provide the pragmatically smoother alternative to evoke the desired reading.

---

31. Further modifying adverbials in de Swart's (1991) account express quality, degree, circumstance and modality, i.e. meaning aspects that do not directly address the tempo-aspectual domain. We exclude these from our analysis.

(20) Referential and quantificational tense with (c)overt adv. modification
    a. *Tell me, what happened at 10 pm?*
       Referential reading with covert referential adverbial:
       – *I was at home, called my dad and went to bed.*
       Referential reading with overt referential adverbial:
       – *<u>At 10</u> I was at home, called my dad and <u>then</u> I went to bed.*
    b. *Wanna go to London?*
       Quantificational reading with covert quantificational adverbial:
       – *Nah, I've been there.*
       Quantificational reading with overt quantificational adverbial:
       – *Nah, I've been there <u>before/several times</u>.*

Both examples are fine with both covert and overt adverbial modification. Nevertheless, depending on the context, one of the two alternatives might represent the more appropriate choice for a speaker in order to enhance a particular reading. This is in line with a conception that "the prototypical adverbial is optional and corresponds syntactically to an adjunct, acting semantically as a modifier" (Maienborn and Schäfer 2012: 1392).[32]

For the purpose of our study of the Present Perfect though, this bipartite picture is too coarse-grained, as it will turn out in the Chapters 3 and 4. Therefore, we stick to Rathert (2012) and an architecture featuring a fourfold distinction of positional, quantificational, durative and "Extended-Now (XN)" adverbials:

(21) Tempo-aspectual adverbials   (Rathert 2012: 238)
    a. Positional adverbials
       i. anaphoric adverbials: *three weeks ago, afterward*
       ii. deictic adverbials: *yesterday, tomorrow*
       iii. clock-calendar adverbials: *on May 1, 1999*
    b. Quantificational adverbials: *once, twice, often, seldom, sometimes*
    c. Adverbials of duration: *until, since, in, for*
    d. Extended-Now adverbials: *ever since*

As an extension, positional adverbials (corresponding to modifying adverbials in de Swart 1991) are now divided into three subgroups. They differ in how they retrieve the value for t_{LOC}. While anaphoric positional adverbials yield their value discourse-based, deictic adverbials do so relative to the deictic center of the speaker. Finally, clock-calendar adverbials represent absolute values that do not depend on the restrictions of the other two types. Furthermore, the two groups of durative and XN-adverbials are added. Intuitively, durative adverbials seem to represent

---

32. This notion of modification is different from de Swart's (1991) modifying adverbials.

a somewhat hybrid type by combining characteristics from both referential and quantificational adverbials:

> [...] duration adverbials characterize a time interval of a particular length; a situation that is specified by a duration adverbial is asserted to cover the whole time referred to by the adverbial. (Musan 2002: 110)

In fact, durative adverbials seem to indicate a temporal frame identical with the time that the predicated eventuality is said to hold (i.e. identical with the event time t_E). This is triggered by a universal quantification over t_E within the interval that is denoted by durative adverbials.[33]

(22) I have been living by myself *for three months*.

In (22), the durative adverbial "for three months" scopes over t_E by universally quantifying over all relevant times included in the denoted interval such that I live by myself is true at each interval included in the interval that is denoted by "for three months". We thus consider durative adverbials to operate on a quantificational level, as well.[34] The assumption that positional and quantificational/durative adverbials scope over different temporal ingredients can be shown with a linguistic test as illustrated in (23). It builds on the premise that the adverbials scope is resolved via answering implicit questions, such as "when?", "how long?" and "how many times?".

(23) Distinguishing referential, quantificational and durative adverbials
   a. When... ?
      i. ✓*three weeks ago, yesterday*
      ii. **twice, often, sometimes*
      iii. **until, since, in, for*
   b. How many times... ?
      i. **three weeks ago, yesterday*
      ii. ✓*twice, often, sometimes*
      iii. **until, since, in, for*
   c. How long... ?
      i. **three weeks ago, yesterday*
      ii. **twice, often, sometimes*
      iii. ✓*until, since, in, for*

---

33. Cf. discussion on the universal vs. existential ambiguity in Iatridou et al. (2003) for sentences like "I haven't seen Mary in a while. Where is she? – *She has been sick*".

34. The position of durative adverbials between reference and quantification is not uncontroversial. Our view is in line with e.g. Móia (2000: 14), but contradicts Musan (2002: 109) who classifies them as a non-quantificational, third group.

(23a) shows that durative adverbials do not answer the implicit question of "when?" which would mean that they scope over t_{LOC}. Instead, they answer the implicit question of "how long?" – which does not aim at temporally locating an eventuality but rather at the question if there is a repetition or an extension of t_E. In the same vein, "how many times…?" aims at t_E, as well.

Finally, we define XN-adverbials to scope over a third tempo-aspectual ingredient, namely the perspective time t_P. In Section 2.1, we defined t_P as the "time from which the given information is viewed" (Kamp 2013: 116). Further, we followed Declerck et al. (2006) in assuming that t_P may lay in the past time-sphere or the present time-sphere, as illustrated in the repeated Figure 2.6. A priori, the exact boundary dividing these two spheres is vague (and might be perceived as gradual). Nevertheless, the present time-sphere is defined to include a period of time which is prior to the speech time t_S (t_0 in Figure 2.6), namely to include the pre-present time-sphere.

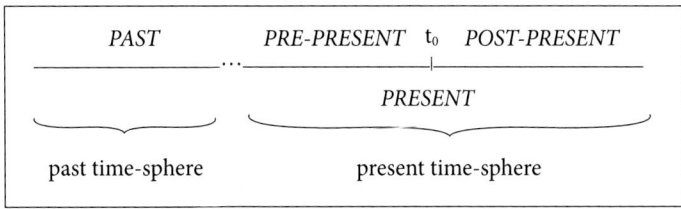

Figure 2.6 Time-spheres and zones (Declerck et al. 2006: 149)

Now, XN-adverbials like "ever since" serve as means to specify the vague temporal range of the present time-sphere. That is, XN-adverbials specify the perspective time t_P and need to satisfy the presupposition of being compatible with the present time-sphere.

The category of XN-adverbials will be particularly crucial in Chapter 4 and the analysis of the PPC_{SP} and its combinations with adverbials. As it will turn out, there is a range of Spanish adverbials that are commonly analyzed as indicating "hodiernality" when combined with the PPC_{SP}, like "today, now, this week". We will argue that, in many cases, they may be analyzed as XN-adverbials (instead of positional adverbials), i.e. that they may be analyzed as scoping over t_P (instead of t_{LOC}). Furthermore, the scope of the XN-adverbials relates to the famous "Present Perfect Puzzle" and the hodiernality constraint of the Spanish PPC_{SP} (cf. also Section 2.5).

Table 2.4 summarizes our assumptions concerning the four categories of tempo-aspectual adverbials as we are going to apply them in our study.[35]

---

[35] As mentioned above, the list of the lexical representatives of the category of the XN-adverbials will be expanded within the analysis of the PPC_{PT} in Chapter 3 and the PPC_{SP} in Chapter 4.

Table 2.4 Tempo-aspectual adverbials

Adverbial	Scope	Implicit question	Example
Positional	t_{LOC}	When?	*three weeks ago, yesterday*
Quantificational	t_E	How many times?	*once, twice, often, sometimes*
Durative	t_E	How long?	*until, since, for*
Extended-Now	t_P	(What is the temporal vantage point?)	*ever since*

2.4 Tense and aspect in discourse

In the Sections 2.1 and 2.2, we have introduced the study of tense and aspect guided by the question of how we can capture the semantics of a particular tense form. To a great extent, this endeavor was based on the semantics of tense forms as isolated discourse units. In this section, we expand the focus by integrating discourse-related phenomena related to the study of tense and aspect. The need of this discourse-based perspective on tense and aspect can be motivated with Kamp et al. (2011):

> It is a ubiquitous feature of natural languages that utterances are interpretable only when the interpreter takes account of the contexts in which they are made [...]. The focus on context dependence has led to an important shift in paradigm, away from the "classical" conception of formal semantics which sees semantic theory as primarily concerned with reference and truth and towards a perspective in which the central concept is not that of truth but of information.
>
> (Kamp et al. 2011: 125)

It follows that for an adequate description of the PPC$_{SP}$ and PPC$_{PT}$, there is a need to understand the functions that the two tense forms fulfill in discourse. This is, in addition to the analysis of truth-conditional meaning, we need to take into account several factors that will be introduced in the present section. In order to narrow down the manifold aspects associated with the term discourse, we want to distinguish two levels which we will call the macro-structure and the micro-structure of discourse. While the former one is supposed to capture what is commonly subsumed under the term of modes of discourse (in the sense of Smith 2003), the latter one aims at syntagmatic relations that may be established between adjacent tense forms on the syntagmatic axis. Since we assume both dimensions to be intrinsically intertwined, they should be understood as exerting mutual influence instead of forming autonomous layers. Nevertheless, we introduce them separately in the following.

2.4.1 The macro-structure: Modes of discourse

The modes of discourse were proposed by Smith (2003):

> The Discourse Modes are classes of discourse passages, defined by the entities they introduce into the universe of discourse and their principle of progression. […] The Discourse Modes grew out of my work on aspect and tense. In studies of situation types in discourse, I noticed interesting differences between passages of different types. (Smith 2003: 1)

The main idea is that a text (also a passage within a text) embodies a particular mode of discourse which correlates with certain peculiarities in the tempo-aspectual domain. Narration and report represent the two principal modes that are commonly employed to relate to eventualities that lay in the past. This bipartite picture traces back to Weinrich (1964) and his study of *Tempusregister* ('temporal registers'). He distinguishes *Erzählte Welt* ('narrated world') and *Besprochene Welt* ('discussed/reported world') and assigns discussing/reporting tense forms and narrating tense forms to the two registers respectively. As it turns out, this distinction accounts for the temporal relations that may hold between adjacent tense forms of past. These may either be temporally related to each other or be anchored discretely with respect to the speech time, the deictic center. In the tradition of Weinrich (1964), the archetype of the Present Perfect functions as a discussing/reporting tense form (cf. below and Section 2.5 for further discussion). Now, as an extension of that approach, Smith (2003: 8) proposes the following modes of discourse: Narrative, description, report, information and argument. The modes are defined based on three features, namely "type of situation", "temporality" and "progression", as exposed in the following.

Narrative / Narration

- *Situations: primarily specific events and states*
- *Temporality: dynamic, located in time*
- *Progression: advancement in narrative time*

The narrative mode (or mode of narration) has gained a lot of attention over the past decades due to the peculiar dynamicity that it evolves while discourse unfolds, as illustrated in (24).

(24) Narration (Smith 2003: 14)
A few days later I called on Dr P and his wife at home […]. *Mrs. P showed me into a lofty apartment, which recalled fin-de-siècle Berlin.* […]. *There were books, there were paintings, but the music was central. Dr. P came in, a little bowed and advanced with outstretched hand to the grandfather clock* […].

Narration is said to include events and states, i.e. all kinds of situations that both bear and depend on a temporal advancement. They are typically restricted to the past. Furthermore, the denoted events and states are temporally related to each other such that temporal progression within the past time-sphere can be achieved. It is crucial to point out that this progression is semantically encoded and not a product of pragmatic inferences. In Chapter 2.1, we introduced the notion of reference time t_R. Following Kamp et al. (2011: 199), we defined t_R as "the time or event to which the story has so far advanced [and] with which the tense of the new sentence establishes a certain anaphoric relation." In this vein, t_R is shifted by events and maintained with states (cf. also section on the micro-structure of discourse below). Now, we can sharpen the concept of t_R and state that it is typical to occur in the mode of narration: whenever there is a narrative discourse mode, t_R gets activated in order to enable the dynamic update of the discourse reference time in terms of narrative progression. There is another link between the semantic pillars of tense (as discussed in Section 2.1) and the modes of discourse. We defined the perspective time t_P as "the time from which the given information is viewed" (Kamp 2013: 116). Moreover, following Declerck et al. (2006: 149), we defined two potential time-spheres as candidates to become t_P, namely the past time-sphere and the present time-sphere. With regard to the discourse mode of narration, we can state that t_P is encoded to lie in the past time-sphere. This is in line with the standard Reichenbachian accounts of past tense forms that assume t_P to precede t_S.[36] In sum, the categories of tense, aspect and discourse mode are intrinsically intertwined, as demonstrated by the inclusion of t_R and the setting of t_P in the past time-sphere as a typical feature of the mode of narration. None of these categories dominates the other ones though. Otherwise, a specific discourse mode or a specific tempo-semantic property could be identified as *the* primordial one that all kinds of phenomena observable in the domain of tense, aspect and the modes of discourse could be traced back to.

Report

- Situations: primarily events, states, general statives
- Temporality: dynamic, located in time
- Progression: advancement anchored to speech time

The report mode is characterized as denoting events, states and general statives. It also allows for a dynamic updated of temporal progression in time. Contrasting with the mode of narration though, the report's temporal advancement and progression is anchored to speech time (and not to other eventualities), as in (25).

---

36. In Reichenbach's (1947) terms: $R \prec S$.

(25) Report (Smith 2003: 16)
A week after Ethiopia started an offensive that it says is aimed at ending the two-year-old war, it is now clear that the whole of Eritrea could become a battlefield. with hundreds of civilians fleeing the region, Colonel Kidane said Ethiopian soldiers continue to skirmish with Eritrean soldiers on the run here in western Eritrea. [...]

In our terminology, the adverbial "a week after Ethiopia started an offensive" does not specify t_{LOC}, i.e. it does not locate an eventuality in the past. Instead, it specifies the perspective time t_P that lies in the present time-sphere. Additionally, any temporal relationship that may hold between the denoted eventualities, such as simultaneity or succession, has to be indicated explicitly via adverbials or has to be inferred based on other mechanisms given that there is no default semantic mechanism (t_R) that would push the reference time forward as it is the case in the narrative mode (cf. also 2.5).

Description

- *Situations: primarily events and states, and ongoing events*
- *Temporality: static, located in time*
- *Progression: spatial advancement through the scene or object*

The description mode denotes temporally anchored situations. Although these are located in time, they are strictly static which leads to the lack of any temporal progression or advancement. "The entities introduced in descriptions are usually states, ongoing events, atelic events" (Smith 2003: 28). There may be spacial advancement though the scene or object.

(26) Description (Smith 2003: 29)
We were in an impressive and beautiful situation on a rocky plateau. It was too high for grass, there was very little earth and the place was littered with boulders, but the whole plateau was covered with a thick carpet of mauve primulas. There were countless thousands of them, delicate flowers on thick green stems. Before us was the brilliant green lake, a quarter of a mile long, and in the shallows and in the streams that spilled over from it the primulas grew in clumps and perfect circles.

Information

- *Situations: primarily general statives*
- *Temporality: atemporal*
- *Progression: metaphorical motion through the text domain*

The information mode primarily features general, atemporal statives. That is, there is no denotation of eventualities that could be located on a virtual timeline, as in (27).

(27) Information (Smith 2003: 17)
When people try to get a message from one individual to another in the party game "telephone," they usually garble the words beyond recognition. It might seem surprising, then, that mere molecules inside our cells constantly enact their own version of telephone without distorting the relayed information in the least. Actually, no one could survive without such precise signalling in cells. The body functions properly only because cells communicate with one another constantly. […]

Given that there is no temporal anchoring of situations, there is no temporal progression either. However, the employment of past and future tense form is not ruled out as they build on the concept of "metaphorical motion through the text domain" (Smith 2003: 20). This enables the use of expressions like "Like I said before" etc.

Argument

- Situations: primarily facts and propositions, general statives
- Temporality: atemporal
- Progression: metaphorical motion through the text domain

The argument mode is quite similar to the mode of information. It is atemporal, thus it lacks temporal progression. Consequently, tense and aspect forms serve as a metaphorical means to navigate through the text – as opposed to the other modes that exploit tense and aspect to locate eventualities on a virtual timeline. In addition to general statives, the mode of argument denotes facts and propositions, as illustrated in (28).

(28) Argument (Smith 2003: 98)
The press has trumpeted the news that crude oil prices are three times higher than they were a year ago. But it was the $10 or $11 price of February 1999, not the one today, that really deserved the headlines. When inflation is taken into account, that 1999 price was the lowest in modern history, while oil has gone above today's seemingly high price several times. And for the past 14 years, at $17.50, oil has been one of the real bargains of the modern age. […]

In the Chapters 3 and 4, we particularly relate the modes of discourse to the study of the PPC_{PT} and PPC_{SP} in order to determine the typical contexts that these occur in. Furthermore, we investigate the PPC_{SP}'s approach of the mode of narration within its referential drift in Chapter 6.

Having introduced this overview of the macro-structure of discourse, we now zoom in on the micro-structure of discourse.

2.4.2 The micro-structure: Syntagmatic relations

This section discusses tempo-aspectual phenomena on the level of the micro-structure of discourse by zooming in on the syntagmatic axis. The underlying premise is that adjacent tempo-aspectual expressions, such as tense forms, mutually impact each other's interpretation in discourse. Or as Moens (1987) puts it:

> [T]he comprehension of discourse involves the construction of a model of the events and situations talked about in the discourse. Or, more accurately, the listener tries to build a structured representation of the temporal relations the speaker claims there to be between these states of affairs. (Moens 1987: 106)

We are going to focus on two aspects of the micro structure of discourse, namely (i) temporal anaphora which is (mainly) tied to the discourse mode of narration and the related discourse-based management of t_R, as well as (ii) so-called actualization effects (in the sense of Declerck et al. 2006) which build on the antagonistic discourse functions of referential and quantificational tense.

Temporal Anaphora
The literature on anaphoricity in the temporal domain has been growing over the past decades. This is mainly due to the success and influence of the Discourse Representation Theory (DRT) by Kamp et al. In Section 2.1, we defined past tense exemplified by the Simple Past as an ordering function:

(29) Referential Simple Past as an ordering function (repeated from Section 2.1)

$[\![\text{Past}_{\text{REF}}]\!]: \lambda t_S \lambda t_E \lambda t_P \lambda t_{\text{LOC}}. \, (t_E \left[\genfrac{}{}{0pt}{}{\subseteq}{\supseteq}\right] t_{\text{LOC}}) \subseteq t_P \prec t_S$

However, such a merely truth-conditional account might miss capturing fundamental parts of meaning typically stored at the level of discourse:

> When a sentence is examined in isolation, and its interpretations are studied, it is necessary to construct implicitly a discourse in which to interpret it. By default, a minimum discourse is usually chosen, with the implication that this will yield the "real," "core," context-independent meaning of the sentence.
> (Fauconnier 1997: 55f.)

This view is supported by tense forms – e.g. the Romance Imperfect – whose function fully evolves in discourse (cf. below). Tense forms introduce discourse entities that enter the referential structure of discourse (cf. Becker and Egetenmeyer 2018). Under certain conditions, these may become available for anaphoric reference. This can be, once again, illustrated with Kamp and Rohrer's (1983) example of temporal anaphora with the French *Imparfait*.

(30) Update vs. retention of t_R in narration   (Kamp and Rohrer 1983: 253)
   a. *Pierre entra,   Marie téléphona.*
      Pierre entered_{SIMPLE PAST} Marie called_{SIMPLE PAST}
      'Pierre came in, [and then] Marie called someone.'
   b. *Pierre entra,   Marie téléphonait.*
      Pierre entered_{SIMPLE PAST} Marie called_{IMPERFECT}
      'Pierre came in, [while] Marie was on the phone.'

The two tense forms in (30a), (both Simple Past) denote a temporal succession of two events ($e_1 \prec e_2$) despite the lack of an adverbial expression indicating that relation (as it might be achieved for instance by "and then" or "immediately"). In the previous section, we have outlined that the discourse mode of narration enables the semantic encoding of temporal relations between several eventualities even without the explicit specification of the location time t_{LOC} via adverbial modification. This is achieved by exploiting the phoric discourse function of the discourse reference time t_R:

> [T]he tense of a clause triggers a presupposition to the effect that the location time [t_{LOC}] of the eventuality which the clause describes stands in a temporal relation p to a reference time r [t_R]; r has to be linked, via a process of anaphoric presuppposition resolution, to an element from the context [...] established by the antecedent discourse.   (Kamp et al. 2011: 201)

Within the DRT-framework, there are two basic types of eventualities, namely events and states. Both have the status of primitive discourse referents (that is, events and states are not meant to represent situation types) and fulfill different functions on the level of discourse and its temporal make-up. While events are supposed to shift t_R forward, i.e. to lend an updated value to t_R, states maintain it. In (30), *téléphona* and *téléphonait* form a minimal pair of these two basic types. The former (the aoristic *Passé Simple*) updates t_R by temporally shifting it forward in time. As a consequence, the calling-event is semantically encoded as having occurred *after* the event of `Pierre enter the room`. Contrarily, the *Imparfait* in (30b) encodes the calling-event as having occurred *simultaneously* to the event of `Pierre enter the room`. In order to describe the underlying mechanisms, DRT makes use of the so-called DRT-boxes which are designed to depict mental states at a given stage of discourse. The boxes indicate the entities that a discourse is composed of at a given stage, i.e. the entities that have been introduced so far and that form the referential structure. Furthermore, the boxes illustrate several kinds of relations that may hold between these. Figure 2.7 encapsulates such a DRT-box for the mini discourse "Josef turned around". "The man pulled his gun from its holster", which is similar to Example (30a). It consists of two events e_1 and e_2 that form a temporal sequence, i.e. that receive an interpretation of $e_1 \prec e_2$.

```
n j t₁ e₁ x t₂ e₂
   Josef(j)
   t₁ ≺ n
   e₁ ⊆ t₁
   e₁ : "turn-around"(j)
   t₁ ≺ t₂
   "the man" (x)
   t₂ ≺ n
   e₂ ⊆ t₂
   e₂ : "pull-gun"(x)
```

Figure 2.7 DRT box (Kamp et al. 2011: 204)
n: now (t_S); j, x: variable for nominal referent; t: t_{LOC} (morphosyntactically covert); e: t_E.

The box reads as "*The following entities and relations have been introduced to the discourse: n, j (Josef), t_1, e_1 (turn aorund), x (the man), t_2 and et_2 (pull gun). The events e_1 and e_2 are predicates of j and x respectively. The interval t_1 temporally precedes n and e_1 is a subset of t_1. The same holds for t_2, which temporally precedes n and which e_2 is a subset of; t_1 precedes t_2.*"

One might deduce that the sequence of two tense forms denoting aoristic past events generally lead to a sequential interpretation of e_1 preceding e_2. This assumption, that would predict that temporal interpretation in discourse depends on tense and aspect features alone, has been updated in SDRT, the Segmented Discourse Representation Theory (Asher and Lascarides 2003). SDRT adds the layer of rhetorical relations (RR) that hold between propositions in discourse and that serve to establish coherence. They have an impact on the temporal interpretation, as well:

(31) Rethorical Relations and temporal interpretation in SDRT
(Asher and Lascarides 2003: 6)
    a. RR-Narration: $e_1 \prec e_2$
       Max fell. John helped him up.
    b. RR-Explanation: $e_1 \succ e_2$
       Max fell. John pushed him.

While the RR of narration causes the interpretation of $e_1 \prec e_2$, the RR of explanation inverses that order (the RR-narration is not to be confused with the discourse mode of narration as discussed in the previous section). That is, both examples in (31) are instances of the narrative discourse mode. Yet, as proposed in the framework of SDRT, there may be different RR holding between several propositions in discourse. Given that our study is not concerned with rhetorical relations in detail, we do not deepen the analysis of RR and their impact on the temporal interpretation. Instead, we focus on the question of how t_R is actually discursively managed by speaker and hearer and how it is modeled.

In general, there are two competing approaches to the question of how to model the discursive update of t_R. Following Bary (2009: 140) (apud Becker and Egetenmeyer 2018: 34), these approaches may be paraphrased as "pushing vs. pulling accounts." The pulling vs. pushing refers to the question of how t_R is actually updated and anaphorically accessed. The pushing account is argued for by Partee (1984), who credits the approach to Hinrichs (1981):

> Hinrichs proposes that each new past-tense event sentence is specified to occur within the then-current reference time, and it subsequently causes the reference time to be shifted to a new reference time which follows the just-introduced event. [...] Intuitively, the reference time introduced by an event-sentence is located "just after" that event [...]. (Partee 1984: 254)

An illustration of this approach is depicted in Becker and Egetenmeyer (2018):

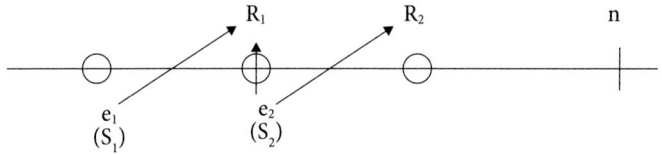

Figure 2.8 The pushing account of t_R (Becker and Egetenmeyer 2018: 34)
e: event; S: state; R: t_R ; n: now (t_S)

When the discursive requirements for temporal anaphora are met and when an event e_1 gets introduced, t_R is shifted just after e_1 providing an anchor for the succeeding e_2. In our terms, t_{R-1} serves as the location time t_{LOC} for e_2. States may also be anaphorically attributed to the current t_R. Nevertheless, these do not cause a shift of t_R but maintain it.

The competing theory of the pulling account is designed in exactly the opposite way. It is argued for e.g. by Kamp (2013) and Becker and Egetenmeyer (2018) whose illustration is depicted in Figure 2.9.

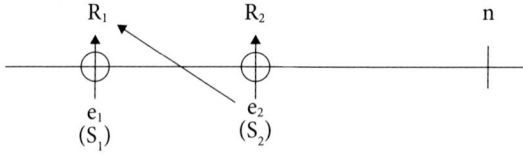

Figure 2.9 The pulling account of t_R (Becker and Egetenmeyer 2018: 34)

Here, t_R is not shifted. Instead, t_R equals the time that the event takes place (i.e. the location time t_{LOC}). At a first glance, the pushing account seems to be more convincing as it intuitively grasps the typical sequential temporal interpretation which is often derived in the narrative mode, as in exemplified above in (30a). However, examples like (31b) are not well captured by the pushing account. Due to an explanation relation, the temporal order is inversed ($e_1 \succ e_2$). The pulling account basically allows for any temporal relation between two events by not determining the temporal relation between them a prioi. In addition, it allows for a better description of how states retrieve their anaphoric referent. In Example (30b), there is a sequence of an event and a state which is interpreted to overlap with e. In other words, the state pulls the reference time t_R introduced by the event.

In sum, there is a correlation between the discourse mode of narration, the use of referential past and temporal anaphora which, in turn, is enabled by exploiting the discourse functions of t_R. In the Chapters 5 and 6, we will discuss whether the PPC_{SP} is able to establish relations of temporal anaphora with adjacent past eventualities.

Quantification and reference in discourse: Actualization effects

In Chapter 2.1, we introduced the opposition of referential vs. quantificational tense. Accordingly, quantificational tense existentially quantifies over t_E and restricts it temporally to the past via a relation of precedence (t_E precedes t_S). Due to the indefinite temporal location of t_E, quantificational tense sometimes is also labelled indefinite tense (cf. Grønn and Stechow 2016), lacking t_{LOC} in its logical form. On the other hand, referential tense assigns a specific temporal location to t_E by assigning it to t_{LOC} – which is why it is also labelled definite tense. The value of t_{LOC} for referential tense forms may be adverbially specified, co-textually retrieved or pragmatically inferred. Again inspired by the research on definiteness in the nominal domain, it turns out that definite and indefinite tense fulfill different functions in discourse. Although it is beyond the scope of our work to review the literature on definiteness in the nominal domain, we summarize, in the following, some of the main insights from the research on the discourse functions of definiteness in the nominal domain based on von Heusinger (2002). In most general and simplified terms, the choice of the definiteness of a nominal phrase is influenced by the referential status of a referent denoted by the respective NP. A referent may be either discourse-new or discourse-old, i.e. previously mentioned (or not) und thus familiar (or not) to both speaker and hearer. In addition to the dimension of definiteness, there is another criterion, namely the one of specificity that is needed in order to account for observable discourse functions of definiteness, as illustrated in (32).

(32)   *A student in syntax I cheated on the exam.*   (von Heusinger 2002: 246)
   a.   *His name is John.*
   b.   *We are all trying to figure out who it was.*

In (32), "a student" is introduced to the discourse as an indefinite noun phrase. However, the indicated potential continuations suggest that the identity of the student may either be known or unknown to the hearer. Accordingly, the indefinite NP "a student" in (32a) is commonly labelled as a specific-indefinite referent, i.e. it is known by the speaker. On the other hand, it is unspecific-indefinite in (32b), i.e. unknown by both hearer and speaker. Table 2.5 illustrates these "identifiability criteria" for definiteness and specificity.

Table 2.5 The identifiability critieria for definiteness and specificity (von Heusinger 2002: 249)

identified by	Definite (+spec)	Indefinite spec.	Indefinite non-spec.
speaker	+	+	−
hearer	+	−	−

Table 2.6 Cross-classification of definiteness and specificity (von Heusinger 2002: 253)

	Discourse-old	Discourse-new
referentially anchored to discourse referents	referential or specific def. NPs	specific indef. NPs
referentially bound by operators	attributive or non-spec. def. NPs	non-spec. indef. NPs

The discourse functions that correspond to these three categories of definiteness are shown in Table 2.6: discourse-new entities get introduced by indefinite NPs that may either (i) be specific, i.e. bound to discourse referents, or (ii) non-specific, i.e. bound by operators (like the existential quantifier). On the other hand, discourse-old entities get introduced by referential or specific definite NPs or attributive or non-specific definite NPs. Applying this picture to the verbal domain to definite and indefinite tense, we can derive a somewhat similar picture. This has been put forth by Declerck et al. (2006). However, the authors reduce their discursive account to the definite vs. indefinite opposition, i.e. they waive the specific vs. non-specific distinction in the temporal domain within their account. In their investigation of the English tense system, the authors point out a typical pattern of a sequence of a Present Perfect followed by a Simple Past. As it turns out, this sequence seems to exploit the discourse function of temporal definiteness in a similar fashion as nominal definiteness does (32b), as discussed above. The Present Perfect, the tense form featuring indefinite tense, existentially quantifies over a discourse-new past eventuality (cf. Section 2.5 for our account of the Present Perfect as an inherently quantificational tense form). Next, the Simple Past functions as a tense form featuring definite tense by picking up that eventuality as discourse-old, i.e. as familiar in order to elaborate on it. This mechanism is illustrated in (33).

(33) Actualization focus (Declerck et al. 2006: 319)
Some idiot has put diesel in the tank instead of petrol. Which of you did that? – I did.

In (33), it seems that the speaker just discovered that somebody must have filled diesel in the tank based an a particular result that (s)he witnesses (perhaps, the speaker is not able to start the engine). As a consequence, (s)he infers a past event at t_E that must have led to the result without really knowing much about it. Next, (s)he referentially picks up the introduced t_E in order to elaborate on it. Metaphorically speaking, one might state that the speaker first sets the stage and then zooms in, as it is done with a camera lens. Declerck et al. (2006: 319) characterize this sequence as a typical discourse function that arises from combining indefinite with definite tense which they label as actualization focus: "[…] the speaker actualizes the event by focussing on […] the situation itself" (Declerck et al. 2006: 299), by adding further information answering questions like "where?", "how?" and "when?", i.e. by actualizing the information about the past eventuality, which is not the primary function of the quantificational tense form in the given sequence.

Here, we already seem to touch on one of the typical discourse functions of the English Present Perfect – and there is reason to assume that this function, triggered by the fundamental semantic category of definiteness, might be exploited in a likewise fashion in languages that dispose of a Present Perfect that is commonly described as being semantically similar to the English PP, i.e. the Spanish *Pretérito Perfecto Compuesto*. In this vein, we consider Example (33) to illustrate what a micro-structural discourse-based account of a Present Perfect adds to common analyses: in isolation, the Present Perfect ("has put") is commonly characterized as denoting an eventuality that has taken place recently and which bears particular "current relevance", i.e. relevance at speech time. This is e.g. in line with the Reichenbachian entry for the Present Perfect ($E \prec S, R$) and also matches the PP's resultative character.[37] However, e_2 ("did") and e_3 ("did") also denote eventualities of a highly resultative character. After all, both e_2 and e_3 relate to results whose relevance is of a very high degree for the speaker at speech time. In other words, both eventualities match the temporal characterization of $E \prec S, R$ – which actually qualifies them to be expressed with a Present Perfect. Nevertheless, the Simple Past is chosen over the allegedly adequate choice of a Present Perfect. This outlines, once again, that the choice of a tense form is not determined by its truth conditions exclusively, but is also influenced by discourse-effects and the question of how a speaker chooses to present, configure and perspectivize the eventualities contained in a given piece of discourse, as well as the relations among these.

---

37. Cf. Section 2.5 for common analyses of the Present Perfect as a cross-linguistic category.

Relying on the mechanism of the actualization focus as proposed by Declerck et al. (2006), we conclude that the syntagmatic interaction between tense forms is crucial for a proper account of how speakers actually employ them. Tense forms denote intervals that represent entities that enter the discourse universe and its referential structure. Depending on the kind of underlying semantic operation of quantification vs. reference, the choice of a tense form is influenced by the referential structure in discourse.

Having introduced fundamental aspects related to the study of tense, aspect, tense forms, adverbials and discourse-effects related to the referred categories, we overview the study of the Present Perfect as a cross-linguistic category in the next section.

2.5 The Present Perfect as a cross-linguistic category

After having introduced the fundamentals of the semantics of tense, aspect, adverbials and discourse, we now turn to the study of the Present Perfect, in particular, to the Present Perfect in the Romance languages. Although this book's focus is synchronic, it is indispensable to expound some of the most important diachronic developments that the Present Perfect is commonly said to have passed through in the major Romance languages, in order to identify current trends of the Present Perfect that can be observed in synchrony. The section is thus divided into a diachronic and a synchronic part.

2.5.1 Diachrony and grammaticalization

This subsection provides a brief overview on the diachronic research on the Romance Present Perfect. The premise behind this endeavour is that the diachronic view helps identify the synchronic status quo, as well as evaluate the latest tendencies. In this vein, it has become common practice to underpin synchronic findings with diachronic trends: the diversity of readings that can be attested in synchrony oftentimes seems to mirror stages of the diachronic evolution. Put differently, some of the synchronically attested readings seem to represent relics of earlier evolutionary stages that have not (yet) become fully extinct (cf. e.g. Becker 2022: 81). In the following, we expound the most influential diachronic theory for the Present Perfect in the Romance languages, the stage model (cf. Harris 1982; Bertinetto and Squartini 2000). It consists of four stages that are characterized as giving rise to particular readings. Harris's (1982) assumptions concerning Stage II have been criticized by Bertinetto and Squartini (2000) though (cf. below). The stages are depicted in Table 2.7.

Table 2.7 Diachronic path of the PP (Bertinetto and Squartini 2000: 406, inspired by Harris 1982)

Evolution	Function of PP
Stage I	the CP is "restricted to present states resulting from past actions, and is not used to describe past actions themselves, however recent" (some Southern Italian vernacular varieties)
Stage II	the CP occurs "only in highly specific circumstances such as contexts aspectually marked as durative or repetitive" parallel to English *I have lived here / been living here all my life; I have often seen him at the theatre* (Galician and Portuguese, many varieties of American Spanish)
Stage III	the CP expresses "the archetypal present perfect value of past action with present relevance" (Castilian Spanish; some varieties of langue d'oil and langue d'oc)
Stage IV	the CP also expresses the preterital or aoristic functions, while the SP is restricted to "formal registers" (Standard French, Northern Italian, Standard Romanian)

In general terms, the theory claims four stages that respectively represent a typical semantic value which is expressed by the PP. While Stage I – the oldest stage, historically located in the transition from Latin to the emerging Romance languages – seems to be almost extinct nowadays (cf. Chapter 4 for the *tenere*-construction in Spanish), stages II – IV are assumed to be nowadays occupied by different Romance languages to different degrees. The following overview provides a detailed characterization of the referred stages, mainly based on Bertinetto and Squartini (2000).

Stage I
At Stage I, the PP is said to denote a resultative state that holds at speech time. A past eventuality is implied but not denoted (cf. Detges 2006 and discussion in Section 4.3 for details). In its purest form, Stage I is characterized as exclusively combining with state predicates. Classical examples for this stage are presented in Example (34).

(34) Stage I-readings
    a. Latin[38]
       i. *Multa bona bene parta habemus*
          many goods well obtained have
          'We possess many well obtained goods.'
      ii. *Te auratam et vestitam bene habet.*
          you bejewelled and dressed well has
          'He keeps you bejewelled and well dressed.'

---

[38] Cited from *Plautus, Trin. 347* and *Plautus, Men. 801* apud Bertinetto and Squartini (2000: 404).

b. French[39]
   Il   est parti depuis deux jours.
   he is gone since two   days
   'He has been gone for two days.'
c. Spanish[40]
   Te   lo tengo dicho.
   you it have said
   'I have (already) told you.'

According to the restriction to states, the Spanish and French examples in (34) do not count as genuine representatives of Stage I. That would be in line with Bertinetto and Squartini (2000: 407) who notice that "no contemporary Romance language exhibits a [PP] with a purely resultative value". However, from a synchronic point of view, they seem to better fit into Stage I than into the other groups. In this vein, the Spanish *tenere*-construction, and even some readings of the French Passé *Composé* (cf. Laca 2009), may be analyzed as pertaining to Stage I by expressing a resultant state which is evoked by an implied eventuality.[41]

Stage II

Stage II represents the next step in the evolution of the PP in the Romance languages in Harris (1982). By contrast, Bertinetto and Squartini (2000) consider Stage II rather a peculiar development, in particular exemplified by the Portuguese PPC_{PT}, which deviates from the common grammaticalization path of the Romance languages. That is, they do not consider Stage II to lead over to Stage III. After all, it remains unclear whether the French and Italian PP historically actually passed through Stage II (cf. Bertinetto and Squartini 2000: 419).

However, the meaning that is commonly discussed as Stage II is expressed in durative and universalized readings. These are aspectual readings that denote an interval starting at some point in the past and reaching up to the speech time. Concerning the aspectual constitution of the interval, there are two possible scenarios. Traditionally, Stage II still is associated with atelic predicates, i.e. with states and activities (cf. Laca 2009: 365). In this scenario, there is a homogeneous state continuously holding throughout the interval. Telic situations, on the other hand, give rise to a (more or less) homogeneous repetition of several culminating instances of the situation. According to Bertinetto and Squartini (2000), Stage II is typically evoked by the PP in Portuguese, Galician and some American varieties of Spanish.

---

39. Example taken from Laca (2009: 362).

40. Example taken from Detges (2018: 260).

41. Detges (2018) also characterizes the PPC_{SP} in *Lo he escrito ahora* ('I have written it now.') as belonging to Stage I; cf. also Chapter 4.

(35) Stage II readings
   a. Portuguese[42]
      Ultimamente o   João tem lido muitos romances.
      recently   the John has read many novels
      'Recently John has read many novels.'
   b. Mexican Spanish[43]
      Has escrito a Fulano?
      has written to Fulano
      'Have you been corresponding with Fulano?'
   c. Galician Spanish[44]
      Aquí tengo comido las mejores ostras de mi vida.
      here have eaten the best   oysters of my life
      'Here I have repeatedly eaten the best oysters of my life.'

In most general terms, the examples provided in (35) can be illustrated with Figure 2.10.

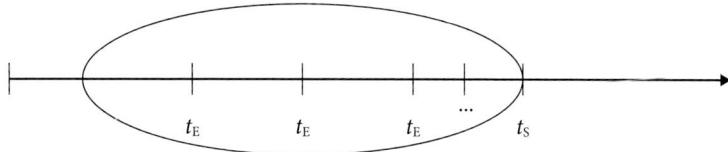

Figure 2.10 Stage II-Present Perfect

What the examples in (35) qualify as original representatives of Stage II is that they evoke their readings without the support of any adverbial expression or other linguistic means. The universal or durative value is inherently expressed by the Present Perfect itself. Nevertheless, Stage II readings can also be achieved by additional means, such as the combination with durative adverbials:

(36) Adverbially forced Stage II readings
   a. Spanish[45]
      Ha vivido solo desde que murió su padre.
      have lived alone since that died his father
      'He has been living by himself since his father died.'

---

42. Example taken from Bertinetto and Squartini (2000: 409).
43. Example taken from Lope Blanch (1972).
44. Example taken from Chamorro (2012: 1).
45. Example taken from García Fernández and Martínez-Atienza (2003: 32).

b. French[46]
   Il   a   vécu ici   toute sa   vie, on   ne   peut pas le   chasser.
   he has lived here   all   his life   one NEG can NEG him chase away
   'He has lived here all his life, we can't chase him away.'

We derive that there is a distinction between Perfects that *allow for* vs. *evoke by default* a particular reading. This is an important aspect for the assumption that Stage II is an actual evolutionary step that a Present Perfect in a given language traverses: a PP that nowadays behaves like the ones indicated in (35), synchronically represents antiquated uses that, for some reason, dismissed the purported regular process of grammaticalization that has been attested for several Romance languages. This very preservation of Stage II and its circumstances has puzzled a lot of researchers. Yet, given that the purported irregularity has been observed for several languages (e.g. Portuguese, Galician, Mexican Spanish), there seems to be a bit of a regularity as well. One might conclude that the preservation of Stage II does not mark an irregularity but rather a peripheral phenomenon which "calls into question the assumption that universal readings constitute a stage in the development of perfects" at all (Laca 2008: 1). In the same vein, Becker (2016) argues that the Portuguese PPC is not an instance of a typical Stage II Perfect but rather an idiosyncratic form that ceased to follow the common grammaticalization path. Due to a range of semantic restrictions that the PPC$_{PT}$ imposes, it seems to be indeed a contestable claim to classify the PPC$_{PT}$ as a regular representative of Stage II (cf. Chapter 3 for a detailed analysis of the PPC$_{PT}$).

Stage III
"Stage III represents an important turning point in the evolution" of the PP given that it "extends its coverage to purely perfective situations" (Bertinetto and Squartini 2000: 414).[47] Stage III includes readings denoting indefinite past actions with current relevance at speech time. Stage III allows for combinations with both telic (37a–i), (37a–iii) and atelic predicates (37a–ii), (37c).

---

46. Example taken from Laca (2009: 362).

47. In our view, it is problematic to define Stage III as denoting a perfective aspect. In our framework, viewpoint aspect is defined based on the relationship between t_E and t_{LOC} – not as the relationship between t_E and t_P. Further, we assume Stage III-Perfects to lack a t_{LOC} due to its indefinite temporal semantics. Consequently, we assume that the Stage III Perfect is not able to denote a perfective viewpoint aspect. However, it typically evokes a bounded reading due to the constellation of t_E preceding t_S (while unbounded readings belong to Stage II).

(37) Stage III readings
    a. Spanish[48]
        i. (*Is the king still alive?*)
           No, ha muerto.
           no has died
           'No, he (has) died.'
        ii. *¿Has estado en Australia?*
           have been in Australia
           'Have you been to Australia?'
        iii. *Ha llegado el rey!*
           has arrived the king
           'The king has arrived.'
    b. Portuguese[49]
        *Tem chegado o rei.
        has arrived the king
        'The king has arrived.'
    c. French[50]
        Il est fatigué parce qu'il a mal dormi de la nuit.
        he is tired because CONJ+he has badly slept PREP the night
        'He is tired because he hasn't slept well at night.'

The examples in (37) denote culminated, bounded eventualities whose temporal location (t_{LOC}) is not specified though. Based on our framework, we argue that the quantificational PP lacks t_{LOC} in its logical form due to its indefinite temporal semantics.

In synchrony, the Stage III PP denoting an indefinite past event with current relevance has been declared to represent a "well-behaved Perfect" (cf. Laca 2008), i.e. the prototypical Present Perfect, as exemplified by the PPC_{SP} (cf. also Bertinetto and Squartini 2000).

Stage IV

Bertinetto and Squartini (2000) label the approaching of Stage IV as the aoristic drift. The main progress from stage III to IV is expressed in an update that qualifies the PP as a preterite or aoristic tense form. As a consequence, it may be employed for telling stories with eventualities located in the past and fully detached from speech time. In other words, it may be employed in the discourse mode of narration.

---

48. Examples taken from Bertinetto and Squartini (2000: 415).

49. Example taken from Bertinetto and Squartini (2000: 409).

50. Example taken from Laca (2009: 362).

According to Bertinetto and Squartini (2000: 417), the aoristic drift is "represented by Standard French, Standard Romanian, northern Italian varieties, Romansh, Ladin, Friulian and Sardinian", the Stage IV Perfect "can be used in any kind of purely perfective contexts and in some cases it is the only existing form." In our framework, the main update from Stage III to IV is expressed in the introduction of a location time t_{LOC} which allows for a perfective viewpoint aspect denoting t_E to be a subset of t_{LOC} ($t_E \subseteq t_{LOC}$). The PP can now be combined with positional adverbials:

(38) Stage IV readings
   a. French[51]
       Il est allé en Inde en 1970.
       he is gone to India in 1970
       'He went to India in 1970.'
   b. Spanish[52]
       ?Ayer he comprado un aire acondicionado y me da calor.
       yesterday have bought a air conditioner and me gives heat
       Yesterday I bought an air conditioner and I'm getting heat [from it]'

The aoristic drift of a PP in a particular language generally triggers profound changes in the functional load of other tense forms. That is, the approach of Stage IV has an impact on the competition of the PP with other tense forms, especially with the Present Tense and the Simple Past. In this vein, the *Passé Simple* in French has ceased to be the default tense form to relate past eventualities, except from formal registers, historical events and literary style (e.g. in the narration of tales, cf. Bertinetto and Squartini 2000: 422, cf. also Becker 2010b). Similarly, the dominance of the Present Perfect in Upper German ('Oberdeutsch') is known for causing a decline of the Preterite (cf. Abraham and Conradie 2001), commonly labelled as *Präteritumschwund* ('decline of the Preterite'). Expressed in a Saussurian-structural terminology, changing the *valeur* of the PP has an impact on the *valeur* of the closely related tense form, such as the Simple Past (and vice-versa).

Overview
The authors conclude that the majority of the Romance language is situated somewhere between Stage III and Stage IV – with some exceptions of languages or dialects that preserved Stage II. An outcome of their theory is the prediction that the PP in the Romance languages typically pursues a path of gradually developing into an aoristic tense form.

---

51. Example taken from Laca (2009: 362).

52. Example taken from Schwenter and Cacoullos (2008: 2). The acceptability of (38b), if acceptable at all, underlies diatopic variation.

Bertinetto and Squartini (2000) classify the Spanish PPC$_{SP}$ as a truly perfectal tense form, i.e. as denoting indefinite past events with a particular present relevance. Their prediction that the PPC$_{SP}$ should, at some point, start to approach Stage IV has already been an object of research over the past years (cf. Chapter 4). Regarding Portuguese, Bertinetto and Squartini (2000) conclude that the PPC$_{PT}$ has not even reached Stage III. This picture is illustrated in Figure 2.11.

| Spanish | Occitan Catalan | Standard Italian | Standard French | Standard Romanian | various North Italian & French vernaculars |

<more perfectal>--<purely aoristic>

Figure 2.11 Aoristic drift of the Romance CP (Bertinetto and Squartini 2000: 422)

There is another aspect that is predicted by the stage model and confirmed by synchronic evidence: the readings associated with Stage II, III and IV seem to form an implicational scale that can be read from right to left. A PP that allows for Stage IV readings, allows for Stage III and Stage II (French). If a PP allows for Stage III, this implies that it also allows for Stage II, as instantiated by Spanish. Table 2.8 illustrates the implicational scale.[53]

Table 2.8 The PP readings forming an implicational scale

	Stage II	Stage III	Stage IV
Portuguese	✓	✗	✗
Mexican Spanish	✓	✓/✗	✗
Peninsular Spanish	✓	✓	✗
French	✓	✓	✓

2.5.2 Synchrony

This section provides a brief overview on the contemporary synchronic analysis of the Present Perfect in the Romance languages, complemented by our own framework introduced in the previous sections.

Readings
There is a great tradition to abstract away from a range of uses of the Present Perfect to a limited set of typical readings (cf. e.g. Comrie 1976: 56ff., Inoue 1979: 562,

---

53. Evidence for Mexican Spanish taken from Lope Blanch (1972); Moreno de Alba (1978); Bertinetto and Squartini (2000), Laca (2009).

Depraetere 1998: 598, Nishiyama and Koenig 2010: 612). The ultimate goal is to generalize over the PP's readings and functions in order to achieve an integrated semantic sketch, i.e. a description that ideally captures all kinds of uses that can be attested in corpora. Ideally, that sketch would even be complemented by a cross-linguistically valid picture. Nevertheless, there is no consensus about the question of how many readings one should minimally assume for the PP. We adhere to Portner (2012: 1219) who distinguishes four readings, namely the resultative reading, the continuative (also: universal) reading, whose variation "is pragmatic in nature" although there is no consensus on "whether the continuative perfect [...] is semantically different from the others, or just pragmatically different", the existential reading and the hot news reading.[54]

(39) Typical PP readings (Portner 2012: 1219)[55]
   a. Resultative reading
      Mary has read Middlemarch.
   b. Continuative reading
      Mary has lived in London for five years.
   c. Existential reading
      The earth has been hit by giant asteroids before (and probably will be again).
   d. Hot news reading
      The Orioles have won!

Curent relevance
One of the guiding questions behind the research on the Present Perfect has always been to detect the actual function of the readings indicated in (39). What is it that leads speakers to choose the Present Perfect? Do particular tempo-aspectual truth conditions allow (or force) a speaker to opt for the PP? Is the choice determined by discourse-based strategies that pertain to the realm of the management of coherence (cf. de Swart 2007; Nishiyama and Koenig 2010)? Or does the choice depend on information structural strategies by establishing a particular relation to a current discourse topic (cf. Inoue 1979; Klein 1992, 1994, 2000; Giorgi and Pianesi 1997; Portner 2003, 2012; Schaden 2009)? It turns out that the majority of the approaches share some version of the concept of *Current Relevance* (CR), a pragmatic meaning component, as a key to a proper analysis. Depraetere (1998) points out the fuzziness of the concept of CR:

---

[54]. Portner's (2012) classification is in the tradition of McCawley (1971); Comrie (1976); Nishiyama and Koenig (2010) (a.o.).

[55]. Portner (2012) mostly feeds his study with English examples.

> Strange though it may seem, the linguists defending the view that the indication of current relevance constitutes the semantics of the present perfect often fail to define this property accurately. In some cases, an intuitive understanding of current relevance is taken for granted […]. (Depraetere 1998: 599)

CR builds on the assumption that a PP, although denoting a past eventuality, mainly asserts on the present. This assertion is of particular relevance at speech time. Dahl and Hedin (2000: 392) define CR as "a condition on the world [of a] continuance of a result", furthermore as a "condition on the discourse, in that the speaker portrays the consequences of an event as somehow essential to the point of what he is saying." With Depraetere (1998), CR may be pinned down to "resultative conversational implicatures":

(40) CR as a "resultative conversational implicature" (Depraetere 1998: 609)
    a. *I have lived in London*
        i. That's why I receive letters from Britain.
        ii. I know how to get to the Tate gallery.
    b. *I have known him well.*
        i. I understand why he is angry.
        ii. I know he does not love his girlfriend.
    c. *I have studied a lot.*
        i. I am clever.
        ii. I feel exhausted.

The examples in (40) characterize CR as a pragmatic meaning component, i.e. as cancelable and context-dependent meaning. Based on the indicated implicates, (40a) may be felicitously uttered as answer on a question like "Why do you keep receiving letters from Britain?" In the same way, (40b) may be an adequate answer on a question like "Why do you think he is angry?" The tradition of relating current relevance to the Present Perfect traces back, once again, to the Reichenbachian analysis (E ≺ S, R) introduced in Section 2.1, where reference time equals speech time. In our approach, this constellation is coded as speech time being a subset of the perspective time ($t_s \subseteq t_p$). As proposed by Dahl and Hedin (2000: 391), the PP suffers a "a gradual relaxation of the requirements on current relevance" when it grammaticalizes into a preterite form, i.e. in the context of the aoristic drift and the progress from Stage III to Stage IV (as discussed in the previous section). We conclude that CR is a pragmatic concept that helps understanding the discourse function of the PP's readings (39) and that arises from the combination of the PP's quantificational temporal semantics and its perspective time that is coded to lie in the present time-sphere.

The Present Perfect: A quantificational tense form
Following Iatridou et al. (2003), the typical PP readings indicated in (39) can be divided into two groups, namely one group consisting of those readings that carry an existential quantifier in their logical form, and another group, consisting of readings that carry a universal quantifier in its logical form, as illustrated in Figure 2.12.[56]

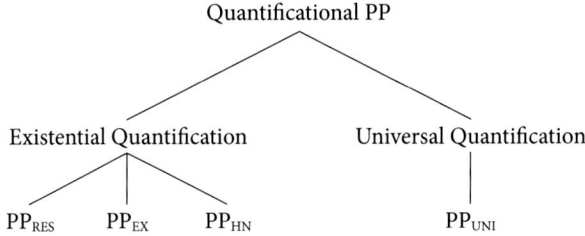

Figure 2.12 The PP as a quantificational tense form
RES: *resultative;* EX: *experiential;* HN: *hot news;* UNI: *universal*

Given this bipartite architecture, the authors speak of the "existential vs. universal ambiguity" linked to the PP. Furthermore, they claim that adverbials turn out to play a crucial role in their evocation:

> The U[*niversal*]-reading is never available to a perfect unless the latter is modified by certain adverbials. (Iatridou et al. 2003: 158)

Situation aspect, e.g. telicity, does not resolve the universal vs. existential ambiguity because existential readings allow for both telic (39c) and atelic (41a) predicates. Due to their somewhat privileged position, existential readings (PP_{RES}, PP_{EX}, PP_{HN}) are evoked by default, i.e. when there is no adverbial modification, as illustrated in (41).

(41) Universal readings and adverbial modification (cf. Iatridou et al. 2003)
 a. *She has been sick.*
  Existential reading
 b. *I haven't seen Mary in a while. Where is she? – She has been sick.*
  Existential or Universal reading
 c. *Mary has been sick lately.*
  Universal reading

For our purposes, the most crucial assumption is that the Present Perfect, in both cases, is an inherently quantificational tense form. This is expressed in its

---

56. Iatridou et al. (2003) do not include the hot news reading into their analysis which, according to our analysis, fits into the first group carrying an existential quantifier, as well.

quantification over t_E, which may be realized as an existential or a universal quantification. That is, the PP does not serve to refer to a definite interval in the past. Applying our terminology from Section 2.1, we thus derive the following claim: the PP lacks a location time t_{LOC} in its logical form such that the PP is a function that takes three arguments (t_S, t_P and t_E) and outputs them in a specific order making use of the temporal relations of precedence, subset of and abutment ($\prec, \subseteq, \succ\!\!\prec$, cf. e.g. Grønn and Stechow (2020: 16) for the abutment relation).

(42) The quantificational Present Perfect (no t_{LOC})
    a. $[\![PP_{RES/EX/HN}]\!]: \lambda t_S \lambda t_E \lambda t_P.\ t_E \prec t_S \subseteq t_P$
    b. $[\![PP_{UNI}]\!]: \lambda t_S \lambda t_E \lambda t_P.\ t_E \succ\!\!\prec t_S \subseteq t_P$

(42a) is similar to the traditional Reichenbachian entry of $E \prec R, S$. The constellation of t_E preceding t_S and t_P allows for the resultative, existential and hot news reading. The logical form of the universal reading indicated in (6b) is a slightly updated one featuring an abutment relation. It is supposed to formalize the PP_{UNI}'s property to denote an eventuality that reaches from (some time in) the past and abuts speech time t_S, which, in turn, is included in the perspective time t_P (the present time-sphere). Compared to our definition of the quantificational Simple Past, the exclusive difference between the two is spelled out in the differing perspective time. While the former denotes it to lie in the past time-sphere, the latter denotes it to lie in the present time-sphere. This constellation is even preserved with instances of the Present Perfect that have already developed into preterite tense forms, as e.g. the French *Passé Composé*, a tense form which is typically analyzed as having pursued the path of the aoristic drift (cf. previous section). As argued by de Swart (2007), a crucial semantic difference between the Stage IV *Passé Composé* and an original narrative tense form (as e.g. the Simple Past) remains:

> [I]t is possible to tell a story in the Passé Composé, because the temporal structuré of the discourse is determined by the rhetorical structure of the discourse, which in turn depends on the connectives, the lexical semantics of verbs and adverbs, and world knowledge about the 'natural' order of events [...]. We conclude that the French Passé Composé is well on its way to become a perfective past tense, but it is not quite there yet. Its orientation towards the speech time makes it a non-anaphoric tense, which means that it is not in essence a narrative tense.
> (de Swart 2007: 2290 ff.)

In other words, the deictic orientation of the *Passé Composé* towards the speech time has not been cancelled yet. This is spelled out in that the perspective time t_P continues to lie in the present time-sphere, as opposed to a referential Simple Past that encodes its perspective time to lie in the past time-sphere. We thus assume the following logical form for a Stage IV Present Perfect disposing of referential temporal semantics:

(43) Referential PP (featuring t_{LOC})

$\llbracket PP_{IV} \rrbracket$: $\lambda t_S \lambda t_E \lambda t_{LOC} \lambda t_P$. $t_E \begin{bmatrix} \subseteq \\ \supseteq \end{bmatrix} t_{LOC} \prec t_S \subseteq t_P$

The referential Present Perfect as defined in (43) turns out to be a somewhat hybrid tense form seeming to denote two competing information at the same time: it refers to a past eventuality but maintains its orientation towards the speech time. This turns it into a highly flexible tense form with a versatile functional load (cf. the prominence-based study of the discourse functions of the PPC$_{SP}$ in Chapter 6).

The PP puzzle
Based on our definition of the PP as a quantificational tense form that, as a consequence, fails to dispose of t_{LOC} in its logical form (which, in turn, is preserved for the semantic operation of reference), we may now be able to derive a new answer to an old question: the Present Perfect puzzle. It traces back to Klein (1992) and refers to the oddity of Present Perfect expressions when combined with (prehodiernal) positional adverbials:

(44) The Present Perfect Puzzle   (Klein 1992: 525)
 a. *Chris has left New York.*
 b. **Chris has left New York yesterday.*
 c. **Chris has left New York last year*

The puzzling aspect about the examples indicated in (44) is that the PP is a proper expression to capture that Chris was in New York the day before. Yet, it is odd to indicate this definite temporal location. In other words, the PP's truth conditions seem to allow for a definite position of the eventuality in question. After all, (44a) is a felicitous and true utterance. Yet, the PP's use conditions seem to block a modification of t_{LOC}. Klein's solution is a pragmatic principle, the "P-Definiteness Constraint":

> In an utterance, the expression of TT and the expression of TSit cannot both be independently p-dennite.   (Klein 1992: 546)

Though not completely equivalent, Klein's TT and TSit correspond to our t_P and t_E, respectively. That is, the "P-Definiteness Constraint" blocks an adverbial specification of the two at the same time. Given the pragmatic nature of that principle, Klein succeeds in accounting for the observation that the PP puzzle seems to lay outside of the realm of the PP's truth conditions.

Our account contrasts with that *pragmatic* assumption by reducing the PP puzzle to the PP's *semantics* : whenever an eventuality is temporally anchored, i.e. modified by a positional adverbial, the addressee of that operation is *not* t_E, but t_{LOC}.[57]

---

57. Cf. Section 2.3 for tempo-aspectual adverbials and their semantic scope. Cf. below and discussion in Chapter 4 for potential exceptions, i.e. for positional adverbials that modify t_P instead of t_{LOC} when combined with a PP.

Now, defining the quantificational PP to lack t_{LOC} in its logical form, the PP puzzle may be explained as follows: the positional adverbial "yesterday" in Example (44b) lacks a point of reference. There is no anchor, no t_{LOC} for this positional adverbial which causes that the expression gets ruled out as odd.

Adverbial modification
Having discussed the PP puzzle, the question arises why the PP combines with adverbials that seem to modify t_{LOC}, such as in (45).

(45) The PP's XN-effect   (Grønn and Stechow 2016: 326)
   a. *[*Yesterday/last week*], I have been to New York.
   b. ✓[*Today/this morning*], I have been to New York.

As a solution, many scholars have defended the Extended-Now theory for the Present Perfect claiming that the PP denotes an XN-interval. The XN approach traces back to McCoard (1978) and has been applied in several studies of the PP, e.g. in Rothstein (2008) for German, English and Swedish or Becker (2020a) for Portuguese and Spanish. The XN-interval is typically characterized as abutting the speech time t_s and stretching to some point in the past, whose "initial point […] can be determined by adverbials, implied by context, or left vague" (Portner 2012: 1232); the XN theory thus provides a particularly suitable account of the universal readings. Concerning (45), it is typically argued that any adverbial that gets combined with the PP need to be consistent with its XN-interval. Since prehodiernal positional adverbials, i.e. adverbials that denote an interval that is temporally prior to the XN-interval and thus detached from the speech time, violate that condition, the oddity of (45a) is predicted. Conversely, adverbials that can be accommodated to the XN-interval, as in (45b), are fine. However, the actual scope of the adverbials indicated in (45) remains unclear. Table 2.9 presents our assumptions concerning the interaction between the PP and tempo-aspectual adverbials based on the approach discussed in Section 2.3.

XN-adverbials may thus be defined as scoping over the perspective time t_P instead of the location time t_{LOC}. Following this approach, we may argue that XN-adverbials, when combined with the PP, do not modify t_{LOC} but specify what is perceived as the perspective time instead. In this vein, the temporal location of `I be to New York` is denoted as anterior to the speech time, as well as to be included in the perspective time ("today, this morning"). This idea can be, once again, illustrated with Botne and Kershner's (2008) notion of the P-domain and the D-domain which stand in an orthogonal relation to each other, cf. Figure 2.13. Given that there is no location time argument called by the PP, its t_E cannot be situated on the D-domain axis. That is, the remoteness condition that impedes prehodiernal adverbials to be combined with the PP actually applies to t_P instead of to t_{LOC}. The perspective time, in turn, is tied to the present time-sphere, which

Table 2.9 Tempo-aspectual adverbials combined with the quantificational PP

Adverbial	Scope	Example
*Positional	*t_{LOC}	* $\begin{bmatrix} \text{Yesterday} \\ \text{Three weeks ago} \\ \text{On May 1,1999} \end{bmatrix}$, Mary has read Middlemarch.
Quantificational	t_E	Mary has $\begin{bmatrix} \text{never} \\ \text{always} \end{bmatrix}$ read Middlemarch $\begin{bmatrix} \text{before} \\ \text{once} \\ \text{many times} \end{bmatrix}$.
Durative	t_E	Mary has lived in London $\begin{bmatrix} \text{for five years} \\ \text{ever since} \\ \text{lately} \end{bmatrix}$.
Extended-Now	t_P	$\begin{bmatrix} \text{Today} \\ \text{This month} \\ \text{This week} \\ \text{Now} \end{bmatrix}$, Mary has read Middlemarch.

qualifies the adverbials "today" and "this morning" to be employed. What speakers perceive as pertaining to the present time-sphere might vary to different degrees in different languages or varieties though.

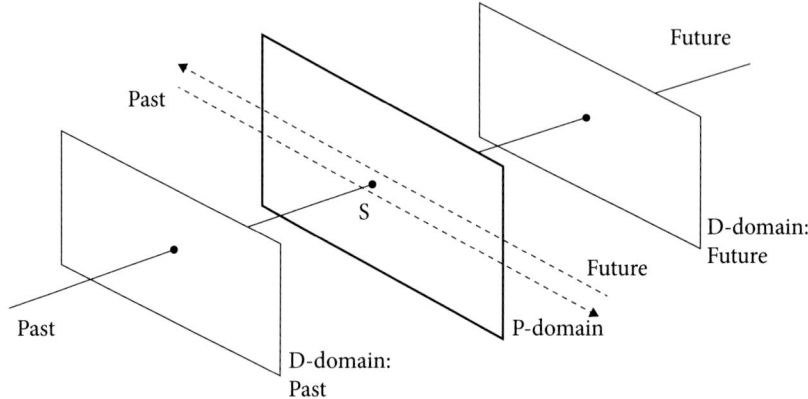

Figure 2.13 Cognitive worlds with three perspectives on time
(Botne and Kershner 2008: 153)

2.6 Conclusion

In this chapter, we introduced the theoretical framework that we are going to apply in our study of the PPC$_{SP}$ and PPC$_{PT}$.

Section 2.1 defined tense as an ordering function taking t_S, t_E, t_P and, under certain conditions, t_{LOC} and t_R as its arguments – and outputting an order based on the semantic relations of precedence, subset of and superset of. In Section 2.5 we furthermore added the relation of abutment for the universal reading of the Present Perfect. We discussed the distinction between referential and quantificational tense that differ in terms of how they treat t_E. While quantificational tense quantifies over t_E (blocking t_{LOC}), referential tense assigns t_E to a location time t_{LOC}.

Section 2.2 introduced the study of situation aspect and viewpoint aspect as relating to the lexical vs. grammatical encoding of boundaries of situations. We defined the perfective vs. imperfective distinction to express the relationship between t_E and t_{LOC}.

In Section 2.3, we discussed the semantics of tempo-aspectual adverbials, i.e. of those adverbials that are relevant to the study of tense forms. The list that we are going to apply in our study consists of positional, quantificational, durative and XN-adverbials. Moreover, we defined their semantic scope based on the idea that each of them functions as specifying the location time t_{LOC}, the event time t_E, or the perspective time t_P. However, adverbials and the referred intervals do not map strictly, which means that particular adverbials may have different readings, i.e. they may be able to scope over more than just one interval.

Section 2.4 divided the study of tense forms in discourse into two intertwined domains: the macro-structure of discourse, i.e. the modes of discourse in the tradition of Smith (2003), and the micro-structure of discourse, i.e. relations between adjacent tense forms on the syntagmatic axis. Here, we particularly focussed on the mechanisms of temporal anaphora based on the dynamic management of t_R and on actualization effects triggered by the exploitation of the complementary discourse functions of definite (referential) and indefinite (quantificational) tense. Further, we discussed some of the typical correlations between the choice of tense forms and the macro- and micro-structure of discourse.

Finally, Section 2.5 introduced the study of the Present Perfect as a cross-linguistic category. Apart from the influential stage model that, in most general terms, predicts the Romance Present Perfect to gradually grammaticalize into an aoristic tense form, we outlined and discussed synchronic approaches to the PP. Most crucially, we defined the Present Perfect as an inherently quantificational, i.e. indefinite tense form that lacks a location time. Furthermore, we divided the its meaning into existential readings, that existentially quantify over t_E (experiential, resultative and hot news) and universal readings, that universally quantify over t_E. The PP's perspective time t_P lies in the present time-sphere, which harmonizes with the PP's effect of current relevance (cf. "resultative conversational implicature" in Depraetere 1998). Due to the missing location time t_{LOC}, the PP impedes combinations with positional adverbials. Quantificational adverbials (scoping over t_E), durative adverbials (scoping over t_E) and XN-adverbials (scoping over t_P) are fine though.

In (46), we summarize the semantics of Simple Past and Present Perfect as developed throughout the chapter.

(46) Simple Past and PP as ordering functions

    a. $[\![\text{Simple Past}_{\text{REF}}]\!]: \lambda t_S \lambda t_E \lambda t_P \lambda t_{LOC}.\ (t_E \begin{bmatrix}\subseteq \\ \supseteq\end{bmatrix} t_{LOC}) \subseteq t_P \prec t_S$
        i. [Oh wait! When I left...] I didn't turn off the stove.
        ii. In 1989, he was a farmer.
    b. $[\![\text{Simple Past}_{\text{QUANT}}]\!]: \lambda t_S \lambda t_E \lambda t_P.\ t_E \subseteq t_P \prec t_S$
        i. She wrote several books on the topic.
        ii. Knicks owner James Dolan recovered from Coronavirus.[58]
    c. $[\![\text{PP}_{\text{RES/EX/HN}}]\!]: \lambda t_S \lambda t_E \lambda t_P.\ t_E \prec t_S \subseteq t_P$
        i. Mary has read Middlemarch.
        ii. The earth has been hit by giant asteroids before (and probably will be again).
        iii. The Orioles have won!
    d. $[\![\text{PP}_{\text{UNI}}]\!]: \lambda t_S \lambda t_E \lambda t_P.\ t_E \succ \prec t_S \subseteq t_P$
    Mary has lived in London for five years.
    e. $[\![\text{PP}_{\text{REF}}]\!]: \lambda t_S \lambda t_E \lambda t_{LOC} \lambda t_P.\ t_E \begin{bmatrix}\subseteq \\ \supseteq\end{bmatrix} t_{LOC} \prec t_S \subseteq t_P$
    Fr. Il est allé en Inde en 1970.
    'He went to India in 1970'

Having outlined our general perspective on tense, aspect, tempo-aspectual adverbials, the discourse-based study of these components, as well as our view on the Present Perfect as a cross-linguistic semantic category, we now turn to the study of the Portuguese PPC$_{\text{PT}}$ and the Spanish PPC$_{\text{SP}}$.

---

58. https://www.washingtonpost.com/sports/2020/04/22/knicks-owner-james-dolan-recovered-coronavirus-set-donate-plasma/, 04/23/2020.

CHAPTER 3

The Portuguese *Pretérito Perfeito Composto*

This chapter presents a detailed study of the Portuguese *Pretérito Perfeito Composto* (PPC$_{PT}$) of the following morphosyntactic form:

(1) Ele tem escrito a   tese.
     he has written the thesis
     'He has been writing (on) his thesis lately.'

The translation indicated in (1), featuring the Present Perfect Progressive, already hints at the PPC$_{PT}$'s peculiar meaning. Concerning the form side, the PPC$_{PT}$ disposes of quite an idiosyncrasy as well: while most of the Romance languages select an auxiliary that traces back to Lt. *habere* (e.g. French *avoir* or Spanish *haber*), the PPC$_{PT}$ selects a form tracing back to Lt. *tenere* (Pt. *ter*). It stands to reason that there have been several accounts that explain the PPC$_{PT}$'s idiosyncratic meaning compositionally based on this very formal peculiarity (cf. e.g. Giorgi and Pianesi 1997: 123, Schmitt 2001). However, we will concentrate on the meaning side only in the following. The chapter is structured as follows.

Section 3.1 provides an overview of the general meaning and meaning effects of the PPC$_{PT}$ according to the literature. As already indicated in Chapter 2.5, the PPC$_{PT}$ is oftentimes characterized as a universal Stage II Perfect. However, additional semantic restrictions and pragmatic meaning components make the PPC$_{PT}$ deviate from standard universal PP readings (as e.g. the Spanish PPC$_{SP-UNI}$).

Section 3.2 briefly reviews the research on the use of the PPC$_{PT}$ according to diatopic variation and the question of whether there are functional differences between the PPC$_{PT}$ in Brazilian Portuguese (BP) and European Portuguese (EP).

Section 3.3 presents our analysis of the PPC$_{PT}$ as a quantificational tense form – which is in line with our general semantic sketch of the cross-linguistic PP as presented in Chapter 2.5. Based on the PPC$_{PT}$'s quantificational semantics, we distinguish three types of readings that can be attested in synchrony. These are (i) indefinite pluractional existential readings (IPEX readings), (ii) universal (durative) readings, and (iii) characterizing readings. The three groups differ with regard to their anchoring in time: the IPEX and universal readings can be conceived of as expressing episodicity in the sense that they denote eventualities that get a temporal index. In other words, they can be located on a virtual timeline. By contrast, the characterizing readings abstract away from concrete eventualities located on a virtual timeline in order to express a generalization that is temporally restricted to the present time-sphere. As it turns out, the characterizing readings seem to represent the more frequent, i.e. the central readings of the two.

Section 3.4 analyzes the interaction between the PPC_PT and tempo-aspectual adverbials. Based on its peculiar semantic restrictions, we expose that the PPC_PT (i) blocks positional adverbials (which is in line with our framework that predicts this incompatibility based on that the PPC_PT does not call for a location time argument), (ii) allows for combinations with durative and extended-now adverbials, and (iii) differentiates between several types of quantificational adverbials: while IPEX, universal and generic-quantificational adverbials are fine, definite-quantificational adverbials are ruled out.

Section 3.5 discusses three combinations that the PPC_PT may establish with adjacent tense forms. These are (i) another PPC_PT, (ii) a *Pretérito Perfeito Simples* (PPS), and (iii) Present Tense. Based on the division between episodic and characterizing PPC_PT's readings introduced in Section 3.3, we discuss (some of) the typical discourse functions of these combinations. As it turns out, most of these functions operate as a rhetorical device. With regard to the macro-structure of discourse, we derive that the PPC_PT typically blocks the modes of narration and description, while it may be employed in the modes of information, argument and report.

3.1 General meaning and meaning effects

The PPC_PT is commonly characterized as having blocked the typical gammaticalization into a Stage III Perfect, i.e. into a tense form that denotes an indefinite eventuality preceding the speech time t_S without abutting it. Instead, the PPC_PT is typically classified as a Stage II Perfect that exclusively gives rise to universal readings – even when lacking adverbial modification – denoting a repetition or an extension of an eventuality abutting speech time (cf. e.g. Ilari 2001; Becker 2016, 2020a, 2022; Cabredo Hofherr et al. 2010; Barbosa Bertucci 2008; Molsing 2006; Schmitt 2001; Oliveira and Leal 2012; Suter 1984; Wigger 2005; cf. below for discussion of whether an eventuality in the scope of the PPC_PT is also expressed to continue to hold beyond the speech time). As a preliminary hypothesis, we may thus assume the semantics of the universal Present Perfect as discussed in Chapter 2.5 and repeated in (2).

(2) The PPC_PT as a universal Present Perfect (preliminary and simplified)
 $[\![PP_{UNI}]\!]: \lambda t_S \lambda t_E \lambda t_P.\ t_E \succ \prec t_S \subseteq t_P$

However, it turns out that there is a range of peculiar semantic restrictions and pragmatic meaning components additionally imposed by the PPC_PT that cannot be derived from (2) and that require a detailed analysis:

> [...] [T]he Present Perfect in Portuguese is overwhelmingly dedicated to universal readings, with some additional felicity conditions, such as discontinuity and length of the XN-interval in the Brazilian varieties [...]. (Laca 2008: 16)

Ilari's (2001) account

For a first approximation, we may follow Ilari (2001), who provides the following characterization of the PPC$_{PT}$'s meaning and meaning effects based on introspective Brazilian data.

(3) The PPC$_{PT}$'s meaning and meaning effects in Ilari (2001)
   a. Expression of iteration
      Ele tem-nos visitado várias vezes / *uma vez.
      he has us visited several times / *one time
      'He (has) been visiting us several times / *once.'
   b. Expression of iteration independently of an adverbial indicating frequency
      Ele nos tem visitado (mais de uma vez).
      he us has visited (more than one time)
      'He has been visiting us more than once.'
   c. Expression of durativity/continuity
      Tenho estado doente.
      have been ill
      'I have been ill lately.'
   d. "Refers" to an interval that starts in the past but does not end in the past[59]
      Le Monde tem sido entregue em São Paulo pelo correio aéreo
      le monde has been delivered in São Paulo by the air mail
      desde 1927 (*desde 1927 até 1968).
      since 1927 (*from 1927 to 1968).
      'Le Monde has been delivered in Sao Paulo by airmail since 1927 (*from 1927 until 1968).'
   e. Telic predicates evoke iterative readings, atelic predicates evoke durative readings
      i. *O Fernando tem publicado na serie Novos Ecritores da*
         o Fernando has published in the series new/young writers by the
         Editora Ática.
         publisher Ática
         'Lately, Fernando has been publishing in the young writers series by Editora Àtica.'.

---

[59]. Within our framework, the PPC$_{PT}$ does not refer to a location time t_{LOC} but quantifies over t_E (cf. Chapter 2.5).

ii. A   este governo   tem faltado vontade política para a
    PREP this government has lacked volition political for the
    solução dos   problemas.
    solution of the problems
    'This government has been lacking the political will to solve the problems.'
f. The PPC$_{PT}$ must not express eventualities that have occurred once; it must not indicate the exact number of occurrences of an eventuality
    i. *Eles têm vindo três   vezes.
        they have come three   times
        *'They came three times.'
    ii. Eles têm vindo muitas vezes/milhares   de vezes.
        they have come lots of times/thousands of times
        'They have been coming many times / thousands of times.'
g. Grammaticality and interpretation of the PPC$_{PT}$ are influenced by the quantification of involved NPs and the presence of adjuncts
    i. O   surto   de meningite tem matado muita gente.
        the outbreak of meningitis has killed a lot of people
        'The meningitis outbreak has been killing a lot of people.'
    ii. *O   surto   de meningite tem matado uma pessoa
        the outbreak of meningitis has killed one person
        (*a zeladora).
        (*the caretaker)
        *'The meningitis outbreak has killed one person (*the caretaker).'
    iii. O   surto de meningite tem matado Pedro, Carlos e   Jose.
        the outbr. of meningitis has killed Pedro, Carlos and Jose
        *'The meningitis outbreak has killed Pedro, Carlos and Jose.'

As indicated in (3a)–(3c), the PPC$_{PT}$ denotes iteration or duration – independently of the presence or absence of adverbials forcing one of the two interpretations. With respect to the iterative reading, it is commonly assumed that there is a vague (but plural) number of repeated instances of e (in our terminology: t_E). It follows that an interpretation of a single eventuality is systematically ruled out by the PPC$_{PT}$ which certainly can be characterized as the most crucial and central property of the PPC$_{PT}$'s. In this vein, the PPC$_{PT}$ prominently distinguishes from "well-behaved" Stage III Perfects denoting a single eventuality (e.g. the Peninsular Spanish PPC$_{SP}$; cf. Laca (2008) for the term of "well-behaved" Perfects.).[60]

---

[60]. As an exception, *tenho dito* ('I have said/spoken') actually may express a single and bounded past eventuality. Becker (2016: 31) speaks of a fossilized use with the particular communicative function of signaling a speech act. According to Hundertmark-Santos Martins (2014: 123), *tenho entendido* ('I have understood') marks a similar case. Cf. also Müller (2017) for further discussion of possible exceptions.

The Extended-Now (XN) approach to the PPC$_{PT}$

The observations discussed so far have been accessibly visualized within Becker's (2020a) account based on the framework of the Extended-Now theory (XN theory). The XN theory has been applied in many studies to the Present Perfect (cf. e.g McCoard 1978 and von Stechow 1998) and has particularly proven as useful in capturing the semantics of the interval-based universal readings of the Present Perfect (cf. Grønn and Stechow 2020: 22).[61] The XN-interval is designed as stretching from some time in the past (delimited by left boundary of the interval) to the speech time (right boundary). This interval has elsewhere also been labelled as the Perfect time span (PTS), a term introduced by Iatridou et al. (2003) and applied e.g. in Rothstein's (2008) study of the Present Perfect in the Germanic languages. The XN is conceived of as "hosting" the denoted eventualities. Applied to the PPC$_{PT}$, Becker's (2020a) proposes an analysis of (4) as illustrated in Figure 3.1.

(4) *Ultimamente a Maria tem ganho a corrida.*
    lately   the Maria has won the race
    'Maria has been winning the race lately.'

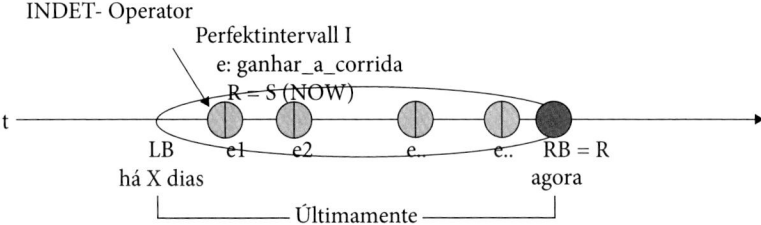

Figure 3.1 An XN analysis of (4) (Becker 2020a: 5)

The analysis illustrated in Figure 3.1 consists of an XN-interval denoted by the XN-adverbial *ultimamente* ('lately'), of a right boundary which equals the speech time, furthermore of a left boundary which is morphosyntactically covert but semantically present *(há x dias,* 'x days ago'). Due to an "INDET-operator", the XN-interval is said to host an indefinite number of occurrences of the eventuality Maria ganhar a corrida. The XN approach in 3.1 thus visualizes the PPC$_{PT}$'s interval-based meaning that gets specified by the INDET-operator.

---

61. Besides the Indefinite Past Theory/Anteriority theory and the Perfect-State theory/Result-State theory, the XN theory represents one of three major cross-linguistic theories of the Present Perfect (cf. e.g. Portner 2012). As noted by Grønn and Stechow (2020), each of the three theories particularly specializes in accounting straightforwardly for the resultative (Perfect-State theory/Result-State theory), experiential (Indefinite Past theory/Anteriority theory) or universal reading (XN theory) of the PP.

The functional split of the PPC$_{PT}$ and the Simple Past

In Portuguese, it is the Simple Past (*Pretérito Perfeito Simples* – PPS) that fills the functional gap caused by the PPC$_{PT}$, by assuming some of the functions that are cross-linguistically often assumed by the PP (cf. e.g. Ferreira 2017):

(5) PPC$_{SP}$ vs. PPC$_{PT}$ (Becker 2020a: 1)[62]
    a. Resultative
        i. Spanish
            Pedro se ha roto la pierna. Le duele mucho.
            Pedro REFL has broken the leg him hurt much
            'Pedro has broken his leg. It hurts a lot.'
        ii. Portuguese
            *O Pedro tem-se quebrado a perna. Doi-lhe muito.
            o Pedro have-REFL broken the leg hurt him much
            'Pedro has broken his leg. It hurts a lot.'
        iii. Portuguese (Simple Past)
            O Pedro quebrou-se a perna. Doi-lhe muito.
            o Pedro broke-REFL the leg hurt him much
            'Pedro has broken his leg. It hurts a lot.'
    b. Existential
        i. Spanish
            ¿Ya has estado en Australia?
            already have been in Australia
            'Have you already been to Australia?'
        ii. Portuguese
            *Você já tem (EP: tens) estado em Austrália? – Sim, já
            you already have been in Australia yes already
            tenho estado três vezes.
            have been three times
            'Have you already been to Australia? – Yes, I have already been there three times.'
        iii. Portuguese (Simple Past)
            - Sim, já estive três vezes.
            yes already was three times
            'Yes, I have already been there three times.'

Both the resultative and the existential reading, which mark prototypical contexts for the PPC$_{SP}$, are incompatible with the semantics of the PPC$_{PT}$ and thus are expressed by using the PPS.

---

62. English translations added.

Continuation of t_E after t_S: Implication or implicature?

Typically, the PPC$_{PT}$'s t_E is interpreted as still holding at speech time, if not even beyond t_S. There has been a debate on whether this continuation should be accounted for in terms of an implication (cf. e.g. Olbertz 2018) or an implicature (cf e.g. Molsing 2007). While the implication-based analysis defines the continuation as an inherent semantic entailment of the PPC$_{PT}$, the implicature-based approach defines it as an optional, cancelable meaning component (cf. e.g. Becker 2016: 28). As it turns out, this question relates to what in the literature is often discussed under the label of scalar implication and scalar implicature (cf. e.g. Carston 1998).

(6) Peter has four kids. (p)
    a. IMPLICATION: *Peter has three kids.* (q$_1$)
       If p is true, it is impossible that q$_1$ is false
       *Peter has four kids but he does not have three kids.
    b. IMPLICATURE: *Peter does not have five kids.* (q$_2$)
       If p is true, q$_2$ can either be true or false
       Peter has four kids. He even has five kids.

The idea is that scalar expressions, such as the number of kids in (6), imply and implicate different meaning components. The implication operates "downwards" the scale, which allows for deriving that Peter has three, two and one kid(s) for sure – on condition that "Peter has four kids" is true. This implication is not cancelable, i.e. a contradicting discursive continuation would result in a logical contradiction as illustrated in (6a). Conversely, the implicature operates "upwards" the scale by implicating that Peter does not have five kids. Traditionally, this is explained based on the maxim of quantity ("Make your contribution as informative as is required (for the current purposes of the exchange)", Grice 1975: 45): If Peter had 5 kids, it would be more pertinent to be precise and to mention the exact number of kids. Nevertheless, adding that he even has five kids is possible for it does not result in a semantic contradiction, as shown in (6b).

Applying these ideas to the study of the PPC$_{PT}$, it turns out that the continuation of t_E after t_S can be conceived of as a scalar implicature as well: the timeline forms a scale, t_S functions as the "vantage point" and there is an implicature upwards the timeline which sugeests that t_E's continuation after t_S is a cancelable meaning component – similar to the implicature of Peter not having five kids in (6b).

Within an alternative approach, this scalar-implicature account of the PPC$_{PT}$ is denied in favor of an implication upwards the timeline, i.e. beyond t_S, as put forth by Olbertz (2018) based on Ilari's (2001) Examples (3g):

(7) a. *O surto de meningite tem matado 298 pessoas.
      the outbreak of meningitis has killed 298 people
      'The meningitis outbreak has killed 298 people.'

b. O   surto   de meningite tem matado muita gente.
    the outbreak of meningitis has killed a lot of people
    'The meningitis outbreak has been killing a lot of people.'

Olbertz (2018: 480f.) assumes that the infelicity of (7a), which "contains a cardinal numeral to quantify the undergoer argument, which has a telicizing effect on the event", suggests that the PPC$_{PT}$ necessarily denotes a continuation of t_E after t_S. According to this analysis, (7b) is fine because of a lacking boundary that delimits t_E as not surpassing t_S. In fact, this analysis would be able to explain the PPC$_{PT}$'s preference of iterative and durative readings based on the implication of continuation alone: if t_E would be unexceptionally denoted as not being concluded at speech time, the PPC$_{PT}$'s incompatibility with singular eventualities and cardinal measurements would be accounted for in a straightforward way.

However, there is data showing that explicitly cancelling the continuation of t_E after t_S does not result in a logical contradiction, as shown in (8).

(8) Cancelling the continuation of t_E after t_S[63]
   a. *Não tem chovido mas choveu   hoje.*
       not has rained but rained-SIMPLE PAST today
       'It has not been raining (lately), but today it rained.'
   b. *Tem chovido mas não choveu   hoje.*
       has rained but not rained-SIMPLE PAST today
       'It has been raining (a lot lately), but today it did not rain.'
   c. *Ele tem estado doente mas ficou bom com a   chegada*
       he has been   ill   bit stayed good with the arrival
       da   mãe.
       of the mother
       'He's been sick but he's been fine with his mother coming.'

In each of these examples, the continuation of the t_E gets explicitly cancelled by means of the Simple Past *(Pretérito Perfeito Composto)* expressing the opposite meaning of the PPC$_{PT}$. Interestingly, the examples might even suggest that a cancelling of t_E may even occur slightly before t_S. We conclude that we consider the examples indicated in (8) as evidence against an implicational account and adhere to the scalar implicature approach.

---

63. Examples (8a) and (8b) were checked with a native speaker of European Portuguese. Example (8c) taken from Campos (1986: 418).

3.2 A note on diatopic variation

Although a variationist approach of the PPC$_{PT}$ lies beyond the scope of our study, we need to briefly revise some aspects related to the potential influence of diatopic variation on the use of the PPC$_{PT}$.

Within Portuguese linguistics, "[t]he most widely studied varieties of Portuguese are European Portuguese (EP) and Brazilian Portuguese (BP)" (Kato and Martins 2016: 15). Accordingly, Barbosa Bertucci (2008) presents a corpus study investigating whether the employment of the PPC$_{PT}$ differs both quantitatively and qualitatively in EP vs. BP. The corpus under scrutiny consists of speeches (representing a rather formal register) and letters (representing a rather informal register) from both EP and BP from the 20th century. The analysis compares occurrences of the PPC$_{PT}$ and the PPS. With regard to EP, the result shows 625 occurrences in total (PPS and PPC) with 564 (90%) instances of the PPS and 61 (10%) instances of the PPC$_{PT}$. With regard to BP, the picture is quite similar. There are 573 occurrences in total (PPS and PPC) with 543 (95%) instances of the PPS and 30 (5%) instances of the PPC$_{PT}$. Apart from the general observation that the PPC$_{PT}$ is rarely used in both varieties in comparison to the PPS, the numbers suggest that the PPC$_{PT}$ is, indeed, "numerically more productive in EP than in BP" (Barbosa Bertucci 2008: 199). This result is confirmed by Becker (2022: 67) who presents a corpus study based on "10 million items for each variety" provided by the *Corpus do Português* (section: 20th century, Davies and Ferreira 2006) that shows the following distribution: 98.7% PPS : 1.3% PPC$_{PT}$ (BP); 98.4% PPS: 1.6% PPC$_{PT}$ (EP) and, in total, 45% PPC$_{PT}$ (BP) : 55% PPC$_{PT}$ (EP). Although the Brazilian PPC$_{PT}$ seems to be slightly less frequent, Barbosa Bertucci (2008) argues that there is no semantic difference between the PPC$_{PT}$ in both varieties. Accordingly, in both varieties the PPC$_{PT}$'s *valeur linguistique*, i.e. its functional load, is similar, particularly with respect to the PPS. This is suggested by further results of her corpus study that indicate similar results regarding the parameters of aspectuality (iterative vs. durative vs. perfective reading), adverbials (presence vs. absence of adverbials), telicity of the underlying predicate, as well as degree of formality:

> A partir da comparação entre vários grupos de fatores (traços aspectuais, presença e/ou ausência de adjunto, telicidade e grau de formalidade) – que auxiliam na interpretação das formas simples e composta – e a variedade do Português, observamos que não existe nenhuma diferença significativa no emprego do Pretérito Perfeito Simples (PPS) e Composto (PPC) no PE e no PB. Sendo assim, podemos concluir

que o PPS e o PPS [*sic*]⁶⁴ possuem características e funções semelhantes nas duas variedades.⁶⁵ (Barbosa Bertucci 2008: 214)

This assumption is e.g. also shared by Schmitt 2001: 404 ("the data relevant to the present discussion are the same in both languages"). To our knowledge, there is no further literature that explicitly studies the diatopic variation of EP vs. BP. Nevertheless, Cabredo Hofherr et al. (2010) study the PPC$_{PT}$ in a northeastern Brazilian dialect that, according to the authors, shows some notable deviations from the Brazilian PPC$_{SP}$ as described elsewhere. Crucially, the peculiarities in the described variety pertain to the restriction of the PPC$_{PT}$ to iterative contexts impeding radical durativity due to a "temporal gap requirement" (Cabredo Hofherr et al. 2010: 75). The authors derive that there seems to be diatopic variation in Brazil that pertains to the question of whether the PPC$_{PT}$ gives rise to universal readings in addition to iterative readings or not (cf. Cabredo Hofherr et al. 2010: 73). In this vein, they put the discussion in Ilari (2001) of whether the PPC$_{PT}$ does (or not) allow for readings featuring radical durativity ("*duratividade absoluta*") down to variation within Brazil.

Given that our framework aims at a general typology of readings (instead of a detailed dialectal study), we opt for including the durative reading in our account in order to derive a cross-dialectal picture (cf. also discussion below in Section 3.3.2).

We summarize the following assumptions:

i. The PPC$_{PT}$ disposes of (almost) identical semantics and functions in EP and BP. There seems to be microvariation though, as e.g. in the northeast of Brazil, whose PPC$_{PT}$ has been characterized by Cabredo Hofherr et al. (2010) as deviating from the default value of the PPC$_{PT}$.
ii. The PPC$_{PT}$ is slightly more frequently used in EP than in BP.

In line with (i), we proceed with our account of the PPC$_{PT}$ without explicitly investigating potential semantic differences between the PPC$_{PT}$ in EP and BP. From (ii), we derive the hypothesis that the key to the PPC$_{PT}$ may lie beyond its truth-conditional meaning, i.e. on the level of discourse and the question of its interplay with further discourse entities on the syntagmatic axis. After all, the different numbers of occurrences in EP and BP suggest that it is possible for a speaker to avoid the PPC$_{PT}$

---

64. PPC.

65. 'From the comparison between various groups of factors (aspectual traits, presence and/or absence of adjunct, telicity and degree of formality) – which assist in the interpretation of simple and composite forms – and the variety of Portuguese, we observe that there is no significant difference in the use of Preterito Perfeito Simples (PPS) and Composto (PPC) in EP and BP. We thus conclude that PPS and PP[C] have similar characteristics and functions in both varieties.'

in particular contexts. That is, there seem to be morphosyntactic alternatives to express the same intended meaning without drawing on the PPC$_{PT}$. In fact, in Section 3.5 and Chapter 5, we propose that the PPC$_{PT}$ may particularly assume the function of contributing to the building of rhetorical coherence in discourse, which turns it into an optional rhetorical device instead of exclusively depending on the truth-conditional requirements of a described situation.

In the next section, we build on the assumptions discussed so far and refine them applying our general framework introduced in Chapter 2.

3.3 Quantificational readings

In Chapter 2, we outlined the quantificational semantics of the cross-linguistic Present Perfect, which is crucially spelled out in the denotation of temporally indefinite past eventualities lacking a location time t_{LOC}. In this section, we apply this approach to the study of the PPC$_{PT}$ and argue that its quantificational semantics give rise to three kinds of quantificational readings: IPEX readings (featuring an indefinite-pluractional event-external quantifier), universal readings (featuring a universal quantifier) and characterizing readings (featuring a temporally restricted generic quantifier).

3.3.1 IPEX readings

IPEX as a combination of indefiniteness and pluractionality
In the context of the XN theory of the PPC$_{PT}$ (cf. Figure 3.1), we discussed Becker's (2020a) covert INDET-operator. This operator is said to cause an indefinite iteration of t_E. Once again, it results from an analogy with the nominal domain. In particular, it is inspired by the semantics of the determiner of plural NPs, such as in Fr. *des chevaliers* ('knights') (Becker 2020a: 3), that denotes an indefinite but plural number of knights.

Cabredo Hofherr et al. (2010); Amaral and Howe (2012) and Molsing (2010) propose to account for the PPC$_{PT}$'s iteration based on a similar semantic notion called pluractionality. The concept of pluractionality is understood as a fundamental semantic component in natural language semantics that, according to Bertinetto and Lenci (2012), may be realized via several linguistic devices, such as reduplication, affixes, free morphemes or lexical tools. The authors, who credit Newman (1980) for introducing the concept, define the following two types of pluractionality:

(9) Types of pluractionality (Bertinetto and Lenci 2012: 852)
   a. Event-internal pluractionality: sub-events holding within a single situation
      Yesterday at 5 o'clock John knocked insistently at the door.
   b. Event-external pluractionality: repetition of an event over several situations
      John swam daily in the lake.

Applying the distinction of event-internal and event-external pluractionality to Ilari's data presented in (3), it becomes clear that the PPC_{PT}'s pluractionality exclusively evokes event-external readings. The PPC_{PT}'s iteration is typically interpreted to stretch over several situations (cf. also Olbertz 2018: 497). After all, it seems unlikely if not odd to attribute a reading like "He has been visiting us several times" (3a) to a single situation. However, Ilari (2001) adduces an example that illustrates that event-internal pluractionality is not ruled out per se by the PPC_{PT}. The example is listed in (10b–ii) together with variations of it manipulating the values of event-external vs. internal quantification and definite vs. indefinite quantification:

(10) PPC_{PT} and pluractionality (inspired by Ilari 2001: 140)
   a. Event-external: ✓ indefinite quantification, ✗ definite quantification
      i. O   carteiro tem tocado várias vezes.
         the   postman   has rung   several times
         'The postman has been ringing the bell several times.'
      ii. *O   carteiro tem tocado duas vezes.
          the postman   has rung   two   times
          'The postman rang twice.'
   b. Event-internal: ✓ indefinite quantification, ✓ definite quantification
      i. O   carteiro tem tocado várias vezes.
         the   postman   has rung   several times
         'The postman has been ringing the bell several times.'
      ii. O   carteiro tem tocado duas vezes.
          the postman   has rung   two   times
          'The postman has been ringing twice lately (over and over).' /
          *'The postman rang twice.'

(10b) indicates that definite event-internal quantification is not ruled out for reasons of grammaticality. However, the referred examples represent semantically highly marked cases. In (10b–ii), the definite quantifier "twice" is incorporated by the predicate. As a consequence, the quantifier phrase scopes over the underlying situation. That is, it is not the PPC_{PT} that gets combined with "twice" but the predicate which, in turn, gets combined with the PPC_{PT}. This crucial difference between event-internal and event-external pluractionality can also be be depicted with the tree structures in the Figures 3.2 and 3.3.

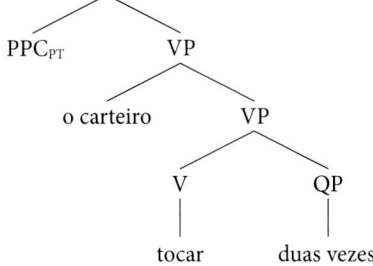

Figure 3.2 PPC_PT allowing for event-internal definite quantification

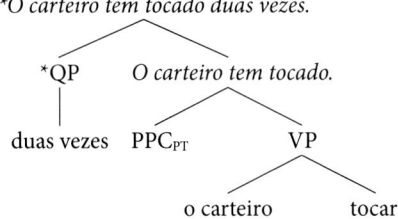

Figure 3.3 PPC_PT impeding event-external definite quantification

We propose combining the aspects covered by both the INDET-operator and the concept of pluractionality by introducing the term "indefinite-pluractional existential reading" (IPEX reading). The reason is that both concepts succeed in accounting for different peculiarities: on the one hand, the PPC_PT systematically rules out the denotation of a single and bounded eventuality, which is predicted by the pluractionality constraint but not by the INDET-operator alone. After all, indefiniteness alone does not impede the denotation of a singular nominal or temporal entity. On the other hand, the PPC_PT's quantification remains indefinite in nearly all of the cases. This is predicted by the INDET-operator but not by the pluractionality constraint alone, which per se would allow for definite pluractionality.

Iterative vs. gradual readings
It is oftentimes the case that the IPEX reading denotes a homogeneous repetition of the eventuality in the scope of the PPC_PT (cf. e.g. (3a) and (3b) in Section 3.1). It turns out though that there may also be a non-homogeneous, gradual scaling of t_E. We consider this type of reading as being associated with the IPEX quantifier, as well. Typically, it occurs in combination with predicates that denote some kind of a non-hompgeneous gradual development. Two types of predicates should be

distinguished, namely (i) incremental theme verbs (cf. Tenny 1994: 18) and (ii) degree achievements or degree verbs (cf. Civardi and Bertinetto 2015). Incremental theme verbs are accomplishments that gradually bear out an internal argument as exemplified in (11a). On the other hand, degree achievements are "step by step achievements" that have a gradual scaling reading without approaching an inherent goal, as exemplified in (11b).

(11) Gradual readings
    a. Incremental theme verbs
        i. *Ao longo de mais de dez anos, os Japanther têm*
           PREP long PREP more PREP ten years the Japanther have
           construído a sua carreira em poucas coisas.
           built the their career in few things
           'Over more than ten years, the Japanthers have built their career on only a few things.'[66]
        ii. *[O] Sporting tem preparado um grande ambiente de*
           the Sporting has prepared a great environment of
           hostilidade para o clássico de amanhã.)
           hostility for the classic of tomorrow
           'Sporting has prepared a big hostile ambience for tomorrow's classic.'[67]
    b. Degree achievements
        i. *[T]êm aumentado os casos de pessoas que viajaram*
           have increased the cases of persons that travelled
           ao exterior.
           PREP abroad
           'The cases of people travelling abroad have been increasing.'[68]
        ii. *[O] clima tem esquentado em relação a uma nova paralisação.*
           the climate has warmed up in relation to a new paralysis
           'The climate has been warming up in relation to a new paralysis.'[69]

---

66. *Bodyspace* (Online journal for music, 09/03/13), http://bodyspace.net/discos/2558-eat-like-lisa-act-like-bart/, 05/11/17, apud Müller (2017: 25).

67. *O Chuto Final* (Online Blog on Football, 01/06/13), https://chutofinal.wordpress.com/tag/sporting/, 05/15/17, apud Müller (2017: 55).

68. *Folha de São Paulo* (02/29/20), https://www1.folha.uol.com.br/equilibrioesaude/2020/02/coronavirus-gera-corrida-sem-necessidade-a-hospitais-de-sp.shtml, 06/30/20.

69. *Estadão* (04/16/19), https://economia.estadao.com.br/noticias/geraljinsatisfeitos-com-pacote-de-bolsonaro-caminhoneiros-ja-falam-em-greve,70002793639, 06/30/20.

We conclude that the PPC$_{PT}$'s indefinite-pluractional event-external quantification gives rise to iterative and gradual readings. The difference between IPEX-gradual and IPEX-iterative readings is that the latter are defined to denote homogenous iterations of equivalent sub-events, while the former denote a concatenation of heterogenous, i.e. not equivalent sub-events. In any case, the number of occurrences of t_E remains indefinite. As an exception to that rule, one might count the case of event-internal pluractionality featuring a definite number of iterations, which is grammatically fine but appears to be semantically highly marked. By semantically highly marked, we intend to couch that expressions as exemplified in (10b–ii) denote truth conditions that will rarely be fulfilled, i.e. that will hardly capture an actually occurring situation in the world.

3.3.2 Universal reading

As already hinted at in Section 3.2, we include the universal reading in our typology of the PPC$_{SP}$'s readings despite Cabredo Hofherr et al.'s (2010) finding that there is no universal reading available in a dialect spoken in the northeast of Brazil. In fact, the PPC$_{PT}$ has been discussed as pertaining to Stage II, i.e. as featuring a universal quantification. After all, there is an abutment-relation ($\succ\prec$) holding between t_E and t_S. In this vein, there is a tradition to assign the PPC$_{PT}$ durative readings (indicating universal quantification) in the case of a combination with an atelic predicate (cf. (3e) and e.g. Schmitt 2001; Wigger 2005; Molsing 2007; Barbosa Bertucci 2008; Leal et al. 2014, Becker 2022, Becker 2020a). Nevertheless, there is a difference between universal quantification in its strictest sense and "universalized" readings, that rather seem to take after the IPEX readings discussed in the previous section. Ilari (2001: 144) discusses both types based on the distinction of *duratividade absoluta* vs. *duratividade intermitente* ('absolute durativity' vs. 'disrupted durativity') as illustrated in Figure 3.4.

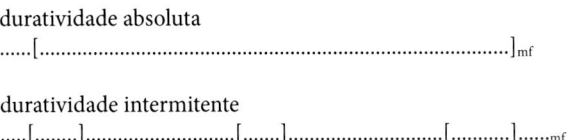

Figure 3.4 *Duratividade absoluta* vs. *duratividade intermitente* (Ilari 2001: 144)
mf: *momento de fala* (speech time (t_s))

In the case of disrupted durativity, there is no rigorously operating "all-quantification". Instead, the quantification seems to hold "only for those [intervals] at which appropriate circumstances for the realisation of the eventuality in question prevail" (Becker 2022: 59), as exemplified by the Simple Past in (12).

(12) "Iterated universal quantification" (Becker 2022: 59)
    a. *Sempre te levei [...] de carro para a escola.*
       always you brought by car to the school
       'I always drove you to school.'

Here, the universal quantifier, which is introduced by *sempre*, can be read as applying to "for instance, a morning during the week, but not a Sunday or a Wednesday night" (Becker 2022: 59). The same mechanism might underly the combination of atelic predicates with the PPC_{PT} forming temporal gaps. In fact, Becker alludes that

> [s]peakers of Portuguese report that they find the use of the PPC in these contexts (which are restricted by an appropriateness condition) slightly more acceptable than in contexts with homogeneous verbal expressions such as stative verbs (*querer*) and activity verbs (*vivir*). (Becker 2022: 59)

Accordingly, the combination of atelic predicates with the PPC_{PT} might generally underly aspectual coercion.[70] In (13), examples of atelic predicates are listed that are coerced from perfectly homogeneous situations into iterated instances of homogeneous situations due to adverbial modification (13a), world knowledge (13b) or the plural semantics of an NP (13c).

(13) Factors that may license iterative readings featuring atelic predicates
    a. Adverbial[71]
       A Maria tem confiado muitas vezes no Manuel.
       the Maria has trusted many times in the Manuel
       'Maria has been trusting Manuel many times lately.'
    b. World knowledge[72]
       Tem dormido bem?
       have slept well
       'Have you been sleeping well?'

---

70. "Typically, coercion is triggered if there is a conflict between the aspectual character of the eventuality description and the aspectual constraints of some other element in the context. The felicity of an aspectual reinterpretation is strongly dependent on linguistic context and knowledge of the world." (de Swart 1998: 360).

71. Example taken from Becker (2020a: 5).

72. Uol (10/04/20), https://www.uol.com.br/vivabem/noticias/redacao/2020/10/04/tem-dormido-bem-busca-por-solucoes-para-o-sono-aumentou-na-pandemia.htm, 10/09/20.

c. NP feat. plural semantics[73]
Tenho estado nas   capitais europeias (a   falar com os
have   been   in the capitals europeans PREP speak with the
nossos aliados).
ours   allies
'I have been in European capitals talking to our allies.'

In (13a), the semantics of the adverbial *muitas vezes* block the denotation of a perfectly homogeneous state and thus force iteration. Example (13b) also denotes temporal gaps in order to appropriately evaluate how the hearer has slept lately (nobody sleeps 24 hours a day). In (13c), it is the plural semantics of *nas capitais europeias* that force an iterated reading (which would not be forced by referring to a single European capital). For ontological reasons, the speaker cannot visit several capitals at the same time.

Now, turning to what Ilari (2001) labelled as *duratividade absoluta*, the question is whether the PPC$_{PT}$ actually does allow for readings whose universal quantifier denotes perfectly homogeneous states that are true at any subinterval of a given interval that they hold at, as exemplified by the Spanish PPC$_{SP}$ in (14).

(14) Universal PPC$_{SP}$ with perfectly homgeneous t$_E$ abutting t$_S$[74]
Ha vivido solo   desde que murió su padre.
has lived alone since that died his father
'He has been living by himself since his father died.'

For each atomic subinterval of the interval, which is delimited by *desde que murió su padre* and the speech time, `vivir solo` is true, i.e. there are no temporal gaps but a perfectly homogeneous state (cf. also Section 2.2 for the properties of states).

With regard to the PPC$_{PT}$, Ilari (2001) formulates the need for a test case featuring a stative predicate that is not coercible into a repetitive interpretation. Based on this test, he concludes that the "durative interpretation of state and activity sentences is, at most, a tendency, which ends up blocked by factors that we hardly know" (Ilari 2001: 144). Cabredo Hofherr et al. (2010) consider the undecisive litrerature regarding the PPC$_{PT}$'s potential to denote *duratividade absoluta* to suggest that it underlies variation. In line with this assumption, we find different judgements of similar data, as shown in (15).

---

[73]. *TVI24* (09/12/19), https://tvi24.iol.pt/internacional/reino-unido/boris-johnson-nega-ter-mentido-a-rainha-para-suspender-o-parlamento, 05/12/20.

[74]. Example taken from García Fernández and Martínez-Atienza (2003: 32).

(15) a. Molsing (2007: 140f.)
   i. *Eu tenho estado doente (desde a   semana passada).*
      I   have been sick   since the week last
      'I have been sick (since last week) / lately.'
   ii. *Eu tenho ficado no   quarto ultimamente.*
       I have stays in the room   lately
       'I have been staying in the room lately.'
   iii. *Eu tenho sido feliz   ultimamente.*
        I   have been happy lately
        'I have been happy lately.'
   b. Becker (2020a: 1)
      *Tenho vivido aqui toda a   minha vida.
      have lived here all ART my   life
      'I have lived here all my life.'
   c. Cabredo Hofherr et al. (2010: 87) (northeastern Brazilian Port.)
      i. **O urso tem dormido na   sua caverna o   inverno inteiro.*
         the bear has slept   in the his cave   the winter whole
         'The bear has been sleeping in his cave all winter.'
      ii. *O Pedro tem dormido na   varanda o   inverno inteiro.*
          the Pedro has slept   in the balcony the winter whole
          'Pedro has been sleeping on the balcony all winter.'
      iii. **Esse livro sempre tem estado na   prateleira da direita.*
           this book always has been in the shelf   of righthand
           'This book has always been on the righthand shelf.'
      iv. **Essa loja tem estado fechada ultimamente.*
          this shop has been   closed lately
          'This shop has been closed for some time.'
      v. *Pedro tem estado muito doente nos   últimos tempos.*
         Pedro has been   very ill   in the las   times
         'Pedro has been very ill lately.'

While readings denoting a perfectly homogeneous state are marked as fine in (15a), they are rated as odd in (15b) and (15c). Cabredo Hofherr et al. (2010) explain the finegrained effects in (15c) based on a distinction between gradable and non-gradable states. The reasoning is that non-gradable states (such as `a loja estar fechada` or `o urso dormir na sua caverna o inverno inteiro` or `o livro estar na prateleira da direita`) denote perfectly homogeneous intervals with the same truth conditions for each atomic subinterval. On the other hand, gradable states denote a set of sub-states that differ in terms of their degree. In `Pedro estar muito doente nos últimos tempos`, **Pedro** is not expected to be sick to the same degree over time. Instead, there are ups and downs such that there is no perfectly homogeneous but a graded universal quantification over t_E. This account would also be able to explain the felicity of eu ser feliz in (15a–iii): the speaker may have been happy to different degrees at different times. This, in turn, is in line with Ilari (2001: 136) who describes the non-homogeneity of the PPC$_{PT}$'s t$_E$ as *escalonamento no tempo* ('grading in time').

As already discussed, we adhere to a typology that includes readings that, in the terminology of Cabredo Hofherr et al. (2010), combine with non-gradable states, irrespectively of potentially underlying variation. This is supported by a quick exploration of sources of online journalism revealing examples as illustrated in (16), which denote perfectly homogeneous states.

(16) Strictly durative readings with the PPC$_{PT}$
    a. *Têm estado quatro destroyers no   mediterrâneo desde há*
       have been four   detroyers in the mediterranean since have
       algum tempo.
       some time
       'There have been four "destroyers" in the Mediterranean since some time ago.'[75]
    b. *A Mesquita de Lisboa tem estado fechada e   assim continuará,*
       the mosque of Lisbon has been closed and so will continue
       por   causa da pandemia.
       because of the pandemic
       'The Lisbon Mosque has been closed and will remain closed because of the pandemic.'[76]
    c. *O restaurante da   Casa do Careto tem estado fechado ao*
       the restaurant of the casa do caerto has been closed to the
       público, devido à   pandemia de Covid-19.
       public due to the pandemic of Covid-19
       'The Casa do Careto restaurant has been closed to the public due to the Covid-19 pandemic.'[77]
    d. *O homem alegou que tem morado na   rua depois de um*
       the man claimed that has lived in the street after of a
       desentendimento com a   família.
       disagreement with the family
       'The man claimed he's been living on the street after a disagreement with his family.'[78]

---

[75]. *Diário de Notícias* (09/13/12), https://www.dn.pt/globo/africa/eua-enviam-dois-navios-de-guerra-para-a-costa-da-libia-2767457.html, 05/12/20.

[76]. *Observador* (04/23/20), https://observador.pt/especiais/como-a-comunidade-islamica-vive-o-ramadao-em-tempos-de-covid-19-espiritualmente-isto-e-muito-violento/, 05/12/20.

[77]. *A Voz de Trás os Montes* (05/06/20), https://www.avozdetrasosmontes.pt/noticia/26819, 05/12/20.

[78]. *Diário do Aço* (04/23/20), https://www.diariodoaco.com.br/noticia/0078136-homem-saca-o-auxalio-emergencial-e-tem-o-dinheiro-furtado, 05/12/20.

e. *No México, o mesmo partido tem estado no poder nos*
   in México the same party has been in the power in the
   últimos 18 anos de democracia.
   last 18 years of democracy
   'In Mexico, the same party has been in power for the past 18 years of democracy.'[79]

f. *Até esta quarta-feira, o metro de Nova Iorque tem estado aberto*
   until this wednesday the subway of New York has been open
   24 horas por dia, durante toda a semana.
   24 hours for day during all the week
   'Until this Wednesday, the New York City subway has been open 24 hours a day, all week long.'[80]

Further evidence is provided by combinations with progressives, which dispose of similar semantics as compared to state predicates: the progressive applied to a predicate ø "is true of a situation s iff ø is true in all relevant subsitutations of s" (cf. Hallman 2009 apud Portner 2012: 1251). Moreover, Cabredo Hofherr et al. (2010: 74) propose the *ainda não*-test ('not yet'), which, once again, should detect the denotation of an interval for which the truth conditions should be homogeneously the same for each part of it.

(17) PPC_{PT} + progressive
   a. *Estar a* + INF[81]
      A KLM tem estado a operar (e continuará em junho) um
      the KLM has been PREP operate and will continue in june a
      voo diário entre Lisboa e Amesterdão.
      flight daily between Lisbon and Amsterdam
      'KLM has been operating (and will continue in June) a daily flight between Lisbon and Amsterdam.'

---

79. *Jornaldo Campus- USPSP* (10/07/18), http://www.jornaldocampus.usp.br/index.php/2018/10/entrevistamos-tres-especialistas-em-ciencia-politica-sobre-as-eleicoes/, 05/12/20.

80. *Observador* (05/06/20), https://observador.pt/2020/05/06/metro-de-nova-iorque-fecha-pela-primeira-vez-na-historia-veja-as-imagens/, 05/12/20.

81. The *estar a* + infinitive construction is the morphosyntactic expression of the progressive in EP. *Observador* (05/20/20), https://observador.pt/2020/05/20/air-france-volta-a-voos-diarios-lisboa-paris-e-retoma-porto-em-6-junho/, 05/20/20.

b. *Estar* + Gerund[82]

Os	russos	têm	estado	trabalhando	na		área de desenvolvimento
the	russians	have	been	working		in the field of	development

de	tecnologias	hipersónicas	já		há	algum	tempo.
of	tecnhologies	hypersonic	already	have		some	time

   'The Russians have been working on the development of hypersonic technologies for some time now.'

c. *Ainda não*[83]

Passos	já		admitiu	aumentar	impostos,	mas	ainda	não	tem	fechado
Passos	already	admitted	raise		taxes	but	yet		not	has	closed

um	acordo	com	o		CDS	nesse		sentido.
a		deal	with	the	CDS	in that	respect	

   'Passos already admitted to raise taxes, but he has not closed a deal with the CDS with respect to this.'

We conclude that there may be sociolinguistic variation that may have an impact on the acceptance of strictly durative, i.e. of strictly universal readings. Yet, we proceed including the universal reading in our framework. In the following, we understand the universal reading of the PPC$_{PT}$ to refer to what we have discussed in the present section under the label of *duratividade absoluta*.

3.3.3 Characterizing readings

In this section, we discuss the characterizing reading as a third variant of the PPC$_{PT}$'s quantificational semantics. Instead of an existential or universal quantifier, it builds on a temporally restricted generic quantifier.

The characterizing reading seems to become more and more central to the PPC$_{PT}$:

> In contemporary Portuguese, a further semantic feature of the PPC is gradually coming to light, at least in particular contexts where the iterative or durative semantics of the PPC acquires a clearly characterising or even generalising quality […] [T]he PPC characterizes a more recent, upcoming habit […] [T]he increasing frequency of characterising or generalising readings in PPC contexts may lead to a conventionalisation of this peculiar feature of the PPC in the long run.
>
> (Becker 2022: 61)

---

[82]. ZAP (03/03/20), https://zap.aeiou.pt/pentagono-alcancar-russia-china-arma-hiprsonica-311662, 05/20/20.

[83]. *Expresso* (05/30/14), https://expresso.pt/politica/passos-so-reage-este-sabado-a-decisao-do-tc=f873154, 05/12/20.

Once again, there is a parallel with the semantics of the noun phrase, that, in most general terms, may denote either a kind or an individual object. Applied to the verbal domain, a proposition with a tempo-aspectual index may denote either a specific, isolated, episodic fact or a general property, a characterizing regularity "which summarizes groups of particular episodes or facts. [...] Other common terms for characterizing sentences found in the literature are (g)nomic, dipsositional, general or habitual." (Krifka et al. 1995: 2f.).

(18) Two types of genericity (Krifka et al. 1995: 2f.)[84]
 a. NP: kind vs. object
  i. *The potato was first cultivated in South America.*
  ii. *This potato was cultivated in my garden.*
 b. Sentential predication: characterizing vs. episodic
  i. *John smokes a cigar after dinner.*
  ii. *Yesterday, John smoked a cigar after dinner.*

While (18a–i) contains an "NP that does not refer to an "ordinary" individual or object, but instead refers to a kind" (Krifka et al. 1995: 2), in (18b–i), "it is the whole generic sentence that expresses regularities which transcend particular facts" (Krifka et al. 1995: 3). Put differently, "kinds [...] abstract away from particular objects, [...] characterizing sentences [...] abstract away from particular events." (Krifka et al. 1995: 4). In the following, we apply these ideas to the study of the PPC$_{PT}$ where we will only be concerned with genericity on the level of propositions, i.e. with the distinction between episodic and characterizing readings.

Characterizing readings temporally restricted to the present time-sphere
As a first hypothesis, we may approach the PPC$_{PT}$ to be able to express a characterizing property that gets temporally restricted to the perspective time, i.e. to the present time-sphere. Following this approach, some of the semantic peculiarities of the PPC$_{PT}$ can be accounted for in a straightforward way: with regard to *A Maria tem confiado no Manuel* ('Maria has been trusting in Manuel'), we yield an interpretation of Maria having regularly trusted in Manuel in the present time-sphere including the pre-present time zone. Although there probably are concrete intervals for which `Maria trust in Manuel` is true, these intervals are not denoted but abstracted away from. That is, they serve as a source for an abstraction, i.e. for the derived characterizing predication. As noted by Krifka et al. (1995), this marks a difference with respect to universally quantified sentences:

---

84. The examples in (18a–ii) and (18b–ii) are modified versions of (18a–i) and (18b–i) that were taken from Krifka et al. (1995).

> [...] although characterizing sentences sometimes have the flavor of universally quantified sentences, these two categories must be kept apart. One reason is that characterizing sentences, in general, allow for exceptions, whereas universally quantified sentences make a claim for every object of a certain sort.
>
> (Krifka et al. 1995: 4)

In other words, the truth conditions of characterizing sentences explicitly allow for exceptions and gaps without becoming false. In this vein, (19a) is true even though there might have been occasions in which John did not smoke a cigar after dinner. Applied to the characterizing interpretation of *A Maria tem confiado no Manuel*, the truth conditions allow for situations in that A Maria confiar no Manuel is false. Conversely, a universally quantified sentence, in its strictest sense and when referring to specific episodes, is not compatible with those gaps (19b).

(19) Characterizing reading vs. universal quantification[85]
  a. *John usually smoked a cigar after dinner.*
  b. *John always smoked a cigar after dinner.*

It should not be derived from (19b) that the adverbial "always" generally blocks a characterizing reading in favor of an episodic reading. Instead, "always" is also compatible with characterizing readings, especially when combined with the PPC_{PT}. This is in line with Becker (pted) who states that a "law-like" reading may be evoked by a PPC_{PT} combined with *sempre*:

> This particular reading distinguishes itself from the typical universal reading associated with sempre in that it abstracts a definite set of individual instances (the all-quantification of *sempre*) and shifts the focus to the general and atemporal character of a gnomic or law-like statement about an entitiy or a state of affairs.
>
> (Becker 2022: 78)

Attributing an atemporal value to the characterizing reading brings up a modal flavor. This is meant to capture that these are not (primarily) situated on and anchored with respect to the temporal dimension. Instead, "they constitute a layer apart", they are "disconnected from the axis of temporal ordering in the unfolding discourse", therefore they do "not belong to the domain of temporality, but to another domain – the 'reign' of modality" (Becker and Egetenmeyer 2018: 55). We will turn back to that issue and the related "conspicuous manifestation of a background structure in discourse" (ibid) when analyzing the PPC_{PT}'s discursive functions in Section 3.5.

In what concerns the semantics of generic expressions and, in particular, characterizing sentences, Krifka et al. (1995: 26) assume a generic quantifier GEN

---

85. Modified versions of examples provided in Krifka et al. (1995).

"underlying characterizing sentences that lack an overt quantificational adverb" yielding the following general formula for generic quantification:

(20) GEN [Restrictor]; Matrix

In the case of characterizing sentences, GEN derives a regular pattern that is abstracted away from episodic eventualities that are expressed in what is labelled the "matrix" in (20). Additionally, the characterizing proposition gets restricted to particular situations or occasions which is spelled out on the level of the restrictor. For example, in (21a), the regular smoking is restricted to situations of Mary coming home. And even (21b), whose morphological form seems to lack a restrictor, is typically interpreted as being restricted to "normal situations with respect to smoking".

(21) The generic quantifier GEN (Krifka et al. 1995: 30f.)
   a. *Mary smokes when she comes home.*
      GEN[s, x;](x = Mary & x comes home in s; x smokes in s)
   b. *Mary smokes.*
      GEN[s, x;](x = Mary & s is a normal situation with respect to smoking & s contains x; x smokes in s)

In the same vein, we assume the GEN-operator to quantify over situations in the scope of the PPC_{PT} that evoke a characterizing reading. The crucial difference to (21a) lies in the PPC_{PT}'s property to temporally restrict the matrix to the PPC_{PT}'s perspective time, i.e. to the present time-sphere. Following the style of Krifka et al. (1995), we may formulate the characterizing PPC_{PT} as proposed in (22).

(22) *A Maria tem confiado no Manuel.*
     GEN[t_P, s, x;](x = Maria & t_P = present time-sphere & s is a normal situation with respect to trusting Manuel & t_P contains s & s contains x & x trusts Manuel in s)

Again, the formula in (22) consists of the generic quantifier, the restrictor and the matrix. The generic quantifier gets restricted to the perspective time t_P, to typical situations with respect to trusting Manuel, as well as to the entity x (Maria). The formula then outputs a meaning that can be read in two different ways: (i) t_P is characterized as GEN(`Maria trust in Manuel`) or (ii) Maria is characterized as GEN(`trust in Manuel`) in t_P. The two readings seem to display two complementary topic-comment structures. Either, it is predicated that Maria generically disposes of a property x (restricted to t_P), or it is predicated that t_P generically disposes of a property x (restricted to Maria).

Further examples of characterizing readings are illustrated in (23).

(23) Adverbially modified characterizing PPC_{PT}
   a. *A Maria tem confiado no Manuel ultimamente.*
      $\text{GEN}[t_P, s, x;](x = \text{Maria} \ \& \ t_P = \textit{ultimamente} \ \& \ s$ is a normal situation with respect to trusting Manuel & t_P contains s & s contains x & x trusts Manuel in s)
   b. *A Maria tem confiado no Manuel geralmente.*
      $\text{GEN}[t_P, s, x;](x = \text{Maria} \ \& \ t_P = \text{present time-sphere} \ \& \ s$ is a normal situation with respect to trusting Manuel & t_P contains s & s contains x & x trusts Manuel in s)
   c. *A Maria tem confiado no Manuel nos últimos anos.*
      $\text{GEN}[t_P, s, x;](x = \text{Maria} \ \& \ t_P = \textit{nos últimos anos} \ \& \ s$ is a normal situation with respect to trusting Manuel & t_P contains s & s contains x & x trusts Manuel in s)
   d. *A Maria sempre tem confiado no Manuel.*
      $\text{GEN}[t_P, s, x;](x = \text{Maria} \ \& \ t_P = \text{present time-sphere} \ \& \ s$ is a normal situation with respect to trusting Manuel & t_P contains s & s contains x & x trusts Manuel in s)

As illustrated, the characterizing reading harmonizes with adverbials that modify the perspective time, i.e. that cotextually define the temporal notion of the present time-sphere (cf. further discussion in Section 3.4).

3.3.4 Overview

We conclude that the PPC_{PT}'s quantificational semantics give rise to three different configurations of IPEX (featuring an existential quantification), universal (universal quantification) and characterizing readings (temporally restricted generic quantification). This tripartite structure is illustrated in Figure 3.5. As discussed, there might be variation within Brazil as to what extent the universal reading can be found in a particular variety.

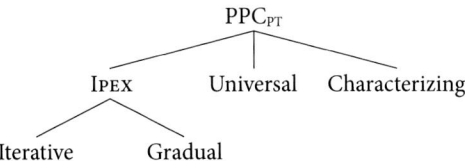

Figure 3.5 The quantificational readings of the PPC_{PT}

A slightly different categorization as a bipartite structure is depicted in Figure 3.6. Here, episodic readings (IPEX and universal readings) are distinguished from characterizing readings. While episodic readings are conceived of as denoting eventualities that receive a temporal index, i.e. that are anchored on a virtual timeline, the characterizing readings represent abstractions. As it turns out in Section 3.5, this alternative architecture helps identify (some of) the discourse functions of the PPC$_{PT}$.

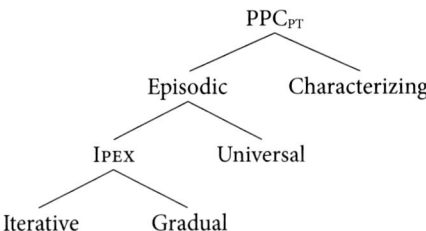

Figure 3.6 The episodic vs. characterizing readings of the PPC$_{PT}$

From a semasiological perspective, it might be worth elaborating on the differences between the *Imperfeito* and the PPC$_{PT}$. After all, the *Imperfeito* is known for evoking continuative, progressive and habitual readings (cf. e.g. Becker 2010a and Leonetti 2018 for the Romance Imperfect), which might be perceived as highly similar to the PPC$_{PT}$'s readings illustrated in Figure 3.6. Therefore, a more detailed revision of the semantics of the Imperfect can be consulted in Section 6.2. For now, the most significant differences between the PPC$_{PT}$ and the Imperfect may be condensed to their diverging temporal perspective. While the *Imperfeito* mostly discursively seeks a temporal anchor due to its "anaphoric character and strong contextual dependency" (Becker 2010a: 79), the PPC$_{PT}$ may be uttered out of the blue, as its point of reference is resolved via its perspective time that lies in the present time-sphere (speech time).[86] The *Imperfeito*, on the other hand, perspectives the past time-sphere. This, essentially, qualifies it to be employed in the discourse mode of narration, which is clearly blocked by the PPC$_{PT}$ (cf. also Section 3.5 below for the relationship between the modes of discourse and the PPC$_{PT}$). Moreover, the PPC$_{PT}$ gives rise to a scalar implicature regarding the continuation of t_E after t_S (cf. Section 3.1), while the *Imperfeito* neither implies nor implicates a continuation of the eventuality in its scope due to its. To sum up, the *Imperfeito* and the PPC$_{PT}$ underly a clear functional division that can be traced back to their diverging temporal semantics although there appear to be aspectual overlaps in their readings.

---

[86]. Cf. Leonetti 2018 though, who discusses exceptions to that rule for the Spanish *Imperfecto*'s continuous and progressive readings.

Having introduced our analysis of the PPC$_{PT}$'s readings in synchrony, we may now derive a new perspective on the question of whether the PPC$_{PT}$ belongs to Stage II, before turning to the next section.

A diachronic note: The PPC$_{PT}$'s evolution as a regular idiosyncrasy?
In Chapter 2, we recapitulated a common categorization of the PPC$_{PT}$ as a universal Perfect of Stage II or as a slightly modified Stage II Perfect imposing additional felicity conditions. However, as noted by (Becker 2022: 56), "[t]o date, the diachronic research on the PPC remains tentative" due to the unsolved question of how the PPC$_{PT}$'s development actually fits into the picture of the Romance Perfect (cf. also Bertinetto and Squartini 2000: 419). Typically, the Stage II Perfect is conceived of as denoting universal quantification over t_E that causes t_E to abut speech time t_S ($t_E \succ \prec t_S$). That condition is synchronically satisfied by the universal readings and, to a certain extent, by the IPEX readings, as well. However, the characterizing readings seem to gradually take over and become more and more frequent by approaching a status of a "conventionalisation [...] in the long run" (Becker 2022: 62). We defined the characterizing readings as lacking the temporal abutment property and to denote a generic quantification within the present time-sphere instead. As a consequence, the characterizing reading seems to escape from the regular grammaticalization path as proposed by Harris (1982) and Bertinetto and Squartini (2000). Instead of focussing its temporal component, leading to an acquisition of Stage III, it promotes a rather modalized value. However, there might be a bit of a regularity in that peculiar development, as well. It is compatible with a picture drawn by another study of cross-linguistic grammaticalization on the level of tense, aspect and modality. Based on a sample of fifty languages, Bybee et al. (1994) infer a pattern of a typical sequence of the values of Iterative < Frequentative < Habitual.[87] The PPC$_{PT}$'s approaching of a characterizing reading instead of a perfective and aoristic meaning would thus remain a rather idiosyncratic evolution within the Romance languages, however represent a rather regular process in the context of a cross-linguistic sample that extends the Romance languages.

---

87. The authors list Tigre, Chacobo, Alawa, Temne, Tem, Maidu, Udmurt, Uigur and Buriat as having developed a form indicating past habituality. Pakerys (2018) shows that in Lithuanian a suffix indicating habituality can be traced back to an originally iterative value, as well.

3.4 Adverbials

Having outlined our framework of the quantificational readings that the PPC$_{PT}$ typically evokes, we can now turn to the question of which tempo-aspectual adverbials are typically combined with these.

In Chapter 2.3, we discussed that, from a cross-linguistic perspective, the Present Perfect typically combines with particular tempo-aspectual adverbials. Despite the set of semantic peculiarities and restrictions imposed by the PPC$_{PT}$, it is remarkable that this picture mostly also applies to the PPC$_{PT}$. To begin with, it is uncontroversial that the PPC$_{PT}$ rules out positional adverbials ("yesterday, three weeks ago"), that try to modify t_{LOC} (24a). This is predicted by the lack of t_{LOC} in the PPC$_{PT}$'s logical form. Given that the PPC$_{PT}$ lacks a location time argument, positional adverbials fail to modify t_{LOC}.

Durative adverbials ("for x months, throughout the time") are fine when combined with the PPC$_{PT}$ (24b). They operate on t_E by emphasizing the abutment relation that holds between t_E and t_S ($t_E \succ \prec t_S$). Durative adverbials receiving an interpretation as being isolated from t_S are blocked, as illustrated in Section 3.1 in Example (3d): while the durative adverbial "from 1927 to 1968" is ruled out, "since 1927" is fine. As already discussed in Chapter 2.3, we assume durative adverbials not to scope over a location time. In fact, an eventuality, that is said to be repeated or to hold throughout an interval, necessarily implies some kind of temporal extent, which, in turn, might be misinterpreted as the location time. However, the referred repetition or duration is explicitly forced by durative adverbials, which makes them scope over t_E.

XN-adverbials serve as means to specify the PPC$_{PT}$'s vague temporal extension of the present time-sphere. The present time-sphere accommodates the PPC$_{PT}$'s perspective time t_P (24c). As shown in Declerck et al. (2006), the present time-sphere also includes the "pre-present time zone", which qualifies XN-adverbials like *ultimamente, nos últimos dias, desde o início, hoje* ('lately', 'over the last days', 'from the beginning on') to be combined with the PPC$_{PT}$. In this vein, XN-adverbials serve as means to increase the t_P's temporal granularity by temporally delimiting it.

(24) Tempo-aspectual adverbials and the PPC$_{PT}$
    a. *Positional
       *Ontem, a   Maria tem confiado no   Manuel.
       yesterday the Maria has   trusted in the Manuel
       *'Yesterday, Maria has been trusting in Manuel.'
    b. Durative
       Ao longo do tempo,   a   Maria tem confiado no   Manuel.
       throughout the time   the Maria has   trusted in the Manuel
       'Throughout the time, Maria has been trusting in Manuel.'

c. Extended-Now
Ultimamente, a Maria tem confiado no Manuel.
lately the Maria has trusted in the Manuel
'Lately, Maria has been trusting in Manuel.'

XN-adverbials and durative adverbials that necessarily follow the PPC$_{PT}$'s abutment condition of t_E and t_S are, in some cases, hardly distinguishable. That is, durative adverbials (when combined with the PPC$_{PT}$) might be interpreted as XN-adverbials in some cases because the PPC$_{PT}$ requires durative adverbials to hold within the present time-sphere. The same holds the other way round: some of the XN-adverbials, that express the present time-sphere to stretch into the past, lend a durative moment that causes an iterated or somewhat unbounded interpretation of t_E. In this vein, adverbials like *até agora, nos últimos tempos, desde o início, ao longo desses últimos meses*, ('until now', 'in recent times', 'since the beginning', 'over the past (few) months') might be interpreted both as quantifying over t_E or as temporally delimiting t_P. We label this the durative-XN ambiguity. For our analysis, this ambiguity does not pose a problem but rather underlines that the denotation of an eventuality included in the present time-sphere abutting speech time marks a if not *the* key to the PPC$_{PT}$'s meaning.

With regard to quantificational adverbials though, the PPC$_{PT}$ imposes some additional restrictions which suggests a division into four subgroups: definite-quantificational, IPEX-quantificational, universal-quantificational and generic-quantificational adverbials. While definite-quantificational adverbials like "once, twice" are ruled out (cf. (25a), cf. footnote 30 though), IPEX-quantificational adverbials are fine (cf. (25b)). Combinations with adverbials of universal quantification like *sempre* and *todas as vezes* yield felicitous expressions (25c), as well as adverbials of generic quantification like "always" or "usually" (25d).

(25) Quantificational adverbials and the PPC$_{PT}$
  a. ˣDefinite quantification[88]
     *A Maria tem confiado no Manuel uma vez / três vezes.
     the Maria has trusted in the Manuel once three times
     *'Maria has been trusting in Manuel once/three times.'
  b. ✓IPEX quantification
     A Maria tem confiado no Manuel várias vezes /muitas vezes /
     the Maria has trusted in the Manuel several times many times
     frequentemente.
     frequently
     'Maria has been trusting in Manuel several times / often / frequently'.

---

[88]. Cf. the discussion of the semantically highly marked but grammatically acceptable case of definite event-internal quantification in Section 3.3.

c. ✓Universal quantification
   A   Maria tem confiado no   Manuel todas   as vezes / sempre.
   the Maria has trusted in the Manuel all the times   always
   'Maria has been trusting in Manuel all the times / always.'
d. ✓Generic quantification
   A   Maria tem confiado no   Manuel geralmente / sempre.
   the Maria has trusted in the Manuel usually   always
   'Maria has been trusting in Manuel usually / always.'

Given that it is a typical function of tempo-aspectual adverbials to force a particular reading when combined with a tense form, it stands to reason that some of the indicated adverbials reflect some of the readings introduced in Section 3.3. As pointed out above, there may be ambiguities, e.g. between XN-adverbials and durative adverbials, since there is not necessarily a strict mapping between particular adverbials and their scope. This is also reflected in that both XN-adverbials and durative adverbials combine with both universal and characterizing readings. Additionally, adverbials of universal quantification also combine with both types of readings. On the other hand, adverbials of IPEX quantification typically combine with the IPEX-quantificational readings, while adverbials of generic quantification typically give rise to characterizing readings. In sum, we draw up the picture summarized in Table 3.1.

Having given an overview of the PPC$_{PT}$'s combinations with adverbials in this section, we proceed with our analysis by discussing (some of) the PPC$_{PT}$'s discursive functions triggered by it interactions with adjacent tense forms.

Table 3.1 Tempo-aspectual adverbials and the PPC$_{PT}$

Adverbial	Scope	Reading	Example	Translation
*Positional	*t$_{LOC}$	✗	ontem, três semanas atrás, em 1999	yesterday, three weeks ago, in 1999
QUANTIFICATIONAL				
*Definite	t$_E$	✗	uma vez, três vezes,	once, three times,
IPEX	t$_E$	IPEX	várias vezes, muitas vezes, já	several times, many times, already
Universal	t$_E$	Universal & Characterizing	sempre, todas as vezes, ainda não	always, each time, not yet
Generic	t$_E$	Universal & Characterizing	sempre, geralmente	always, typically
Durative	t$_E$	Universal & Characterizing	por muitos anos, durante esses oito meses, ao longo do tempo, através dos tempos	for many years, during that 8 months, throughout the time, throughout the time
Extended-Now	t$_P$	Universal & Characterizing	ultimamente, nos últimos dias, desde o início, hoje	lately, over the last days, from the beginning, today

3.5 Discourse

In this section, we extend the analysis of the PPC$_{PT}$ by discussing (some of) its typical functions and related meaning effects in discourse. The resulting list is not supposed to provide an exhaustive coverage of each discourse function that the PPC$_{PT}$ may assume, but to provide a first classification capturing (some of) its most important functions. First, we zoom in on the micro-structure of discourse analyzing combinations that the PPC$_{PT}$ may establish with adjacent tense forms. These combinations are PPC$_{PT}$ + PPC$_{PT}$, PPC$_{PT}$ + *Pretérito Perfeito Composto* (PPS) and PPC$_{PT}$ + Present Tense. Next, we synthesize our assumptions and derive expectations concerning the employment of the PPC$_{PT}$ from a macro-structural perspective of discourse. We derive the assumptions based on our framework discussed in the previous sections and feed them with further data from the literature or, when necessary, with examples of additional corpus queries. In this vein, this section prepares the corpus study presented in Chapter 5, where we apply the assumptions generated in the present section to the exploration of new data in order to see if they prove to be valid.

3.5.1 PPC$_{PT}$ + PPC$_{PT}$

Based on our framework exposed in the previous sections and chapters, we assume that the discursive combination of two instances of a PPC$_{PT}$ creates a "set-like" reading, i.e. a collection of an unordered set of PPC$_{PT}$ eventualities leading towards the present time-sphere, as exemplified in (26).

(26) a. *Contra todas as expectativas, diagnósticos e prognósticos, o Gonçalo <u>tem sobrevivido, tem lutado</u> e <u>ultrapassado</u> as mais duras etapas.*
'Against all expectations, diagnoses and prognoses, Goncalo has been surviving, fighting and overcoming the toughest stages.'[89]

b. *"Temos sido capazes, quer o Ministério da Saude, quer o Governo, de responder de forma a manter o SNS que já tantas vezes foi ameaçado pela oposição de desmantelamento. Ele <u>tem funcionado, tem resistido</u> e vai continuar a resistir", sustentou.*
'"We have been able, both the Ministry of Health and the Government, to respond in a way that maintains the NHS that has been threatened so many times by the opposition with dismantling. It has worked, it has resisted and it will continue to resist", he said.'[90]

---

[89]. Blog *Novamente* (05/21/13), https://www.novamente.pt/nunca-acontece-aos-outros/, 01/11/18. In examples that are supposed to illustrate certain aspects of discursive meaning, we omit glossing due to the increased length of the sentences under consideration.

[90]. *Diário de Notícias* (08/27/13), https://www.dn.pt/portugal/secretario-de-estado-diz-que-sns-vai-continuar-a-resistir-3389546.html, 01/11/18.

Each instance of the PPC$_{PT}$ included in the examples denotes an eventuality abutting speech time, independently of whether it receives an episodic or a characterizing reading. When there is a second PPC$_{PT}$ (e.g. *tem lutado* in (26a)), it receives the same interpretation. That is, adjacent instances of the PPC$_{PT}$ represent somewhat isolated elements that do not encode a discourse-semantic relation between them.

However, pragmatic inferences, e.g. based on world knowledge, may be drawn concerning their temporal relation, as exemplified in (27).

(27) [O] *P.S.A. que é o exame específico que eu falei antes... hoje aponta zero... vírgula cinco... quando o limite é quatro né?... e eu <u>tenho feito</u> exame de vez em quando... <u>tem dado</u> isso daí.*
'The P.S.A., which is the specific test which I told you about before... nowadays the result is zero point five... while the maximum is four, you see? and I have been doing the test from time to time and the result has always been this.'[91]

In (27), it seems to be likely that the repeated subeventualities denoted by PPC$_{PT-1}$ and PPC$_{PT-2}$ are interpreted as being geared: the first instance of `eu fazer exame` is followed by the first instance of `dar isso daí`. The second instance of `eu fazer exame` is followed by the second instance of `dar isso daí`, and so on. Although the PPC$_{PT}$ is not a referential but quantificational tense form denoting indefinite past eventualities, (27) thus suggests that temporal relations between PPC$_{PT-1}$ and PPC$_{PT-2}$ may be pragmatically inferred. Interestingly, (27) contains a characterizing interpretation which is also the case in the following example:

(28) [O]*lha eu gosto muito de pescar mas ultimamente que eu <u>tenho ido</u> num <u>tem dado</u> muita sorte não [...].*
'I like fishing very much, but recently, whenever I have gone fishing, I haven't been very lucky [...].'[92]

In (28), a temporal relation between PPC$_{PT-1}$ and PPC$_{PT-2}$ is explicitly encoded by *ultimamente que* (which would not be the case if *ultimamente que* would be lacking). Again, there are two instances of the characterizing reading where the second gets interpreted with regard to the first one. This time, the first instance of `eu ir pescar` is followed by the first instance of `não dar muita sorte`. The second instance of `eu ir pescar` is followed by the second instance of `não dar muita sorte`, and so on. One might wonder if this suggests that PPC$_{PT}$ may actually provide a discourse reference time functioning as a location time for the succeeding PPC$_{PT}$. However, we maintain our assumption that there is no t$_{LOC}$ (and

---

91. Example taken from Olbertz (2018: 497).
92. Example taken from Olbertz (2018: 496).

no discourse reference time t_R) associated with the temporal semantics of the PPC_{PT}. This is particularly in line with the assumption that the rather atemporal, modalized characterizing reading does not express episodic eventualities. Thus, there is no temporal reference at all. Nevertheless, it seems that the characterizing reading systematically allows for situations as restrictors that are discursively set by a preceding PPC_{PT}. In (29), it is illustrated how the corresponding formulation and its difference to a characterizing PPC_{PT} in isolation may look like.

(29) Preceding PPC_{PT} restricting the generic quantifier of a succeeding PPC_{PT}[93]
   a. *A Maria tem confiado no Manuel.*
      GEN[t_P, s, x;](x = Maria & t_P = present time-sphere & s is a normal situation with respect to trusting Manuel & t_P contains s & s contains x & x trusts Manuel in s)
   b. *Ultimamente que eu tenho ido pescar num tem dado muita sorte.*[94]
      GEN[t_P, PPC_{PT}-s, x;](x = Ø & t_P = present time-sphere & PPC_{PT}-s is a normal situation with respect to eu ir pescar & t_P contains PPC_{PT}-s & PPC_{PT}-s contains x & x dar muita sorte in PPC_{PT}-s)

3.5.2 PPC_{PT} + *Pretérito Perfeito Simples*

Here, we discuss two discourse functions of the PPC_{PT} when combined with the *Pretérito Perfeito Simples* (PPS). These are (i) the establishment of a contrast between episodicity expressed by the PPS on the one hand and characterizing abstractions expressed by a characterizing PPC_{PT} on the other hand, as well as (ii) perspectival bridging, which can be achieved with both episodic and characterizing PPC_{PT} readings.

Contrasting episodicity and genericity
The combination of a characterizing PPC_{PT} and a PPS may result in a contrast between episodic eventualities that are temporally anchored in time and expressed by a PPS and, on the other hand, modalized abstractions, i.e. characterizing statements that express a temporally restricted general property expressed by the PPC_{PT}. As it turns out, contrasting episodicity and genericity may serve as a rhetorical device: by exploiting the interplay between episodicity and genericity, a speaker may convincingly deduct generalizations based on actual episodes.

---

93. (29a) repeated from Section 3.3.

94. Repeated from Section 3.5.

(30) a. General principle → isolated fact
A Red Hot *tem procurado* uma seleção criteriosa de material, o que <u>aconteceu</u> também neste projeto com a escolha de Randy Scruggs para supervisor musical.
'Red Hot has been looking for a careful selection of material, which also happened in this project with Randy Scruggs' choice for music supervisor.'[95]

b. General Principle ← Isolated fact
Muitas pessoas <u>têm morrido,</u> porque <u>confiaram</u> no porteiro, que <u>usou</u> uma chave de fenda num certo pino do elevador em pane para o abrir.
'Many people have died because they trusted the doorman, who used a screwdriver on a certain pin in the elevator to open it.'[96]

In (30a), the PPC$_{PT}$ first characterizes the Red Hot (probably referring to the band Red Hot Chili Peppers) as having been looking for a careful selection of material in the present time-sphere. Next, this general statement gets substantiated by an episodic fact that somewhat justifies the generalizations expressed by the PPC$_{PT}$. The opposite effect is illustrated in (30b), where the general principle is derived as a plausible inference based on episodic instantiations. In both cases, there is an interplay between an abstraction in form of a general principle and a concrete episodic instantiation, linked by the tie of rhetorical coherence.[97]

Perspectival bridging
Another typical function fulfilled by the PPC$_{PT}$ when combined with a PPS in discourse may be labelled perspectival bridging. As discussed above, the PPC$_{PT}$ denotes an interval that starts at some time in the past and abuts the speech time. This qualifies the PPC$_{PT}$ to mediate between two perspective times, one lying in the past time sphere and another one lying in the present time-sphere, by conjoining them as exemplified in (31). In metaphorical terms, we may think of this as functioning as a bridge between the two perspective times.

(31) PPC$_{PT}$ + PPS: perspectival bridging
Há 5 dias encontrei 2 gatinhos recém nascidos no contentor do lixo e <u>trousse-os</u> para casa e até hoje *tem corrido* tudo bem, <u>mas hoje</u> um deles esta constantemente a miar e não sei o que ele tem [...].

---

95. Example taken from Leal et al. (2014: 410).

96. *Saúde e Alimentação* (Blog, 05/09/12), http://paoesaude.blogspot.com/2012/05/se-o-elevador-avariar.html, 08/31/17, apud Müller (2017: 28).

97. In the terminology of rhetorical relations (cf. e.g. Jasinskaja and Karagjosova 2020), one might analyze the PPC$_{PT}$ in (30a) as a nucleus that gets elaborated by the PPS and the PPC$_{PT}$ in (30b) as standing in a result relation with respect to the PPS.

'5 days ago I found 2 newborn kittens in the dumpster and brought them home and until today everything has been fine, but today one of them is constantly meowing and I don't know what he has.'[98]

Although there is no need to merge the two perspective times explicitly by means of a specialized form, the PPC$_{PT}$ creates a smooth transition from the past time-sphere to the present time-sphere, which may be exploited in order to achieve explicit temporal coherence.[99]

3.5.3 PPC$_{PT}$ + Present Tense

Next, we discuss the interplay between the PPC$_{PT}$ and Present Tense that gives rise to two typical discourse functions. The first one is particularly associated with characterizing PPC$_{PT}$ readings that contrast their temporally restricted generic predication with a non-restricted generic predication expressed by Present Tense. The second function is associated with episodic PPC$_{PT}$ readings and its potential to substantiate a generic predication expressed by the Present Tense.

Contrast of characterizing PPC$_{PT}$ vs. generic Present Tense
The characterizing PPC$_{PT}$ may not only contrast with an episodic PPS as discussed above, but also with another general expression, i.e. with a generic Present Tense. The contrasting moment is derived by the following difference: while the generic expressed by a Present Tense holds in general, the characterizing PPC$_{PT}$ is temporally restricted to the perspective time, i.e. to the present time-sphere. The confrontation of the two is exemplified in (32a), where the "two degrees of genericity" meet.

(32) a. *Eu <u>sou</u> uma pessoa que <u>gosta</u> de ver tv. Mas ultimamente <u>tenho lido</u> (muito).*
'I'm a person who likes to watch TV. But lately I've been reading (a lot).'[100]
b. *<u>Fazem-me</u> falta uns óculos. Mas não <u>tenho tido</u> dinheiro.*
'I could use some glasses. But I haven't had any money.'[101]

---

98. *Bolinhas de Pelo* (Blog about cats; 07/21/13), http://bolinhas-de-pelo.blogspot.com/2009/09/como-tratar-de-um-gatinho-recem-nascido.html, 08/15/17, apud Müller (2017: 24).

99. In Chapter 4, we observe the function of perspectival bridging with universal readings of the Spanish PPC$_{SP}$, as well. Thus, it seems that perspectival bridging marks (one of) the typical discourse functions associated with universal or universalized PP readings.

100. Example taken from Becker (2022: 61).

101. Example taken from Suter (1984: 160).

Following Becker (2022), Example (32a)

> [...] contrasts two habits – the habit of watching tv and that of reading books. The utterance marked by the PPC characterizes a more recent, upcoming habit and represents an instance of what Smith (2003: 24) has labelled in her ontology of situations as generalising statements (such as e.g. drink beer or play the guitar).
>
> (Becker 2022: 61)

The same effect can be found in (32b) where the "real" generic expresses the need of glasses while the restricted generic expresses the lack of money. In (33), the speaker seems to play around with the two types of genericity: it is claimed to be a general fact (é *um facto*) that the temporally restricted, characterizing predication (*tem sido* and *têm sido*) holds.

(33) Que Portugal não <u>tem sido</u> um país de romancistas – como o <u>têm sido</u>, por exemplo, a Inglaterra, A França, a Rússia – <u>é</u> *um facto incontestado*.
'That Portugal has not been a country of novelists – as it has been, for example, England, France, Russia – is an undisputed fact.'[102]

PPC_{PT} providing evidence for generic Present Tense
The second function that we want to discuss refers to the cooperation of Present Tense and a characterizing PPC_{PT}. Instead of a contrast, they are linked in order to provide mutual evidence, as exemplified in (34).

(34) a. [O]s *jogadores não <u>merecem</u> contestação, porque <u>têm feito</u> tudo o que deve ser feito.*
'The do not deserve criticism, because they have done everything that should be done.'[103]
b. [D]<u>eve</u> *ser substituido porque <u>tem tido</u> uma intervenção inadequada ao setor.*
(S)he should be replaced because there has been an inappropriate intervention in the sector.'[104]

In both examples, the PPC_{PT} contributes an explanation relation which supports the generic claim expressed by the preceding Present Tense. The speaker wants the hearer to accept and believe what he says, i.e. (s)he wants her/his propositions to

---

102. Example taken from Suter (1984: 159).

103. *Diário das Notícias* (12/16/06), https://www.dn.pt/arquivo/2006/nao-podemos-ter-complexos-por-jogar-em-alvalade-650143.html, 06/30/20.

104. *Sapo* (12/19/15), https://www.sapo.pt/noticias/atualidade/acidentes-mortais-de-trabalho-na-construcao_5675697ca4cc9f1451b51469, 06/30/20.

enter the common ground shared by the interlocutors.[105] In order to achieve that goal, the restrictive generic expressed by the PPC$_{PT}$ helps establish argumentative coherence.

The same effect can also be exploited in the opposite way, as exemplified in (35). Here, the generic expressed by the Present Tense explains and justifies the restrictive generic, i.e. the characterizing PPC$_{PT}$.

(35) O Governo <u>tem dado</u> grande atenção à Saúde porque <u>sabe</u> que falhou redondamente.
'The government has paid great attention to health because it knows it has failed miserably.'[106]

Having discussed some of the typical micro-structural discourse functions of the PPC$_{PT}$, we turn to the macro-structure of discourse.

3.5.4 The macro-structure of discourse

Based on our framework discussed in the present chapter, we derive the following assumptions with regard to the relationship between the macro-structure of discourse and the PPC$_{PT}$ (cf. Section 2.4 and the modes of discourse in the sense of Smith 2003). The PPC$_{PT}$ does not qualify to be employed in narrative discourse:

(36) Narration
*Ontem, fui à cidade, vi que tinha uma corrida e a Maria tem ganho a corrida.
*'Yesterday, I went downtown, saw that there was a race and Maria has been winning the race'.

This is due to the PPC$_{PT}$'s perspective time that lies in the present time-sphere, as well as t_E's indefiniteness. As a consequence, there is no discourse-semantic encoding of temporal relations (precedence and simultaneity) between eventualities expressed by the PPC$_{PT}$ and adjacent past eventualities. Yet, this does not block the general potential that a PPC$_{PT}$ may be employed in a narrative text, e.g. in indirect speech. After all, even within an allegedly homogeneous discourse mode, there may be shifts from one mode to another.

---

105. Common ground (CG) stands for an influential pragmatic theory that assumes a list of propositions that speakers jointly work on and presuppose in communication. The term traces back to Stalnaker's (1978) seminal work on assertion, a speech act that serves as a tool to update CG (repeated footnote 5 from Chapter 2.1).

106. O *Público* (12/25/19), https://www.publico.pt/2019/12/25/politica/noticia/governo-dado-atencao-saude-sabe-falhou-redondamente-1898452, 06/29/20.

The description mode is blocked, as well, due to its static nature:

(37) Description
*A gente mora num casa lindona: a cozinha é nova, na varanda tem muito espaço e o jardim tem encantado as crianças.
'We live in a wonderful house: the kitchen is new, there is a lot of space on the balcony and the garden has been enchanting the children.'

Though located in time, descriptions block any kind of temporal advancement in favor of a "spatial advancement through the scene or object". Even the characterizing PPC_{PT} does not suit the report mode due to its property to still dispose of a temporal component.

The modes of information (38a) and argument (38b) generally allow for the employment of the PPC_{PT}.

(38) a. Information
A China tem vendido muitos milhões de máscaras.
'China has been selling many millions of masks.'[107]
b. Argument
O Governo tem dado grande atenção à Saúde porque sabe que falhou redondamente.
'The government has paid great attention to health because it knows it has failed miserably.'[108]

While the information mode primarily denotes facts, propositions and general statives, the argument mode mainly denotes general statives. The micro-structural discursive functions associated with the rhetoric exploitation of the contrast between episodicity and genericity (cf. previous section) thus pertain to Information and Argument. These two modes particularly presuppose an elaborated rhetorical structure in order to convince a hearer, or, at least, in order to connote to be a trustworthy source. Furthermore, it follows that Information and Argument are the typical modes that the PPC_{PT}'s characterizing readings get employed in.

The report mode, in which the PPC_{PT} may occur as well, is defined as denoting primarily events, states and general statives that may be dynamically located in time. Yet, these are relatively anchored to the speech time. The mode of report thus mainly contrasts with Information and Argument in terms of temporality: while

---

107. *Ribatejo News* (04/05/20), https://ribatejonews.net/2020/04/05/covid-19-china-vendeu-4-mil-milhoes-de-mascaras-desde-marco/, 06/30/20.

108. *O Público* (12/25/19), https://www.publico.pt/2019/12/25/politica/noticia/governo-dado-atencao-saude-sabe-falhou-redondamente-1898452, 06/29/20.

the former is defined to be a temporal mode, the latter are defined to be atemporal. As a consequence, we assume the PPC$_{PT}$'s episodic readings to prevail in reports.

(39) Report
 É o nevoeiro no Tejo que tem feito um navio buzinar toda a noite.
 'It's the fog on the Tagus that has been making a ship honk all night.'[109]

Having outlined our approach to the functions that the PPC$_{PT}$ fulfills in discourse in (i) combination with adjacent tense forms (micro-structure of discourse) and (ii) with respect to the modes of discourse (macro-structure of discourse), we have generated expectations that we apply in our corpus study in Chapter 5 in order to test if they prove to be valid when applied to new data.

3.6 Conclusion

In this chapter, we presented a detailed account of the PPC$_{PT}$ following the framework introduced in Chapter 2. The chapter started with an outline of the PPC$_{PT}$'s general meaning and meaning effects according to the literature. The central aspects of its idiosyncratic meaning are expressed in its (purported) preservation of Stage II. In other words, the PPC$_{PT}$ blocks the cross-linguistically typical PP value of denoting a single and bounded indefinite past eventuality preceding the speech time. Instead, it denotes universalized readings that, additionally, are restricted by conditions that have often been described as resulting in durative and iterative readings: the predicate in the scope of the PPC$_{PT}$ is denoted to be iterated up to, or to hold until, the speech time. The quantification remains indefinite, i.e. the number of occurrences of t_E cannot be counted. Furthermore, the PPC$_{PT}$ implicates (i.e. does not imply) a continuation of t_E after t_S.

On the basis of these observations, we argued that the PPC$_{PT}$'s quantificational semantics derive three major groups of readings in synchrony. These are (i) IPEX readings, including iterative and gradual readings, that trace back to an indefinite-pluractional event-external quantifier, (ii) universal readings, i.e. durative readings, that trace back to a universal quantifier and (iii) characterizing readings, that trace back to a generic quantifier that gets restricted to the PPC$_{PT}$'s perspective time, i.e. to the present time-sphere.

This classification reveals a crucial insight with respect to the PPC$_{PT}$'s position in a cross-linguistic context. Despite its semantic peculiarities, it preserves its quantificational temporal semantics by giving rise to the three referred readings.

---

[109]. O *Público* (01/02/20), https://www.publico.pt/2020/01/02/local/noticia/nevoeiro-tejo-navio-buzinar-noite-1898997, 06/29/20.

What might come as a surprise is that this aspect turns the PPC$_{PT}$ into a typical Present Perfect, given that quantificational temporal semantics can be considered as (one of) the core meaning components of the cross-linguistic Present Perfect (cf. Section 2.5).

With respect to adverbial modification, we argued that IPEX readings are typically combined with IPEX-adverbials (scoping over t_E), and universal and characterizing readings are typically combined with universal, generic, durative (scoping over t_E) or XN-adverbials (scoping over t_P). Instead of a strict mapping though, this represents a tendency.

For the purpose of our study, we have defended to proceed with the assumption that there is no significant semantic difference between the PPC$_{PT}$ as used in Brazilian Portuguese vs. European Portuguese, although the previous literature has identified subtle quantitative differences between those two macro-varieties, as we consider this generalization to be compatible with our research goal of detecting and describing discourse functions of the PPC$_{PT}$. It is important to stress that point especially with regard to the corpus study reported in Chapter 5, that draws on data from BP. However, it stands to reason that diatopic variation still calls for fine-grained research in the future. This concerns both the study of the readings that the PPC$_{PT}$ evokes in several macro- and micro-varieties, which still marks a highly understudied field, as well as the implementation of our discursive account presented in this book. As a working hypothesis, one might assume the quantitative differences between BP and EP to be due to diasystematic-variational factors. However, as discussed in Section 3.3.2, previous work has also identified semantic differences with regard to micro-variation within Brazil. Accordingly, the durative reading, which is included in our general account of the PPC$_{PT}$ for the macro-variety of BP, is blocked in a northeastern variety of Brazil.

On the level discourse, we first zoomed in on the micro-structure by investigating typical discursive functions established by the interplay of the PPC$_{PT}$ with adjacent tense forms on the syntagmatic level. With regard to the characterizing readings, we discussed the following three combinations.

- Combined with another PPC$_{PT}$, we argued that the first PPC$_{PT}$ is able to provide the restrictor for the generic quantifier, i.e. for the characterizing reading of the second PPC$_{PT}$.
- Combined with a PPS, we discussed the function of a contrast between (restrictive) genericity (expressed by the PPC$_{PT}$) and episodicity (expressed by the PPS). Conceived of as a rhetorical device, we argued that the PPC$_{PT}$ helps establish argumentative coherence by instantiating general principles by isolated episodes, as well as the other way round.

- Combined with a Present Tense, we discussed the function of a contrast between a generic proposition expressed by the Present tense and a temporally restricted generic predication expressed by the PPC_{PT}. Again, this combination may be exploited in order to create a rhetorical effect associated with argumentative coherence. Instead of a contrast, the two generic propositions may also be conjoined in order two achieve a communicative goal. In this case, the two generic propositions elaborate or explain each other.

With regard to the episodic reading, we discussed the following two combinations.

- Combined with another PPC_{PT}, we argued that the two tense forms may establish a "set-like" reading featuring an unordered set of episodic (i.e. IPEX or universal) eventualities that lead up to the speech time. Due to their missing location time and discourse reference time, they remain semantically isolated. Yet, temporal relations might be inferred based on pragmatic inferences.
- Combined with a PPS, the episodic reading may function as a perspectival bridge mediating between a perspective time lying in the past time-sphere (expressed by a PPS) and a succeeding perspective time lying in the present time-sphere (expressed by a PPC_{PT}). Though not necessarily required, this may establish a smooth transition between the two time-spheres. This function might also be fulfilled by the characterizing PPC_{PT} though.

With regard to the macro-structure of discourse, we concluded that the PPC_{PT} may be employed in the discourse modes of argumentation and information. This is mainly due to their atemporal character that matches to the PPC_{PT}'s characterizing reading and its potential to serve as means to draw up an elaborated rhetorical structure. Moreover, we concluded that the PPC_{PT} may be employed in the mode of report where we expect to prevailingly find episodic readings. In reports, past eventualities are anchored relative to the deictic center, i.e. to the speech time. Conversely, the narrative and the descriptive mode block the use of the PPC_{PT}.

In sum, we have exposed our account of the PPC_{PT} and, in particular, derived a list of functions that we assume the PPC_{PT} to typically fulfill in discourse, based on its interactions with adjacent tense forms. In Chapter 5, we present a corpus study where we test if these assumptions prove to be valid when applied to new data.

The next chapter introduces the study of the Spanish PPC_{SP} based on the same structure as followed in the present chapter. The comparative approach aims to expose how the quantificational semantics of the Present Perfect lead to radically different readings and discourse functions in the case of the Spanish PPC_{SP}.

CHAPTER 4

The Spanish *Pretérito Perfecto Compuesto*

Following a similar structure as in the previous chapter, this chapter presents a detailed study of the Spanish *Pretérito Perfecto Compuesto* (PPC$_{SP}$) of the following form:

(1) Juan ha escrito la carta.
    Juan has written the letter
    'Juan has written the letter.'

The chapter is structured as follows.

Section 4.1 provides an overview of the general meaning and meaning effects of the PPC$_{SP}$. This includes the identification of its typical readings (resultative, experiential, hot news, and universal readings) one the one hand, and of the current relevance meaning component on the other hand. Thus, the PPC$_{SP}$ can be categorized as widely following the default quantificational semantics of the cross-linguistic "well-behaved" Perfect by denoting an indefinite past eventuality that is relevant at the speech time in some way.

Section 4.2 briefly reviews the research on the use of the PPC$_{SP}$ according to diatopic variation and on the related functional differences in the many varieties within the Spanish-speaking world. We proceed to hypothesize that our framework might be applicable to the description of any particular variety. However, we mostly focus on Peninsular Spanish when discussing data.

Section 4.3 presents, based on our framework, detailed definitions of the quantificational readings of the PPC$_{SP}$ that branch into existential (experiential, resultative and hot news) and universal readings. Each of these readings is identified as representing a different realization of the PPC$_{SP}$'s quantificational semantics.

Section 4.4 discusses the question of whether the PPC$_{SP}$ (already) disposes of a referential reading as well. After all, it is expected that the PPC$_{SP}$, at some point, will acquire referential semantics. In particular, the case of the "hodiernal perfective" reading is discussed as representing an ambiguous use between quantification and reference. Accordingly, "hodiernal perfectives" might function as triggering the PPC$_{SP}$'s referential drift.

Section 4.5 analyzes the interaction between the PPC$_{SP}$ and tempo-aspectual adverbials, as well as potential scope ambiguities. In line with our general framework, the quantificational readings block positional adverbials (which is due to the missing location time argument). Instead, they allow for combinations with durative, extended-now and quantificational adverbials. Conversely, the semantics of a (potential) referential PPC$_{SP}$ would allow for combinations with positional adverbials.

Section 4.6 analyzes several combinations that the PPC$_{SP}$ may establish with adjacent tense forms. These are (i) PPC$_{SP}$ + PPC$_{SP}$, (ii) PPC$_{SP}$ + *Indefinido*, and (iii) PPC$_{SP}$ + *Pluscuamperfecto* and *Imperfecto*. Based on the distinction between the quantificational PPC$_{SP}$ and a (potential) referential PPC$_{SP}$, the section's goal is to discuss typical discourse functions of both types. In this vein, the quantificational readings mainly fulfill functions related to perspectivizing (perspectival shift and perspectival bridging) and to the actualization focus exploiting the distinct discourse functions of quantificational and referential tense forms. On the other hand, the referential PPC$_{SP}$ is discussed as bearing the potential to cataphorically anchor a succeeding *Imperfecto* or *Pluscuamperfecto*. That is, the discourse functions of the (potential) referential PPC$_{SP}$ turn out to significantly differ from the ones of the quantificational PPC$_{SP}$, which again emphasizes the great barrier between the two fundamental semantic operations of quantification and reference. With regard to the macro-structure of discourse, we derive that the quantificational PPC$_{SP}$ typically blocks the modes of narration and description, while it may be employed in the modes of information, argument and report. Interestingly, these restrictions are similar to the one imposed by the Portuguese PPC$_{PT}$. On the other hand, the referential PPC$_{SP}$ might appear in narratives.

4.1 General meaning and meaning effects

The quantificational readings

As opposed to the Portuguese PPC$_{PT}$, the PPC$_{SP}$ is commonly analyzed as a "well-behaved" Perfect, i.e. as a cross-linguistically prototypical Present Perfect (cf. e.g. Laca 2008). In most general terms, that means that the PPC$_{SP}$ widely follows the quantificational semantics of the cross-linguistic PP as discussed in Chapter 2.5. Accordingly, there is a great consensus that the PPC$_{SP}$ principally denotes an indefinite past eventuality with particular relevance at speech time, which is spelled out by a range of typical readings:

> [...] la posibilidad de referir a situaciones perfectivas temporalmente indeterminadas, de las que pueden surgir inferencias sin la necesidad de hacer afirmaciones temporales muy definidas. Consideramos que éste es el significado básico del Pretérito Perfecto Compuesto.[110] (Henderson 2005: 2)

---

110. '[...] the potential of referring to temporarily undetermined perfect situations, of which inferences can arise without the need to make very definite temporal statements. We consider this to be the basic meaning of the Preterito Perfecto Compuesto.' Note that in our framework, indefinite tense impedes to "refer" to t_E. Instead, there is a quantification over t_E.

According to Howe and Schwenter (2003), "the following four uses [...] are found, to differing degrees, in all dialects of Spanish spoken throughout the world."

(2) The PPC$_{SP}$'s readings (Howe and Schwenter 2003: 62f.)
    a. RESULTATIVE: present state resulting from past action
       Maria se ha ido.
       'Maria has left.'
    b. EXPERIENTIAL: situation has held at least once in the past
       Juan ha visitado Italia.
       'Juan has visited Italy.'
    c. CONTINUATIVE: situation begun in past continues at present
       He llorado mucho desde ese dia.
       'I have cried a lot since that day.'
    d. HOT NEWS; situation in the very recent past presumably being conveyed for the first time
       El presidente de la republica ha fallecido.
       'The president of the republic has died.'

In line with the hypothesis that these readings might partly reflect the diachronic development of the PPC$_{SP}$, they do in fact resemble the ones discussed by the diachronic stage model for the PP (cf. Chapter 2.5 and Harris 1982; Bertinetto and Squartini 2000). Accordingly, the resultative, continuative and experiential readings seem to represent the stages I–III, respectively. The hot news reading might be situated somewhere between Stage III and IV (cf. Schwenter 1994b: 995 who states that "hot news perfects [are] more like perfectives than other perfect functions", cf. also Section 4.3.3).

In line with our general framework of analyzing the cross-linguistic Present Perfect as an inherently quantificational tense form, each of the readings illustrated in (2) represents a different outcome of the PPC$_{SP}$'s quantificational semantics. That is, the bipartite quantificational structure discussed in Chapter 2.5 applies to the PPC$_{SP}$'s branching into readings of existential quantification on the one hand, and readings of universal quantification on the other hand. While the former include the resultative, experiential and hot news reading, the latter refer to what is labelled as the continuative reading in (2). This composes the preliminary architecture depicted in Figure 4.4. In Section 4.4, we discuss if the PPC$_{SP}$ (already) additionally disposes of a referential reading, as well. Moreover, Chapter 6 is dedicated in particular to the PPC$_{SP}$'s referential drift and the study of its position between quantification and reference.

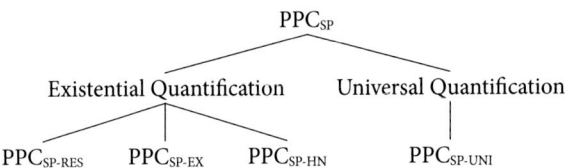

Figure 4.1 The PPC$_{SP}$ as a purely quantificational tense form (preliminary)
PPC$_{SP\text{-}RES}$: *resultative reading; PPC$_{SP\text{-}EX}$* : *experiential reading; PPC$_{SP\text{-}HN}$* : *hot news reading; PPC$_{SP\text{-}UNI}$* : *universal reading.*

Current Relevance (CR)

In line with Section 2.5, the pragmatic meaning component of current relevance (CR) is commonly assumed to play a central role for the Spanish PPC$_{SP}$.

(3) *Juan ha escrito la carta.*
Juan has written the letter
'Juan has written the letter.'

Applied to (3), CR is supposed to capture that the indefinite past eventuality of `Juan escribir la carta` is of certain relevance at the speech time (cf. e.g. Carrasco Gutiérrez 2008: 25, Hurtado González 1998: 55, Schwenter and Cacoullos 2008). Semantically, it may be motivated by tracing it back to the strong orientation towards the speech time, i.e. to the configuration of the perspective time lying in the present time-sphere.

Dahl and Hedin (2000: 392) cross-linguistically define CR as "a condition on the world [of a] continuance of a result", furthermore as a "condition on the discourse, in that the speaker portrays the consequences of an event as somehow essential to the point of what he is saying." This quote points at the distinction of truth conditions, associated with the extra-linguistic world, and the inner-linguistic level of discourse, where discourse entities and propositions are getting introduced, discussed, and linked to each other making use of certain linguistic means (e.g. CR). That means, on the one hand, the CR effect for p Juan having written the letter presupposes that p actually is of relevance at the speech time, or, at least, that it bears the ontological potential.[111] On the other hand, CR functions as a subjective means that a speaker may choose to construct, impose or emphasize a relation of current relevance between a temporally indefinite past eventuality and the speech time. Put differently, the PPC$_{SP}$'s CR component enables a speaker to linguistically add and

---

111. In most general terms, this realistic concept of meaning has been most prominently put forth in truth-conditional correspondence theories, very much in the tradition of "Early Wittgenstein" and the principle of "Einen Satz verstehen, heißt, wissen, was der Fall ist, wenn er wahr ist" ('To understand a proposition means to know what is the case if it is true.', Wittgenstein 2016: 33).

perspectivize a connection holding between a temporally indefinite past eventuality and the speech time, given that the truth-conditional requirements on the world to do so are satisfied. Depraetere (1998: 600) states that "[t]heoretically speaking, any situation which occurred in the past affects the present." This may be best illustrated with the verb *morir* ('(to) die'). While the demise of a person necessarily bears the ontological potential to affect the speaker's speech time in some relevant way, one can choose between highlighting its CR by employing the PPC$_{SP}$ (4a) – or not, by employing the *Indefinido* which lacks the CR component (4b).

(4) a. *Mi abuelo ha muerto.*
my grandfather has died
'My grandfather has died.'
b. *Mi abuelo (se) murió.*
my grandfather REFL died
'My grandfather died.'

In Peninsular Spanish, both alternatives in (4) are fine. One of their semantic differences is thus spelled out in two different ways of relating the father's demise to the speech time (cf. e.g. Carrasco Gutiérrez 2008: 25).

Following Depraetere (1998), CR may be pinned down to the notion of "resultative conversational implicatures" (cf. Section 2.3). Accordingly, resultative conversational implicatures that are triggered by the PPC$_{SP}$ may give rise to discursive coherence by explicitly establishing smooth transitions between propositions, as illustrated in (5).

(5) *Juan ha visitado Londres.* ('Juan has visited London.')
a. *Deberíamos preguntarle sobre un buen hotel.*
'We should ask him about a good hotel.
b. *No podemos irnos de vacaciones otra vez porque ha gastado muchísimo dinero.*
'We can't go on vacation again because he (has) spent a lot of money.'

These implicatures are cancelable and context-dependent. Their inference can be accounted based on the theory of conversational implicatures as proposed by Grice (1975) and the related communicative principles of cooperation and conversational maxims. The sentence *Juan ha visitado Londres* may thus be coherently accommodated to a theoretically infinite number of potential scenarios. As exemplified, it may be uttered as an answer to the question if anybody knows a good hotel in London (5a) or e.g. as a pertinent reaction by somebody who ran out of money because his son Juan has gone to London (5b).

In sum, the current relevance meaning component turns the PPC$_{SP}$ into a tense form that, in addition to the denotation of mere truth-conditional meaning, particularly contributes to the establishment of discourse coherence.

4.2 A note on diatopic variation

Although our approach does not aim at a cross-dialectal study, we proceed with a brief overview of the diatopic variation that underlies the use of the PPC$_{SP}$. As opposed to the Portuguese PPC$_{PT}$, there has been a lot of research on the diatopic variation of the PPC$_{SP}$. This is mostly motivated by the observation that the PPC$_{SP}$'s *valeur linguistique*, i.e. its functional load, varies significantly across the many varieties within the Spanish-speaking world:

> No hay en todo el paradigma verbal del español ninguna otra unidad sujeta a tanta variación dialectal como el PC: constatamos, por una parte, su práctica inexistencia en algunas regiones y, por la otra, un desarrollo que le lleva a desplazar a la forma simple en otras.[112] (Azpiazu Torres 2019: 209)

Apart from studies on the use of the PPC$_{SP}$ in Standard Peninsular Spanish (cf. e.g. Howe 2013; Hurtado González 1998; Bartens and Kempas 2007; Burgos 2015; Kempas 2002, 2006b, 2009), there has been research on, for instance, general trends in the Latin American varieties (Westmoreland 1988; Laca 2009; Burgos 2015), including Peruvian Spanish (Howe 2013), Argentinian Spanish (Kempas 2002, 2006b, 2009; Rodrigues Parrinha 2014, 2015), Mexican Spanish (Lope Blanch 1972; Spitzová and Bayerová 1987; Jara 2009; García Fajardo 2011), Spanish spoken in Chile, Paraguay and Uruguay (Henderson 2010), on seven capitals in the Hispanic world (De Oliveira 2010), on seven regions in Spain (Kempas 2008a), as well as on Spanish spoken in Alicante (Schwenter 1994a), Granada (Montoro del Arco 2017) and the Canary Islands (Serrano 1995). These studies have the common goal to investigate the position that the PPC$_{SP}$ assumes within the respective tense and aspect system, particularly with respect to the functions of the *Indefinido* :

> [...] [E]s la gran variación con la que se opone al Pretérito o PS en las diferentes áreas hispanohablantes, hasta el punto de que esta oposición se ha convertido en uno de los rasgos gramaticales que permite identificar, siquiera burdamente, la procedencia de algunos hablantes.[113] (Azpiazu Torres 2019: 209)

In Azpiazu Torres (2019), we find a detailed and contemporary overview (cf. Table 4.2). Building on a general picture proposed in Veiga Rodríguez (2014), she

---

112. 'There is no other unit in the entire verbal paradigm of Spanish subject to as much dialectal variation as the PC: We note, on the one hand, its practical non-existence in some regions and, on the other, a development that leads to the displacement of the simple form in others.

113. 'It is the great variation with which it opposes the Preterite or PS [Simple Past] in the different Spanish-speaking areas, to the extent that this opposition has become one of the grammatical features that makes it possible to identify, even crudely, the origin of some speakers.'

builds a fine-grained cross classification which is mainly fed with data from previous studies. Therefore, Azpiazu Torres (2019: 126) differentiates the following values that the PPC$_{SP}$ may assume in a given variety.

- P1: *eventos continuados o plurales sin determinación temporal,*[114]
- P2: *evento anterior temporalmente indeterminado con consecuencias en el presente,*[115]
- P3: *evento anterior temporalmente determinado, incluido en un lapso temporal que llega al presente,*[116]
- P3b: *valor aorístico.*[117]

Roughly comparing these values to the stages discussed in Bertinetto and Squartini (2000), P1 and P3b correspond to the stages II (universal reading) and IV (aoristic reading), while Stage III is split into P2 and P3 that refer to existential readings with different restrictions on the denoted eventuality (cf. Section 4.4 for a detailed discussion of P3). The reason why the aoristic value is labelled as P3b (instead of P4) is supposed to account for the fact that even the aoristic PPC$_{SP}$ preserves its orientation towards the speech time, i.e. keeps one of its very much Perfect-like meaning components.

	Subsistema A		Subsistema B			
	Variedad A1	Variedad A2	Variedad 61a	Variedad B1b	Variedad B2a	Variedad B2b
P1	+	+	−	−/+	+	+
P1 + P2	+	+	−	−/+	+	+
P1 + P2 + P3	+	−	−	−	+	−/+
P1 + P2 + P3 + P3b	−	−	−	−	+	−/+
Regiones	Esp. peninsular, variedades cultas de Perú y Bolivia	México, Colombia, Venezuela, Canarias…	Noroeste peninsular	Río de la Plata	Habla popular de Bolivia	Centro peninsular, hablas populares de Perú, Ecuador (?)

Figure 4.2 Functional load of the PPC$_{SP}$ according to diatopic variation (Azpiazu Torres 2019: 204)

---

114. 'Continuous or plural events without temporal determination'.
115. 'Previous event temporarily undetermined with consequences in the present'.
116. 'Previous event temporarily determined, included in a time frame that reaches the present'.
117. 'Aoristic value'.

The varieties A1 and A2 form the subsystem A. On the one hand, this group contains Peninsular Spanish, as well as the *variedades cultas* spoken in Peru and Bolivia – characterized by the presence of P3. On the other hand, the American varieties spoken in Mexico, Colombia and Venezuela, as well as the variety spoken on the Canary Islands form variety A2 – characterized by the absence of P3. In the tradition of Harris (1982) and Bertinetto and Squartini (2000), these two varieties (A1 and A2) have probably received most attention as they are often considered as the two major representatives of the PPC_{SP}. The varieties B1a–B2b form the subsystem B. The northwest of Spain, representing B1a, is declared to generally abstain from the PPC_{SP}. Thus, it is hardly ever used but replaced by the *Indefinido* in respective contexts. In the context of the sociolinguistic situation in the northwest of Spain, language contact with Galician and Portuguese might have (had) an impact on this peculiarity. In most general terms, both the Portuguese and Galician PPC are equivalently restricted to contexts of iteration or duration reaching up to the speech time (cf. Wigger 2005: 18) causing an increased use of the Simple Past. This influence thus might contribute to the dominance of the Simple Past over the PPC_{SP} in the northwest of Spain. However, it does not account for the attested omission of the PPC_{SP}, which is even more radical than in Portuguese and Galician. As a potential additional factor resulting in such a significant deviation, Azpiazu Torres (2019: 164) points out that speakers might be particularly insecure due to the differences between the Peninsular Standard and the Galician Standard. The opposite trend can be observed in the colloquial language in Bolivia, where the PPC_{SP} is said to occupy each of the four values. Furthermore, due to heterogeneous evidence presented in the literature, B1b (Río de la Plata) is not definitely specified regarding P1 and P2. Similarly, B2b (including *Centro Peninsular*) is not definitely specified with respect to the values of P3 and P3b. Azpiazu Torres (2019: 173) speaks of a "heterodoxy" due to differences in terms of what speakers find acceptable or not. In other words, apart from diatopic variation, there might be inter-subjective variation influencing the usage and acceptance of the PPC_{SP} within the variety B2b as an additional factor, which is not well studied yet.[118]

For our investigation of the discourse functions of the PPC_{SP}, we will exclusively focus on data from *Español Peninsular* and *Centro Peninsular*, particularly in the corpus study and the experimental study in the Chapters 5 and 6. These varieties seem to represent what might be considered the standard use of the PPC_{SP} within the Spanish peninsula. Moreover, Figure 4.2 suggests that these two varieties dispose of the most innovative ones as they seem the first ones to approach P3b (following the aoristic drift; in our terminology: referential drift). In other words,

---

118. In fact, the results of our experiment reported in Chapter 6 are compatible with that assumption.

they might be the first varieties to abolish the status of exclusively disposing of quantificational semantics in favor of additionally approaching referential semantics. We expect this development to come along with profound changes regarding the PPC$_{SP}$'s discursive potential.

4.3 Quantificational readings

In this section, we present a detailed study of the PPC$_{SP}$'s quantificational readings, i.e. of the existential readings (resultative, experiential and hot news) on the one hand, and the universal reading on the other hand. As discussed in Chapter 2, the quantificational readings quantify over t_E, either existentially or universally. Accordingly, their temporal semantics may be captured as follows.

(6) Quantificational readings[119]
    a. Existential: $[\![PPC_{SP-RES/EX/HN}]\!]$: $\lambda t_S \lambda t_E \lambda t_P. \, t_E \prec t_S \subseteq t_P$
       i. Maria se   ha ido.
          Maria REFL has left
          'Maria has left.'
       ii. Juan ha visitado Italia.
          Juan has visited Italy
          'Juan has visited Italy.'
       iii. El presidente de la republica ha fallecido.
          the president of the republic has died
          'The president of the republic has (just) died.'
    b. Universal: $[\![PPC_{SP-UNI}]\!]$: $\lambda t_S \lambda t_E \lambda t_P. \, t_E \succ \prec t_S \subseteq t_P$
       He llorado mucho desde ese dia.
       He llorado mucho desde ese dia.
       'I have cried a lot since that day.'

Again, the crucial observation that follows from (6) is that the quantificational readings of the PPC$_{SP}$ do not call for a location time argument. Due to the PPC$_{SP}$'s indefinite temporal semantics, the PPC$_{SP}$ thus particularly qualifies to be employed in contexts where t_{LOC} is not required, or simply not of interest.

The existential readings may be paraphrased as "there is at least one t_E prior to the speech time t_S which, in turn, is included in the perspective time t_P, i.e. in the present time-sphere, for which the eventuality in the scope of the PPC$_{SP}$ is true". (6-a-i) expresses that Maria *has* gone, i.e. that she *is* gone, independently of *when* she has left. In (6-a-ii), the mere information of Juan having been to Italy (or not)

---

119. Spanish examples taken from Howe and Schwenter (2003: 62f.).

is at stake. Third, in (6-a–iii), the information of the president having died, presented as breaking news, postpones the question of when exactly the president has actually died.

The universal reading, on the other hand, may be paraphrased as "there is a stretched or iterated t_E prior abutting the speech time t_S, which, in turn, is included in the perspective time t_P, i.e. in the present time-sphere, for which the eventuality in the scope of the PPC_{SP} is true." In this vein, (6b) expresses that the speaker has been crying again and again, independently of when exactly the crying took place. That is, the PPC_{SP-UNI}'s abutment relation ($\succ\prec$) does not specify t_{LOC} either. Instead, there is a universal quantification over t_E. In the same vein, durative adverbials rather answer the implicit question of "how long?" instead of "when?" (cf. Section 4.5).

In the following, we analyze the PPC_{SP}'s quantificational readings in detail.

4.3.1 Experiential reading

Comrie (1976: 58) defines the experiential reading as indicating "that a given situation has held at least once during some time in the past leading up to the present." Thus, the experiential reading may be paraphrased as an expression of having x-ed before, as exemplified in (7).

(7) ¿Ya/ alguna vez has estado en Londres? – Sí, ya he estado
already ever have been in London yes already have been
en Londres.
in Londres
'Have you already / ever been to London?' – 'Yes, I have already been to London.'
PPC_{SP}(I be to London) = 1 iff I be to London ∈ {*speaker's experiences*}

As an answer to the question of A, B accesses a set of everything they have ever done before the speech time. Therefore, the perspective time t_P (included in the present time-sphere) serves as a vantage point for the evaluation of these experiences. The set contains all of the experiences the speaker has made in her/his life. If be to London is an element of this set (or not), B answers that (s)he *has* been to London before (or not). In line with the quantificational semantics of the experiential reading component, there is no location time required.

In Section 2.5, we introduced that the experiential reading is typically analyzed as representing a third evolutionary step in the diachronic path of the PP in the Romance languages, by following on the resultative and universal reading. While resultative readings typically prefer telic situations, universal readings typically prefer atelic situations. Now, one of the crucial diachronic achievements of the experiential reading can be traced back to its potential to be employed with both telic and atelic situations. That is, due to its distinguished grammaticalized status, the experiential reading can be combined with any predicate, independently of its situation aspect, as illustrated in (8).

(8) a. PPC$_{SP-EX}$ with atelic situation aspect (state and activity)
    i. Ya he vivido en Londres.
       already have lived in Londres
       'I have already lived in London.'
    ii. Ya he caminado mucho.
       already have walked much
       'I have already walked a lot.'
b. PPC$_{SP-EX}$ with telic situation aspect (accomplishment and achievement)
    i. Ya he corrido 10 kilómetros por montaña.
       already have run 10 kilometers PREP mountain
       'I've already run 10 kilometers up the mountain.'
    ii. Ya he ganado la loteria.
       already have won the lottery
       'I have already won the lottery.'

A terminological note on experiential readings as a hyponym of the existential readings

In our view, the "experience-driven" interpretation of examples like (7) transparently motivates the term experiential reading. In the same vein, several studies of the PPC$_{SP}$ employ the term for the Spanish PPC$_{SP}$, e.g. Schwenter (1994a); Bartens and Kempas (2007); Kempas (2008a); Carrasco Gutiérrez (2008), Rodrigues Parrinha (2014, 2015), Burgos (2015); Xiqués (2015). Furthermore, we conceive of the experiential reading as a concrete realization of the existential readings (cf. Figure 4.4), which is in line with e.g. McCawley (1971); Mittwoch (1988); Iatridou et al. (2003) and Molsing (2006).[120] We consider this note on terminology as worth mentioning because some studies of the cross-linguistic PP exclusively make use of the term existential reading (cf. e.g. de Swart 2007; Nishiyama and Koenig 2010; Portner 2012) or seem to conceive of the two as synonyms (cf. e.g. Vlach 1993; Michaelis 1994, Lindstedt 2008).

---

[120]. Rothstein (2008: 114) inverts this structure by conceiving of the existential reading as a hyponym of the experiential readings. However, we consider the common property of the resultative, experiential and hot news reading of carrying an existential quantifier to suggest the approach illustrated in Figure 4.4.

4.3.2 Resultative reading

The direct resultant state

We adhere to Nishiyama and Koenig (2010: 612) by defining the resultative reading as the "reading where the direct resultant state of a past event still continues" at t_S. In this vein, the PPC_{SP-RES} disposes of a specialized form of current relevance, which the experiential PPC_{SP} lacks. The difference between the resultative and the experiential reading is expressed in the opposition of CR combined with a direct resultant state vs. CR lacking a direct resultant state:

(9) PPC_{SP-RES} vs. PPC_{SP-EX}[121]
   a. PPC_{SP-RES}: [+] DIRECT RESULTANT STATE, [+] CR
      He   terminado la   carta.
      have finished   the letter
      I have finished the letter.
   b. PPC_{SP-EX}: [−] DIRECT RESULTANT STATE, [+] CR
      El hombre ha   estado en la Luna.
      the man   have been   in the moon
      Mankind has been to the moon.
   c. PPC_{SP-RES} or PPC_{SP-EX}: [±] DIRECT RESULTANT STATE, [+] CR
      He   terminado la   carta.
      have finished   the letter
      I have finished the letter.

The examples illustrated in (9) represent versions of the existential readings featuring quantificational temporal semantics causing the denotation of a temporally indefinite past eventuality with particular relevance at speech time (which is due to the inclusion of t_S in the present time-sphere). (9a) denotes a direct resultant state which is a written letter, i.e. an effected object. It is derived based on the lexical semantics of the underlying predicate of writing a letter: having finished writing a letter necessarily entails a the result of a written letter. Consequently, the direct resultant state as entailed by the PPC_{SP-RES} presupposes a telic predicate. As discussed in Section 2.2, telic predicates contain logical endpoints, i.e. inherent boundaries which may be defined "by the properties of the elements they separate" (Dahl 2013: 48). Applied to the PPC_{SP-RES}, these properties are (i) the past eventuality `finish the letter` and (ii) its direct resultant state of the letter being finished. On the other hand, there is no direct resultant state in (9b), such as "mankind is on the moon". Here, the underlying state predicate of `el hombre estar en la Luna` lacks an aspectual boundary which impedes the derivation of a direct resultant

---

[121]. Examples taken from Kempas (2008a: 398), translations added.

state – if not a direct object adding a telic boundary is involved (cf. Section 2.2 for the telicizing potential of object NPs). (9c) is ambiguous, i.e. it may evoke a resultative or an experiential reading. A potential scenario for uttering the resultative reading would be "I have finished the letter. Now, I finally have the time to do other things." Conversely, an experiential reading would fit a context like "I have done a lot today. I have washed the car and I have finished the letter." However, the differences remain highly subtle for examples like (9c). In fact, Comrie (1976: 59) points out that "most of the familiar European languages" do not have distinct morphological forms for the resultative vs. experiential division such that these often give rise to an ambiguity. As an exception to that pattern, Comrie refers to the rare case of Chinese that disposes of a productive toneless suffix -*guo* yielding the experiential reading:

(10) Morphosyntactic distinction of PP$_{RES}$ and PP$_{EX}$ in Chinese (Comrie 1976: 59)
    a. nǐ chī-le yúchì-le méi-you
         'Have you eaten the shark's fin?'
    b. nǐ chī-**guo** yúchì méi-you
         'Have you ever eaten shark's fin?'

The translations of these examples suggest that English allows for an explicit disambiguation of the resultative and the experiential reading by adding particular tempo-aspectual adverbials, which also holds for Spanish, as exemplified by means of *ya [...] una vez* in (11).

(11) Ya   he   terminado la   carta una vez.
     already have finished   the letter once
     I have already finished the letter before/once.

We conclude that the direct resultant state associated with the PPC$_{SP-RES}$ is a lexically triggered meaning component which presupposes verbal telicity of the underlying predicate (again, predicate is understood as referring to the entire verbal phrase including potential verb-internal objects). In fact, this harmonizes with the common diachronic assumption that the PPC$_{SP-RES}$ represents the older and more specialized stage that developed into the PPC$_{SP-EX}$ by gradually loosening its requirement of exclusively combining with telic predicates in favor of the functionally more versatile meaning component of CR, that does allow for the combination with atelic predicates.

Delimiting PPC$_{SP-RES}$ from the tener + *participle construction*
Apart from the PPC$_{SP-EX}$, there is another closely related construction that needs to be disentangled from the PPC$_{SP-RES}$, namely the resultative construction featuring *tener* ('(to) have') instead of *haber* as its auxiliary. Not only on the form side, but

also one the meaning side, the two have to be distinguished, as suggested by the English translations provided in (12).

(12) PPC$_{SP\text{-}RES}$ vs. resultative construction
    a.   *He   escrito   un   libro.*
        have written a   book
        'I have written a book.'
    b.   *Tengo escrito   un   libro.*
        have written a   book
        'I have a book written.' (i.e. 'I am the author of a book.')[122]

The crucial syntactic difference between the two pertains to the syntactic position of the participle. Figure 4.3b illustrates for the resultative construction featuring *tener* that the participle is embedded in the verb-internal DP as an adjective, which particularly accounts for that the participle and the DP (*un libro*) agree in gender and number, as e.g. in *Tengo hecha ya la comida* ('I have already prepared the meal' in the sense of 'The meal is already prepared (because of me) and it is here with me'). On the other hand, the participle of the PPC$_{SP}$ arises from the predicate's retrieval of tense, aspect and mood information, i.e. from the combination with the tense form PPC$_{SP}$, as illustrated in the simplified syntactic structures in Figure 4.3a.

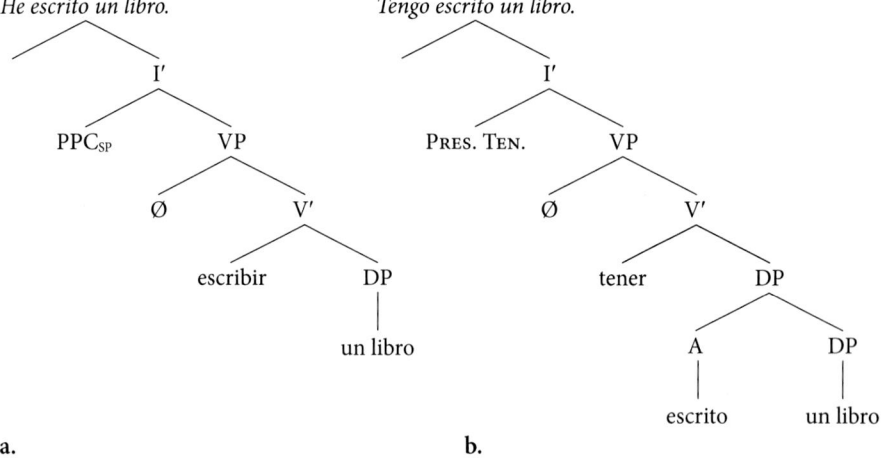

Figure 4.3 Simplified syntactic structures of PPC$_{SP\text{-}RES}$ and resultative construction

Semantically, the two differ, as well. In most general terms, resultatives may be defined as

---

122. Example and translation taken from Detges (2000: 350).

[…] those verb forms that express a state implying a previous event. The difference between the stative and the resultative is as follows: the stative expresses a state of a thing without any implications of its origin, while the resultative expresses both a state and the preceding action it has resulted from.

(Nedjalkov and Jaxontov 1988: 6)

In the same vein, Detges (2000) motivates the semantic difference between the two based on the opposition of implication vs. denotation. He argues that the resultative *tener* construction *denotes* a resultant state *implying* a past event, while the PPC$_{SP-RES}$ *denotes* a past event *implying* a resultant state. This inverse structure is illustrated in Table 4.1.

Table 4.1 *tener* vs. *haber* (inspired by Detges 2000: 349)

	Denoted	Implied	Semantic role of subject
tener+PART.	Present Result	Past Event	Somehow related to Result
haber+PART.	Past Event	Present Result	Agent of Past Event

The illustrated antithetical structure is complemented by further contrasts: while for the *tener* construction, the grammatical subject's referent is perceived as being somehow *related* to the result of the construction, it *may* be the agent of the past event. On the other hand, the PPC$_{SP-RES}$'s grammatical subject's referent *may* be related to the result and *is* the agent of the past event. Rosemeyer (2014: 43) corroborates these observations, arguing that the resultative construction lacks a Davidsonian event argument, as opposed to the PPC$_{SP-RES}$, which is in line with Maienborn (2003), who proposed that copula verbs as stative constructions generally lack an event argument. Accordingly, Rosemeyer (2014: 52) states that resultative constructions block combinations with adverbials trying to modify the lacking event argument, as e.g. locative adverbials, as it may be illustrated with (13).

(13)   Resultative construction blocking specification of temporal location
       *Tengo escrito un libro hace poco/ esta mañana.
        have written a   book recently   this morning
       'I have a book written recently/ this morning.'

It is particularly interesting that the resultative construction in (13) does not even allow for the adverbial *(esta mañana)*, which, on the basis of our framework, might be analyzed as modifying the perspective time instead of the missing event time (cf. Section 4.5 for the interaction of the PPC$_{SP}$ and tempo-aspectual adverbials). That means that the resultative construction does not only seem to lack t_E but also t_P. Given that we defined tense as an ordering function of t_E, t_P t_S (and, depending on the tense form, t_{LOC} and t_R), the resultative construction should in fact not be considered an actual tense form: t_E and t_P are, at most, implied, but not denoted.

Having delimited the PPC$_{SP-RES}$ from (i) the resultative construction, based on the relation between the event and the resultant state, as well as from (ii) the experiential reading, based on a distinction between mere current relevance vs. a lexically triggered direct resultant state, we proceed to the next reading, the hot news reading (PPC$_{SP-HN}$).

4.3.3 Hot news reading

A third representative of the existential readings marks the hot news reading (PPC$_{SP-HN}$):

(14) El   presidente de la   república ha fallecido.
      the president of the republic has passed away
      'The president of the republic has passed away.'[123]

The PPC$_{SP-HN}$ expresses a "breaking news character" which can be traced back to its interpretation of t_E being temporally located quite close to t_S. That is, the PPC$_{SP-HN}$ comes along with a quite narrow present time-sphere which accommodates the perspective time t_P. Again, the PPC$_{SP-HN}$ lacks a location time t_{LOC}, i.e. the PPC$_{SP-HN}$'s function in (14) is not to express *when* exactly the president died. Instead, its aims at expressing *that* the president has died *very recently*. Moreover, hot news readings

> [...] emphasize the significance and recency of the past event itself, not its present results. Diachronically, hot news uses arise later than other perfect functions, as the perfect construction gradually loses its connection to the present. This shift of focus from the present to the past makes hot news perfects more like perfectives than other perfect functions. (Schwenter 1994b: 995)

Put differently, the PPC$_{SP-HN}$ may be considered as a quite innovative use that particularly triggers or accompanies the PPC$_{SP}$'s grammaticalization into a past tense, which Schwenter (1994b) associates with a "shift of focus from the present to the past". In Chapter 6, we deepen the idea of a focal shift from the present domain to the event domain within a prominence-based account. While Schwenter (1994b) attributes the shift to the diachrony, we assume that a prominence-based structuring of the post-state vs. the event domain synchronically mediates between different readings that, in turn, give rise to different discourse functions.

With regard to the effect of current relevance, the PPC$_{SP-HN}$ may give rise to a resultative conversational implicature. Thus, (14) may be felicitously uttered as an answer to e.g. "Why is our session cancelled?" However, it seems that the

---

123. Example taken from Howe and Schwenter (2003: 62f.).

"breaking news character" of the hot news reading in fact rather focusses the "significance of the past event" (cf. Schwenter 1994a) that causes a decline of CR. Cross-linguistically, Dahl and Hedin (2000: 391) observe the same tendency for the PP that is said to suffer "a gradual relaxation of the requirements on current relevance" when it grammaticalizes into a preterite form.

4.3.4 Universal reading

The $PPC_{SP\text{-}UNI}$ crucially differs from the existential readings by denoting a universal quantification causing t_E to abut t_S ($t_E \succ\!\prec t_S$) instead of preceding it. Due to this difference, the PPC_{SP} generally tends to "favor" either the universal reading or the existential readings over one another in a given variety. While the Mexican PPC_{SP} is often described as giving rise to the universal reading per default (cf. e.g. Bertinetto and Squartini 2000), the "well-behaved" peninsular PPC_{SP} generally requires specific adverbial support in order to derive the universal reading due to the privileged status of the existential readings (cf. García Fernández 1999: 346, Laca 2008: 5). An adverbial forcing the universal reading is e.g. *siempre* ('always') (cf. also the more detailed discussion of the interplay of the PPC_{SP} and tempo-aspectual adverbials in Section 4.5.) In fact, the PPC_{SP} cross-linguistically shares this constraint with a range of languages, as Iatridou et al. (2003: 157) point out that the universal reading "is never available to a perfect unless [it] is modified by certain adverbials." In (15), the $PPC_{SP\text{-}UNI}$ is forced by means of *desde que*.

(15) $PPC_{SP\text{-}UNI}$
 a. *Ha vivido solo desde que murió su padre.*
    have lived alone since that die his father
    'He has been living by himself since his father died.'[124]
 b. *Ha estado enfermo desde que se marchó su hermano.*
    have been sick since that REFL leave his brother
    'He has been sick since his brother left.'[125]

The $PPC_{SP\text{-}UNI}$ is oftentimes characterized as lacking an aspectual boundary:

> There is an old intuition according to which universal readings involve states, i. e. unbounded and homogeneous situations, embedded under the Perfect, whereas existential readings involve events, i. e. bounded and therefore non-homogeneous situations (Mittwoch 1988). For Spanish, it is widely known that universal readings are much easier to get with states, with habituals and with progressives than with any other types of predicate (García Fernandez 2007). (Laca 2008: 4)

---

124. Example taken from García Fernández and Martínez-Atienza (2003: 42).

125. Example taken from García Fernández and Martínez-Atienza (2003: 38).

Following Lohnstein (2011: 268ff.), we have defined states as denoting a perfectly homogeneous interval imposing the very same truth conditions for each atomic part of it (definition repeated from Chapter 2.2):

(16) $P_{STATE}(x)$ is true in an interval i, iff $P_{STATE}(x)$ is true for every $t \subset i$ of length 0.[126]

In line with Laca (2008), this definition matches the semantics of the PPC_{SP-UNI} exemplified in (15). In fact, one might argue that (15b) does not denote a perfectly homogeneous interval under a gradual reading of being sick in the sense that one's degree of sickness might vary over time. However, being "very sick" at t_1 and "a little bit sick" at t_2 would both satisfy the truth conditions of being sick. Still, the PPC_{SP-UNI} does not always denote such a rigorous all-quantification. As discussed in Chapter 3 in the context of the Portuguese PPC_{PT}, the universal quantifier may be restricted by appropriateness conditions to situations that the underlying predicate typically occurs in (cf. Becker 2022: 59). This is exemplified in (17) where the speaker does not intend to express that (s)he has been drinking beer permanently ever since. Instead, the universal quantifier is restricted to situations that represent typical occasions for drinking a beer.

(17) *Desde siempre he bebido cerveza, con y sin alcohol.*
since ever have drunk beer with and without alcohol
'I have always drunk beer, alcoholic and non-alcoholic.'

That is, the universal quantifier included in the PPC_{SP-UNI} also combines with iterated and habitual meanings. From a cross-linguistic perspective, this is not exceptional, keeping in mind that e.g. the Portuguese PPC_{PT} has grammaticalized this very meaning component. The fact that continuative, iterative and habitual meanings are closely related is e.g. also demonstrated by the Romance Imperfect, that disposes of each of them (cf. e.g. Becker 2010a; Leonetti 2018, cf. also Section 6.2).

Competition with Present Tense
While the existential readings may compete with the *Indefinido* (Simple Past), the universal reading may compete with the Present Tense, in particular in sentences featuring *desde que* ('since'):

(18) Present Tense (competing with PPC_{SP-UNI}) (García Fernández 2007: 98)
 a. *Vive solo desde que murió su padre.*
  lives alone since that die his father
  'He has lived / he lives by himself since his father died.'
 b. *Está enfermo desde que se marchó su hermano.*
  is sick since that REFL leave his brother
  'He has been / he is sick since his brother left.'

---

126. 0 should be conceived of as infinitesimally 0.

García Fernández (2007: 111) proposes an approach to the distribution of the PPC$_{SP-UNI}$ vs. Present Tense based on their difference with regard to a potential continuation of the predicate after the speech time. Accordingly, the PPC$_{SP-UNI}$ may denote both a continuation of the predicated eventuality after t_s *and* the limitation of t_E to t_S. By contrast, the Present Tense only allows for the future-continuative reading. In other words, the PPC$_{SP-UNI}$ is said to *implicate* a continuation while the Present Tense *implies* continuation. A linguistic test to illustrate that assumption could be designed as the one indicated in (19).

(19) ?*Está /Ha estado enfermo desde que se marchó su hermano, pero ahora*
   is   has been   sick   since that REFL leave his brother but now
   está mejor.
   is   better
   'He is / has been sick since his brother left, but now, he feels better.'

The Present Tense version blocks the canceling of t_E's continuation due to a logical incompatibility. Accordingly, p$_1$ (*Está enfermo desde que se marchó su hermano*) implies ¬ p$_2$ (*ahora está mejor*). On the other hand, the PPC$_{SP-UNI}$ and t_E's continuation are compatible because p$_1$-PPC$_{SP-UNI}$ does not imply ¬ p$_2$. Further evidence in favor of the assumption that the PPC$_{SP-UNI}$'s t_E is implied (not denoted) to continue beyond t_S can be derived from Iatridou et al. (2003). The authors argue that universal readings are odd with individual-level predicates, as shown in (20), and claim that this observation holds cross-linguistically.

(20) Universal reading with individual-level predicate
   a. *He has had brown eyes since he was born.[127]
   b. ?*Ha tenido ojos marrones desde que nació.*

Since the continuation of t_E after t_S is not cancelable with individual-level predicates, there is a clash with the property of the universal reading that *does* allow for cancelling the implicated (not implied) continuation and which should block examples like (20b).

Current Relevance or direct resultant state?
Above, we discussed current relevance (resultative conversational implicature) and the direct resultant state as being associated with the PPC$_{SP-EX}$ and PPC$_{SP-RES}$, respectively. Given that the PPC$_{SP-UNI}$ (i) lacks an aspectual boundary and (ii) is able to cancel t_E's implicated continuation after the speech time, we assume that the PPC$_{SP-UNI}$ does not denote a direct resultant state. However, the PPC$_{SP-UNI}$ may give rise to current relevance effects, i.e. to resultative conversational implicatures, as illustrated in (21).

---

127. Example taken from Iatridou et al. 2003: 160.

(21) *He vivido aquí desde siempre.*
'I have always lived here.'
a. *Conozco bien la zona.*
'I know the area well.'
b. *Vengo de una familia tradicional.*
'I am from a traditional family.'
c. *Me quedo aquí.*
'I am staying here.'

The indicated scenarios suggest that the PPC$_{\text{SP-UNI}}$ expression of always having lived at a certain place may give rise to a range of implicatures and thus may be felicitously uttered as an answer to several questions. In this vein, it may mean that the speaker knows a good restaurant (21a), that the speaker is socially integrated in the society of the town (21b), or that he will not move away because this would break with a great familiar tradition (21c). Again, we assume that the potential to derive CR effects can be traced back to the PPC$_{\text{SP}}$'s temporal configuration of setting its perspective time to lie in the present time-sphere.

4.3.5 Overview

We conclude that the quantificational readings of the PPC$_{\text{SP}}$ can be conceived of as branching into existential (t_E is prior to t_S) and universal (t_E abuts t_S) readings. The existential readings furthermore branch into experiential (PPC$_{\text{SP-EX}}$), resultative (PPC$_{\text{SP-RES}}$) and hot news readings (PPC$_{\text{SP-HN}}$), as illustrated in Figure 4.4 in Section 4.1. Each of these readings has in common (i) that the perspective time is included in the present time-sphere, (ii) that the past eventuality at t_E gets quantified over (either existentially or universally) and (iii) that there is no location time included in the temporal make-up.

Having introduced the different manifestations of the PPC$_{\text{SP}}$'s existential semantics in the present section, we proceed to the question of whether the PPC$_{\text{SP}}$ (already) disposes of referential semantics, i.e. of a referential reading, as well.

4.4 Is there a referential reading?

Having classified the PPC$_{SP}$ as a cross-linguistically "well-behaved" PP due to its purely quantificational core meaning so far, we have to discuss whether there is a referential PPC$_{SP}$, as well.[128] It is generally expected that the PPC$_{SP}$ will develop, at some point, into a referential tense form as indicated in (22). Triggered by the referential drift, the (potentially) resulting PPC$_{SP\text{-}REF}$ qualifies to combine with positional adverbials that modify its location time (cf. Section 2.5). It remains unclear though if the PPC$_{SP}$ synchronically already disposes of such a a referential reading.

The semantics of the potential referential PPC$_{SP\text{-}REF}$

In Chapter 2.5, we characterized the referential PP (exemplified e.g. by the French *Passé Composé*) based on the following semantic form:

(22) Referential PPC$_{SP}$

$[\![PPC_{SP\text{-}REF}]\!]: \lambda t_S \lambda t_E \lambda t_{LOC} \lambda t_P.\; t_E \begin{bmatrix}\subseteq \\ \supseteq\end{bmatrix} t_{LOC} \prec t_S \subseteq t_P$

First of all, the referential PPC$_{SP}$ maintains its orientation towards the speech time such that t_S continues to be included in t_P, i.e. in the present time-sphere. Yet, the most striking update associated with the PPC$_{SP\text{-}REF}$ is expressed in the inclusion of the location time t_{LOC}. This causes t_E to be referentially assigned to t_{LOC}, as opposed to an existential or universal quantification over t_E. Furthermore, this update introduces a viewpoint aspect, i.e. a perfective viewpoint (t_E as a subset of t_{LOC}) or an imperfective viewpoint (t_{LOC} as a subset of t_E).

Evidence for the PPC$_{SP\text{-}REF}$

In fact, there are attested uses that might be considered as "hodiernal perfective" uses (cf. e.g. Bartens and Kempas 2007; Schwenter and Cacoullos 2008), i.e. uses that suggest that the PPC$_{SP}$ already disposes of referential configurations:

> [...] the Peninsular PP is well-established as a hodiernal perfective, because it is near categorical in hodiernal contexts, in which, moreover, its rate is not significantly lower even in the presence of specific temporal adverbials.[129]
> (Schwenter and Cacoullos 2008: 31)

---

128. Cf. Laca (2008) for the notion of "well-behaved" Perfects.

129. Cf. Chapter 6 for empirical data suggesting that the claim that the PPC$_{SP}$ "is near categorical in hodiernal contexts" appears to be too strong, as the *Indefinido* still seems to be preferred over the PPC$_{SP}$ in hodiernal-narrative contexts.

Similarly, Azpiazu Torres (2019: 127) assumes that the Peninsular Spanish variety is able to denote definite eventualities that are temporally restricted by the condition to be included in a *lapso temporal del Perfecto* ('perfect time span') which enables the combination with certain adverbials like *este mes, esta semana* ('this month', 'this week', cf. also Figure 4.2 in Section 4.2).[130] Examples of those "hodiernal perfective uses" are illustrated in (23).

(23) Evidence for a referential PPC$_{SP}$?
    a. *Hoy he visitado a mi abuela en el hospital.*
       today have visited PREP my grandmother in the hospital
       'Today I (have) visited my grandmother in the hospital.'[131]
    b. *¿Has visto esta mañana el atasco Extremadura?*
       have seen this morning the traffic jam Extremadura
       'Did you see this morning the traffic jam [on] Extremadura?'[132]
    c. *Estoy cansado porque me he despertado a las cinco de*
       I am tired because me have woken up a the five PREP
       la mañana.
       the morning
       'I am tired because I woke up at five in the morning.'[133]

The tempo-aspectual adverbials that the PPC$_{SP}$ combines with in the indicated examples might be interpreted as positional adverbials modifying the location time t_{LOC} (cf. Section 2.3 and the detailed analysis of the interaction of tempo-aspectual adverbials and the PPC$_{SP}$ Section 4.5). This interpretation thus presupposes a location time in the temporal make-up of the PPC$_{SP}$. Accordingly, t_E gets attributed to an adverbially provided t_{LOC} like *today* or *this week*. Given that t_E and t_{LOC} are interpreted as standing in an inclusion relation ($t_E \subseteq t_{LOC}$), the PPC$_{SP}$ denotes a perfective viewpoint aspect.

On the level of discourse, (24) might be considered as providing further evidence.

---

130. Cf. the results of the experiment reported in Chapter 6 though, that suggest that even in hodiernal contexts, the *Indefinido* is slightly preferred over the PPC$_{SP}$, which contradicts the characterization of the PPC$_{SP}$ as a "hodiernal perfective".

131. Example taken from Azpiazu Torres (2019: 134).

132. Example and translation taken from Schwenter and Cacoullos (2008: 17).

133. Example taken from Bartens and Kempas (2007: 155).

(24) Discursive evidence for a referential PPC$_{SP}$?[134]
   a. *O sea ha esperado a acabar de hablar con Nicolás, lo que había empezado, ha tardado su minuto y luego ya ha cogido la llamada.*
   'I mean he waited to finish talking with Nicolás what he had started, he took his minute and then he finally answered the call.'[135]
   b. *Qué te decía yo? – dijo, sin preámbulos. Esta mañana cuando he salido al jardín Gladys me ha llamado, como anoche. Ya estaba fuera, esperándome. He ido a su instalación, me he asomado a la ventana de su dormitorio y, ¿adivinas lo que he visto entre sus patas?*
   'What did I tell you? – she said, without any introduction. This morning, when I went into the garden Gladys called me, as last night. She was already outside, waiting for me. I went to her cabin, peeked through her bedroom window and guess what I saw between her paws?' [Gladys is a panther][136]

Both examples in (24) clearly share narrative properties. Instead of denoting eventualities that only get a temporal interpretation relative to the speech time, they denote past eventualities that are dynamically updated and temporally anchored relatively to each other. Crucially, they furthermore feature the anaphoric tense forms *Pluscuamperfecto* (24a) and *Imperfecto* (24b) that presuppose that the perspective time lies in the past time-sphere (cf. Becker 2010a, 2020b).[137] As illustrated in (25), this should be incompatible with the semantics of the quantificational PPC$_{SP}$, which, after all, sets its perspective time to lie in the present time-sphere, and that lacks a location time t_{LOC} and a discourse reference time t_R.

(25) PPC$_{SP}$ + *Pluscuamperfecto* : perspectival clash
   Cuando [llegó/ *ha llegado] Maria, los invitados ya se habían ido.
   'When Maria arrived, the guests had already left.'[138]

In sum, it seems that the uses presented in (23) and (24) might be best accounted for by means of a referential approach. However, it remains unclear why prehodiernal adverbials would actually be ruled out by a referential PPC$_{SP}$. Put differently, the temporal boundary that separates the hodiernal and the prehodiernal time-sphere remains to be motivated as an additional temporal constraint within the referential

---

134. We omit glossing in sentences that illustrate discursive phenomena due to their increased length.

135. Example and translation taken from Schwenter and Cacoullos (2008: 16).

136. Example and translation taken from Laca (2008: 6f.).

137. Cf. Chapter 6 for a detailed account of PPC$_{SP}$ + *Imperfecto*.

138. Example taken from Carrasco Gutiérrez (2008: 26), translation added.

approach. On the other hand, it might be *the* cue that mediates between the clearly separated semantic categories of quantification and reference, i.e. that actually triggers the reanalysis of the quantificational PPC$_{SP}$ as a referential PPC$_{SP}$ (cf. also "The quantificational/referential ambiguity as a transitional context?" below and Chapter 6).

Arguments supporting a purely quantificational account

Within an alternative perspective, it might be argued that the discussed examples do not provide evidence for a referential PPC$_{SP}$, given that a purely quantificational account might be able to account for them as well. According to this line of argumentation, the examples shown in (23) rather exhibit pseudo-perfective uses due to adverbial scope ambiguities: the adverbials *esta mañana* and *hoy* do not actually modify the location time but function as XN-adverbials specifying the perspective time, i.e. the temporally vague extension of the present time-sphere. This approach is particularly able to account for the PPC$_{SP}$'s peculiar tendency of its temporal restriction to hodiernal eventualities. Assuming that purportedly positional adverbials actually function as XN-adverbials that modify the perspective time (instead of t$_{LOC}$), the effect of hodiernality may be traced back to the fact that the PPC$_{SP}$'s perspective time must be included in the present time-sphere. This impedes the employment of prehodiernal adverbials like "yesterday" but allows for adverbials like "today", "this morning", 'this week' (cf. also the discussion of the Present Perfect puzzle in Section 2.5). Applying this analysis to (23a), the adverbial "today" specifies the perspective time that the speaker asserts on. In other words, "today" explicitly emphasizes that the perspective time does not escape from the present time-sphere. In what concerns the past eventuality `visitar a mi abuela` on the other hand, t$_E$ is expressed to precede the speech time and remains indefinite.

The application of the purely quantificational account to (23c) featuring the adverbial "at five in the morning" calls for further elaborations. After all, "at five in the morning" seems to be too specific for specifying the present time-sphere (instead of a location time). It might be argued though that the adverbial "at five in the morning" gets interpreted as being incorporated into the predicate. In this scenario, it gets interpreted as a fixed expression where `despertarse a las cinco de la mañana` is expressed as an indefinite past eventuality that precedes the speech time. This interpretation is particularly supported by the fact that the utterance explicitly aims for creating the PP-typical current relevance effect by means of "I am tired because + PPC$_{SP}$". Accordingly, t$_E$ of the predicate `despertarse a las cinco de la mañana` remains indefinite in (23c), as its temporal perspective focusses the speech time.

In fact, the results of the experiment reported in Chapter 6 of this book may be interpreted as supporting the purely quantificational view. They suggest that, even in hodiernal contexts, the *Indefinido* is still preferred over the PPC$_{SP}$ in narrative contexts. Put differently, even in hodiernal contexts the PPC$_{SP}$ has not yet fully turned into a perfective tense form. However, similarly to the purely referential anaylsis as discussed above, the purely quantificational account also faces problems. The claim that t_E remains temporally indefinite in examples like (23) might be too strong, as the visiting of the grandmother must have taken place hodiernally, i.e. the there actually seems to be some kind of temporal restriction of t_E. Finally, we assume that the ambiguous nature of the so-called hodiernal-perfective uses as exemplified in (23) may actually hint at a bridging context of diachronic relevance for the PPC$_{SP}$'s referential drift.

The quantificational/referential ambiguity as a transitional context?

As discussed above, both the referential and the quantificational account felicitously capture meaning components of the uses presented in (23) and (24). We interpret this ambiguity, i.e. that the PPC$_{SP}$ ambiguously vacillates between a quantificational and a referential semantic configuration, not to pose an analytical problem but to hint at ongoing diachronic dynamics. Assuming the PPC$_{SP}$ to acquire referential semantics in the long run (which is in line with the assumption of a so-called aoristic drift of the Romance PP, cf. Bertinetto and Squartini (2000) and Section 2.5), the question arises how the referential drift is actually initiated. According to grammaticalization theory, reinterpretation processes triggered by ambiguities are right at the heart of grammaticalization. This is captured by the three stages which are assumed to typically guide grammaticalization processes according to Heine (2003):

i. *There is a linguistic expression A that is recruited for grammaticalization.*
ii. *This expression acquires a second use pattern, B, with the effect that there is ambiguity between A and B.*
iii. *Finally, A is lost, that is, there is now only B.* (Heine 2003: 579)

Applied to the PPC$_{SP}$, the first stage refers to a purely quantificational semantic configuration, while the second stage applies to the addition of a referential configuration creating the ambiguity discussed above. In this vein, XN-adverbials like "today" and "this week", that initially scope over t_P, may gradually suffer a reinterpretation towards being interpreted as positional adverbials scoping over t_{LOC}, which is possible due to the inclusion of a location time argument in the semantics of the PPC$_{SP}$, as illustrated in (22). Since these adverbial scope ambiguities suggest that it is problematic to base the study of the PPC$_{SP}$'s referential drift on combinations with particular tempo-aspectual adverbials alone, the present study aims for complementarily focussing on the PPC$_{SP}$'s functions on the level of discourse beyond its potential to combine with particular adverbials. For now, we proceed with the assumption that there might already be a referential PPC$_{SP}$ available in synchrony, as illustrated in the updated sketch of the PPC$_{SP}$-readings in Figure 4.4.

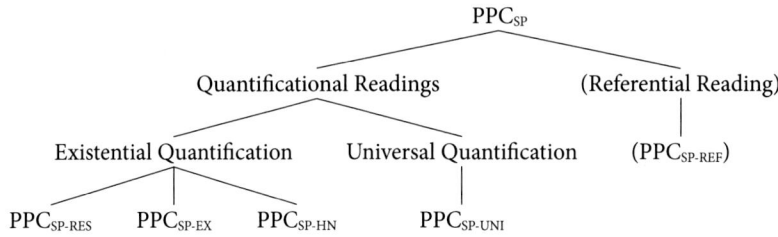

Figure 4.4 Updated typology of the PPC$_{SP}$'s readings

We move the further discussion of the referential reading to Section 4.6, where we discuss syntagmatic combinations of the PPC$_{SP}$ with adjacent tense forms in detail, to Chapter 5, where we report a corpus study on the discourse functions of the PPC$_{SP}$, as well as to Chapter 6, where we pick up the question of the diachronic evolution of the PPC$_{SP}$ in terms of its referential drift. Here, we report an empirical study of testing the acceptability of cases where the PPC$_{SP}$ functions as an anaphoric anchor for a succeeding *Imperfecto*.

4.5 Adverbials

In this section, we discuss the interaction of the PPC$_{SP}$ and tempo-aspectual adverbials in detail. As outlined in Section 2.3, the analysis is based on the four groups of positional, quantificational, durative and extended-now (XN) adverbials.

With regard to positional adverbials, the quantificational PPC$_{SP}$ is, in most general terms, consistent with the cross-linguistic trend to block positional adverbials.

(26) Positional adverbials
  a. *Maria ha comprado un coche ayer.
     Maria has bought a car yesterday
     'Yesterday, Maria bought a car.'
  b. ?Maria ha comprado un coche hoy.
     Maria has bought a car today
     'Today, Maria bought a car.'[139]

---

[139]. The question mark does not call into question the felicity of (26b) but refers to the unclear scope of the adverbial *hoy*. That is, it remains unclear if *hoy* actually functions as a positional adverbial modifying t$_{LOC}$, cf. Section 4.4.

This is widely uncontroversial concerning prehodiernal positional adverbials (26a) and also connectives that try to modify t_R and t_{LOC}:

> [...] [S]pecific or "definite time" (Dahl 1985: 137) adverbials, such as *ayer* 'yesterday,' calendar dates, clock times, co-occurring *cuando* 'when,' and other temporal clauses [...], should disfavor the PP, as should 'connective' adverbials (cf. Bonami et al. 2004; Fernández 1999: 3188–3192) such as *primero* 'first,' *antes* 'before,' *despues, entonces, luego* 'afterward, then,' *al final* 'in the end' [...], because temporal specification or anchoring to another situation presumably detracts from (focusing on the result associated with) a current relevance interpretation (Dahl and Hedin 2000: 395; cf. Fleischman 1983: 199).
>
> (Schwenter and Cacoullos 2008: 16)

However, there is evidence (cf. e.g. Kempas 2002, 2006a; b, 2009; Holmes and Balukas 2011; Montoro del Arco 2017) concerning micro-variation and varieties allowing for the PPC$_{SP}$ to be combined with prehodiernal positional adverbials. As discussed in Section 4.4, it remains unclear whether hodiernal-positional adverbials (e.g. XN-adverbials like *hoy, esta mañana*) are blocked when combined with the quantificational PPC$_{SP}$ (26b), which would mean that they presuppose referential semantics, or whether they are fine, receiving an interpretation as scoping over the perspective time t_P.

Apart from positional adverbials, the are no further specific restrictions (as e.g. for the Portuguese PPC$_{PT}$ as discussed in Chapter 3): while quantificational adverbials existentially or universally quantify over their event time t_E (27a), XN-adverbials specify the temporal range of the perspective time, i.e. the range of the present time-sphere (27b). Durative adverbials are ambiguous between quantifying over t_E or modifying t_P (27c). This ambiguity is due to the condition imposed by the PPC$_{SP-UNI}$ that durative adverbials must abut the speech time.

(27) a. Quantificational
        i. *Ha ido dos veces a Buenos Aires.*
          has gone two times to Buenos Aires
          '(S)he has gone/been twice to Buenos Aires.'[140]
        ii. *Siempre ha vivido solo.*
          always has lived alone
          '(S)he has always lived by herself/himself.'[141]
   b. Extended-now
        i. *Maria ha comprado un coche hoy.*
          Maria has bought a car today
          'Maria bought a car today.'

---

140. Example taken from Laca (2008: 2).

141. Example taken from Laca (2008: 5).

ii. *Maria ha comprado un coche esta semana.*
Maria has bought a car this week
'Maria bought a car this week.'
c. Durative and XN[142]
i. *Ha vivido solo durante dos meses.*
has lived alone during two months
'(S)he has lived by herself/himself for two months.'
ii. *Ha vivido solo últimamente.*
has lived alone lately
'(S)he has lived by herself/himself lately.'

There is no one-to-one correspondence between the PPC_{SP}'s readings and the adverbials indicated in (24), as exemplified by the XN-adverbial "today" in (28). The contexts supplied in the square brackets suggests a situation in which a respective reading might be evoked by the PPC_{SP} combined with *hoy*.

(28) The XN-adverbial *today* and the PPC_{SP}
a. Universal reading
Ha escrito la carta hoy [durante todo el día].
'She has been writing the letter today [all day long].'
b. ?Hodiernal-referential reading
Ha escrito la carta hoy [a las cinco cuando tenía ganas].
'She has written the letter today [at five when she felt like it].'
c. Experiential reading
[¿Qué ha hecho hoy?] Ha escrito la carta hoy.
'[What has she done today?] She written the letter today.'
d. Resultative reading
Ha escrito la carta hoy. [Finalmente, podemos enviar la carta.]
'She has written the letter today. [Finally, we can send the letter.]'
e. Hot news reading
[Me acaban de decir:] Ha escrito la carta hoy!
'[I have just been told:] She has written the letter today!'

Table 4.2 summarizes our assumptions concerning tempo-aspectual adverbials and their scope when combined with the PPC_{SP}. The indicated question marks for the positional-hodiernal adverbial refer to the unclear scope of the adverbial *hoy*. That is, depending on its use, it remains unclear if *hoy* actually functions as a positional adverbial modifying t_{LOC} or as an XN-adverbial specifying t_P, which gives rise to an ambiguity as discussed in Section 4.4.

---

142. Both examples taken from Laca (2008: 5).

Having discussed our view on the PPC$_{SP}$'s interactions with adverbials in this section, we proceed to the discussion of the PPC$_{SP}$'s combinations with adjacent tense forms.

Table 4.2 Tempo-aspectual adverbials and the PPC$_{SP}$

Adverbial	Scope	Example	Translation
*Positional-prehodiernal	*t$_{LOC}$	*ayer,* *hace tres semanas,* *en 1999*	yesterday, three weeks ago, in 1999,
?Positional-hodiernal	?t$_{LOC}$	*hoy,* *esta mañana,* *a las cinco*	today, this morning, at five
Existential Quantification	t$_E$	*una vez,* *tres veces,* *muchas veces,* *ya,* *todavía no*	once, three times, several/many times, already, not yet,
Universal Quantification	t$_E$	*siempre,* *todas las veces*	always, each time
Durative	t$_E$	*desde la semana passada,* *durante muchos años*	since last week, for many years
Extended-now	t$_P$	*últimamente, los últimos dias, desde entonces, hoy*	lately, over the last days, ever since, today

4.6 Discourse

In this section, we discuss typical functions that the PPC$_{SP}$ fulfills in discourse. These functions are not supposed to form an exhaustive list but to be a first approximation (that may also inspire future studies). We mainly focus on the PPC$_{SP}$'s interaction with adjacent tense forms on the syntagmatic axis, i.e. on the micro level of discourse (Sections 4.6.1 and 4.6.2) before deriving assumptions concerning the macro-structure of discourse, i.e. the modes of discourse (Section 4.6.3).

Previous work

So far, there is little research on the subject of the PPC$_{SP}$'s interplay with adjacent tense forms. Among those is Moreno-Torres Sánchez's (1999) sketch of the interactions between the PPC$_{SP}$ and the *Indefinido*. His analysis points out the rhetorical relations that typically hold between the two tense forms. It builds on two relations of temporal inclusion (background and elaboration) and, on the other hand, two relations of temporal sequence (narration and explanation), as exemplified in (29).

(29) Rhetorical relations in Moreno-Torres Sánchez (1999: 244)
  a. *Escenario*: e_2 is a state that includes e_1 ($e_1 \subset e_2$)
     Juan entró$_{e1}$ en la habitación. La habitación estaba$_{e2}$ escura.
     'John entered the room. The room was dark.'
  b. *Narración*: e_1 precedes e_2 ($e_1 \prec e_2$)
     Juan cogió$_{e1}$ un vaso de cerveza. Se lo bebió de un trago$_{e2}$.
     'Juan took a glass of beer. He drank it in one gulp.'
  c. *Explicación*: e_2 precedes e_1 ($e_2 \prec e_1$)
     Juan entró$_{e1}$ en el bar. Había oído$_{e2}$ un ruido.
     'Juan entered the bar. He had heard a noise.'
  d. *Elaboración*: e_2 is part of e_1 ($e_2 \subset e_1$)
     Los niños construyeron$_{e1}$ un castillo de arena. Luís hizo$_{e2}$ la torre.
     'The children built a sand castle. Luis made the tower.'

This list suggests that there are typical patterns of how particular rhetorical relations are established by particular tense forms. While the *Imperfecto* seems to typically indicate a background relation (29a), the *Pluscuamperfecto* (Past Perfect) seems to serve to establish the rhetorical relation of explanation featuring temporal precedence (29c). However, neither do *Imperfecto* and *Pluscuamperfecto* exclusively function as discursively establishing the rhetorical relations of background and explanation, nor does it mean that there are no other ways to establish those relations. As discussed in Section 2.4, narration is typically achieved by combining two instances of the Simple Past, i.e. the *Indefinido* (29b). Building on these rhetorical notions, Moreno-Torres Sánchez (1999) derives the sketch presented in Table 4.3 for discursive combinations of the PPC$_{SP}$ and the *Indefinido*.

It suggests that PPC$_{SP}$ + PPC$_{SP}$ is able to create the relations of *narración*, *elaboración* and *retroceso* (*retroceso* complies with *explicación* in (29)), while the relation of *escenario* (background) is blocked. Furthermore, PPC$_{SP}$ + *Indefinido* enables two relations, namely *elaboración* and *retroceso* while *narración* is blocked. We may derive that narration is typically achieved by the combination of the same tense form for e_1 and e_2, i.e. by combining either two instances of the PPC$_{SP}$ or the *Indefinido*. However, there is a crucial difference between these two constellations: while the referential *Indefinido* is able to establish a discourse reference time t_R, which enables the discourse-semantic encoding of temporal relationships between e_1-e_n, the quantificational PPC$_{SP}$ lacks this component. Instead, the achieved narrative progression relies on pragmatic inferences. As discussed in Section 4.4 though, a referential PPC$_{SP}$ could be an exception to this principle as the PPC$_{SP-REF}$ might be able to discourse-semantically establish narrative passages.[143]

Table 4.3 Temporal relations between PPC$_{SP}$ and Indefinido according to Moreno-Torres Sánchez (1999: 245)[144]

Rel. discursiva	PPC$_{SP}$ + PPC$_{SP}$	Indefinido + Indefinido
Narratión ($e1 \prec e2$)	Hoy me he levantado a las 7 y he desayunado en la cama.[a]	Esta mañana me levanté a las 7 de la mañana y desayuné en la cama.[b]
Elaboratión ($e1 \supset e2$)	Juan se ha comprado una casa. Su hermano le ha arreglado el papeleo.[c]	Juan se compró una casa. Su hermano le arregló todo el papeleo.[d]
Escenario ($e1 \subset e2$)	✗	✗
Retroceso ($e1 \succ e2$)	Juan se ha comprado una casa. Le ha tocado la lotería.[e]	Juan se compró una casa en París. Le tocó la lotería.[f]
Rel. discursiva	**PPC$_{SP}$ + Indefinido**	**Indefinido + PPC$_{SP}$**
Narratión ($e1 \prec e2$)	✗	Esta mañana me levante a las 7. Durante todo del día he trabajado en casa.[g]
Elaboración ($e1 \supset e2$)	Hoy hemos trabajado mucho. Estuvimos primero en la obra y luego…[h]	✗
Escenario ($e1 \subset e2$)	✗	✗
Retroceso ($e1 \succ e2$)	Juan se ha comprado una casa. Le tocó la lotería.[i]	✗

The next combination, *Indefinido* + PPC$_{SP}$, seems to be highly marked, as also stated by Kempas (2017):

---

143. However, the fact that the PPC$_{SP-REF}$'s perspective time remains to be included in the present time-sphere would still mark a theoretical problem; cf. Chapter 6 for further discussion and a prominence-based account.

144. Translations for Table 4.3: a: 'Today I have gotten up at 7 o'clock and I have had breakfast in bed.'; b: 'Today I got up at 7 o'clock and had breakfast in bed.'; c: 'Juan has bought a house. His brother has arranged the paperwork for him.'; d: 'Juan bought a house. His brother arranged all the paperwork for him.'; e: 'Juan has bought a house. He has won the lottery'; f: 'Juan bought a house in Paris. He won the lottery'; g: 'This morning I got up at 7. I have been working at home all day.'; h: 'We have worked hard today. We were first at the construction site and then…'; i: 'Juan has bought a house. He won the lottery.'

> [PPC$_{SP}$ and *Indefinido*] solo pueden aparecer en el orden PPC + PPS, (prácticamente) nunca en el orden opuesto [...]. No obstante, en secuencias de este tipo, la mayoría de las veces se utiliza un mismo tiempo.[145]   (Kempas 2017: 241)

Moreno-Torres Sánchez (1999) considers the sequence as giving rise to a narration relation. Interestingly though, the corresponding example features a universal PPC$_{SP}$ which is adverbially forced by *durante todo el día*. Due to the abutment relation between the PPC$_{SP-UNI}$'s t_E and the speech time, we doubt that the example actually displays a narration relation. After all, the contained PPC$_{SP}$ does not receive its temporal interpretation based on a relative relation to the *Indefinido* but based on a relative anchoring with respect to the speech time. Instead of relating two sequentialized events in the past, it rather seems that there is a perspectival shift from the past time-sphere to the present time-sphere, such that e_1 and e_2 remain temporally isolated from one another. In macrostructural terms, we may say that there is a shift from narration ("This morning, I got up at 7") to report ("I have been working all day long at home"). While the former typically establishes temporal relations right between eventualities, the latter relates them to the deictic center, i.e. to the speech time, which is included in the perspective time.

In the following, we analyze the potential combinations indicated in Table 4.3 in detail. Additionally, we also take the combinations of PPC$_{SP}$ + *Pluscuamperfecto* (Past Perfect) and *Imperfecto* (Imperfect) into account. Therefore, we mainly apply the framework discussed in Section 2.4, i.e. we discuss actualization effects, perspectival shifting, as well as the discourse functions of a potential PPC$_{SP-REF}$.

4.6.1 PPC$_{SP}$ + PPC$_{SP}$

Similarly to the Portuguese PPC$_{PT}$, two instances of the PPC$_{SP}$ denote an unordered set of two indefinite past eventualities. By contrast though, the PPC$_{SP}$ may denote singular eventualities which enables the interpretation of a narrative temporal sequence. However, such an interpretation is based on pragmatic inferences instead of discourse-semantic reasoning: while the referential *Indefinido* establishes a discursive reference time t_R anchoring the succeeding referential *Indefinido*, the PPC$_{SP}$'s perspective time remains included in the present time-sphere such that there is neither t_R, nor t_{LOC} due to the PPC$_{SP}$'s indefinite quantificational semantics. As a consequence, the temporal relation of succession that holds between the two eventualities in (30a) is implicated.

---

145. '[PPC$_{SP}$ and Indefinido] may only appear in the order PPC + PPS, (practically) never in the opposite order [...]. However, in sequences of this type, most of the time the same tense form is used.'

(30) PPC$_{SP}$ and inferred temporal relations (taken from Table 4.3)
   a. *Hoy me he levantado a las 7 y he desayunado en la cama.*
      I got up at 7:00 this morning and had breakfast in bed.
   b. *Hoy he desayunado en la cama y me he levantado a las 7.*
      Today I had breakfast in bed and got up at 7:00.

The assumption that the temporal succession of the two denoted past eventualities is not discourse-semantically encoded but pragmatically implicated is particularly supported by (30b). Switching the syntactic position of the two eventualities suggests a non-narrative, "enumerating" reading, which may read as an answer to "What have you done today?". Based on that enumerating character, it is likely to infer a chronology for (30b) that is reversed with respect to the syntactic presentation of the respective eventualities, i.e. a reading of getting up *before* having breakfast in bed.[146] Nevertheless, (30a) seems to be the more likely, the more convenient candidate to express the intended meaning for several factors. With reference to Dowty (1986) and Zwaan (1996), Dery (2012: 19f.) discusses the influence of the syntactic order of eventualities on their chronological interpretation under the label of the iconicity principle (IP). IP predicts that the default way of sorting a chronologically unordered set of eventualities relies on their syntax that is supposed to mirror their chronological order. In other words, if a speaker describes (or constructs) a situation of $e_1 \prec e_2$, then e_1 most likely also precedes e_2 syntactically, as exemplified in (30a). Similarly, this principle is spelled out in Grice's (1975) maxim of manner and its requirements to "avoid ambiguity" and, in particular, to "be orderly". Given the pragmatic nature though, a violation of IP does not result in a logical contradiction. The assumption that the two eventualities of getting up and having breakfast in bed in (30a) enter the discourse universe as an unordered instead of an ordered set instead set has been put forth in a similar way for the referential *Passé Composé* (PC) in French. As outlined in Chapter 2.5, the PC is commonly characterized as having diachronically reached stage IV which qualifies it to describe and express aoristic past eventualities. Moreover, PC felicitously combines with positional adverbials due to the presence of a location time that may be modified. However, de Swart (2007) still ascribes the PC a narrative *potential* (as opposed to a clearly narrative function). She alludes that "even this very liberal perfect construction is not an inherently narrative tense, because it maintains its orientation towards the speech time." (de Swart 2007: 2305). Yet,

---

146. The example might be confusing in the sense that it seems to be contradicting to get up, i.e. to leave the bed, in order to have breakfast in bed. However, such a reading is fine under an interpretation of getting up at t_1, preparing breakfast in the kitchen at t_2 and having breakfast in bed at t_3.

> [...] it is possible to tell a story in the Passé Composé, because the temporal structure of the discourse is determined by the rhetorical structure of the discourse, which in turn depends on the connectives, the lexical semantics of verbs and adverbs, and world knowledge about the 'natural' order of events [...].
>
> (de Swart 2007: 2284)

As a consequence,

> [...] any temporal relation can be established between two sentences in the Passé Composé: posteriority, overlap (simultaneity, inclusion), and temporal inversion.
>
> (de Swart 2007: 2290)

We conclude that the "set-like" combination of two instances of the quantificational PPC_{SP} may lead to several temporal relations that may be inferred by means of pragmatic reasoning, i.e. based on the verb semantics of e_1 and e_2, on likely rhetorical relations that may hold between the eventualities, as well as on world knowledge. In line with de Swart (2007), this assumption would also hold for a referential PPC_{SP}.

4.6.2 PPC_{SP} + *Indefinido*

In this subsection, we discuss three typical micro-structural discourse functions associated with the combination of a quantificational PPC_{SP} with an *Indefinido*. These are (i) actualization focus, (ii) perspectival shift and (iii) perspectival bridging. While (i) and (ii) are typically achieved by the combination with an existential PPC_{SP} reading, (iii) seems to represent a common discourse function of the universal PPC_{SP} reading. Furthermore, (i) exploits the contrast between a quantificational tense form (PPC_{SP}) and a referential tense form *(Indefinido)*, while (ii) and (iii) exploit the contrast between two contrastive perspective times lying in the present (PPC_{SP}) or the past time-sphere *(Indefinido)*.

Actualization Focus
In Section 2.4, we discussed the discourse function of actualization focus as typically arising from the combination of a quantificational tense form with a referential tense form. Applied to Spanish, the quantificational tense form PPC_{SP} existentially quantifies over (i.e. introduces) a discourse-new past eventuality. Next, the definite *Indefinido* referentially picks it up as discourse-old, i.e. as familiar. According to Declerck et al. (2006: 299), the speaker actualizes the event by "focussing on [...] the situation itself, by adding further information answering questions like "where?", "how?" and "when?", which is not the primary function of the quantificational PPC_{SP}.

(31) Actualization Focus
   a. *Es tal la frialdad entre ambos que, como presidentes, solo se <u>han reunido</u> una vez y <u>fue</u> en un país ajeno.*
      'Such is the coldness between the two that, as presidents, they have only met once, and that was in a foreign country.'[147]
   b. *El galés y el croata <u>han vivido</u> situaciones similares en los dos últimos agostos. Modric <u>estuvo</u> sin entrenarse con el Tottenham los meses de julio y agosto de 2012, con el fin de lograr ser transferido al Real Madrid.*
      'The Welshman and the Croatian have experienced similar situations in the last two August. Modric was without training with Tottenham in July and August 2012, in order to achieve a transfer to Real Madrid.'[148]

(31) exemplifies typical actualizing sequences achieved by the combination PPC$_{SP}$ and *Indefinido*. Metaphorically speaking, in (31a), the speaker first sets the stage by introducing the past eventuality of `los presidentes reunirse` to the discourse universe. Second, the speaker zooms in by providing further information about the just introduced eventuality, i.e. by elaborating that the meeting took place in a foreign country. The same applies to (31b), where `vivir situaciones similares` is introduced to the discourse by means of the PPC$_{SP}$ and then provided with detailed information by means of the *Indefinido*. In fact, the link between the two propositions reminds of the rhetorical relation of elaboration, as discussed by Moreno-Torres Sánchez (1999) (cf. Table 4.3). Following Jasinskaja and Karagjosova (2020), the elaboration relation may be defined as a relation holding

> […] between two discourse units where the second describes the same state of affairs as the first one (in different words) […]. Usually, […] the second description [is] more detailed and longer (e.g. Mann and Thompson (1988)) […].
> (Jasinskaja and Karagjosova 2020: 4)

However, assuming that PPC$_{SP}$ + *Indefinido* necessarily triggers an elaboration might be misleading. After all, definite reference to an entity, which was previously introduced by means of an indefinite form, must not necessarily express an elaboration relation. Evidence for that assumption is shown in (32).

(32) Indefinite vs. definite NP/tense form and rhetorical relations
   a. A man$_{INDEF}$ came into the room. Then, he$_{DEF}$ left.   (NARRATION)
   b. Some idiot has put$_{INDEF}$ diesel in the tank instead of petrol. The car broke$_{DEF}$ down.   (RESULT)

---

147. *El País* (07/25/18), https://elpais.com/internacional/2018/07/24/estados_unidos/1532393319_751954.html, 06/23/20.

148. *ABC* (08/31/13), http://abcblogs.abc.es/tiro-al-blanco/public/post/bale-y-modric-el-que-la-persigue-la-consigue-15763.asp/, 01/29/18.

In rhetorical structure theory, (32a) clearly exemplifies a narration relation ("a man came into the room ≺ he left"). In (32b), a result relation, that also implies temporal sequence, holds between the two propositions expressed by an indefinite Present Perfect ("has put") and a definite Simple Past ("broke"). In other words, the management of the information status of nominal and eventive discourse entities by means of indefinite and definite forms needs to be disentangled from rhetorical relations. However, the actualization focus actually oftentimes *does* correlate with the elaboration relation.

Turning back to the PPC$_{SP}$, we now may shed new light on an example discussed in Azpiazu Torres (2015: 347), where the actualization focus appears to hold between two passages within a larger piece of discourse (instead of between two single propositions).

(33) *Al menos 24 personas <u>han muerto</u> y más de 80 <u>han resultado</u> heridas este sábado por una explosión causada por una fuga de gas en la refinería de Amuay, una de las tres que conforman el Centro Refinador de Paraguaná (CRP), el más grande de Venezuela y uno de los más grandes del mundo, según <u>han informado</u> fuentes oficiales. Stella Lugo, gobernadora de Falcón, Estado del noroeste del país en el que se encuentra la refinería, <u>declaró</u> que entre las víctimas mortales se halla un niño de 10 años. La gobernadora <u>indicó</u> que pese a que el incendio persiste, "la situación está controlada". "La gente presumía que era un terremoto", <u>relató</u> Lugo. El vicepresidente Elías Jaua <u>declaró</u> que la mayoría de los muertos son efectivos de la Guardia Nacional, según informa la cadena de televisión Globovisión. Jaua <u>resaltó</u> que se vio afectado el Destacamento de la Guardia Nacional, que se encontraba en el lugar para custodiar la refinería y que la onda expansiva afectó a varias comunidades.*[149]

'At least 24 people have been killed and more than 80 injured this Saturday by an explosion caused by a gas leak at the Amuay refinery, one of the three that make up the Paraguaná Refining Center (CRP), the largest in Venezuela and one of the largest in the world, official sources said. Stella Lugo, the governor of Falcón, the northwestern state where the refinery is located, said a 10-year-old boy was among the fatalities. The governor said that although the fire persists, "the situation is under control. "The people presumed it was an earthquake," Lugo said. Vice President Elías Jaua said most of the dead are National Guard troops, according to Globovisión. Jaua said the National Guard Detachment, which was on the scene to guarding the refinery and that the shock wave affected several communities.'

---

[149]. Cited in Azpiazu Torres 2015 as: *El País* (08/25/12), http://internacional.elpais.com/internacional/2012/08/25.

Azpiazu Torres (2015) explains the sequential order of the first part containing the PPC$_{SP}$ and the second part containing the *Indefinido*, which she assumes to typically occur in the language of the press, based on a "first voice" (PPC$_{SP}$) of the article who seeks to catch the reader's attention, and, on the other hand, a second voice (*Indefinido*), a "less sonorous but more fluid" voice. We agree with Azpiazu Torres's (2015) intuition. However, we assume that the impressionistic notions of the "first" and "second voice" can be motivated in a more consistent fashion by tracing them back to the opposition of quantificational vs. referential tense and their actualizing discursive interplay. Accordingly, the first part of the passage, that exclusively consists of the PPC$_{SP}$, sets the stage by introducing indefinite events to the discourse. At some point, the *Indefinido* "takes over" signaling that the events under discussion are now discourse-old, i.e. familiar. Accordingly, further details are added. In this vein, we assume that the (rather subjective) impression of a first ("more sonorous") and a second ("less sonorous") voice is an effect set off by the indefinite-definite contrast.

Perspectival shift
The perspectival shift refers to the discourse function of indicating a change of perspective from the past time-sphere towards the present time-sphere or vice-versa. While the *Indefinido* qualifies to perspectivize the former, the PPC$_{SP}$ perspectivizes the latter per default. The perspectival shift as indicated by the combination of an *Indefinido* and the PPC$_{SP}$ is exemplified in (34a) and illustrated in Figure 4.5.

(34) a. *EL PAÍS <u>ha tenido</u> acceso a decenas de documentos y grabaciones con los detalles de los 12 días que <u>duró</u> aquel plan médico caótico y a todas luces insuficiente que <u>fue</u> el pilar básico de la "medicalización" de las residencias madrileñas.*
'EL PAÍS has had access to dozens of documents and recordings with the details of the 12 days that that chaotic and clearly insufficient medical plan lasted, which was the basic pillar of the "medicalization" of the residences in Madrid.'[150]
b. *Desde que <u>empezamos</u> la campaña, <u>hemos cuadriplicado</u> el tráfico en nuestra página de Internet.*
'Since we started the campaign, we have quadrupled the traffic on our website.'[151]

---

150. https://elpais.com/espana/madrid/2020-06-21/los-12-dias-de-la-operacion-bicho-el-fiasco-del-plan-de-la-comunidad-de-madrid-para-salvar-las-residencias.html, 06/22/2020.
151. Example taken from Henderson (2005: 5).

In (34a), the interplay of the PPC$_{SP}$ and the *Indefinido* is exploited in order to create a two-dimensional perspectival structure. First, the present time-sphere sets the stage for discussing the journalistic investigations that took place (the access to the documents and recordings), next, the perspective time gets shifted towards the past time-sphere that accommodates the past eventualities under discussion. Effectively, there is a split between (i) the object (the "chaotic medical plan"), which is temporally located and perspectivized in the past time-sphere and (ii) the discussion of the object on a metalevel, which is perspectivized in the present time-sphere. Figure 4.5 illustrates how this perspectival shift might be conceived of on a timeline.

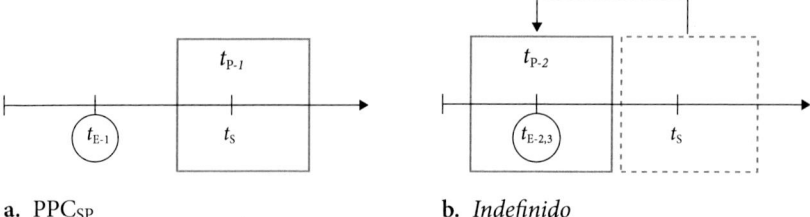

a. PPC$_{SP}$ b. *Indefinido*

Figure 4.5 Perspectival shift in Example (34a)
t_{P-1}: present time-sphere; t_{P-2}: past time-sphere; t_{E-1}: *ha tenido acceso a decenas de documentos*; t_{E-2}: *duró 12 días*; t_{E-3}: *fue el pilar básico*.

The concept of a perspectival shift between the two time-spheres also applies to (34b), where the order of the two tense forms is reversed. Here, the perspective time is shifted away from the past time-sphere *(empezamos la campaña)* to the present time-sphere *(hemos cuadriplicado el tráfico)*.

Perspectival bridging
While the perspectival shift as discussed above functions as contrasting the two time-spheres, we assume perspectival bridging to "melt" the two by creating a smooth transition, as exemplified in (35). We assume the function of perspectival bridging to be particularly associated with the PPC$_{SP-UNI}$ due to its property of denoting t_E to abut t_S.

(35) PPC$_{SP-UNI}$ as a perspectival bridge between the past and present time-sphere
    a. *Esta mañana me <u>levanté</u> a las 7. Durante todo del día <u>he trabajado</u> en casa.*
       'I got up at 7 this morning. I've been working at home all day.'[152]
    b. *[…] el martes 31 de marzo se <u>detectó</u> el pico de la pandemia con 9.222 positivos […]. Desde entonces, <u>ha ido bajando</u> progresivamente hasta llegar a los 3.045 de hoy. De esta manera, la cifra de nuevos positivos se <u>aproxima</u> a la de nuevos curados […].*

---

152. Example taken from Moreno-Torres Sánchez (1999), cf. Table 4.3.

'On Tuesday, March 31st, the peak of the pandemic was detected with 9,222 positives. Since then, it has progressively declined to 3,045 today. This brings the number of new positives close to the number of new cases cured.'[153]

In (35a), the *Indefinido* denotes a past eventuality whose temporal location marks the beginning of a universal quantification that reaches into the present time-sphere and abuts the speech time. In (35b), the bridging is even more explicit due to the Present Tense that follows the bridging PPC$_{SP\text{-}UNI}$. Perspectival bridging may be used as means to establish particularly explicit transitions between the time-spheres. Figure 4.6 illustrates the discourse function of perspectival bridging associated with the PPC$_{SP\text{-}UNI}$.

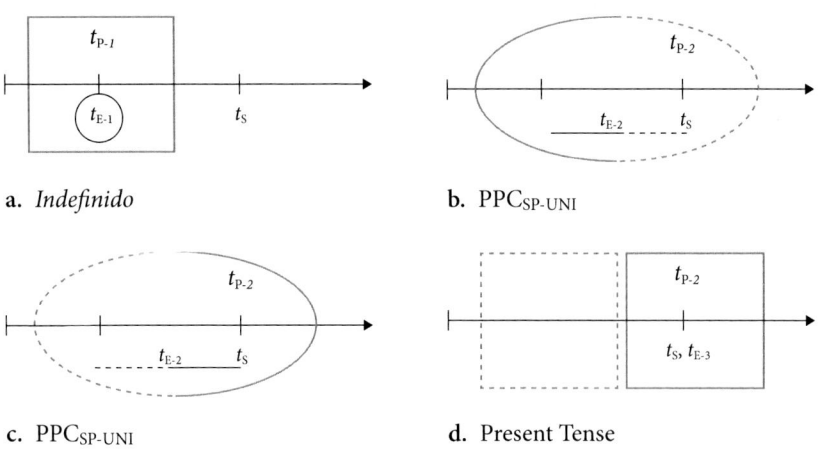

a. *Indefinido*   b. PPC$_{SP\text{-}UNI}$

c. PPC$_{SP\text{-}UNI}$ d. Present Tense

Figure 4.6 Perspectival bridging in Example (35b)
$t_{P\text{-}1}$: past time-sphere; $t_{P\text{-}2}$: present time-sphere; $t_{E\text{-}1}$: *detectó el pico de la pandemia*; $t_{E\text{-}2}$: *ha ido bajando progresivamente desde entonces*; $t_{E\text{-}3}$: *la cifra de nuevos positivos se aproxima la de nuevos curados*.

4.6.3 PPC$_{SP}$ + *Pluscuamperfecto/Imperfecto*

In this subsection, we discuss the potential of the PPC$_{SP}$ to combine with an *Imperfecto* and a *Pluscuamperfecto*. While the quantificational PPC$_{SP}$ is predicted to cause a perspectival clash, the semantics of the referential PPC$_{SP}$ might allow for these combinations. This suggests that PPC$_{SP}$ + *Imperfecto/Pluscuamperfecto* may serve as a test case concerning the status of the PPC$_{SP\text{-}REF}$ (cf. Chapter 6).

---

153. *ABC* (04/15/20), https://www.abc.es/sociedad/abci-espana-pais-mas-fallecidos-coronavirus-relacion-numero-habitantes-202004141440_noticia.html, 06/22/20.

Quantificational PPC$_{SP}$ clashing with Pluscuamperfecto/Imperfecto
The quantificational PPC$_{SP}$'s orientation towards the speech time causes a perspectival clash in examples where a *Pluscuamperfecto* or an *Imperfecto* presupposes a perspective time lying in the past time-sphere, as illustrated in (36).

(36) PPC$_{SP}$ + *Pluscuamperfecto*: perspectival clash
Cuando [llegó/ *ha llegado] Maria, los invitados ya se habían ido.
'When Maria arrived, the guests had already left.'[154]

The *Pluscuamperfecto* presupposes a reference point in the past that it gets relatively interpreted to (cf. e.g. Meisnitzer 2015: 80, Haßler 2016: 88, Becker 2020b). That is, the *Pluscuamperfecto* requires that the past time-sphere is perspectivized such that t_E retrieves an interpretation relative to another past eventuality. However, this contradicts the PPC$_{SP}$'s property to generally set its t_P to be included in the present time-sphere. Accordingly, as put forth by Carrasco Gutiéirrez (2008), combining a PPC$_{SP}$ with a *Pluscuamperfecto* most likely leads to a perspectival clash, as illustrated in Figure 4.7.

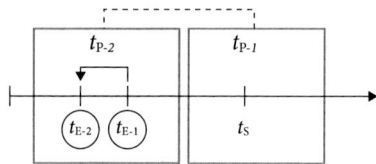

Figure 4.7 Perspectival clash in Example (36)
t_{P-1} : present time-sphere; t_{P-2}: past time-sphere; t_{E-1}: *Maria ha llegado*; t_{E-2}: *los invitados se habían ido*.

On the other hand, the *Indefinido (llegó)*, supported by *cuando*, sets its t_P to be included in the past time-sphere, which enables the anchoring of the Past Perfect's perspective time t_P. In other words, the Past Perfect gets interpreted relatively to a time in the past provided by *cuando* + *llegó*. There should be the same effect with combinations with an *Imperfecto*, as illustrated in (37), a modified version of (36).

(37) ?Cuando ha llegado Maria, Juan le contaba todo.
when has arrived Maria Juan her told everything
'When Mary arrived, John was telling her everything.'

The *Imperfecto* is commonly described as "an anaphoric tense that systematically requires some kind of discourse antecedent to be licensed (in contrast with the autonomous nature of other tenses like […] pretérito indefinido […]" (Leonetti

---

154. Example taken from Carrasco Gutiéirrez (2008: 26), translation added.

2018: 392, cf. also Becker 2010a: 80).[155] Moreover, the *Imperfecto* is typically described as perspectivizing an event's inside, as "a stativizer device that instructs the hearer to view a past situation from inside" (Leonetti (2018: 405). Again, this contradicts the quantificational PPC$_{SP}$, whose perspective time is disjoined from the event time such that there is a perspectival clash of $t_E \prec t_S$, t_P (PPC$_{SP}$) vs. t_E, $t_P \prec t_S$ (*Imperfecto*).

Referential PPC$_{SP}$ anchoring Imperfecto/Pluscuamperfecto?
Assuming a referential PPC$_{SP}$ as discussed in Section 4.4, the anchoring of an *Imperfecto* or a *Pluscuamperfecto* might be semantically possible. Although the PPC$_{SP-REF}$ continues to set its perspective time in the present time-sphere – which, again, should cause perspectival clashes with tense forms that perspectivize the past time-sphere – the promotion of the event domain triggered by the inclusion of a location time t_{LOC} and the related potential to provide the discourse reference time t_R for adjacent tense forms might improve the overall acceptability. In fact, there is data suggesting that the PPC$_{SP}$ actually may function as such an anchor in discourse:

(38) PPC$_{SP}$ + *Imperfecto*
 a. *Esta mañana cuando he salido al jardín Gladys me ha llamado, como anoche. Ya estaba fuera, esperándome.*
  'This morning when I went out to the garden Gladys called me, like last night. She was already outside, waiting for me.'[156]
 b. *Hoy he hecho las fotos de imagen para QBO27 y tras el estudio, nos hemos ido al campo a por su entorno y la bonita luz! Hacía frío, pero teníamos lana a raudales!*
  'Today I took the image photos for QBO27 and after the studio, we went to the country for its environment and the beautiful light! It was cold, but we had plenty of wool!'[157]
 c. *Hoy he vuelto al cole. Cuando he salido de casa estaba nevando, lo que me ha facilitado el camino* […].
  'I went back to school today. When I left the house, it was snowing, which made my way easier.'[158]

---

155. However, Leonetti (2018) argues that continuous and habitual readings (in contrast to stage-level-state readings, progressive readings and narrative readings) do not require an anteceding reference point. For these cases, Leonetti assumes that the *Imperfecto*'s retrieval of an implicit antecedent is not of anaphoric nature.

156. Example taken from Laca (2008: 6). Cited by Laca as "REAL ACADEMIA ESPAÑOLA: Banco de datos (CREA) [en línea]. Corpus de referencia del español actual. http://www.rae.es [IX-2008]".

157. Official facebook post by a professional photographer (02/20/18), https://pt-br.facebook.com/gusgeijo/photos/hoy-he-hecho-las-fotos-de-imagen-para-qbo27-y-tras-el-estudio-nos-hemos-ido-al-c/1576144725826492/, 06/24/20.

158. *Lorezingarita* (Blog, 02/23/09), https://lorezingarita.wordpress.com/nesna/, 06/24/20.

In each of these examples, a PPC$_{SP}$ anchors an *Imperfecto* that anaphorically picks up a discursively provided reference time and perspectivizes a past eventuality expressed by a PPC$_{SP}$ from its inside. In other words, the PPC$_{SP}$ functions as a temporal cataphora. For example, in (38a), t_E *estaba fuera* gets referentially assigned to a location time provided by *cuando he salido*.

The cataphoric potential as evidence for the PPC$_{SP-REF}$?
As already pointed out, the examples listed in (38) still face the theoretical problem of a perspectival clash (perpspectivized past vs. present time-sphere). Still, the PPC$_{SP-REF}$'s inclusion of a location time and the related promotion of the event domain might be the critical factor that might enable cataphoric uses. Thus, one might derive that the PPC$_{SP}$'s discursive potential to cataphorically anchor a succeeding *Imperfecto* might serve as a discursive test case to determine the status of the referential PPC$_{SP}$ in a given variety. In particular, this discourse-based approach would represent a meaningful extension of the standard approach of testing the PPC$_{SP}$'s potential of combining with particular adverbials. After all, testing for adverbials might be problematic due to scope ambiguities as discussed in Section 4.5. We thus conclude that there is a link between the potential of phoricity and the question of whether the PPC$_{SP}$ already disposes of a referential reading (in a given variety). In Chapter 6, we develop, discuss and test this discourse-based approach to the PPC$_{SP}$'s referential drift in detail within a prominence-based theory.

4.6.4 The macro-structure of discourse

Based on the observations concerning the PPC$_{SP}$ and its functions on the micro-level of discourse discussed in the previous subsections, we may derive the following general assumptions with regard to the modes of discourse. Generally, the quantificational PPC$_{SP}$ does not qualify to be employed in narrative discourse (39). It has to be kept in mind though that the notion of narration as a discourse mode has to be distinguished from narration as a rhetorical relation, which, in fact, may be established between two instances of the PPC$_{SP}$ (cf. Table 4.3).

(39) Narration ✗
 a. **Ayer, he ido al centro y he visto que había una fiesta.*
  'Yesterday I went downtown and saw that here was a party.'
 b. *?Hoy, he ido al centro y he visto que había una fiesta.*
  'Today I went downtown and saw that there was a party.'

Furthermore, the incompatibility of the PPC$_{SP}$ with the narrative discourse mode does not impede a PPC$_{SP}$ from appearing in a narrative text. It may e.g. occur in indirect speech, embedded in another mode of discourse. As outlined in Chapter 2.4, there may be shifts from one mode to another even within allegedly homogeneous passages. The (potential) referential PPC$_{SP}$ on the other hand, may appear in the narration mode and might allow for a relative anchoring of several denoted past eventualities with respect to each other, as well as the inclusion of a backgrounded *Imperfecto*, as indicated in (39b), a typical property of narrative passages.

The description mode is blocked due to its static nature. Though located in time, it blocks temporal advancement in favor of a "spatial advancement through the scene or object". In this vein, both the PPC$_{SP-UNI}$ and PPC$_{SP-EX}$ in (40) are infelicitous under a purely descriptive reading. However, the example might be accommodated by a shift to the mode of information that, in turn, allows for the use of the PPC$_{SP}$ (cf. below).

(40) Description ✗
*Vivimos en una casa maravillosa: La cocina es nueva, hay mucho espacio en el balcón y [el jardín ha sido verde últimamente / y la piscina ha sido barata].
'We live in a wonderful house: The kitchen is new, there is a lot of space on the balcony and the garden has been green.'

The modes of information (41a), argument (41b) and report (41c) enable the use of the PPC$_{SP}$. While the information mode primarily denotes facts, propositions and general statives, the argument mode mainly denotes general statives. Both are particularly adequate environments due to the PPC$_{SP}$'s denotation of indefinite past eventualities relatively anchored to the speech time. The same holds for the report mode, which is defined as denoting primarily events, states and general statives that may be dynamically located in time.

(41) a. Information ✓
Cuando hasta los niños desayunaban vino: cómo ha cambiado nuestra relacioín con el alcohol.
'When even the children were having wine for breakfast: how our relationship with alcohol has changed.'[159]

b. Argument ✓
Mi respuesta sería inequívocamente sí. Sobretodo porque han hecho pensar que no todos los productos financieros son para todas las personas.
'My answer would be unequivocally yes. Especially since they have made us think that not all financial products are for everyone.'[160]

---

[159]. El *País* (07/20/20), https://verne.elpais.com/verne/2020/06/16/articulo/1592315341_911723.html, 07/20/20.

[160]. *Las Provincias* (Blog, 11/09/11), https://blogs.lasprovincias.es/nimioeconomia/2011/11/09/que-riesgo-tienen-los-bonos-patrioticos-de-la-comunitat-hay-que-invertir/, 07/20/20.

c. Report ✓
Hoy, he ido al centro.
'Today I went downtown.'

In sum, the most crucial distinction to be drawn with respect to the modes of discourse in the context of the study of the discourse functions of the PPC$_{SP}$ pertains to the division of the narrative mode vs. the non-narrative modes. After all, this opposition seems to directly interact with the PPC$_{SP}$'s potential to sequentialize, foreground and background past eventualities with respect to each other, as well as with their phoric potential.

In Chapter 5, we test if the assumptions concerning the discourse functions of the PPC$_{SP}$ discussed in the present section are compatible with new data.

4.7 Conclusion

In this chapter, we presented a detailed account of the PPC$_{SP}$ based on our framework developed in Chapter 2.

The quantificational PPC$_{SP}$

The most crucial insight from a theoretical and cross-linguistic perspective is expressed in the observation that the PPC$_{SP}$ widely follows the default quantificational semantics of the PP: the PPC$_{SP}$ mostly denotes indefinite past eventualities with current relevance while it does not take a location time t_{LOC} as an argument. We labelled this default configuration the quantificational PPC$_{SP}$. As opposed to referential tense forms, the quantificational PPC$_{SP}$ introduces a past eventuality to the discourse universe, i.e. it quantifies over t_E, but does not refer to it. Accordingly, the PPC$_{SP}$ focusses the perspective time t_P that is set as being included in the present time-sphere. We further analyzed the range of interpretations that the PPC$_{SP}$'s quantificational semantics give rise to: existential readings denote its t_E to precede t_S, as expressed by the resultative, experiential and hot news reading, whereas the universal (continuative) reading denote its t_E to abut t_S, which creates a "state-like" interpretation.

With regard to potential combinations with tempo-aspectual adverbials, the quantificational PPC$_{SP}$ typically combines with quantificational, durative and XN-adverbials while blocking positional adverbials. Furthermore, the hodiernality effect, that excludes prehodiernal adverbials but allows for hodiernal adverbials, may be accounted for assuming that hodiernal adverbials function as XN-adverbials (instead of as positional adverbials). This scope ambiguity motivates the hodiernal boundary, as XN-adverbials need to be compatible with the present time-sphere,

Chapter 4. The Spanish *Pretérito Perfecto Compuesto* 155

a condition that is not fulfilled by prehodiernal adverbials. Nevertheless, as discussed in Section 4.4, some so-called "hodiernal-perfective" uses may also call for an analysis according to which the PPC$_{SP}$ already disposes of a referential configuration. In this scenario, it would remain to be motivated where the temporal restriction to the hodiernal time-sphere actually stems from.

Concerning the level of discourse, we first zoomed in on the micro-structure by investigating typical discursive functions established by the interplay of the PPC$_{SP}$ with adjacent tense forms. We discussed the following combinations.

With regard to PPC$_{SP}$ + PPC$_{SP}$, we argued for a "set-like" reading, i.e. an enumeration of past eventualities that do not denote a specific chronological order. However, pragmatic inferences allow for ordering the eventualities, e.g. based on world knowledge or on the iconicity principle suggesting a parallel structure of the syntactic order and the actual temporal order. Combined with an *Indefinido*, we discussed the actualization focus as exploiting the contrastive discourse functions of the (i) quantificational (indefinite) PPC$_{SP}$ and (ii) the referential (definite) *Indefinido*: while the PPC$_{SP}$ introduces an indefinite eventuality, the *Indefinido* elaborates on the event by adding further details.

Additionally, we discussed the function of perspectival shifting based on a perspectival contrast between the PPC$_{SP}$ (t$_P$ incuded in the present time-sphere) and the *Indefinido* (t$_P$ included in the past time-sphere). This function helps establish two perspectival levels that are discussed, e.g. a level that is concerned with what actually happened in the past, and, on the other hand, a level anchored in the present time-sphere, where the past gets discussed and evaluated.

The third function of perspectival bridging is particularly associated with the universal reading. It conjoins a perspective time lying in the past time-sphere (*Indefinido*) with a perspective time lying in the present time-sphere in order to create a coherent transition between the two time-spheres in an explicit fashion.

In comparison to the Portuguese PPC$_{PT}$ as discussed in the previous chapter, it is noticeable that the PPC$_{PT}$ and the quantificational PPC$_{SP}$ do hardly differ with respect to their macro-structural discourse potential despite their radically different readings. We consider that this observation once again emphasizes their common root of bearing quantificational temporal semantics that causes their similar deployment on the macrostructural level of discourse.

The referential PPC$_{SP}$ and the referential drift

In addition to the quantificational PPC$_{SP}$, we discussed the (potential) referential PPC$_{SP}$. According to standard diachronic theories (cf. Chapter 2.5), the referential PPC$_{SP}$ is expected to be available at some point. According to our framework, the most crucial update brought by the referential drift is expressed in the inclusion of a location time t_{LOC} and the related potential of introducing a discourse reference time t_R. Based on this semantic sketch, some of the assumptions for the quantificational PPC_{SP} do not apply to the referential PPC_{SP}. Most crucially, the $PPC_{SP\text{-}REF}$'s inclusion of a location time does allow for combining with positional adverbials. Thus, under a referential reading, adverbials like *hoy* ('today') or *esta mañana* ('this morning') are no longer ambiguous between functioning as positional or XN-adverbials, i.e. between scoping over t_{LOC} or t_P, in favor of an interpretation as positional adverbials. In this vein, readings that are commonly labelled as "hodiernal perfective" readings, might be best accounted for as diachronically fulfilling a transitional function bridging between the quantificational and the referential PPC_{SP} readings as they seem to be compatible with both. In fact, we concluded that this very ambiguity makes it plausible to assume that the referential drift is a highly gradual process that gets triggered by a reinterpretation of the quantificational reading as a referential reading.

Concerning the level of discourse, we discussed the $PPC_{SP\text{-}REF}$'s potential of cataphorically anchoring a succeeding anaphoric *Imperfecto* or *Pluscuamperfecto*. These combinations are predicted to be odd with a quantificational PPC_{SP}, but might be fine with a referential PPC_{SP} (in spite of a remaining perspectival clash). We derived that the potential cataphoric function of the PPC_{SP} may represent a new discursive test case for the question of whether the PPC_{SP} already disposes of referential semantics in a given variety. In this vein, the discussed discursive approach may add a new perspective to the study of the referential drift. After all, it does not run the risk of being corrupted by the scope ambiguities related to the adverbial domain. We concluded to move the detailed discussion of the referential PPC_{SP} to Chapter 6.

Having exposed our account of the Portuguese PPC_{PT} and the Spanish PPC_{SP} in the previous and the present chapters in detail, we proceed by presenting a corpus study that we have performed to test if our assumptions apply to new data.

CHAPTER 5

Corpus study

In this chapter, we present a corpus study of the Portuguese PPC$_{PT}$ and the Spanish PPC$_{SP}$. The goal is to examine if the assumptions and hypotheses of our framework discussed in the previous chapters prove as empirically valid when applied to new data. The chapter is structured as follows.

Section 5.1 introduces the composition of the corpus, which was manually gathered based on subtitles of movies and series regarding the Spanish data, as well as transcripts of a political talk show and political speeches regarding the Portuguese data. Besides motivating this approach, which especially concerns variational factors that need to be taken into account in the analysis of the Portuguese PPC$_{PT}$, the section discusses the methods used for computational analyses of the data.

Section 5.2 presents the analysis concerning combinations of the PPC with tempo-aspectual adverbials. This endeavour is mainly guided by the questions of (i) how frequently the PPC is adverbially modified and (ii) which distribution of positional, durative, XN and quantificational adverbials we can find in the data. The results for the second question widely match our framework which predicts a dominance of quantificational and XN-adverbials. Strikingly though, the data suggest for both languages that the PPC does not receive adverbial modification in the overwhelming majority of the cases. Furthermore, many of the attested adverbials are ambiguous in terms of their scope. We derive to keep the assumption that adverbials may represent a problematic test case for an analysis of the discursive potential of the PPC. In particular, that means that the status of the referential PPC$_{SP}$ should not be discussed based on combinations with (potential) positional adverbials alone. Instead, combinations with adjacent tense forms may provide evidence.

Section 5.3 presents a qualitative exploration of the data concerning combinations of the PPC with tense forms present in the cotext. In line with our framework, the data suggest that there are differences in how the PPC$_{PT}$ and PPC$_{SP}$ are (mostly) employed in discourse: in the analyzed data, the characterizing PPC$_{PT}$ mainly functions as a rhetorical means exploiting the interplay between episodicity and genericity in order to gain argumentative power in planned, elaborated language of distance. On the other hand, the Spanish PPC$_{SP}$ mainly functions as a means to shape the discursively managed perspectival and event-referential structure. Furthermore, the data suggest that the episodic readings of the Portuguese PPC$_{PT}$ assume discourse functions that overlap with the PPC$_{SP}$'s. From a cross-linguistic perspective, this suggests that their discourse functions are more similar than it might be expected.

Concerning the referential PPC$_{SP}$, the qualitative data exploration reveals very few examples that may be argued to actually depict referential readings featuring an anaphorical attribution of t_E to a location time t_{LOC}. However, there are examples that show that the PPC$_{SP}$ may function as a cataphoric anchor of an *Imperfecto*. This observation suggests that the PPC$_{SP}$ synchronically may dispose of readings that have already passed a first step in the transition from a purely quantificational to a referential reading. We conclude to investigate the cataphoric potential of the PPC$_{SP}$ in detail in Chapter 6, hypothesizing that it assumes a transitional function mediating between quantification and reference.

5.1 Introduction

5.1.1 Composition of the corpus

For the purpose of the study, we manually constructed a corpus containing data from Brazilian Portuguese and Peninsular Spanish.

The Spanish corpus
The Spanish subcorpus consists of subtitles of the Netflix series *La Casa de Papel* (Season 1), a heist crime drama (2017) and *Élite* (Season 1), a thriller teen drama (2018), as well as of the movie *El Bar*, a black comedy thriller (2017). Each of these series/movies was created by Spanish screenwriters, which suggests that the data represent what might be considered the conventionalized standard with respect to the use of the PPC$_{SP}$ in Peninsular Spanish.[161] The subtitles mainly consist of spontaneous dialogues that involve a high amount of turn taking, i.e. spoken language featuring a highly dynamic management of the common ground, as well as many discourse moves related to the introduction and discussion of eventive discourse entities (i.e. eventualities). Furthermore, they provide a glance into the question of how the perspectival structure is dynamically managed in discourse, as many shifts between the present- and the past time-sphere are to be expected. Although scripted dialogues do not represent real spontaneous speech, they are supposed to be an authentic imitation, which qualifies them as a valuable source of evidence, at least for the purposes of our study. While research concerning e.g. phonological or lexical variation might, in fact, be corrupted by the artificiality of scripted dialogues,

---

161. *La Casa de Papel* was created by Álex Pina, *Élite* created by Carlos Montero and Darió Madrona, *El Bar* written by Jorge Guerricaechevarría and Álex de la Iglesia.

we consider the data to be appropriate for the study of subtle discursive mechanisms underlying the choice of tense forms. From a methodological perspective, subtitles technically provide very tidy data in the sense that their formal shape is predestinated for computational analysis, as there are no spelling or typing errors and almost no stop words or fillers that might distract the automatic extraction of relevant data points. Last but not least, an analysis of the use of the PPC_{SP} in movie and series subtitles has not yet been carried out to our knowledge. A detailed overview of the composition of the Spanish corpus is illustrated in Figure 5.1. The data show a PPC_{SP} density of 1,234 per 103,361 tokens (11.94/1000 tokens). Strikingly, the PPC_{SP} ratios are almost identical across the three sources.

Table 5.1 The Peninsular Spanish Corpus

	Source	Tokens	PPC	/1000
Movie/Series	Total	103,361	1,234	11.94
	La Casa de Papel, Season 1	54,264	676	12.46
	El Bar	10,168	121	11.90
	Élite, Season 1	38,929	437	11.23

The Portuguese corpus
Concerning the Portuguese PPC_{PT}, we decided to exclusively concentrate on Brazilian data. As discussed in Section 3.2, we adhere to the working hypothesis that the PPC_{PT} is based on the same semantics in both Brazilian and European Portuguese. Different frequencies in European and Brazilian corpora should not arise from different semantics and meaning effects but might suggest stylistic variation, which, together with further potential factors, lies beyond the scope of the present study. The pursued discursive approach to general strategies of how the PPC_{PT} is employed in discourse does not take into account inner-Brazilian variation either, such as discussed in Cabredo Hofherr et al.'s (2010) study of a northeastern Brazilian dialect (cf. Section 3.2). Since the Brazilian PPC_{PT} has been characterized as being marked as pertaining to a rather formal and literary style of language (cf. Becker 2022: 67), we decided not to create a parallel corpus with regard to the Spanish part. The goal to create a perfectly comparative corpus was thus outweighed by the need of data representing those communicative situations that the PPC_{PT} most naturally occurs in. This procedure, on the one hand, avoids a methodological problem concerning the critical number of observations needed for deriving reliable results and inferences, as it has to be kept in mind that the PPC_{PT} is generally rarely used. In addition, our semantic account of the PPC_{PT} presented in Chapter 3 supports a genre-specific selection of the data. As discussed, we expect the shaping of the rhetorical structure of an argument to be a discourse function of the PPC_{PT}, which is derived from its role as a sophisticated rhetorical means that

evolves its impact in argumentative discourse (discourse mode of argumentation). In particular, it is the characterizing reading that we expect to predominantly operate on an argumentative level by adding elaborated rhetorical support for episodic or generic propositions. This suggests focussing on data that are more likely to include passages representing the argumentation mode, combined with the tendency of well-planned and elaborated contributions containing a (rather) dense flow of information. In the tradition of Koch and Oesterreicher's (1985) account of linguistic variation, these properties may be subsumed under the term of language of distance, that seems to be a factor promoting the use of the PPC$_{PT}$. In the corresponding model, language of immediacy and language of distance constitute two basic pillars that form a scale, each representing communicative situations that are supposed to impose typical linguistic properties. The authors characterize language of distance as tending to feature a spatiotemporal separation between speaker and hearer (e.g. in a monologue), further as a public speech or text that aims at being objective, lacking affective and expressive speech in favor of a planned and elaborated contribution with a dense flow of information. While language of immediacy is conceived of as conceptually oral although it may be written text, language of distance is conceived of as conceptually written language although it may be spoken text. Applying these concepts to competing zones, a particular linguistic variant may be favored by particular communicative situations. For example, on the level of morphosyntactic variation, the Portuguese *mesóclise* in *amar-te-ei* ('I will love you') is commonly analyzed as being restricted to formal and written language (cf. e.g. Ilari and Basso 2008: 172), while the unmarked *te amarei/amarei-te* ('I will love you') does not underly such a restriction. Turning back to the study of the PPC$_{PT}$ and the composition of our corpus, language of distance obviously represents a good candidate for rather formal, perhaps even literary language that, crucially, seems to be preferred by the PPC$_{PT}$ (cf. Becker 2022: 67), as well as for rhetorically sophisticated argumentative discourse (cf. Chapter 3). This obviously contrasts with the Spanish corpus, which is composed of series and movies that prevailingly consist of dialogues of language of immediacy. In line with these considerations, as well as in order to verify that the PPC$_{PT}$ disprefers communicative situations of language of immediacy, Table 5.2 shows a query performed on two Brazilian Netflix series (3%, Season 1, *O Mecanismo*, Season 1) and a Brazilian movie (*Cidade de Deus*), i.e. on a corpus constructed in parallel fashion with respect to the Spanish corpus. The shown frequencies turn out to be too poor for the purposes of our study, indeed, with only 13 occurrences per 67,093 tokens (0.19 per 1,000 tokens). Even adding 100,000 tokens to the corpus would amount to a meager output of approximately 26 PPC$_{PT}$ data points, a way too small number to derive reliable results. Movies and series thus seem to pertain to a genre that predominantly consists of communicative situations that do not provide a quite natural discursive environment for the PPC$_{PT}$.

Table 5.2 Poor PPC_PT frequencies in Brazilian series/movies

Subcorpus	Source	Tokens	PPC	/1000
Movie/Series	total	67,093	13	0.19
	3%, Season 1	26,939	4	0.15
	Cidade de Deus	12,414	3	0.24
	O Mecanismo, Season 1	27,740	6	0.22

Instead, we gathered transcripts of the Brazilian TV show *Roda Viva* for the Portuguese corpus, i.e. oral data that may be characterized as conceptually written (language of distance). *Roda Viva* is a show where

> [...] political leaders, writers, philosophers, artists, and notable people [are] interviewed. [...] Roda Viva features a host presenter, who serves as a mediator, and several journalists from news outlets. In the program the guest sits on a swivel chair in the middle of a circle of journalists, who are in a higher position. The interviewed person turns to answer the journalist asking the question.
> (https://en.wikipedia.org/wiki/Roda_Viva, 08/03/20)

Transcripts of the show have been published by the project *Memória Roda Viva*, an initative by of the *Fundação Padre Anchieta*, the *Fundação de Apoio à Pesquisa do Estado de São Paulo (Fapesp)* and the *Universidade Estadual de Campinas (Unicamp)*, providing open-access to transcripts from 1986 until today for scientific research. Our subcorpus *Roda Viva* includes 49 transcribed episodes that were picked by the name of the guest following an alphabetical order (A-E) and that were broadcasted between 2000 and 2009.[162]

Additionally, we gathered political speeches given by Jair Bolsonaro (24 speeches given in 2019), Dilma Rousseff (12 speeches given in 2011, 2014, 2015), Lula da

---

162. The transcripts were retrieved from https://rodaviva.fapesp.br/entrevistas/1 (accessed 06/08/22). Our corpus includes the following 49 interviews: Aécio Neves (2005), Alberto Goldman (2005), Alexandre de Moraes (2005), Alfredo Bosi (2002), Aloisio Mercadante (2002), Amyr Klink (2000), Anthony Garotinho (2006), Antônio Carlos Biscaia (2006), Antonio Carlos G. Costa (2000), Antonio Carlos Valente (2007), Antonio Nóbrega (2004), Arany Santana (2004), Armênio Guedes (2008), Armínio Fraga (2002), Arnaldo Cohen (2000), Arnaldo Jabor (2005), Benedita da Silva (2002), Benjamin Steinbruch (2005), Bernardinho (2007), Bolivar Lamounier (2005), Cacá Diegues (2005), Caio Luiz de Carvalho (2001), Carlos Artur Nuzman (2003), Carlos Guilherme Mota (2000), Carlos Lyra (2008), Carlos Minc (2008), Carlos Saldanha (2006), Carlos Velloso (2005), Celso Amorim (2008), César Maia (2005), Ciro Gomes (2005), Claudio Abramo (2004), Claudio Fonteles (2004), Claudio Humes (2005), Claudio Lembo (2006), Cristovam Buarque (2006), D. João de Orleans e Bragança (2008), D. Tomas Balduino (2005), Daniel Filho (2001), Danilo Miranda (2006), Delcídio Amaral (2005), Denise Stoklos (2001), Dilma Rousseff (2006), Drauzio Varella (2004), Dulce Maria Pereira (2000), Carlos Dunga (2009), Eduardo Gianetti (2005), Elza Soares (2002), Emilia Viotti da Costa (2001).

Silva (15 speeches given in 2010) and Michel Temer (25 speeches given in 2016), also representing language of distance (oral but conceptually written), with a high amount of argumentative discourse.[163]

Table 5.3 The Brazilian Portuguese Corpus

Subcorpus	Source	Tokens	PPC	/1000
Political Speech	total	102,206	96	0.94
	Jair Bolsonaro	18,137	7	0.39
	Dilma Rousseff	22,747	22	0.97
	Lula da Silva	22,138	17	0.77
	Michel Temer	39,184	50	1.28
Talkshow	Roda Viva	638,094	358	0.56

As illustrated in Table 5.3, the PPC_{PT} ratios amount to 96/102,206 tokens for political speech (0.94/1000 tokens) and 358/638,094 for *Roda Viva* (0.56/1000 tokens). There are remarkable differences though within the subcorpus of political speech. The frequencies of the PPC_{PT} suggest a scale ranging from Jair Bolsonaro, whose speeches contain the lowest number of PPC_{PT} occurrences, to Lula da Silva who, together with Dilma Roussef, occupies an interim position on the scale, to Michel Temer, whose speeches dispose of the highest PPC_{PT} ratio. Assuming the PPC_{PT} to represent an optional linguistic variant that is diastratically and diamesically marked, this finding matches common characterizations of the language that the referred politicians make use of. This particularly applies to the extremes of the scale, i.e. to Jair Bolsonaro and Michel Temer. As Jair Bolsonaro mainly pursues politics that might be, in most general terms, characterized as pertaining to the global trend of populism, he tends to make use of simple language, as e.g. in his catchy slogan of *Brasil acima de tudo, Deus acima de todos* ('Brazil above everything, God above everyone'). This style may be best characterized as being opposed to formal language, that is marked as high with respect to the diaphasic and diastratic level of variation. In this vein, Bolsonaro tends to language of immediacy (as opposed to distance), disposing of affective and also expressive speech, which might explain why in his speeches, the PPC_{PT} occurs more rarely as compared to the others.

The opposite trend can be observed in the speeches given by Michel Temer, whose language is, indeed, commonly characterized as highly formal and distantial.

---

163. The speeches are available on the following websites (accessed 01/11/21): Jair Bolsonaro: https://www.gov.br/planalto/pt-br/acompanhe-o-planalto/discursos, Dilma Rousseff: http://www.biblioteca.presidencia.gov.br/presidencia/ex-presidentes/dilma-rousseff/discursos/discursos-da-presidenta, Lula da Silva: http://www.biblioteca.presidencia.gov.br/presidencia/ex-presidentes/luiz-inacio-lula-da-silva/entrevistas/2o-mandato/2010, Michel Temer: http://www.biblioteca.presidencia.gov.br/presidencia/ex-presidentes/michel-temer/discursos-do-presidente-da-republica.

In fact, his peculiar style of language has been labelled as "michelês", criticized as an *instrumento de exclusão* ('an instrument of exclusion') and been accused for *falar difícil não é falar bem* ('to speak difficult is not to speak well.').[164] We consider this characterization of Temer's language to match well the finding of a higher PPC$_{PT}$ ratio in his speeches as compared to the others.

In sum, the creation of the Spanish and Portuguese subcorpora was guided by the goal to investigate the PPC's discourse functions in its most natural discursive environments, i.e. in those communicative situations that it most frequently and typically occurs in. The potential benefits of a perfectly homogeneous, i.e. parallel corpus with regard to genre and mode of discourse was outweighed by the peculiar semantic restrictions imposed by the PPC$_{PT}$, its general low frequencies, as well as its specialization in argumentative discourse featuring language of distance.

5.1.2 Analysis of the data

The data were analyzed using R Studio (R Core Team 2017), "a free software environment for statistical computing and graphics".[165] In particular, the analysis was mostly carried out using the packages *tidyverse* (Wickham et al. 2019) for data wrangling and visualization, as well as *tidytext* (Silge and Robinson 2016) for text mining and text analysis. The procedure was the following. The raw texts were loaded into R, tokenized, i.e. segmented into uni-, bi- or trigrams (depending on the task) and filtered for the relevant data points.

For the Spanish data, we created bigrams, i.e. chunks of two tokens, and filtered the first position of those for *he, has, ha, hemos, habéis* or *han*, i.e. for the conjugated forms of the PPC$_{SP}$ auxiliary *haber*. This procedure almost exclusively output PPC$_{SP}$ data points. Data points that we might have missed using this technique are instances of the PPC$_{SP}$ with eliptical auxiliaries, as well as cases disposing of 1+n token(s) in between the auxiliary and the participle.

With regard to the Portuguese data, we filtered bigrams for *tenho, tens, tem, temos, têm* i.e. for the conjugated forms of the PPC$_{PT}$ auxiliary *ter*. Next, we filtered the output for regular and irregular participles using regular expressions. Furthermore, we checked trigrams making use of the same technique in order to detect cases containing 1+n tokens in between the auxiliary and the participle (e.g. *tem-se mostrado fundamental* 'has been proving fundamental').

---

164. Cf. https://www1.folha.uol.com.br/poder/2016/11/1832080-conheca-o-micheles-idioma-falado-pelo-presidente-da-republica.shtml, 11/25/20 and https://novaescola.org.br/conteudo/5026/a-mesoclise-de-temer-e-um-instrumento-de-exclusao, 11/25/20.

165. https://www.r-project.org.

5.1.3 Overall frequencies

Figures 5.1 and 5.2 provide a first look at the overall frequencies of the verbs in the data for both Spanish and Portuguese. They show the distribution of verbal lemmas combined with the PPC$_{PT}$ and PPC$_{SP}$, as well as general distributions of verbs. Given the size of the corpora (Portuguese: 102,206 + 638,094 = 740,300 tokens; Spanish: 103,361 tokens), the annotation (lemmatization) concerning the general distributions of the verbs shown in Subfigure 5.1b and Subfigure 5.2b was carried out automatically by means of the Natural Language Processing toolkit *udpipe* (Wijffels 2019), an R package for automatic annotations based on pre-trained,

a. PPC$_{PT}$

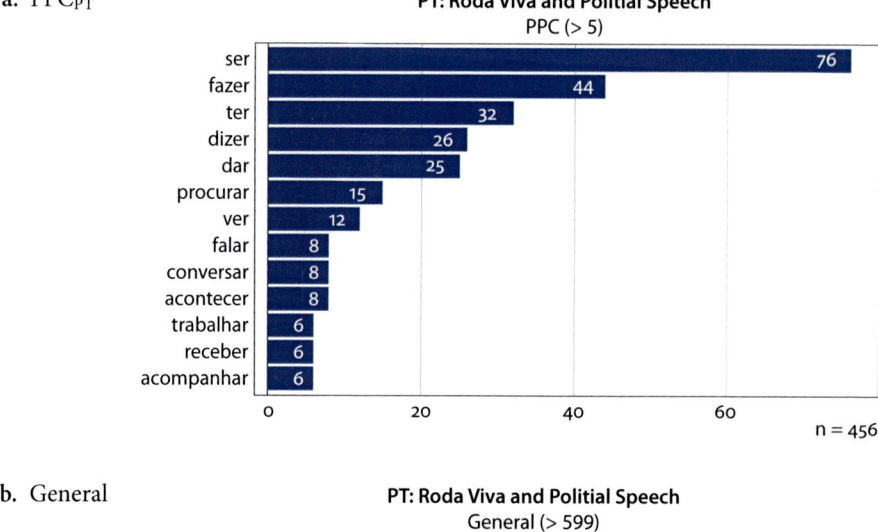

b. General

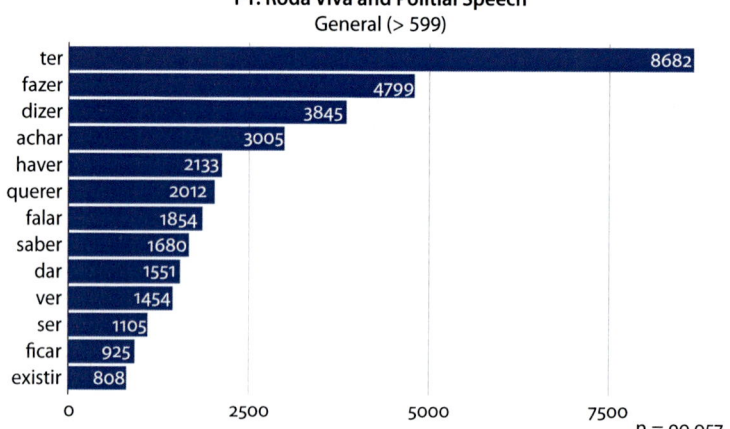

Figure 5.1 Distribution of verbs: PPC$_{PT}$ vs. general

machine-learned algorithms.[166] The package contains models for several languages including Spanish and Portuguese. The lemmas of the verbs realized by means of a PPC, as presented in Subfigure 5.1a and Subfigure 5.2a, were annotated manually.

In total, the Portuguese corpus contains 90,057 verbs. Among these, *ter* ('(to) have') is the most frequent one with 8,682 occurrences, followed by *fazer* ('(to) do') and *dizer* ('(to) say'). Interestingly, this picture is not mirrored in the distribution of the verbs combined with the PPC$_{PT}$. Here, *ser* ('(to) be') is, by far, the most frequent verb, followed by *fazer* and ter. That means that 16.67% of the PPC$_{PT}$ participles trace back to the lemma ser, while only 1.23% in the overall data stem from the lemma *ser*. Even though one might not expect an identical distribution for both

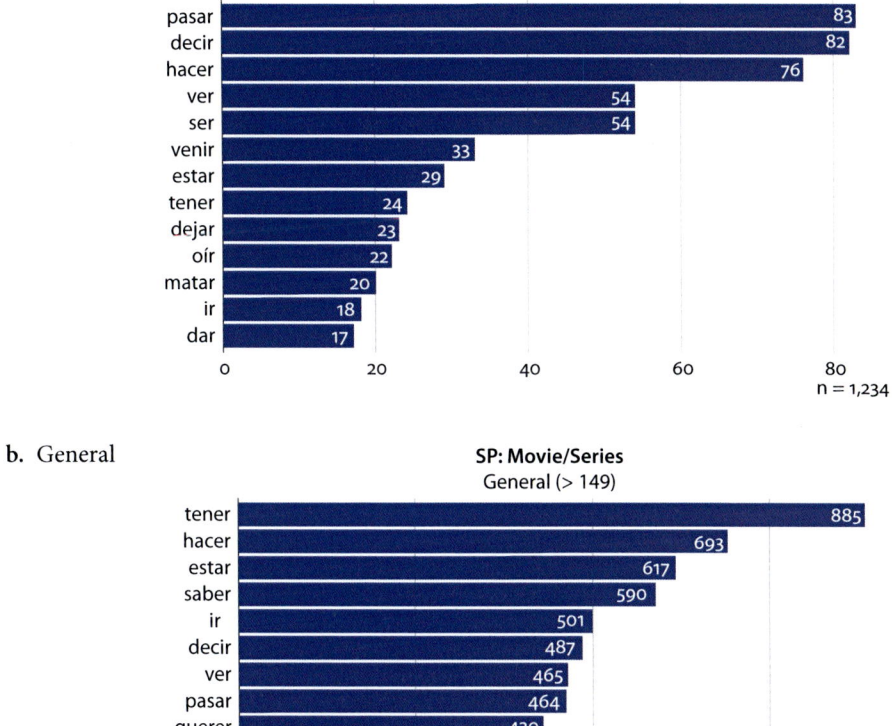

Figure 5.2 Distribution of verbs: PPC$_{SP}$ vs. general

---

166. Cf. https://cran.r-project.org/web/packages/udpipe/.

sets, we assume this striking difference to be semantically motivated: the generic meaning of *ser* harmonizes with the unbounded and mostly characterizing value of the PPC$_{PT}$. In fact, the data suggest that the PPC$_{PT}$ generally prefers to combine with atelic verbs, as illustrated in Figure 5.1a:

- 3 telic: *dizer, acontecer, receber* ('(to) say', 'happen', 'receive')
- 8 atelic: *ser, ter, procurar, ver, falar, conversar, trabalhar, acompanhar* ('(to) be', 'have', 'search', 'see', 'speak', 'work', 'escort')
- 2 contingent: *fazer, dar* ('(to) make', 'give')

The label of "contingent" refers to those verbs that are sensitive to their VP-internal argument. For example, the telicity value of *fazer* is labile between assuming a telic or an atelic aspectual value depending on the semantics of the object, as e.g. in telic *fazer a mala, fazer 30 anos* ('(to) pack the bag', 'turn 30') vs. atelic *fazer sol, fazer esporte* ('(to) be sunny', 'do sports'). The general preference of atelic verbs is furthermore supported by the observation that one of the telic verbs, *dizer*, is generally considered to represent a fossilized fixed expression, which, as opposed to the default semantics of the PPC$_{PT}$, may actually express a single and bounded past eventuality. In this vein, Becker (2016: 31) speaks of a fossilized use with the particular communicative function of signaling a speech act.

All in all, there are seven verbs occurring in the list of the 13 most frequent verbs combined with the PPC$_{PT}$ that do not appear in the list of the 13 generally most frequent verbs. These are *procurar, conversar, acontecer, trabalhar, receber, acompanhar* ('(to) search', 'chat', 'work', 'receive', 'escort'), while seven verbs appear in both lists (*ser, fazer, ter, dizer, dar, ver, falar* ('(to) be', 'make', 'have', 'say', 'give', 'see', 'speak').

Turning to the Spanish data, the distribution of atelic vs. telic verbs is much more balanced than in the Portuguese data, as illustrated in Figure 5.2:

- 5 telic: *pasar, decir, venir, dejar, matar* ('"(to) pass', 'say', 'come', 'leave', 'kill')
- 4 atelic: *ser, estar, tener, ir* ('(to) be', 'be', 'have', 'go')
- 4 contingent: *hacer, ver, oír, dar* ('(to) make', 'see', 'hear', 'give')

In our view, this finding reflects the highly productive status of the PPC$_{SP}$ in the sense that it does not show a preference for predicates of a particular situation type. Furthermore, there are only three verbs appearing in the PPC$_{SP}$ list missing in the general distribution. These are *venir, oír, matar* ('(to) come', 'hear', 'kill'). The depicted verbal distributions in Figure 5.2 are thus more similar in the Spanish than in the Portuguese corpus in Figure 5.1.

We conclude that these first findings once more emphasize the discussed differences between the PPC$_{PT}$'s and the PPC$_{SP}$'s. While the PPC$_{PT}$ is the more specialized tense form, the PPC$_{SP}$ is much more productive, as suggested by the insights concerning telicity and overall frequencies of verbs.

5.2 Adverbials

This section presents a corpus analysis with regard to the PPC's combinatorial possibilities with adverbials. The analysis builds on an annotation of presence vs. absence of tempo-aspectual adverbials, as well as the type of the respective adverbial according to our framework featuring quantificational adverbials (e.g. "always, twice, sometimes, already"), durative adverbials (e.g. "for two months"), XN-adverbials (e.g. "today, this month, now") and positional adverbials (e.g. "yesterday, last year, afterwards"). Furthermore, the annotation includes adverbials that are ambiguous between durative and XN, i.e. adverbials that abut t_S (e.g. "over the past month, until now"), and adverbials that are ambiguous between positional and XN, i.e. positional adverbials located within the present time-sphere (e.g. "today at three o'clock, today in the morning").[167]

5.2.1 Expectations

We expect that the data show that both PPC_{PT} and PPC_{SP} predominantly combine with quantificational and durative adverbials, i.e. with adverbials that scope over t_E in line with the PPC_{PT}'s and PPC_{SP}'s quantificational semantics.

Furthermore, we expect to find no unambiguously positional adverbials in the Portuguese data at all. With regard to the Spanish data, we refrain from formulating expectations concerning occurrences of positional adverbials. Nevertheless, we do explore the Spanish data for positional adverbials keeping in mind the question of whether the PPC_{SP} (already) disposes of a referential reading. Since we argued that adverbials do not provide adequate means to approach this problem – which is due to potential scope ambiguities – neither absence nor presence of positional adverbials in the data would help verify or falsify a related hypothesis.

In the following, we present and discuss three figures per variety, illustrating (i) the overall distribution of adverbially modified vs. non-modified occurrences of the PPC, (ii) distributions of the types of adverbials and (iii) distributions of the adverbials by their exact lexical type.

5.2.2 Portuguese

All in all, 377/454 PPC_{PT} datapoints (83.04%) lack a tempo-aspectual adverbial. Conversely, 77 instances (16.96%) dispose of tempo-aspectual modification by means of an adverbial. The proportions within the two Portuguese subcorpora are illustrated in Figure 5.3.

[167.] Thanks to student assistant David Wick (project *C02: Tense and Aspect in Discourse*, CRC 1252, University of Cologne) for annotating presence vs. absence of tempo-aspectual adverbials.

168 The Spanish and the Portuguese Present Perfect in Discourse

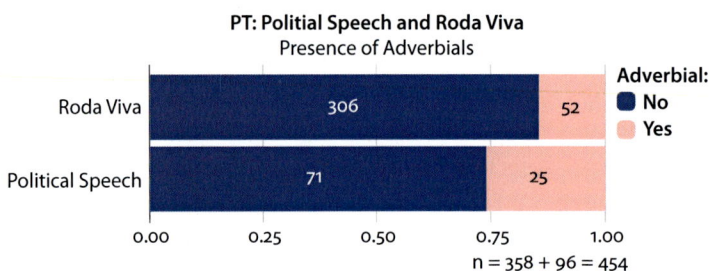

Figure 5.3 Tempo-aspectual adverbials combined with PPC$_{PT}$: Yes vs. no

The high frequency of non-modified instances of the PPC$_{PT}$ once again emphasizes the PPC$_{PT}$'s highly grammaticalized status for being able to denote its specialized meaning independently of explicit tempo-aspectual adverbial modification. Recall that this is a crucial property against the backdrop of the cross-linguistic trend that universal or universalized readings of the Present Perfect mostly do presuppose adverbial modification (cf. Iatridou et al. 2003). For our study of the PPC$_{PT}$'s discourse functions (cf. Section 5.3), we derive the general assumption that we should prominently take into account non-modified instances of the PPC$_{PT}$, as these seem to represent the more common and frequent case. Although the analysis of potential combinations with tempo-aspectual adverbials oftentimes helps test for particular meaning effects – which has actually proven to be an adequate analytical tool both (i) in diachronic corpus studies where adverbials sometimes might represent the only evidence to determine the meaning of a reading, as well as (ii) in the investigation of the question of which readings the PPC$_{PT}$ disposes of synchronically – non-modified PPC$_{PT}$ expressions generally should receive significant attention.

Most of the adverbials receiving adverbial modification turn out to belong to the group of adverbials that are ambiguous between durative and XN-adverbials. That is, they are ambiguous between scoping over t_E (abutting t_S) and scoping over t_P (specifying the present time-sphere which accommodates t_P), such as *nos últimos anos* ('over the past years'), *até agora* ('until now') or *o tempo inteiro* ('all the time'). Another frequent type is represented by quantificational adverbials, such as *muitas vezes* ('many times), *freqüentemente* ('frequently/often') or *sempre* ('always'). The proportions are illustrated in Figure 5.4.

As expected, there is no positional adverbial in the data at all. This is in line with the PPC$_{PT}$'s semantic configuration that, as discussed in Chapter 3, does not call for a location time t_{LOC} as an argument. Moreover, the data lack unambiguously durative adverbials that might be interpreted as being disjoined from the speech time. That is, the durative adverbials that appear in the data denote an abutment of the speech time (such as *nos últimos anos* ('over the past years'), cf. above). This impedes

Chapter 5. Corpus study   169

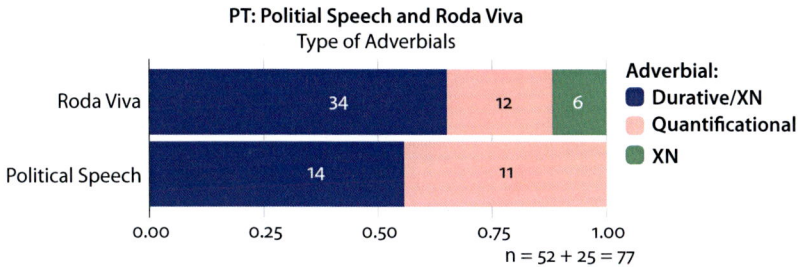

Figure 5.4 Types of adverbials combined with PPC$_{PT}$

a clear-cut delimitation of the contained durative adverbials from XN-adverbials, as illustrated in (1). The adverbial *ao longo desses últimos meses* ambiguously scopes over t$_E$ or t$_P$, i.e. it may be interpreted both as a universal or as an XN-adverbial.

(1) [...] <u>*ao longo desses últimos meses*</u> *o PFL tem buscado um veio para tentar pedir o impeachment do presidente Lula.*[168]
'Over the past few months the PFL has sought a vein to try to impeach president Lula.'

Figure 5.5 illustrates the adverbials by their exact lexical type. The list shows that the most frequent adverbials in the data are *ao longo do tempo* and *hoje*. Both adverbials express a temporal extension abutting speech time and, thus, serve as tools to underline the typical XN effect of the PPC$_{PT}$, i.e. the extension of the present time-sphere that accommodates both episodic (IPEX and universal) and characterizing readings.

5.2.3 Spanish

In the following, we present our results for the Spanish data. All in all, 1,116 of the 1,234 PPC$_{SP}$ datapoints (90.44%) lack a tempo-aspectual adverbial. Conversely, 118 instances (9.56%) dispose of actual tempo-aspectual modification. Again, we derive from this observation that the study of the PPC$_{SP}$ needs to prominently take into account non-modified examples as these seem to represent the more common use. The 9:1 distribution of modified vs. non-modified also turns out to be quite stable across the three subcorpora, as illustrated in Figure 5.6.

Similar to the Portuguese data, the tempo-aspectual adverbials combined with the PPC$_{SP}$ do not strictly follow a fourfold categorization of quantificational, durative, XN and positional adverbials. Instead, many adverbials again turn out to

---

168. *Roda Viva,* Claudio Lembo (2006). PFL = *Partido da Frente Liberal.*

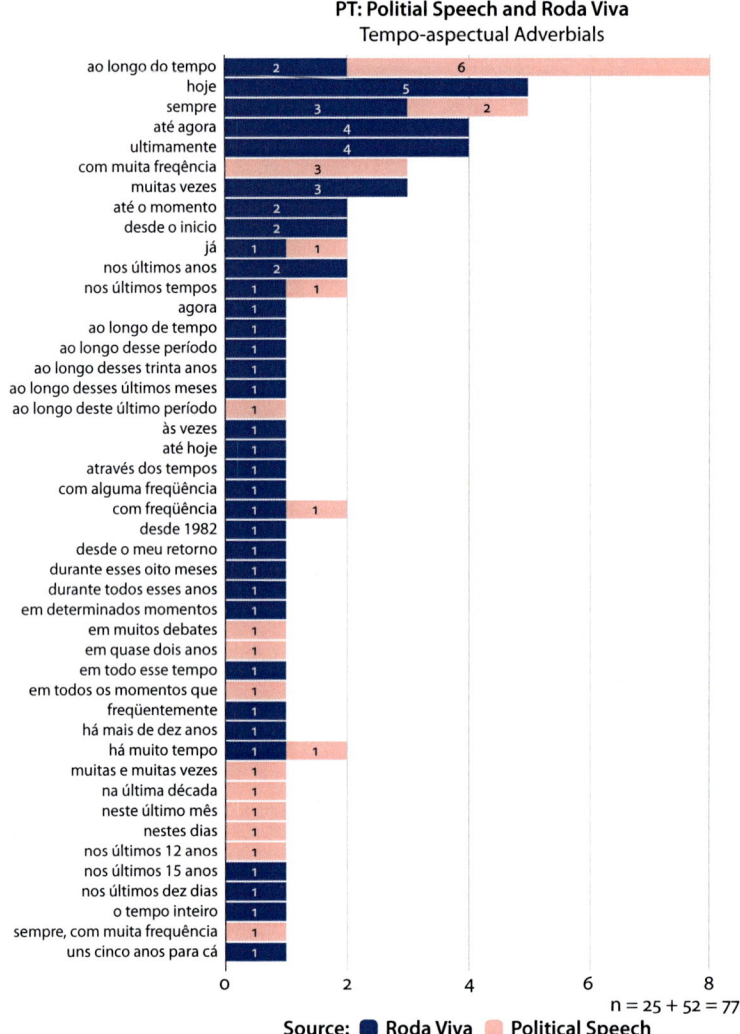

Figure 5.5 Lexical types of adverbials combined with PPC$_{PT}$

show ambiguities, e.g. *hasta ahora, estas últimas horas* (until now, (during) the last hours') that are ambiguous between durative and XN, i.e. between scoping over t_E or t_P. Furthermore, adverbials like *esta tarde, esta noche* ('this afternoon, this night/tonight) remain ambiguous between XN- and positional adverbials, i.e. between scoping over t_P and a potential location time t_{LOC} (cf. also discussion below and examples in (3)).

Chapter 5. Corpus study 171

As illustrated in Figure 5.7, the most frequent adverbials turn out to be quantificational adverbials, such as *ya* ('already'), *nunca* ('never') or *muchas veces* ('many times'), which underlines the significance of the PPC$_{SP}$'s quantificational semantics as one of its central properties. The rest of the adverbials mostly pertain to durative adverbials, such as *a lo largo del tiempo* ('throught time') or *cinco minutos* ('five minutes') and XN-adverbials, such as *hoy* ('today') or *últimamente* ('lately').

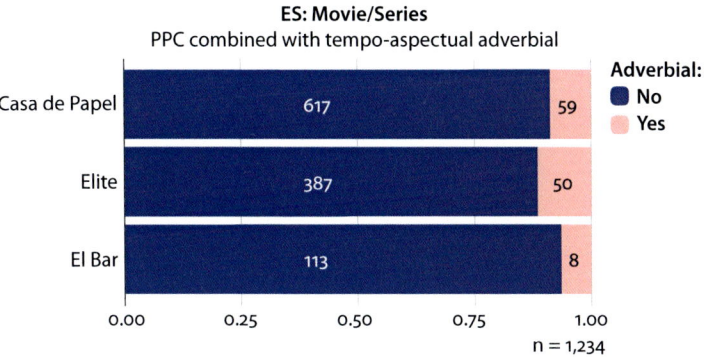

Figure 5.6 Tempo-aspectual adverbials combined with PPC$_{SP}$: Yes vs. no

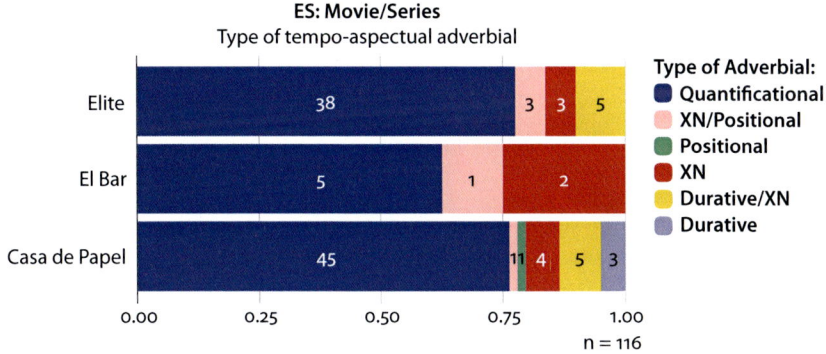

Figure 5.7 Typs of adverbials combined with PPC$_{SP}$

Figure 5.8 lists the tempo-aspectual adverbials contained in the data by their exact lexical type according to their frequency. Again, there is a similar distribution of the data across the three subcorpora in proportional terms: the quantificational adverbial *ya* ('already') is uniformly the most frequent one, followed by quantificational *nunca* ('never'), *antes* ('before') and *alguna vez* ('ever/once').

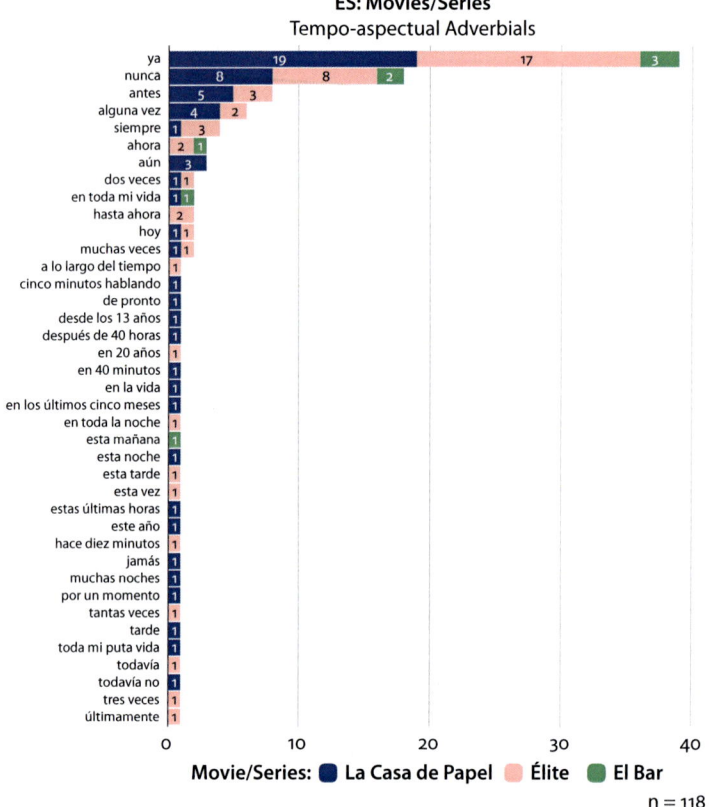

Figure 5.8 Lexical types of adverbials combined with PPC$_{SP}$

Are there positional adverbials in the Spanish data?
The existence of positional adverbials may serve as a tool to detect referential PPC$_{SP}$-readings (cf. Section 4.4). As it turns out, the adverbials presented in Figure 5.7 include a single unambiguous case of a positional adverbial, i.e. of an adverbial scoping over t_{LOC} presupposing a referential reading. The example is depicted in (2).

(2) Positional adverbial as evidence for the referential PPC$_{SP}$?
Mire… Estaba aquí… pensando en mis cosas y… <u>de pronto se me ha ocurrido pensar</u>: ¿qué clase de música escuchará este hombre cuando se ducha todas las mañanas?[169]
'Look… I was here… thinking about my stuff and… suddenly it occurred to me: what kind of music will this man listen to when he showers every morning?

---

169. *La Casa de Papel*, 01/06.

The mini-discourse in (2) is designed as a narration, i.e. featuring referential temporal semantics. This is expressed, on the one hand, by the *Imperfecto* – which directs the perspective time to the past time-sphere and which refers to a temporal anchor provided by (or inferred from) the discourse. Moreover, *de pronto* ('suddenly') updates the discourse reference time t_R (cf. Section 2.1) and, at the same time, temporally anchors the succeeding referential PPC_{SP} eventuality `se me ocurrir pensar`. This discourse-semantic, anaphoric assignment of the PPC_{SP} presupposes referential semantics featuring a location time (as discussed e.g. in Section 4.4). However, as the data only show a single example clearly suggesting a referential configuration, it seems dubious that the PPC_{SP} already disposes of a productive referential reading in addition to its quantificational core meaning.

Interestingly, the data further contain five ambiguous cases featuring adverbials that might be interpreted both as positional and XN-adverbials, i.e. as ambiguous between scoping over t_{LOC} or t_P:

(3) XN vs. positional ambiguity
    a. *Elena… …yo sé que te gusto. Lo noté en tu mirada desde que entraste al bar por primera vez. <u>Esta mañana me has salvado</u> la vida. Cuando aquellos hijos de puta querían joderme, tú me defendiste.*[170]
       'Elena… …I know you like me. I could see it in your eyes when you first walked into the bar. You saved my life this morning. When those sons of bitches wanted to fuck me over, you defended me.'
    b. *¿Qué dices? [Samu] Marina. ¿Qué tal? Te estuve llamando anoche. Te <u>he llamado</u> también <u>hoy a primera hora</u>. ¿Todo bien? Sí, estaba un poco cansada y se me acabó la batería del móvil.*[171]
       'What do you say? [Samu] Marina. How are you? I was calling you last night. I called you today at first, too. Everything okay? Yes, I was a little tired and my cell phone battery ran out.', 01/05.
    c. *¿Qué haces? Suéltame. ¿Quieres que tu madre sepa lo que te pasó esta mañana? [ríe] ¿Y tú quieres que mi hermano se entere de por qué <u>has venido esta tarde</u>? ¡Que me sueltes!*[172]
       'What are you doing? Let go of me. Do you want your mother to know what happened to you this morning? And you want my brother to know why you came here this afternoon? Let go of me!'

---

170. *El Bar.*
171. *Élite,* 01/05.
172. *Élite,* 01/06.

d. *Nos han pillado, joder.* – [Guzmán] *¿Qué pasa?* – [Lu] *¡Mierda! – ¿Cómo que nos han pillado? – Mierda. No te preocupes, tío. Estará al caer, <u>he quedado con él hace diez minutos</u>. Además, aquí no te va a ver nadie, no te rayes.*[173]
'We've been fucking caught. – What's going on? – [Lu] Shit! – What do you mean, we re busted? – Shit. Don't worry, man. He'll be here any minute. I have met him ten minutes ago. Besides, nobody will see you here, don't get scratched.'

e. <u>*Esta noche… he llamado*</u> *a un amigo. Le he contado lo difícil que es mantener el orden y la armonía aquí dentro, y le he… dicho que he tenido que matar, que he ordenado matar… a una mujer.*[174]
'Tonight… I called a friend. I told him how difficult it is to maintain order and harmony in here, and I… I told him I had to kill, that I had ordered the killing… of a woman.'

Each of the illustrated examples is compatible with both a referential (adverbial modifying t_{LOC}) and a quantificational reading (adverbial modifying t_P). Applied to (3a), the adverbial *esta mañana* may thus either be interpreted as modifying a location time that the event gets assigned to, or as an XN-adverbial specifying the temporal extension of the present time-sphere that is perspectivized. In the latter reading, the adverbial would thus define that the speaker asserts on the present time-sphere, which is perceived as beginning in the morning and reaching to the speech time, and, furthermore, it is asserted that there is an indefinite past eventuality as denoted by default by the PPC_{SP}'s quantificational semantics (cf. Sections 2.3 and 4.5). However, the surrounding discourse may provide cues that might turn one of the two readings more likely. In (3a) and (3b), a referential reading seems to be the more likely choice. Both examples contain, apart from the PPC_{SP}, the tense forms *Imperfecto* (*querían* and *estaba*) and *Indefinido* (*noté, entraste, defendiste* and *estuve, acabó*), i.e. tense forms that are typically included in narrative discourse due to their ability to establish temporal relationships between one another. This is opposed to a temporal anchoring relative to the speech time (that functions as the deictic center) typically established by the quantificational PPC_{SP}. Furthermore, the *Imperfecto* is compatible with a perspective time that lies in the past time-sphere, which clashes with those discourse modes that perspectivize the present time-sphere. Thus, in both (3a) and (3b), it is the interplay with adjacent tense forms that suggests to resolve the ambiguity triggered by the tempo-aspectual adverbial in favor of a referential reading.

In (3c) and (3d), the hearer might rather opt for a quantificational interpretation, again due to the surrounding discourse. In both examples. the perspective

---

173. *Élite*, 01/01.

174. *La Casa de Papel*, 01/05.

time remains in the present time-sphere which is suggested by the use of Present Tense (*haces, quieres* and *pasa, va*) and imperatives (*suéltame, sueltes* and *no te preocupes, no te rayes*).[175]

Finally, (3e) does not dispose of a clear discursive hint. On the one hand, the concatenation of several instances of the PPC$_{SP}$ suggests a reading of an unordered set of indefinite past eventualities that may receive a chronological order based on pragmatic inferences, e.g. driven by world knowledge or their morphosyntactic presentation (cf. Section 4.6). On the other hand, a referential interpretation featuring a discursively updated reference time t_R serving as a location time t_{LOC} for the denoted eventualities remains plausible, as well.

Based on these observations, we again derive that the PPC$_{SP}$'s potential to evoke referential readings needs to be primarily investigated on a discursive level, in particular in order to handle the problem of potential scope ambiguities associated with tempo-aspectual adverbials, as illustrated in (3).

5.2.4 Discussion

First of all, the most striking observation that follows from the data is that both PPC$_{PT}$ and PPC$_{SP}$ do not combine with tempo-aspectual adverbials in the majority of the cases (83.04% and 90.44%). One the one hand, this underlines the highly grammaticalized status of both tense forms, that mostly derive their typical readings and meanings independently of adverbial modification. On the other hand, this observation again raises the question of the actual function of tempo-aspectual adverbials. Our findings may suggest the following scenarios.

In the first scenario, the PPC disposes of certain readings that are very frequent and thus seem to represent the PPC's default meaning. These readings are often explicitly emphasized by particular adverbials that match their meaning. In this scenario, a high frequency of quantificational adverbials would suggest that the PPC, in fact, denotes quantificational readings in most of the cases, also in those that lack adverbial modification.

In the second scenario, the PPC disposes of certain readings that are infrequent, i.e. that represent marked uses. These readings presuppose additional adverbial enforcement in order to be derived. In fact, as exposed by Iatridou et al. (2003), there is a cross-linguistic tendency that universal readings need to be explicitly evoked by means of adverbials. In this scenario, the high frequency of quantificational adverbials would contradict the assumption that the quantificational value is an inherent semantic feature of the PPC independently of adverbial modification.

---

175. Independently of the question of whether imperatives are temporally anchored in time or not, the crucial point is that they do not shift the perspective away from the present time-sphere towards the past time-sphere either way.

In the third scenario, there is no link between the frequency of readings and the frequency of adverbials. The usage of adverbials rather depends on truth-conditional needs, as well as on the speaker's choice of how to coherently construct a discourse passage. In other words, adverbials may instantiate particular readings that are compatible with the PPC's abstract semantics. In this scenario, frequencies of adverbials do not relate to quantitative patterns of the PPC's readings at all.

Each of the three scenarios can be motivated based on particular examples and thus should taken into consideration when an adverbial gets combined with the PPC. The first scenario (the distribution of the adverbials maps onto the overall distribution of the readings) motivates the congruence between the inherently quantificational PPC_{SP} and the dominance of the quantificational adverbials combined with the PPC_{SP}. The second scenario (the distribution of the adverbials inverts the picture of the overall distribution of the readings) matches the PPC_{SP-UNI}'s need of adverbial modification in Peninsular Spanish. In this vein, the universal reading may be considered a rather peripheral reading requiring explicit enforcement which causes an increased number of durative or durative/XN-adverbials. The third scenario applies to those cases where the adverbial does not directly interact with a particular reading but rather adds fine-grained truth-conditional meaning, which seems to be predominantly the case with the PPC_{PT}. In this vein, tempo-aspectual adverbials may e.g. add details about quantification ("three times, sometimes, always") or information concerning the granularity of the present time-sphere ("today, this month, this year, up to now"), that the PPC's abstract meaning lacks but is compatible with.

As discussed above, we conclude to proceed with the PPC's interactions with adjacent tense forms in the following. This perspective seems not only to provide a new glance into the question of how the PPC is integrated and employed in discourse, but also to furnish new evidence beyond the level of tempo-aspectual adverbials in the study of the potential referential drift of the PPC_{SP}.

5.3 The micro-structure of discourse

In this section, we present the results of a qualitative analysis of the data concerning the micro-structural functions of the PPC, i.e. its discursive interactions with adjacent tense forms. This is guided by the hypotheses discussed in the Chapters 3 and 4. The method is qualitative and explorative in the sense that we do not determine quantitative ratios regarding frequencies of particular discursive functions. The goal is to elaborate a classification of how the PPC is typically employed in the data, without weighting the functions according to frequency.

5.3.1 Expectations

In most general terms, we expect the PPC$_{PT}$ and PPC$_{SP}$ to mainly operate on different levels due to their diverging semantic configurations.

Portuguese
In Section 3.5, we defined the PPC$_{PT}$'s readings as splitting into (rather modal) characterizing and (rather temporal) episodic readings. Recall that this notion of episodicity as opposed to genericity is not to be confused with temporal definiteness. In this vein, the notion of genericity aims at abstractions, i.e. generalizations derived from concrete instantiated eventualities, while episodicity refers to concrete eventualities, that may be temporally indefinite though, as exemplified by the episodic PPC$_{PT}$ readings (universal and IPEX readings) that are derived based on indefinite temporal semantics.

We have argued that the characterizing PPC$_{PT}$ deviates from common grammaticalization tendencies observed for the Present Perfect by deriving a generic quantification which is temporally restricted to the present time-sphere. On the level of discourse, we expect this reading to function as an elaborated rhetorical means shaping the argumentative structure based on exploiting the contrast or consistency of generic and episodic (expressed e.g. by a Simple Past) propositions. In this vein, we expect the PPC$_{PT}$ to serve as a tool to help the speaker achieve the communicative goal of making the hearer believe (or commit to) a certain proposition. Furthermore, we expect to find fine-grained graduations between two levels of genericity based on an interplay with the Present Tense: in addition to "original" generic expressions (e.g. "She is a teacher", "Paris is the capital of France"), the characterizing PPC$_{PT}$ yields a temporally restricted generic expression predication.

With regard to the episodic PPC$_{PT}$, we expect to find a function that overlaps with the discourse functions of the Spanish PPC$_{SP}$, particularly with the universal PPC$_{SP}$. This pertains to the establishment of transitions between the past and the present time-sphere, i.e. to the shaping of the perspectival structure.

Spanish
In Section 4.6, we defined the PPC$_{SP}$ to branch into quantificational and potential referential readings. The quantificational readings are furthermore defined as branching into existential (resultative, experiential, hot news) and universal readings.

Regarding the discourse functions of the existential readings, we mainly expect to detect (i) actualization effects and (ii) perspectival shifts. While (i) refers to the introduction of a discourse-new, indefinite past eventuality (by means of a PPC$_{SP}$) that subsequently gets referentially picked up by a definite Simple Past, (ii) refers to the perspectival shifting between the present and past time-sphere.

In addition to these default functions associated with the PPC$_{SP}$'s quantificational readings, we assume that the data may contain examples featuring a referential PPC$_{SP}$, as well. Discourse functions that would suggest the existence of referential readings are temporal anaphora and cataphora. The former refers to the discursive resolution of the PPC$_{SP}$'s location time t$_{LOC}$, the latter turns the PPC$_{SP}$ into a cataphoric anchor for succeeding anaphoric tense forms, such as *Imperfecto* or *Pluscuamperfecto*.

The formulated expectations concerning the discourse functions for both PPC$_{PT}$ and PPC$_{SP}$ are summarized in Table 5.4.

5.3.2 Portuguese

In the following, we present the results of the exploration of the 454 PPC$_{PT}$ datapoints with regard to the micro-structural effects established by combinations of the PPC$_{PT}$ with other tense forms. To a great extent, the results are consistent with our expectations formulated in Table 5.4. Unexpectedly though, the data suggest that the PPC$_{PT}$ additionally enables actualization effects and perspectival shifts, i.e. functions that we expected to detect in the Spanish data. That is, there seem to be more similarities between the PPC$_{PT}$'s and PPC$_{SP}$'s discourse functions than assumed. In the following, we present a selection of examples that we consider to be representative for an illustration of the several discourse functions.

Table 5.4 Expected discourse functions for PPC$_{PT}$ and PPC$_{SP}$

	Comb. with	Level	Function
Characterizing PPC$_{PT}$	SP	Argumentative structure	Contrasting generic and episodic propositions
Episodic PPC$_{PT}$	SP, PT	Perspective	Bridging between past time-sphere and present time-sphere
Quantificational PPC$_{SP}$	SP	Event reference	Introduction and actualization based on (in)definiteness
		Perspective	Shift between past time-sphere and present time-sphere
	PT	Perspective	Maintenance of present time-sphere
Referential PPC$_{SP}$	IMP, PQP	Event reference	Temporal cataphora: discursive anchoring of an anaphoric tense form

SP: Simple Past; PT: Present Tense; IMP: *Imperfecto* ; PQP: *Pluscuamperfecto*.

5.3.2.1 *Characterizing* PPC_{PT}

Contrast or consistency with episodicity

As expected, many occurrences of the PPC_{PT} in the data show a characterizing PPC_{PT} grounding an episodic proposition, as illustrated in (4).

(4) *Olha, eu <u>vou ser</u> também mais uma vez muito sincero, como <u>tenho sido</u> o tempo inteiro: não é mau que o governador de minas seja lembrado; tradicionalmente isso ocorre.*[176]
'Look, I will also be very honest (once) again, as I have been all along: it is not bad that the governor of mines is remembered; traditionally that happens.'

The isolated fact p (e.g. "Once again, I will be honest (now)" is conceived as a consistent episodic instantiation of the underlying characterizing background q ("I have been honest all along"). Here, the episodic eventuality is expressed by the periphrastic Future Tense. It seems that integrating the PPC_{PT}, the speaker Aécio Neves may more likely achieve his communicative goal of making the hearer believe p. He promises that he will answer honestly and the audience should believe that because he (claims that he) has already been answering honestly throughout the whole interview: if generic q is true, episodic p should be true as well. Conceived of as an analogy to the scientific principles in the tradition of Popper (1935), (4) is based on a deductive principle: a general assumption, conceived of as a rule, gets deducted from and applied to a concrete empirical (episodic) observation. Further examples are listed in (5).

(5) Characterizing PPC_{PT} → isolated episode (deduction)
   a. *Muito obrigado ao meu bom Deus por essa missão. E sei que Ele me <u>dará</u> muito mais do que sabedoria para conduzir o destino dessa nação, como já <u>tem me dado</u> boas parcerias, dentro da política nacional, como Davi Alcolumbre, para vencermos esses obstáculos.*[177]
   'Thanks a lot to my good God for this mission. And I know that He will give me much more than wisdom to lead the destiny of this nation, as He has already given me good partnerships, within national politics, like David Alcolumbre, to overcome these obstacles.'
   b. *Eu <u>digo</u> isso porque em entrevistas que <u>tenho dado</u> as pessoas me perguntam: a sua interinidade não atrapalha a história da governabilidade?*[178]
   'I say this because in interviews I have been giving people ask me: does your temporariness not hinder the history of governability?'

---

176. *Roda Viva*, Aécio Neves (2005).

177. Jair Bolsonaro (01/22/19).

178. Michel Temer (06/22/16).

c. *No geral, os nossos votos <u>têm ultrapassado</u> 340, 350, e se contar os ausentes por causa da madrugada, nós <u>chegaremos</u> a 377 votos na câmara dos deputados.*[179]
Overall, our votes have been exceeding 340, 350, and if we count those absent because of the dawn, we will reach 377 votes in the Members' Chamber.

In (5a), episodic p "God will give me more than wisdom" is deduced from characterizing q "God has been giving me good partnerships", in (5b), episodic p "I say this" is deduced from characterizing q "I have been giving interviews and people asked", and in (5c), episodic p "we will reach 377 votes" is deduced from characterizing q "we have been exceeding 340, 350".

The data show that the very same argumentative tie between an episodic and a characterizing proposition may also be exploited the other way round, as illustrated in (6).

(6) *Eu acho que a violência, especialmente aquela que <u>tem se dado</u> ao longo do tempo, porque <u>deu-se</u> uma no Rio de Janeiro, mas o fato é que é uma violência permanente em relação a mulher, em todos os estados brasileiros.*[180]
'I think that (the) violence, especially that which has taken place over time, because it happened in Rio de Janeiro, but the fact is that it is a permanent violence against women, in all Brazilian states.'

Here, the characterizing proposition q (e.g. "the violence which has taken place over time" gets provided with episodic evidence p (e.g. "it happened in Rio de Janeiro"), where p justifies and underpins the claimed generalization q. In this configuration, the relationship between p and q reminds of the inductive principle: based on an empirical (episodic) observation, an abstract, generalized regularity is derived. Or, applying the terminology of rhetorical relations, the PPC$_{PT}$ functions as a nucleus that p stands to in a relation of explanation. Further examples are listed in (7).

(7) Isolated episode → characterizing PPC$_{PT}$ (induction)
a. *O que nós <u>temos feito</u> – já <u>iniciamos</u> esse processo – é focar mais nos títulos de curto prazo, ou que tenham algum vencimento em curto prazo.*[181]
'What we have been doing – we have already started this process – is to focus more on short-term securities, or securities that have some short-term maturity.

---

179. Michel Temer (06/30/16).

180. Michel Temer (05/31/15).

181. *Roda Viva*, Armínio Fraga (2002).

b. *Desde então, <u>pusemos</u> em marcha ações decisivas. Nosso esforço <u>tem dado</u> grandes resultados.*[182]
'Since then, we have set in motion decisive actions. Our efforts have been yielding great results.'
c. *Não tenho dúvidas de que a CELAC <u>tem sido</u> um catalisador desse processo. <u>Foram</u> necessários coragem e sentido de responsabilidade histórica por parte dos presidentes Raúl Castro e Barack Obama, para dar esse importante passo.*[183]
'I have no doubt that CELAC has been a catalyst in that process. It took courage and a sense of historical responsibility on the part of Presidents Raul Castro and Barack Obama to take this important step.'

In (7a), characterizing p "we have been focussing on short-term securities" is induced from episodic q "we already started that process", in (7b), characterizing p "our efforts have been yielding great results" is induced from episodic q "since then, we have set in motion decisive actions", and in (7c), characterizing p "CLEAC has been a catalyst of this process" is induced from episodic q "it took courage to take this important step".

P and q may also be conceived as a contrast, i.e. as to two propositions that conflict with each other, as illustrated in (8).

(8) Isolated episode contradicting general principle
 a. *O nosso querido presidente Macri também <u>tem alcançado</u> avanços expressivos numa série de outras áreas, apesar dos desafios que <u>encontrou</u> ao assumir o governo do seu país.*[184]
 'We follow with interest and admiration President Macri's efforts to revive Argentina's economy and make it more integrated with the world. Our beloved President Macri also been making significant advances in a number of other areas, despite the challenges he encountered in taking over his country's government.
 b. *O que eu acho que o governo do presidente Lula <u>tem feito</u> [,] e <u>foi feito</u> pouco no passado[,] é um esforço de encontrar compensações adequadas para o paraguai.*[185]
 'What I think the government of President Lula has been doing, and little has been done in the past, is an effort to find adequate compensation for Paraguay.

---

182. Dilma Rousseff (09/23/14).
183. Dilma Rousseff (01/28/15). CELAC = *Comunidad de Estados Latinoamericanos y Caribeños.*
184. Jair Bolsonaro (04/02/19).
185. *Roda Viva*, Celso Amorim (2008).

In (8a), characterizing p "President Macri has been making significant advances" contrasts with episodic q "he encountered challenges" and in (8b), characterizing p "the government has been doing an effort" contrasts with episodic q "little has been done in the past". Interestingly, the characterizing PPC$_{PT}$ is used to express a positive action by the president in both examples. Thus, the semantics of the PPC$_{PT}$ seem to be systematically exploited to present the president's surmounting of obstacles and challenges as a generic property (instead of episodic eventualities).

Furthermore, the data contain examples where the speaker seems to be indecisive between employing a characterizing PPC$_{PT}$ or an episodic Simple Past which results in a revision of the tense form choice. Some of these examples are listed in (9).

(9) Competition between PPC$_{PT}$ and Simple Past
   a. *Alexandre, eu não fui, apesar de líder, eu não tenho ido a essas reuniões de partido, até por razões...*[186]
      'Alexander, I didn't go, despite being a leader, I haven't been going to those party meetings, even for reasons…'
   b. *Nós sabemos que o senhor é uma pessoa muita católica, que o senhor tem rezado bastante, rezou muito e tem rezado muito.*[187]
      'We know that you are a very Catholic person, that you have been praying a lot, prayed a lot and have been praying a lot.'
   c. *[…] porque nestes dias eu tenho tido a felicidade, sem embargo de contar apenas 20 dias – hoje estou fazendo o vigésimo dia de governo, ainda interino, mas eu tive a felicidade de rever, presidente Giacobo, a câmara dos deputados e o senado federal trabalhando ativamente.*[188]
      '[…] because these days I have had the happiness, even though I have only counted 20 days – today I am doing the twentieth day of government, still acting, but I had the happiness to review, president giacobo, the chamber of deputies and the federal senate working actively.'
   d. *Quem contou e recontou essa história, quem tem contado ao longo desses trinta anos foram os blocos afros, movimentos esses dos quais eu faço parte desde o início.*[189]
      'Who told and retold this story, who has been telling it over the past thirty years are the afros blocks, movements of which I have been a part since the beginning.'

---

186. *Roda Viva*, Delcídio Amaral (2005).
187. *Roda Viva*, Delcídio Amaral (2005).
188. Michel Temer (06/02/16).
189. *Roda Viva*, Arany Santana (2004).

In the respective examples, the speaker seems to be vacillating between characterizing q "I haven't been going" and episodic "I didn't go" in (9a), characterizing q "you have been praying a lot" and episodic "you prayed a lot" in (9b), characterizing q "I have been (being) lucky" and episodic "I was lucky" in (9c), and characterizing q "who told this story" and episodic "who has been telling this story" in (9d). Since the amendments in the examples are realized in both directions (PPC_{PT} to PPS and vice-versa), speakers seem to be aware of the differences between characterizing and episodic propositions, which is not only perceived on a truth-conditional level, but also on a discursive level shaping the rhetorical structure of an argument.

Contrast or consistency with genericity
Another frequent pattern suggested by the data regarding the syntagmatic combination of the PPC_{PT} with other tense forms concerns the interplay with "real" generic expressions. As discussed above, the characterizing PPC_{PT} may be described as bearing a "reduced" generic meaning due to its temporal restriction to the present time-sphere. The corpus suggests that speakers exploit an effect of gradience between the two, again in order to achieve the communicative goal of making the hearer believe a proposition p, or to let p enter the common ground. Typically, it is the Present Tense that contributes the generic expression in the examples.

(10) *Olha, eu acho que em termos de desenvolvimento tecnológico, nós temos hoje um CPQD que [...] é uma instituição extremamente forte e tem produzido um desenvolvimento possivelmente mais focado em determinados campos [...].*[190]
'Look, I think in terms of technological development, we have today a CPQD that [...] is an extremely strong institution and has produced a development possibly more focused on certain fields [...]'

In (10), there might be a higher chance for the speaker Antonio Carlos Valente to achieve his communicative goal to successfully assert p "CPQD is a strong institution" when supported by a "weaker generic", i.e. by characterizing q ("CPQD has been producing a development"). Again, this rhetorical device may also be employed the other way round where a generic expression supports a characterizing PPC_{PT}, as illustrated in (11).

---

190. *Roda Viva*, Antonio Carlos Valente (2007). CPQD = *Centro de Pesquisa e Desenvolvimento em Telecomunicações*.

(11) Generic expression and characterizing PPC$_{PT}$: consistency
   a. *No Brasil, estamos fazendo isso. Ao mesmo tempo em que <u>diminuímos</u> a pobreza e a desigualdade social, <u>protegemos</u> o meio ambiente. Nos últimos 12 anos, <u>temos tido</u> resultados extraordinários.*[191]
   'In Brazil, we are doing this. While reducing poverty and social inequality, we are protecting the environment. In the last 12 years, we have been having extraordinary results.'
   b. *Nós <u>precisamos ensinar</u> as novas gerações a viver a cidadania, então eu <u>tenho falado</u> muito do protagonismo juvenil.*[192]
   'We need to teach the new generations how to live citizenship, so I have talked a lot about youth protagonism.'
   c. *O legislativo não <u>pode</u> invadir a competência do poder de igual maneira o judiciário não <u>poderia fazê-lo,</u> como não <u>tem feito</u>.*[193]
   'The legislature cannot invade the power in the same way the judiciary could not, as it has not.'

In (11), generic p "we protect the environment" is linked with characterizing q "we have been having extraordinary results", in (11b), generic p "we need to teach the new generations how to live citizenship" expressing deontic necessity is linked with characterizing q "I have been talking a lot about youth protagonism", and in (11c), generic p "the legislature cannot invade the power" expressing deontic necessity is linked with characterizing q "the judiciary has not been invading the power". Also here, we consider the discourse function of the PPC$_{PT}$ to be tied to the enhancement of the insertion of a generic predication expressed by the Present Tense. The two propositions may also be constructed as contradicting each other though, as illustrated in (12).

(12) Generic expression and characterizing PPC$_{PT}$: contrast
   a. *<u>É importante que se busque</u> na função legislativa aquilo que é interesse maior do país, o que <u>não tem acontecido</u> em determinados momentos.*[194]
   'It is important that the legislative function seek out what is in the country's best interests, which has not been happening at certain times.'

---

191. Dilma Rousseff (09/23/14).
192. *Roda Viva,* Antônio Carlos G. Costa (2000).
193. Michel Temer (05/31/16).
194. *Roda Viva,* Antônio Carlos Biscaia (2006).

b. *Eu <u>tenho</u> uma admiração muito grande, uma paixão muito grande pela literatura, mas infelizmente <u>não tenho podido</u> acompanhar essa minha paixão na dimensão que eu gostaria de ter.*[195]
'I have a great admiration, a great passion for literature, but unfortunately I have not been able to keep up with that passion in the dimension that I would like to have.'

c. *Eu acho que essa experiência <u>tem sido</u> muito dura, mas o PT é muito maior do que fatos como esses e com relação a algumas pessoas.*[196]
'I think this experience has been very hard, but the pt is much bigger than facts like these and with some people.'

In (12a), generic p "it is important that" expressing deontic necessity contradicts characterizing q "it has not been happening", in (12b), generic p "I have a great passion for literature" contradicts characterizing q "I have not been able to read", and in (12c), generic p "the PT is much bigger" contradicts characterizing q "this experience has been very hard".

5.3.2.2 Episodic PPC$_{PT}$ readings

Perspectivizing
As hypothesized, the data suggest that the PPC$_{PT}$ may contribute to the perspectival structure, as exemplified in (13).

(13) *Eu <u>acompanhei</u> com muito cuidado, com muito interesse o que lá acontecia e <u>verifiquei</u> uma coisa curiosa, porque nós <u>temos pregado</u> muito ao longo do tempo a pacificação do país, a harmonia entre todos os brasileiros, a harmonia entre os poderes do estado.*[197]
'I followed with great care, with great interest what was happening there and I verified something curious, because we have been preaching a lot over time the pacification of the country, the harmony between all Brazilians, the harmony between the powers of the state.'

Here, the speaker Michel Temer makes a separatation between a perspective located in the past time-sphere (*acompanhei, verifiquei, acontecia*) and a perspective located in the present time-sphere. The switch to the present time-sphere is signalled by means of the PPC$_{PT}$ (*temos pregado*), which sets the perspective time to lie in

---

195. *Roda Viva*, Antonio Nóbrega (2004).

196. *Roda Viva*, Delcídio Amaral (2005). PT = *Partido dos Trabalhadores*.

197. Michel Temer (07/14/16).

the present time-sphere. Further examples of perspectival effects triggered by the PPC$_{PT}$ are illustrated in (14).

(14) PPC$_{PT}$ indicating a perspectival shift
   a. *Eu <u>tenho tido</u> a impressão, em todo esse tempo e no contato com o senhor, de que <u>houve</u> um convencimento pessoal da sua parte, alguma coisa humana lhe <u>tocou,</u> alguma coisa da sua história, do Alexandre Moraes como pessoa <u>teve</u> um envolvimento, alguma coisa que <u>tocou</u> muito de perto.*[198]
   'I have had the impression, in all this time and in the contact with you, that there was a personal conviction on your part, something human touched you, something from your history, from the Alexandre that had as a person had an involvement, something that touched very closely.'
   b. *A minha leitura enviesada – sem dúvida – é de que ele <u>passou</u> bem no teste; [que] <u>foi</u> possível ser flexível; [e] que nós <u>incorporamos</u> algumas lições, como a importância de se já ir explicitando [a tendência] [....], a partir do diagnóstico dos choques – que é o que nós <u>temos procurado</u> fazer.*[199]
   'My biased reading – no doubt – is that he passed the test well; [that] it was possible to be flexible; [and] that we have incorporated some lessons, such as the importance of already explaining [the trend] from the diagnosis of shocks – which is what we have been trying to do.'
   c. *Prefeito, em uma entrevista que o senhor <u>deu</u> em 96, para a revista da folha de S.Paulo, o senhor <u>dizia</u> que <u>detinha,</u> na época, uma tecnologia nos padrões brasileiros de disputa eleitoral que lhe <u>dava</u> uma grande vantagem, que <u>era</u> justamente o conhecimento que o senhor <u>tinha</u> desse mundo da eleiçao baseada na propaganda eleitoral pela televisão e tudo isso que hoje <u>tem funcionado</u> muito. Mas o senhor <u>dizia</u> também que não <u>tinha</u> grupo político, que <u>fazia</u> política sozinho e se <u>definia</u> como um franco atirador.*[200]
   In an interview you gave in 1996 for the magazine folha de s.paulo, you said that you had, at the time, a technology in the Brazilian standards of electoral competition that gave you a great advantage, that it was precisely the knowledge that you had of this world of election based on television advertising and all this that has worked a lot today. But you also said that you had no political group, that you made politics alone and defined yourself as a sniper.'

In each of these examples, the PPC$_{PT}$ appears in the cotext of past tense forms that perspectivize the past time-sphere. The PPC$_{PT}$ thus creates opposition to these past

---

198. *Roda Viva*, Alexandre de Moraes (2005).

199. *Roda Viva*, Armínio Fraga (2002).

200. *Roda Viva*, César Maia (2005).

tense forms to establish a shift towards the present time-sphere. In (14a) e.g., the present time-sphere accommodates the interviewer's analysis of the interviewee's performance so far, which is expressed by the PPC$_{PT}$ "I have had the impression", whereas the past time-sphere ("there was a personal conviction, something touched you, touched very closely") accommodates situations that led to the interviewer's opinion.

Actualization
The analysis unexpectedly revealed that the PPC$_{PT}$ may also contribute to actualization effects as discussed in the context of the Spanish PPC$_{SP}$, as illustrated in (15).

(15) *Alexandre, eu estou notando o seguinte: você <u>tem falado</u> em todas as dimensões do problema e tal, mas se <u>referiu</u> muito pouco ao judiciário.*[201]
'Alexander, I am noticing the following: you have spoken in all the dimensions of the problem and such, but you referred very little to the judiciary.'

Here, the PPC$_{PT}$'s indefinite, quantificational tense ("you have been speaking in all the dimensions of the problem") is followed by a definite, referential Simple Past ("you referred"), which zooms in on the previously introduced eventuality and elaborates on it by providing detailed information. Actualization thus seems to be another discourse function (besides shaping the perspectival structure) that the Portuguese PPC$_{PT}$ and Spanish PPC$_{SP}$ share. Further examples are illustrated in (16).

(16) Episodic (universal and IPEX) PPC$_{pt}$ and actualization effects
  a. *Nesse ponto, <u>tenho tido</u> conversas ótimas, inclusive <u>tive</u> o privilégio de ter uma conversa maravilhosa com um homem que eu admiro demais: o presidente do banco central, Armínio Fraga [presidiu o banco entre 1999 e 2003].*[202]
  'At this point, I have had great conversations, including the privilege of having a wonderful conversation with a man I admire too much: the president of the central bank, Armínio Fraga [presided over the bank from 1999 to 2003].'
  b. *E o PMDB <u>tem dado</u> demonstrações disso durante esses oito meses: <u>votou</u> praticamente em todas as matérias relevantes com o governo, e no senado foi fundamental para a gente ter aprovado tudo.*[203]
  'And the PMDB has been giving demonstrations of this during these eight months: it voted on practically all relevant matters with the government, and in the Senate it was fundamental for us to have approved everything.'

---

201. *Roda Viva*, Alexandrea de Moraes (2005).
202. *Roda Viva*, Caio Luiz de Carvalho (2001).
203. Roda *Viva*, Aloisi Mercadante (2002). PMDB = *Partido Movimento Democrático Brasileiro*.

c. *Entre outras coisas [que] o senhor <u>tem criticado,</u> o senhor também <u>disse</u> agora há pouco que [o judiciário] pode estar envolvido com crimes diretamente.*[204]
'Among other things [that] you have been criticizing, you have also just said that [the judiciary] may be involved with crimes directly.'

d. *Eu acho que a história do Brasil <u>tem tido</u> períodos melhores, aqui em São Paulo também <u>teve</u> períodos melhores.*[205]
'I think the history of Brazil has had better periods, here in Sao Paulo also had better periods.'

e. *Os países que integram a CELAC […] <u>têm privilegiado</u> a integração regional. Em 2008, numa reunião no Brasil, os Chefes de Estado e de Governo latino-americanos e caribenhos <u>foram</u> capazes de formular uma agenda própria, representativa dos interesses da América Latina e do Caribe.*[206]
'The countries that make up CELAC have favored regional integration. In 2008, at a meeting in Brazil, the Latin American and Caribbean Heads of State and Government were able to formulate their own agenda representing the interests of Latin America and the Caribbean.'

Interestingly, the listed examples might also be interpreted as characterizing readings that, in turn, give rise to the rhetorical discourse function of exploiting the generic-episodic contrast for argumentative purposes, as discussed above. This suggests that the episodic vs. characterizing reading distinction correlates with an argumentative vs. actualization distinction on the level of discourse. The episodic PPC_{PT}, on the one hand, denotes indefinite eventualities spread over the timeline, which (still) qualifies them as typical universalized readings. This, in fact, motivates their partially overlapping discourse functions (of shaping the perspectival structure and actualization function) with the Spanish PPC_{SP}. On the other hand, the characterizing reading denotes abstractions of regular patterns that represent a rather modalized layer, that is situated beyond the temporal discourse structure and that does not directly contribute to the event-referential structuring (cf. also Becker and Egetenmeyer 2018: 55). In sum, the potential ambiguities concerning the discourse functions in (16) correlate with potential ambiguities with regard to the readings in the shown examples (cf. also discussion).

---

204. *Roda Viva*, D. Tomas Balduino (2005).

205. *Roda Viva*, Emilia Viotti da Costa (2001).

206. Dilma Rousseff (01/28/15).

5.3.3 Spanish

In the following, we present an exploration of our corpus with regard to micro-structural effects established by combinations of the PPC$_{PT}$ with other tense forms. Again, we present a selection of examples that we consider to be representative for an overview and an analysis of how the PPC$_{SP}$ contributes to the micro-structural organization in discourse.

5.3.3.1 Quantificational PPC$_{SP}$

Perspectival shift

The PPC$_{SP}$ is defined as denoting its perspective time t$_P$ to lie in the present time-sphere, independently of its reading. Contrarily, the *Indefinido* (Simple Past) is defined as denoting its perspective time to lie in the past time-sphere. According to these definitions, (one of) the crucial differences between PPC$_{SP}$ and *Indefinido* is spelled out by the configuration of the perspective time. In line with our expectations, lots of combinations of PPC$_{SP}$ and *Indefinido* in our corpus turn out to exploit this contrast in order to create perspectival shifts between the past and the present time-sphere. This is exemplified in (17), where the speaker chooses to differentiate between "then" and "now" (cf. also Declerck et al. 2006: 200).

(17) *Imagino que <u>has visto</u> la foto que <u>subió</u> a Internet. Yo no <u>subí</u> esa foto.*[207]
'I imagine you've seen the picture that was uploaded to the internet. I didn't upload that picture.'

In (17), the speaker manages to discuss two temporal perspectives at the same time. One the one hand, they focus the present time-sphere asking whether the hearer has seen the picture or not. Next, the speaker perspectivizes the past time-sphere, i.e. the time when the uploading of the photo occurred. Once again, (17) emphasizes a crucial observation that follows from our discourse-based approach to the PPC: the propositions `la foto subir a Internet` and `yo no subir esa foto` both represent prototypical candidates to become PPC$_{SP}$ expressions. After all, they denote significantly resultative meanings. Furthermore, their temporal semantics remain indefinite (i.e. there is no location time) and they do not add additional details to a discourse-old eventuality answering questions like "when, where, who". In other words, both express indefinite eventualities that entail a resultant state of particular relevance holding at speech time. However, these cues are overridden by the discourse function of perspectival shifting causing that an *Indefinido* instead of a PPC$_{SP}$ is employed..

---

[207]. La *Casa de Papel*, 01/01.

A selection of further examples is listed in (18).

(18) Perspectival shift (PPC$_{SP}$ vs. *Indefinido*)
   a. *Que me <u>escayolaran</u> el brazo <u>ha sido</u> lo más emocionante que me <u>ha pasado</u> este año.*[208]
      'Having my arm put in a cast was the most exciting thing that's happened to me this year.'
   b. *<u>Dijo</u>: "No me toquéis". Y yo no le <u>he tocado</u>.*[209]
      He said, "Don't touch me." And I haven't touched him.'
   c. *Lo <u>siguieron</u> hasta el bar. – Pero a ver, esto ya <u>ha pasado</u> antes, y nadie <u>ocultó</u> nada, ¿eh?*[210]
      'They followed him to the bar. – But let's see, this has happened before, and nobody hid anything, huh?'
   d. *Tokio me <u>ha dicho</u> que el plan no se te <u>ocurrió</u> a ti, pero no le <u>has dicho</u>.*
      'Tokio told me you didn't come up with the plan, but you didn't tell him.'

In each of the examples, the speaker differentiates between a past and a present perspective. In (18a) e.g., the speaker contrasts the past event of putting the arm in cast and the discussion of that past event, considered from the vantage point of the present time sphere. Similarly, in (18b), the speaker does not relate what happened right after the past event of "said" – which would create a narrative chain – but, again, chooses to report the result of the indefinite past event "I haven't touched him" from the vantage point of the present time-sphere (cf. also Section 2.1 for the closely related distinction of *Besprochene Welt* ('discussed world') vs. *Erzählte Welt* ('narrated world') in Weinrich 1964).

Perspectival maintenance

As opposed to perspectival shifting, the PPC$_{SP}$ may also set the perspective time to maintain in the present time-sphere although discussing a past eventuality, e.g. when combined with another PPC$_{SP}$. Once again, this demonstrates that the choice of a tense form is not strictly guided by truth conditions imposed by the extra-linguistic world alone, but also influenced by co-existing inner-linguistic alternatives of how to present and configure eventualities and their relationship with respect to other entities present in discourse. Combining two past eventualities expressed by a PPC$_{SP}$ causes that potential temporal relations holding between those eventualities – such as simultaneity, inclusion or precedence/succession – are not

---

208. La *Casa de Papel*, 01/02.

209. El bar.

210. El bar.

semantically encoded.[211] Instead, they are typically derived based on pragmatic reasoning, i.e. based on world knowledge, verb semantics or other discursive cues (cf. Section 4.6). It follows that the pragmatically inferred chronology can be cancelled and reinterpreted without causing logical contradictions. Also, a chronological order may be derived based on the iconicity principle that suggests that the syntactic order of the eventualities correlates with their chronological interpretation. As discussed in Chapter 4.6, the concatenated PPC$_{SP}$ expressions in Example (19) denote an unordered set of $\{e_1$ engañarme, e_2 llevarme a un baño, e_3 hacerme una foto desnuda$\}$.

(19) *Es que me han engañado, me han llevado a un baño y me han hecho una foto desnuda.*[212]
 'It's that I've been tricked, they took me to a bathroom and took a naked picture of me.'

There is a range of possible interpretations, as indicated in (20). The most likely interpretation is indicated in (20a): the temporal interpretation of $e_1 - e_3$ mirrors their syntactic presentation, i.e. e_2 and e_3 are most likely interpreted as being connected by a narrative relation of succession, while the two form a subset of e_1, which means that they contribute an elaboration to e_1. However, alterantive interpretations would not result in semantic contradictions.

(20) Possible temporal inferences for (19)
 a. $e_1 \supseteq [e_2 \prec e_3]$
 b. $e_1 \prec e_2 \prec e_3$
 c. $e_1 \succ e_2 \succ e_3$
 d. $e_1 \succ e_2 \prec e_3$
 e. $e_1 \prec e_2 \succ e_3$
 f. ...

Further examples of concetanations of several instances of the PPC$_{SP}$ are illustrated in (21).

(21) PPC$_{SP}$ + PPC$_{SP}$ maintaining the present time-sphere
 a. *A ver, Nacho, ese señor ha tosido, ha escupido sangre, ha tocado las paredes, el suelo, el móvil...*[213]
 'Let's see, Nacho, this man has coughed, spat blood, touched the walls, the floor, the cell phone...'

---

211. This does not apply to contexts containing positional adverbials like *después, antes, cuando, mientras* ('afterwards', 'before', 'when', 'while'), that do semantically denote temporal relations.

212. *La Casa de Papel*, 01/02.

213. *El bar.*

b. *Hija, son las dos. La niña se ha despertado y ha vomitado un poquito [...].*[214]
'Daughter, it s two o clock. The child has woken up and vomited a little [...].'

c. *Enhorabuena, porque uno de ustedes lo ha conseguido, ha grabado una imagen de aquí dentro y se la ha enviado a la policía.*[215]
'Congratulations, because one of you has succeeded, has recorded an image from here and has sent it to the police.'

d. *Ha sido provocado por una rehén que no ha cumplido mis normas y ha tratado de contactar... con este teléfono.* [216]
'(S)he has been provoked by a hostage who has not complied with my rules and has tried to contact... with this phone.'

e. *He incumplido la primera norma. He matado a un rehén.*[217]
'I have violated the first rule. I have killed a hostage.'

f. *Esta noche... he llamado a un amigo. Le he contado lo difícil que es mantener el orden y la armonía aquí dentro, y le he... dicho que he tenido que matar, que he ordenado matar... a una mujer.*[218]
'Tonight... I called a friend. I told him how difficult it is to maintain order and harmony here, and I... I told him that I had to kill, that I had ordered to kill... a woman.'

In each of these examples, the PPC$_{SP}$ makes sure that, although denoting several past eventualities, the perspective time is maintained in the present time-sphere. This impedes the transformation of the discourse mode into a narration in favor of maintaining the discourse mode of report. That is, the denoted indefinite past eventualities are relatively anchored to the deictic center and remain discourse-semantically isolated with respect to one another. Potential temporal relations are derived based on pragmatic inferences.

Another frequent pattern features questions expressed by the PPC$_{SP}$ answered by a PPC$_{SP}$, as illustrated in (22). Instead of answering by means of a definite tense form – as e.g. observed in examples of actualization (cf. below) – the indefinite PPC$_{SP}$ maintains the perspective time in the present time-sphere. This function seems to override the use of an *Indefinido* in the examples indicated in (22).

---

214. *La Casa de Papel*, 01/02.

215. *La Casa de Papel*, 01/02.

216. *La Casa de Papel*, 01/03.

217. *La Casa de Papel*, 01/05.

218. *La Casa de Papel*, 01/05.

(22) Perspectival maintenance: PPC$_{SP}$ answering PPC$_{SP}$
   a. *¿Qué <u>ha pasado</u>? – <u>Han reventado</u> una cámara.*
   'What happened? – A camera has been blown up.'[219]
   b. *¿De dónde la <u>has sacado</u>? – La <u>he encontrado</u> por ahí. – Y no <u>ha dicho</u> nada.*[220]
   'Where did you get it? – I found it over there. – And she didn't say anything.'
   c. *[…] lo ha conseguido, <u>ha grabado</u> una imagen de aquí dentro y se la <u>ha enviado</u> a la policía.*[221]
   '[…] he's done it, he's recorded an image from in here and sent it to the police.'
   d. *¿Qué <u>ha dicho</u>? – <u>Ha dicho</u>: "¡No me toquéis!"*[222]
   'What did he say? – He said, "Don't touch me!"'
   e. *Bueno, nadie lo <u>ha visto</u>. – Pero <u>ha sonado</u> a disparo. – Oh, Señor.*[223]
   'Well, no one has seen it. – But it sounded like a shot. – Oh, Lord.'
   f. *¿Qué <u>ha pasado</u>? – Le <u>han pegado</u> un tiro a ese. – ¿Al del pan con tomate?*[224]
   'What happened? – That one's been shot. – The one with the tomato bread?'
   g. *No las tengo. – ¿Cómo? ¿Las <u>has perdido</u>? – No, las <u>he escondido</u>.*[225]
   'I don't have them. – What? You lost them? – No, I hid them.'

Actualization
In Section 4.6, we defined the discourse function of actualization following Declerck et al. (2006) as typically arising from combining an indefinite tense form with a definite tense form.

> [A]n indefinite present perfect is normally only used to introduce a 'bygone' situation into the discourse (i. e. to establish a domain in the pre-present zone), not to go on speaking about it after this has happened. In order to do that we normally switch to the past tense. (Declerck et al. 2006: 461)

First, an indefinite, quantificational tense form (PPC$_{SP}$) existentially quantifies over, i.e. introduces, a discourse-new past eventuality. Next, the definite, referential tense form *(Indefinido)* referentially picks up the eventuality as discourse-old,

---

219. *La Casa de Papel*, 01/01.

220. *El bar.*

221. *La Casa de Papel*, 01/02.

222. *El bar.*

223. *El bar.*

224. *El bar.*

225. *El bar.*

i.e. as familiar. According to Declerck et al. (2006: 299), the speaker actualizes the event by "focussing on [...] the situation itself", by adding further information answering questions like "where?", "how?" and "when?", which is not the function of the quantificational tense form in the given sequence: An example from the data is exemplified in (23).

(23) ¿Esa herida cómo te la <u>has hecho</u>? – Me <u>pegué</u> contra una puerta.[226]
'How did you get that wound? – I hit a door.'

Again, the discursive strategy to exploit the discursive interplay of indefinite and definite tense in order to establish the effect of actualization overrides the fact that me pegar contra una puerta would qualify to become a PPC$_{SP}$ expression (resultative reading) when observed in isolation. After all, person B still suffers from the direct resultant state of the underlying predicate, i.e. from a wound, while talking to person A. (24) lists a selection of the many examples contained in our corpus that belong to the group of actualized eventualities.

(24) PPC$_{SP}$ + Indefinido: actualization focus
    a. ¿Que qué cojones te <u>ha dicho</u>? – No <u>escuché</u> nada.[227]
       'What the fuck did he say to you? – I didn't hear anything.'
    b. <u>He oído</u> disparos. ¿Estás bien? Eso <u>fue</u> cuando <u>mataron</u> al barrendero y al otro.[228]
       'I heard gunshots. Are you okay? That was when they killed the sweeper and the other one.'
    c. <u>He entrado</u> porque mi coche está aquí y <u>olvidé</u> algo muy importante en el maletero, muy importante.[229]
       'I got in because my car is here and I forgot something very important in the trunk, very important.'
    d. Lo <u>he visto</u>. Le <u>clavaron</u> un hierro a mi hermano y sangraba mucho. Vamos. Ven. Ven.[230]
       'I've seen it. My brother was hit with an iron and he was bleeding badly. Let's go. Come. Come.'

---

226. *Élite*, 01.
227. *La Casa del Papel*, 01/06.
228. *El bar*.
229. *La Casa de Papel*, 01/01.
230. *La Casa de Papel*, 01/01.

e. [...] *que lo <u>han fichado</u> por mi culpa. <u>Lo grabaron</u> a través de mi móvil. Porque <u>quise</u> encenderlo.*[231]
'[...] that he's been booked because of me. They recorded it through my cell phone. Because I wanted to turn it on.'

f. *¿Qué <u>has tomado</u> esta vez? – Que Pablo no me <u>drogó</u>. Que solo <u>fumamos</u> un poco y ya está.* [232]
'What did you take this time? – Pablo didn't drug me. We just smoked a little and that was it.'

g. *¿Cómo la <u>habéis encontrado</u>? – Un vecino <u>aseguró</u> haber visto a un grupo de jóvenes.*[233]
'How did you find her? – A neighbor claimed to have seen a group of young people.'

h. *<u>He hecho</u> lo que me has pedido. Porque <u>pensé</u> que no te atreverías. Y era la única forma.*[234]
'I've done what you asked. Because I thought you wouldn't dare. And it was the only way.'

i. *<u>Han detenido</u> a mi hermano por mi culpa. <u>Estaba</u> tan cabreado con él que <u>creí</u> que había sido capaz de matarla.*[235]
'My brother has been arrested because of me. I was so pissed off at him that I thought he was capable of killing her.'

The listed examples emphasize the idea that the typical sequence of PPC$_{SP}$ followed by an *Indefinido* is, indeed, motivated based on the discourse functions of definite and indefinite tense, as discussed in detail Section 4.6. Furthermore, the data suggest that the actualization focus seems to be a productive figure not only in the language of the press as suggested by Azpiazu Torres (2015) under the label of the first voice (PPC$_{SP}$) and second voice *(Indefinido)*. The dialogues in the shown examples, that consist of short utterances and high amounts of turn-takings, also depend on an economic management of the referential discourse structure. In this vein, the actualization focus seems to be part of a more general mechanism contributing to the management of eventive discourse entities, that is not restricted to a particular register.

---

231. *La Casa de Papel,* 01/01.
232. *Élite,* 01/03.
233. *La Casa de Papel,* 01/09.
234. *Élite,* 01/04.
235. *Élite,* 01/09.

5.3.3.2 Referential PPC$_{SP}$

All in all, the data suggest that the PPC$_{SP}$ is employed as a quantificational, non-narrative tense form in the overwhelming majority of the cases. This is i.a. expressed in the very low number (if any at all) of positional adverbials combined with the PPC$_{SP}$ (cf. discussion of potential positional adverbials included in the data in Section 5.2). Put differently, the data lack unambiguously referential uses, i.e. anaphoric uses where t$_E$ gets referentially attributed to a location time t$_{LOC}$. However, the corpus turns out to contain a few examples featuring a PPC$_{SP}$ that functions as a cataphoric anchor for a succeeding *Imperfecto*. In these cases, it seems that the PPC$_{SP}$ actually affiliates with an *Imperfecto* in order to form narrative passages containing past eventualities that are temporally related to one another, instead of relatively anchored to the speech time. This is illustrated in (25).

(25) *Cuando he vuelto a la carpa, había una situación muy grave, de riesgo, en el tejado de la Fábrica y... creía que uno de los rehenes estaba en peligro, así que he dado... orden de disparar.*[236]
'When I returned to the tent, there was a very serious situation, of risk, on the roof of the Factory and I thought one of the hostages was in danger, so I gave the order to shoot.'

In most general terms, the *Imperfecto* is an anaphoric tense form that seeks to discursively resolve its temporal reference (cf. also Sections 4.6 and 6.2). Typically, the *Imperfecto*'s location time t$_{LOC}$ is provided either by an adverbial expression or by the definite tense form *Indefinido*. In (25) though, it is the PPC$_{SP}$ which, in combination with *cuando*, provides the required location time. Strikingly, this use is not consistent with the quantificational semantics of the PPC$_{SP}$: the quantificational PPC$_{SP}$ is oriented towards the speech time, i.e. sets its perspective time to lie in the present time-sphere which causes that the denoted past eventuality remains indefinite. As a consequence, the quantificational PPC$_{SP}$ is supposed not to provide "access" to t$_E$ that would license further discursive operations, such as the creation of a discourse reference time t$_R$ functioning as the location time t$_{LOC}$ for a succeeding *Imperfecto* (cf. also Section 2.4). Further examples of the cataphoric function of the PPC$_{SP}$ are illustrated in (26).

(26) Cataphoric PPC$_{SP}$ anchoring an *Imperfecto*
    a. *¿Dónde estaba el Profesor cuando se han escapado 16 rehenes? ¿Dónde estaba cuando le han abierto la cabeza a Oslo?*[237]
    'Where was the Professor when 16 hostages escaped? Where was he when Oslo's head was split open?'

---

236. La *Casa de Papel*, 01/04.

237. La *Casa de Papel*, 01/09.

b. *Es que antes, cuando he visto a Mónica Gaztambide y he visto que estaba viva, que estaba bien, me he venido abajo y creo que no he reaccionado como ella esperaba.*[238]
'It's just that before, when I saw Monica Gaztambide and I saw that she was alive, that she was fine, I broke down and I don't think I reacted as she expected.'

c. *Me ha pillado de... sorpresa, porque no lo sabía. Lo mismo que no sabía que eras del Atleti.*[239]
'It has caught me off guard... surprise, because I didn t know it. The same thing I didn't know you were from Atleti.'

d. *Siéntate con nosotros. ¿Necesitas un tenedor? – He estado en Egipto, pero no se comía así. – ¿Qué tenemos que ver nosotros con Egipto?*[240]
'Sit down with us. Do you need a fork? I've been to Egypt, but they didn't eat like this. What do we have to do with Egypt?'

e. *No soportaba más miradas de pena o de condescendencia. – ¿Has visto como me miraba Nadia?*[241]
'I couldn't stand any more looks of pity or condescension. – Have you seen the way Nadia looked at me?'

f. *Samuel, ¿has visto cómo me miraba la gente?*[242]
'Samuel, did you see how people looked at me?'

g. *¿Yo qué sí? Antes he visto eso y... Y me ha llamado la atención. No sabía lo que era.*[243]
'What do I know? I've seen that before and... And it has caught my attention. I didn't know what it was.'

h. *Me he imaginado muchas veces el momento en el que decidíamos que éramos novios. Muchas. Pero así no era ninguna, te lo aseguro. ¿Tienes por ahí tu máquina del tiempo?*[244]
'I have imagined many times the moment when we decided that we were engaged. Many times. But that was none, I assure you. Do you have your time machine out there?'

---

238. *La Casa de Papel*, 01/08.

239. *La Casa de Papel*, 01/05.

240. *Élite*, 01/04.

241. *Élite*, 05.

242. *Élite*, 01/08.

243. *La Casa de Papel*, 01/04.

244. *Élite*, 01/04.

i. A ver.. Samu, no <u>ha pasado</u> nada. Solo <u>querían</u> asustarla, ya esta.[245]
'Let's see… Samu, nothing has happened. They just wanted to scare her, that's all.'

Each of these examples contains a PPC$_{SP}$ that, together with an *Imperfecto*, may be interpreted as forming a mini discourse of narration. Crucially, a temporal relationship is established between the PPC$_{SP}$ and the *Imperfecto*. For example, in (26-a), the PPC$_{SP}$ *se han escapado 16 rehenes* is temporally included in the *Imperfecto* (*el profesor estaba dónde*). In other words, the *Imperfecto* anaphorically retrieves its temporal anchor (provided by *cuando* + PPC$_{SP}$) and gets backgrounded with respect to that anchor based on an inclusion relation creating an interpretation of simultaneity. While this discourse-semantic encoding of a temporal relationship between the PPC$_{SP}$ and an adjacent tense form is predicted to be blocked by a purely quantificational PPC$_{SP}$, it might be compatible with the semantics of a referential PPC$_{SP}$ as discussed in Section 4.4. In this sense, we consider the examples listed in (26) as highly relevant discursive evidence for the grammaticalization status of the PPC$_{SP}$ (referential drift). In Chapter 6, we take up this question in more detail, discussing further implications and problems from a theoretical point of view based on a prominence-based account, complemented with further empirical evidence.

5.3.4 Discussion

To a great extent, the expectations formulated in Section 5.3.1 turned out to be consistent with the data.

Portuguese
In the data, the Portuguese PPC$_{PT}$ turned out to be oftentimes employed in order to shape the structure of an argument by establishing effects of contrast or consistency with episodic propositions – that may not only be denoted by the Simple Past, but e.g. also by Future Tense – in order to gain argumentative power. This finding matches well the genre-specific properties of the Portuguese subcorpus favoring elaborated and well-planned language of distance, as well as the discourse mode of argument. In fact, this rhetorical discourse function of the PPC$_{PT}$ may be analyzed as a means to contribute to the generation of quasi-logical arguments in the tradition of the seminal account of rhetoric and argumentation by Perelman and Olbrechts-Tyteca (1971: §45).[246] In their framework, quasi-logical arguments repre-

---

245. *Élite* 01/02.

246. The cited source is an officially digitalized version (E-Book) that lacks page numbering, as it is structured into paragraphs.

sent one of the three major techniques of argumentation (together with arguments based on the structure of reality and arguments establishing the structure of reality):

> Quasi-logical arguments claim to be similar to the formal reasoning of logic or mathematics. [...] Since there are formal proofs of recognized validity, quasi-logical arguments derive their persuasive strength from their similarity with these well-established modes of reasoning. [...] Sometimes the speaker will mention the formal reasoning to which he makes reference, availing himself of the prestige of logical thought. [...] By making this charge, one takes advantage of the prestige of rigorous thought. (Perelman and Olbrechts-Tyteca 1971: §45)

The property of quasi-logical arguments of contributing to a highly prestigious kind of argumentation correlates with PPC_{PT}'s variational status as being diastratically and diamesically marked as high. In this sense, the discussed deductive and inductive reasoning expressed by the interplay between the characterizing PPC_{PT} and episodic propositions seem to apply/imitate the principles of logic to/on the level of the argumentative structure in discourse.

Similarities between the PPC_{PT}'s and PPC_{SP}'s discourse functions

The episodic PPC_{PT} turned out to give rise to transitional perspectival effects, i.e. perspectival shifts from the past time-sphere to the present time-sphere. Surprisingly, the data also revealed that the episodic readings of the PPC_{PT} may contribute to actualization effects, that we exclusively expected to detect in the Spanish data. That is, the PPC_{PT} may be employed to introduce an iterated t_E that gets referentially picked up, elaborated and provided with further details by a definite tense form as discourse unfolds. We assume that the PPC_{PT}'s actualizing potential once again motivates its classification as a Present Perfect, as the PPC_{PT} and PPC_{SP} share more discourse functions than previously expected. However, this similarity correlates with the PPC_{PT}'s split into episodic and characterizing readings. While the episodic PPC_{PT}'s denoted eventualities remain indefinite, they are spread over the virtual timeline pertaining to the temporal domain which qualifies them to contribute to the discursive management of the event-referential structure. This does not hold for the characterizing PPC_{PT} on the other hand, which motivates the characterizing PPC_{PT}'s peculiar discourse functions. This is also in line with Becker and Egetenmeyer (2018) who postulate that the temporal domain – as opposed to the modal domain – is associated with a continuous updating of the referential structure:

> The habitual nature of the exposed eventualities disqualifies them from belonging to the primary story line characterized by its continuous updating.[247] As is well

---

247. "Habitual" is another term used in the literature for "characterizing", cf. Krifka et al. (1995: 3).

known, "habituality" does not belong to the domain of temporality, but to another domain – the "reign" of modality. This is the reason why habitual eventualities are situated beyond the temporal level of discourse structuring and ordering, i.e., they constitute a layer apart. (Becker and Egetenmeyer 2018: 55)

Spanish
With regard to the Spanish data, our expectations turned out to be consistent with the data to a great extent, as well. The corpus showed many examples featuring functions of perspectivizing and actualization. This suggests that the PPC$_{SP}$ productively contributes to the discursive shaping of the event-referential structure, as well as to the shift between the present- and the past time-sphere.

Moreover, the Spanish subcorpus contained examples where a PPC$_{SP}$ is employed in order to cataphorically anchor a succeeding *Imperfecto*, as exemplified in (26). As discussed in Section 2.5, it is assumed that the PPC$_{SP}$, at some point, will develop into a referential tense form that is able to denote perfective and aoristic past eventualities that allow for narrative uses. In our framework, this development is expressed in the transition from a quantificational to a referential tense form. Given the gap between these two categories, the cataphoric function of the PPC$_{SP}$, as attested in the data, might assume a bridging function in the transition from the quantificational to the referential PPC$_{SP}$. It may signal that the PPC$_{SP}$ already allows for innovative operations as temporal cataphora. Before the PPC$_{SP}$ ultimately turns into a referential, definite tense form taking a location time as an argument (allowing for combinations with prehodiernal, positional adverbials), there is first an attentional shift towards the event domain expressed in the licensing of cataphoric operations. In Chapter 6, we discuss and empirically investigate this case in detail by proposing a prominence-based approach to the question of why the PPC$_{SP}$'s indefinite event domain is released for discursive operations although the perspective time t_P is still maintained to lie in the present time-sphere.

The PPC between truth conditions and discourse: a case for use conditions?
The findings furthermore support the assumption that tense form choice is influenced by a range of factors, i.e. not only by truth conditions but also by inner-linguistic factors that contribute to the framing of a linguistically described situation. This is in line with the claim that "the nature of reality does not dictate the way that reality is represented in people's mind" (Pinker 2007: 4), discussed in the introduction. Furthermore, this was shown by examples employing a Simple Past instead of a PPC while the PPC would have been adequate from a purely truth-conditional perspective, as e.g. in the repeated example in (27).

(27) *Imagino que <u>has visto</u> la foto que <u>subió</u> a Internet. Yo no <u>subí</u> esa foto.*[248]
'I imagine you've seen the picture that was uploaded to the internet. I didn't upload that picture.'

When observed in isolation, the proposition expressed by the *Indefinido* (*yo no subí*) would perfectly match the PPC$_{SP}$'s truth conditions. After all, the proposition "I didn't upload the picture" is highly relevant at the speech time, which would be adequately captured by the semantic configuration indicated in (28a).

(28) Quantificational PPC$_{SP}$ vs. Referential *Indefinido*
    a. ⟦PPC$_{QUANT}$⟧: $\lambda t_S \lambda t_E \lambda t_P. t_e \prec t_s \subseteq t_p$
    b. ⟦SIMPLE PAST$_{REF}$⟧: $\lambda t_S \lambda t_E \lambda t_P \lambda t_{LOC}. (t_E \genfrac{}{}{0pt}{}{\subseteq}{\supseteq} t_{LOC}) \subseteq t_P \prec t_S$

Independently of whether "I didn't upload the picture" would represent a resultative, experiential or hot news reading, it is the perspectivizing of the present time-sphere and lacking location time argument that qualify the PPC$_{SP}$ as a good candidate for capturing the intended meaning. However, the use of the *Indefinido* instead of the PPC$_{SP}$ may be accounted for assuming that the discourse-structural demand of emphasizing an actualization overrides the truth-conditional cue. The speaker thus chooses to zoom in on the situation by shifting the perspective time towards the past time-sphere, i.e. to the eventuality under discussion, by means of an *Indefinido*, which is based on the semantic configuration indicated in (28b). Concerning future work, it seems to be promising to discuss whether the discursive cues imposed by the inner-linguistic structure impacting tense choice form additionally to truth conditions can be approached based on the concept of use-conditional meaning, a concept tracing back to Kaplan (1999) and Recanati (2004) (cf. Gutzmann 2013):

> Use-conditional content affects the conditions under which a sentence can be uttered felicitously, not the conditions that have to be fulfilled in order to make a sentence true. Hence, using a UCI [*use-conditional item*] that is not licensed by the utterance context leads to infelicity, but does not render a sentence false [...]. We are dealing with two separate criteria to evaluate a sentence.
> (Gutzmann 2013: 33)

The idea that the felicitousness of a word or utterance that is imposed by its use conditions complements its truth conditions has been argued to account for meaning effects on many levels, as illustrated in (29). The formula are written "informally in a fraction-like fashion with the use-conditional content on top of the truth-conditional one" (Gutzmann 2013: 5), i.e. as $\frac{\text{use condition}}{\text{truth condition}}$.

[248.] *La Casa de Papel*, 01/01.

(29) Examples for use-conditional content complementing truth conditions in Gutzmann (2013)

a. Lessing was a Kraut = $\dfrac{\text{Generally, I don't like Germans}}{\text{Lessing was a German}}$

b. Hans-i (German) = $\dfrac{\text{Familiar relationship between the speaker and Hans}}{\text{Hans}}$

c. John, Mary loves. = $\dfrac{\text{The speaker's mental representation of John is active}}{\text{Mary loves John}}$

d. Carl did finish his book. = $\dfrac{\text{It is true that Carl finished his book}}{\text{Carl finished his book}}$

e. How tall Michael is! = $\dfrac{\text{It is unexpected how tall Michael is}}{\emptyset}$

In (29a), *Kraut* may be uttered felicitously if the speaker does not like Germans. Otherwise, it would be infelicitous to refer to a German by *Kraut*. Similarly, it is a relationship of familiarity that licensed to address *Hans* as *Hansi* in (29b). (29c) illustrates the impact of use conditions beyond the word level, i.e. on the sentence level. Here, the information-structural topicalization of John is licensed by "the speaker's mental representation of John is active", which turns the syntactically marked variant of "Mary loves John" felicitous. Similarly, in (29d) it is the verum focus that licenses the explicit insertion of *did* as felicitous. In (29e), there is even no truth-conditional content at all, as the exclamative-like utterance of *How tall Michael is* seems to express use-conditional meaning exclusively. In sum, the use-conditional approach aims at a formal synthesis of functional and formal perspectives on meaning. As it turns out, it might provide a fruitful tool for the analysis for the study of the competition of tense forms. In (30), it is illustrated how an application of a use-conditional account to potential competing zones of PPC$_{SP}$ vs. *Indefinido* might look like.

(30) ¿Qué ha dicho? – _____ "¡No me toquéis!"[249]

a. Ha dicho: = $\dfrac{\text{maintain t}_P}{\text{(s)he said}}$

b. Dijo: = $\dfrac{\text{shift t}_P \text{ / actualization}}{\text{(s)he said}}$

The formulization exemplified in (30) might provide a way to record the multidimensional impacts on tense form choice on the micro structure of discourse discussed in this chapter. Furthermore, it might offer a way to integrate the study PPC$_{SP}$'s and also PPC$_{PT}$'s interplay with the micro-structural discursive dimension

---

249. 'What did (s)he say? – [(S)he (has) said]: Don't touch me!'

into a more general theory of how tense forms are employed. However, a systematic exploration of the approach applied to the study of PPC$_{PT}$ and PPC$_{SP}$ lies beyond the scope of our study, but remains as a promising enterprise for future work on theoretical perspectives on the PPC$_{PT}$ and PPC$_{SP}$, as well as on tense forms in general.

Summing up, the idea that inner-linguistic discursive conditions and truth conditions jointly impact the choice of the PPC is, again, illustrated in Figure 5.9.

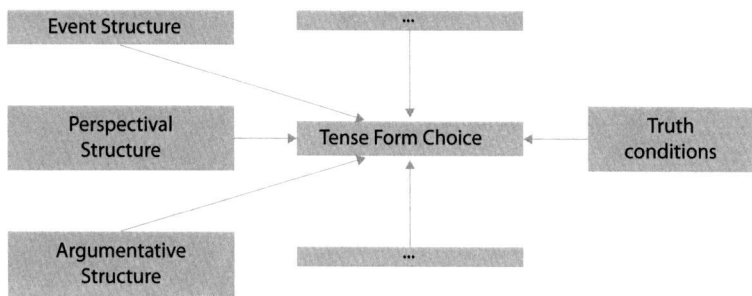

Figure 5.9 Micro-structural discursive factors complementing truth conditions in tense form choice

As indicated by the boxes containing dots, the list is not meant to illustrate an exhaustive classification of the range of micro-structural factors influencing tense form choice. However, it emphasizes the idea of the certainly highly diverse impacts on tense form choice, as also suggested by our corpus data.

5.4 Conclusion

In this chapter, we presented a corpus study whose goal was to investigate the discourse functions of PPC$_{PT}$ and PPC$_{SP}$. This was approached by studying first their interplay with tempo-aspectual adverbials, and second their interaction with adjacent tense forms. The study was guided by the general hypothesis that both PPC$_{PT}$ and PPC$_{SP}$ share the inherent semantic feature of denoting quantificational temporal semantics, even if spelled out differently, which should reveal similarities between the two tense forms on the level of discourse as well. With regard to the Spanish PPC$_{SP}$, we additionally checked for evidence concerning referential uses of the PPC$_{SP}$.

We created a corpus consisting of Spanish subtitles of movies and series (containing 103,361 tokens in total) and, on the other hand, transcripts of a Brazilian talk show and of political speeches by Brazilian politicians (containing 638,094 + 102,206 = 740,300 tokens in total). The well-known fact that PPC$_{PT}$ and

PPC$_{SP}$ significantly differ quantitatively in terms of their overall frequencies was reflected in the data in that the Spanish data showed much higher PPC ratios than the Portuguese data.

The analysis of combinations with tempo-aspectual adverbials revealed the PPC$_{PT}$'s preference of quantificational and durative/XN-adverbials, as well as a lack of positional adverbials. The Spanish data, on the other hand, suggested a clear preference of quantificational adverbials, moreover, low numbers of potential positional adverbials. However, the study confirmed the assumption that an analysis of the PPC should not be exclusively built on combinations with tempo-aspectual adverbials. The data showed a range of examples of adverbials featuring scope ambiguities, i.e. adverbials that are e.g. ambiguous between positional and XN-adverbials (scoping over t_{LOC} vs. t_P), such as *esta mañana, esta tarde, hoy* ('this morning', 'this afternoon', 'today'). Furthermore, the data quite consistently showed for each subcorpus that the PPC does not receive adverbial modification at all in the majority of the cases. We derived the need to particularly focus on the PPC's interaction with adjacent tense forms.

The study of the PPC's syntagmatic interplay with tense forms was guided by the hypotheses and assumptions discussed in the previous chapters. The Portuguese subcorpus showed two general tendencies: on the one hand, the characterizing PPC$_{PT}$ seems to be typically employed in elaborated, planned language of distance in order to establish effects of consistence between generic and episodic propositions. In this vein, the characterizing PPC$_{PT}$ represents a rhetorical device that helps structure an argument in order to make a hearer believe or commit to a proposition. This suggests that the PPC$_{PT}$ has specialized in the discourse mode of argumentation where it is able to contribute prestigious quasi-logical arguments in the sense of Perelman and Olbrechts-Tyteca (1971). On the other hand, the episodic PPC$_{PT}$ (still) shows functions that overlap with the PPC$_{SP}$'s, namely the functions of actualization and perspectivizing (perspectival shift and perspectival maintenance).

The Spanish data suggested that the indefinite, quantificational semantics of the PPC$_{SP}$ productively contribute to the discursive management of the event-referential structure, as well as to the perspectival structure. The former function refers to highly productive actualizations expressed in the introduction of an indefinite past eventuality that, in the following, gets picked up by a referential, i.e. definite tense form. The latter function shifts or maintains the perspective time with respect to the past and present time-sphere.

Moreover, the study shed new light on the question of the potential referential configuration of the PPC$_{SP}$. As discussed, hodiernal-perfective uses contained in the data could neither verify nor falsify a truly referential PPC$_{SP}$ due to scope ambiguities. Besides, unambiguously anaphoric uses featuring prehodiernal positional adverbials suggesting that the PPC$_{SP}$ has already grammaticalized into a productive referential tense form were lacking in the data, as well.

However, the analysis revealed examples of cataphoric uses of the PPC$_{SP}$ providing an anchor for an adjacent *Imperfecto*. These examples represent a highly interesting case for the PPC$_{SP}$'s referential drift, i.e. its transition from quantificational towards referential temporal semantics. They bear both quantificational and referential components at the same time: on the one hand, their perspective time remains situated in the present time-sphere; on the other hand, there seems to be an attentional shift to the event domain such that the indefinite past eventuality gets promoted, licensing the attachment of an anaphoric tense form (e.g. *Imperfecto*). In the final chapter, we investigate in detail the idea that the cataphoric use of the PPC$_{SP}$ may trigger the PPC$_{SP}$'s referential drift, hypothesizing that it assumes a bridging function between quantification and reference, before the PPC$_{SP}$ finally productively allows for temporally definite uses. Figure 5.10 summarizes the findings concerning the discourse functions of PPC$_{PT}$ and PPC$_{SP}$ according to their readings.

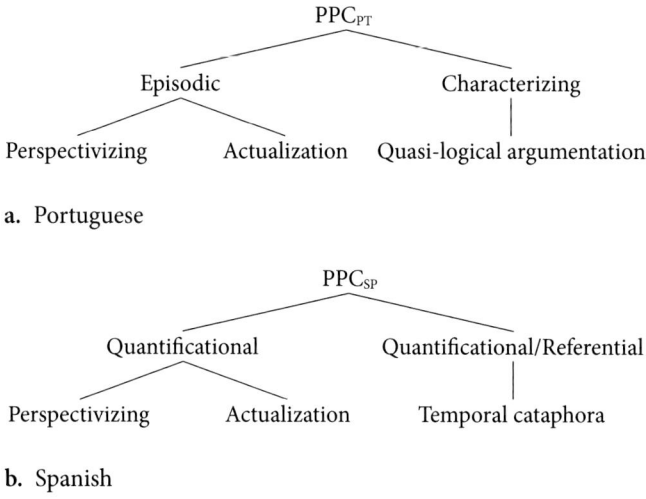

Figure 5.10 Discourse functions of PPC$_{PT}$ and PPC$_{SP}$

PPC$_{PT}$ escaping from stage II and PPC$_{SP}$ approaching stage IV?

We may now "zoom out" and return to a more general discussion and relate our findings to the overall diachronic development commonly assumed for the PPC in the Romance languages (cf. Section 2.5) in the tradition of Harris (1982) and Bertinetto and Squartini (2000). With regard to the Portuguese PPC$_{PT}$, we have given a preliminary answer in Section 3.3 hypothesizing that the split of the PPC$_{PT}$ into episodic (universal and IPEX) and characterizing readings correlates with a diverging status with respect to the model: while the episodic readings still pertain to stage II, the characterizing readings have escaped from stage II (which may actually account for why the PPC$_{PT}$'s has not approached stage III). On a truth-conditional level, the difference between the episodic and characterizing readings remains subtle. This is e.g. expressed in the lack of an exact linguistic test to distinguish them (e.g. based on potential combinations with particular tempo aspectual adverbials), as well as in reading ambiguities. In fact, these ambiguities might explain why the reinterpretation of the universal/IPEX quantifier as a generic/characterizing quantifier has been realized by speakers at all. Moreover, the discursive study has shown that the PPC$_{PT}$'s reading split correlates with a discourse-functional split. That is, the episodic and characterizing readings turn out to license different discursive operations that can be transparently motivated based on their diverging semantic configurations. With regard to Spanish, the PPC$_{SP}$ spreads over stage II (universal reading) and stage III (existential readings). Additionally, there are uses that might be classified as being situated somewhere in between stage III and IV, as discussed and studied in detail in the final chapter. Figure 5.11 summarizes these discussed ideas. Strikingly, there seems to be a correlation between the stages assumed by the model and the discourse functions of the respective readings. Stages II and III lead to discourse functions related to the shaping of the perspectival and event-referential structure, which holds for both PPC$_{PT}$ and PPC$_{SP}$. Thus, these functions may be considered cross-linguistically as the core discourse functions of the PPC. By contrast, the readings deviating from stages II and III lead to innovative

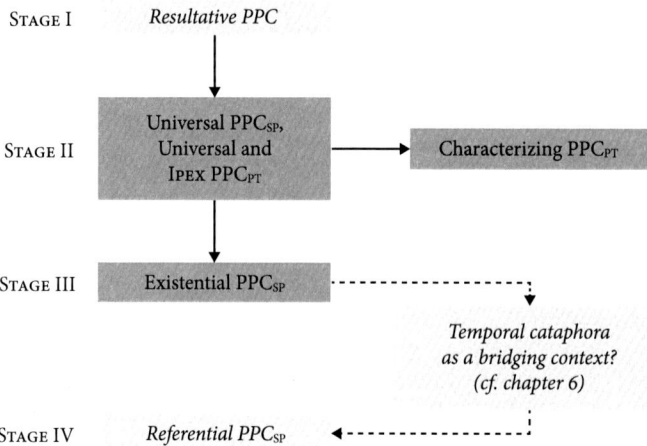

Figure 5.11 Grammaticalization path of the PPC$_{PT}$ and PPC$_{SP}$ as suggested by our analysis

discourse functions, as exemplified by the characterizing PPC$_{PT}$ on the one hand, and the PPC$_{SP}$ approaching stage IV on the other hand.

As indicated in the figure, the next chapter presents a detailed analysis of the PPC$_{SP}$'s transition between stages III and IV. The account is based on the concept of prominence, in particular, on a prominent event domain that mediates between the quantificational PPC$_{SP}$ and a referential PPC$_{SP}$. Furthermore, the chapter reports an experimental case study testing acceptability judgements for cataphoric PPC$_{SP}$ uses featuring a prominent event domain.

CHAPTER 6

The PPC$_{SP}$'s referential drift

In this chapter, we focus on the PPC$_{SP}$'s referential drift, i.e. the PPC$_{SP}$'s transition from a purely quantificational tense form to a referential tense form. In the terminology of the diachronic stage model discussed in Section 2.4, this drift has been traditionally labelled as an aoristic drift and is associated with the transition from stage III to stage IV (cf. Bertinetto and Squartini 2000). We argue that a micro-structural discourse-based perspective provides evidence for investigating the PPC$_{SP}$'s referential drift. In particular, the PPC$_{SP}$'s cataphoric potential of anchoring adjacent past eventualities is discussed on grounds of a prominence-based theory and experimentally tested. The chapter is structured as follows.

Section 6.1 reviews common approaches to the PPC$_{SP}$'s referential drift. Accordingly, a "gradual relaxation of the degree of recentness" (Comrie 1976: 61) is expected to guide the PPC$_{SP}$'s development which is expressed in a stepwise extension of a temporal boundary separating the prehodiernal sphere (past time-sphere) from the hodiernal sphere (present time-sphere). Additionally, the PPC$_{SP}$'s indefiniteness is assumed to contribute to the decline of the temporal remoteness constraint.

Section 6.2 discusses the PPC$_{SP}$'s potential to cataphorically anchor a backgrounded *Imperfecto*, i.e. whether an anaphoric tense form may be attached to the PPC$_{SP}$. The standard characterization of the quantificational PPC$_{SP}$ would predict a semantic clash for this operation. Yet, the corpus study presented in Chapter 5 revealed counterevidence. We derive that a particular semantic configuration of the PPC$_{SP}$, which is on its way to acquire referential semantics, may license those uses. Arguing that the cataphoric potential of the PPC$_{SP}$ may serve as a test case for whether a PPC$_{SP}$ is approaching (or not) referential semantics in a given variety, we aim for complementing common approaches by focussing on the PPC$_{SP}$'s micro-structural potential beyond the level of tempo-aspectual adverbials.

Section 6.3 introduces the concept of prominence as a "basic underlying organizational principle of linguistic structuring" (Himmelmann and Primus 2015: 52) and identifies two competing domains denoted by the PPC$_{SP}$. These are the post-state domain on the one hand and the event domain on the other hand. We argue that while the quantificational PPC$_{SP}$ highlights its post-state as the prominent domain, the approaching of referential semantics is triggered by the innovative highlighting of the event domain. The event domain then functions as a structural attractor providing access to the event. This, in turn, licenses the micro-structural discursive operation of establishing explicit temporal relationships between the PPC$_{SP}$'s past eventuality and other past eventualities present in discourse, which is exemplified by the PPC$_{SP}$'s cataphoric anchoring of an adjacent *Imperfecto* as discussed in Section 6.2.

Section 6.4 reports an experiment testing the acceptability of the PPC$_{SP}$'s cataphoric function as licensed by a prominent event domain. Investigating the attachment of a progressive *Imperfecto,* the results show quite controversial acceptability scores among speakers of Peninsular Spanish. This suggests that the PPC$_{SP}$ has not yet acquired referential semantics (which also holds for hodiernal contexts), but seems to be on its way to do so. That is, there seems to be a currently ongoing change featuring a transitional reading located between quantification and reference. Furthermore, the results suggest that the PPC$_{SP}$'s cataphoric potential follows the temporal remoteness constraint as well, which is commonly assumed to impact the felicitous use of the PPC$_{SP}$. This is expressed in higher acceptability scores for hodiernal (present time-sphere) than for prehodiernal (past time-sphere) contexts. With regard to the methodological dimension, the proposed shift towards investigating the PPC$_{SP}$'s micro-structural potential by means of measuring acceptability scores is argued to represent a fruitful approach for future studies, that might particularly take into account the dimension of diatopic variation in the study of the referential drift.

6.1 The PPC$_{SP}$ between quantification and reference

As discussed in Section 2.4, the PPC$_{SP}$ is expected to develop into an original past tense form at some point (cf. e.g. Bertinetto and Squartini 2000: 416, Schwenter and Cacoullos 2008: 32). This would qualify the PPC$_{SP}$ i.a. to be combined with positional adverbials (like *yesterday*) modifying a location time. In the very influential terminology of the diachronic model discussed in Bertinetto and Squartini (2000), this development is expressed in the acquisition of stage IV triggered by the aoristic drift, an evolution that is expected to mainly affect the aspectual domain. In a recent publication by Azpiazu Torres (2021), the aspectual nature of the aoristic drift has been reinterpreted as a temporal upgrade by means of a reorganization of the temporal vectors of simultaneity and anteriority in the tradition of Rojo (1974) and Rojo and Veiga (1999). In our account and terminology, building on more general semantic notions, this evolution is labelled as the referential drift. This is in order to emphasize the significant semantic transition which pertains to the development from a purely quantificational, i.e. an indefinite tense form that lacks a location time t_{LOC}, to a referential, i.e. a definite tense form, that takes t_{LOC} as an argument (cf. e.g. Chapter 4).

However, the referential drift does not only come along with this significant truth-conditional update but also triggers profound changes with regard to the PPC$_{SP}$'s functions in discourse. In the terminology of Smith's (2003) modes of discourse, the quantificational PPC$_{SP}$ is typically employed in the mode of report: it primarily denotes events, states and general statives, whose temporal advancement is based on a relative anchoring to the speech time. In this vein, a potential sequential interpretation of the two eventualities in (1) is pragmatically inferred, e.g. based on verb semantics, the syntactic order of the eventualities or on world knowledge. That is, there is no discourse-semantically encoded relation (which would be based on a dynamic shifting of a discourse reference time t_R, cf. also discussion in Section 4.6).

(1) *A ver, Nacho, ese señor <u>ha tosido</u>, <u>ha escupido</u> sangre, <u>ha tocado</u> las paredes, el suelo, el móvil...*[250]
'Let's see, Nacho, this man coughed, spat blood, touched the walls, the floor, the cell phone...'

On the other hand, a referential PPC$_{SP}$ qualifies to be employed in the discourse mode of narration. That is, under a referential reading, the PPC$_{SP}$ in (1) may denote a sequential interpretation of the two eventualities. This is due to the property of the discourse mode of narration of denoting specific events and states that underly a dynamic temporal progression that advances in narrative time. The referred past eventualities thus may establish temporal relations with one another, such as temporal precedence or inclusion, as e.g. also achieved by the referential Simple Past (*Indefinido*) in (2).

(2) *A ver, Nacho, ese señor <u>tosió</u>, <u>escupió</u> sangre, <u>tocó</u> las paredes, el suelo, el móvil...*
'Let's see, Nacho, this man has coughed, spat blood, touched the walls, the floor, the cell phone...

Summing up, the quantificational PPC$_{SP}$'s denotes indefinite past eventualities that remain isolated in discourse with respect to adjacent past eventualities, i.e. they do not license the attachment of further past eventualities. This property blocks the discourse mode of narration. In this vein, (1) might be interpreted as a report. By contrast, the referential PPC$_{SP}$ *may* be employed in the discourse mode of narration due to its updated semantic configuration. Moreover, it licenses the discourse-semantic attachment of adjacent past eventualities based on particular temporal relations, such as anaphoric or cataphoric operations.

---

250. *El bar* (example taken from Chapter 5).

From several studies recapitulated in Azpiazu Torres (2019), we can derive that the Peninsular PPC$_{SP}$ has already started to approach the referential drift.[251] Accordingly, the PPC$_{SP}$ already seems to have consolidated its potential of denoting past eventualities that are temporarily determined, though still restricted to a time frame reaching up to the present (i.e. the present time-sphere). Furthermore, the author attributes an even more innovative use to the macro variety *Centro Peninsular*, where the PPC$_{SP}$ already seems to be approaching an aoristic value. That is, in the center of Spain, the PPC$_{SP}$ seems to have already started to oust the Preterite in more and more contexts, at least in those that are typically characterized as hodiernal contexts (cf. Azpiazu Torres 2019: 204). In fact, the notion of hodiernality – separating prehodiernal from hodiernal contexts – traditionally has been characterized as a factor affecting the PPC$_{SP}$'s grammaticalization. Accordingly, the PPC$_{SP}$ is commonly assumed to follow a path of a gradual extension of the temporal boundaries that define the limits of what speaker and hearer consider as belonging to the past and the present time-sphere.

"Gradual relaxation of the degree of recentness"

This approach is very much in the tradition of Schwenter (1994b). Analyzing the PPC$_{SP}$ in the Alicante variety, Schwenter (1994b) proposes a fine-grained breakdown of what the author calls the PPC$_{SP}$'s "road to perfective". Schwenter's proposal is depicted in Figure 6.1. The stages do not comply with the stages I–IV in Bertinetto and Squartini's (2000) model but are supposed to zoom in on the transition between stages III and IV. Crucially, the formation of the past value of the PPC$_{SP}$ spoken in Alicante is said to be triggered by a "gradual relaxation of the degree of recentness" (in the sense of Comrie 1976: 61). In other words, there is a temporal constraint of hodiernality that keeps getting expanded.

Stage 1 corresponds to an experiential reading denoting an indefinite past eventuality of particular current relevance. Stage 2 adds the hot news reading, i.e. the denotation of past eventualities whose temporal distance to the speech time remains minimal. Next, stages 3 and 4 relax the conditions of temporal remoteness by allowing for past eventualities that satisfy the temporal condition of hodiernality. Stages 5 and 6 consolidate the PPC$_{SP}$'s potential to be used for hodiernal past eventualities as the default tense form for these contexts. Finally, stage 7 abolishes the temporal boundary of hodiernality in favor of an extension towards all "past (perfective) situations." Azpiazu Torres (2019: 141) assumes that the immediate past

---

[251]. This notion of Peninsular Spanish excludes the northeast of Spain and the Canary Islands whose PPC$_{SP}$ is assumed to disprefer the PPC$_{SP}$ (cf. Azpiazu Torres 2019: 294 and overview in Section 4.2).

Table 6.1 The grammaticalization path of the PPC$_{SP}$ in Alicante Spanish from anterior to perfective (Schwenter 1994a: 99)

Stage	Function
1	PP used solely for anterior functions in situations with a "particular aspectual profile" (Fleischman 1983: 195)
2	PP begins to take on recent past functions, given that situation described is considered currently relevant, such as "hot news" use
3	PP used for immediate/recent past situations which are not considered currently relevant
4	PP used for recent past situations occurring on the same day, along with the older Preterite
5	PP used for most "today" past situations, especially those with temporal adverbial modification
6	PP ousts Preterite as the form used for "today" past perfective situations. Hodiernal/prehodiernal distinction also obtains in both narrative and non-narrative contexts
7	PP gradually extended to all past (perfective) situations, regardless of their remoteness from point of speech. The PP becomes a general past perfective, supplanting the Preterite, which is retained in written and more formal spoken registers

(corresponding to Schwenter's (1994a) hot news reading) pertains to events that speaker and interlocutor share and that the hodiernal past more or less pertains to events that have occurred on the same day. However, as e.g. also Xiqués (2021: 190), she calls into question the assumption that speakers strictly follow a clear-cut division separating a prehodiernal from a hodiernal time-sphere:

> [N]os resulta difícil creer que los hablantes son capaces de establecer los límites cronológicos de lo "simultáneo" o de lo que esta o no vigente en el momento de la elocución con tanta precisión. Las formulaciones de este tipo, como la famosa regla académica de las 24 horas que se dicto para el francés ya en el siglo XVII (y terminó descartándose después), no dejan de ser meros desiderátums de los propios gramáticos que tienen poco con ver con el funcionamiento real de la lengua (cf. Fournier 1998, 398ss.; Azpiazu 2017[a], 544).[252] (Azpiazu Torres 2019: 107)

Instead of defining the referred temporal boundary as being delimited by the hodiernal vs. prehodiernal time-sphere, it thus may be more pertinent to conceive of the

---

252. 'We find it difficult to believe that speakers are capable of establishing the chronological limits of what is "simultaneous" or what is or is not in force at the time of elocution with such precision. Formulations of this type, such as the famous academic rule of 24 hours that was dictated for French already in the seventeenth century (and ended up being discarded later), are no more than mere desiderata of the grammars themselves that have little to do with the actual functioning of the language (cf. Fournier (1998: 398ff.); Azpiazu Torres (2017: 544).'

temporal constraint of hodiernality as being constituted by the rather vague notions of the present and past time-spheres (as discussed in Section 2.1). Accordingly, there might be contexts in which eventualities that took place prehodiernally are actually attributed to the present time-sphere. The other way round, there might also be contexts in which hodiernal eventualities are perceived and coded as pertaining to the past time-sphere. That is, we assume the hodiernal vs. prehodiernal division to correlate with the present vs. past time-sphere division. That means that contexts that are inner-linguistically perceived as hodiernal need not be perfectly consistent with the strict notion of a 24 hours lasting day in the extra-linguistic world.

Temporal indeterminacy

A slightly different view on the grammaticalization path of the PPC$_{SP}$ emphasizes the role of temporal indeterminacy as a crucial factor. This is proposed by Schwenter and Cacoullos (2008) and Holmes and Balukas (2011) who present quantitative corpus studies on the influence of a range of factors (dis)favoring the PPC$_{SP}$ in competing zones with the Simple Past (*Indefinido*). Schwenter and Cacoullos (2008: 33) argue for Peninsular Spanish that the PPC$_{SP}$ has already become the default tense form for hodiernal perfectives and, furthermore, is more and more extending into a past perfective, suggested by its status to be preferred in temporal indeterminate contexts:

> The quantitative analysis of naturally-occurring speech data shows that the PP's shift to perfective is advancing in the context not specified for temporal reference: temporally indeterminate past contexts. It remains to be discovered whether indeterminate reference is a locus of change in temporal systems more generally.
> (Schwenter and Cacoullos 2008: 33)

Holmes and Balukas (2011) corroborate this view with a similar finding that qualifies temporal indeterminate contexts as favoring the PPC$_{SP}$.

We understand that the authors assume that the reason why temporally indeterminate contexts favor the PPC$_{SP}$'s grammaticalization into a past perfective tense form lies in the fact that these escape from the restrictions imposed by the hodiernality constraint, which, as a consequence, vanishes in the long run.

In sum, the PPC$_{SP}$'s development into a past tense form seems to be affected by two factors in a parallel fashion. On the one hand, the temporal remoteness constraint of hodiernality keeps getting gradually loosened, which, at some point, enables past reference. On the other hand, the PPC$_{SP}$ has the strong preference to denote temporally indefinite events, which, at some point, enables a decline (instead of a loosening) of the hodiernality boundary.

Temporal semantics vs. discourse functions

As discussed in Section 2.4, the modes of discourse (Smith 2003) correlate with particular tempo-aspectual requirements that tense forms employed in a particular mode need to meet. Due to this correlation, one cannot disentangle whether it is the referential semantics of a particular tense form that triggers its discursive potential or whether it is the other way round. However, it seems that the common accounts of the PPC$_{SP}$'s grammaticalization mainly focus on the PPC$_{SP}$'s upgraded tempo-aspectual profile. They do so by focussing on the stepwise extension of the remoteness constraints associated with the PPC$_{SP}$, e.g. tested on the base of (in)felicitous combinations with particular adverbials. Accordingly, the PPC$_{SP}$'s growing potential to occur in narratives and to denote temporal relations seems to be considered as a rather secondary effect of updated temporal semantics.

Assuming a parallel evolution of the two components of updated temporal semantics and the updated discursive potential though, we want to shift the perspective to the level of discourse hypothesizing that this offers another way of linguistic evidence of the PPC$_{SP}$'s referential drift. In this vein, we consider the micro-structural discourse-based perspective as an extension of existing accounts.

The inverse hypothesis is that we may derive states that the PPC$_{SP}$ gradually licenses more and more discourse functions associated with narration, e.g. the discourse-semantic establishment of temporal relations between adjacent past eventualities, such as temporal precedence and succession, as well as fore- and backgrounding. In the long run, this comes along with the development of referential semantics, i.e. with a location time licensing combinations with positional adverbials.

Perspectival clash

However, within this reversed perspective that primarily focusses the discursive dimension, it actually remains unclear how and why the PPC$_{SP}$, at some point, starts to allow for innovative operations on the level of discourse. In particular, there even seems to be a competing force: it is commonly assumed that even the referential Perfect (e.g. the French *Passé Composé*) maintains its perspective time to lie in the present time-sphere (cf. de Swart 2007). Thus, the puzzle arises of how the maintenance of perspectivizing the present time-sphere is compatible with micro-structural operations that are typical for the mode of narration. After all, there should be a perspectival clash. In Section 2.1, we briefly discussed Botne and Kershner's (2008) distinction between the P-domain and the D-domain (cf. repeated Figure 6.1). The two domains instantiate two "different cognitive worlds." While past and future are associated with the D-domain, anteriority and posteriority are associated with the P-domain. Accordingly, indefinite past eventualities expressed by the quantificational PPC$_{SP}$ are typically situated on the axis of the

P-domain, interpreted as anterior to the speech time. That is, the quantificational PPC$_{SP}$'s past eventuality does not pertain to the past time-sphere which is, in turn, located on the axis of the D-domain. In Weinrich's (1964) terms, the distinction of the D-domain and P-domain corresponds to the distinction of *Erzählte Welt* ("narrated world") and *Besprochene Welt* ("discussed/reported world").

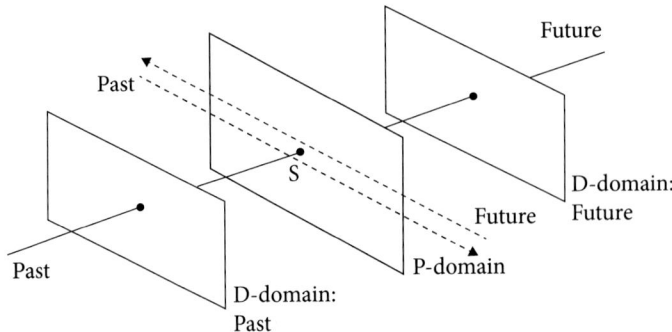

Figure 6.1 Cognitive worlds with three perspectives on time
(Botne and Kershner 2008: 153)

It follows that from a theoretical point of view, the transition of the quantificational PPC$_{SP}$ (which perspectivizes the present time-sphere) towards a referential PPC$_{SP}$ (which licenses the perspectivizing of the past time-sphere) marks a significant update. The transition presupposes that the denoted eventuality may escape from the P-domain (present time-sphere) in order to enter the past of the D-domain (past time-sphere), that is clearly detached from the speech time. Table 6.2 summarizes the idea that the PPC$_{SP}$ updates its discourse functions which, in turn, correlates with an update of its semantic configuration. In the next section, we propose that the gap indicated by the question mark may be filled by a particular discourse function of the PPC$_{SP}$ attested in our corpus study presented in Chapter 5, namely the licensing of the attachment of an anaphoric *Imperfecto*.

Table 6.2 The PPC$_{SP}$ between quantification and reference

Discourse	Type of PPC$_{SP}$	Temporal semantics
t_E denotes an indefinite, isolated event; temporal relations with adjacent eventualities are, at most, pragmatically inferred	Quantificational	$\lambda t_S \, \lambda t_E \, \lambda t_P. \; t_E \prec t_S \subseteq t_P$
⇓⇓	?	⇓⇓
t_E denotes a definite event featuring a location time; temporal relations with adjacent eventualities are discourse-semantically encoded	Referential	$\lambda t_S \, \lambda t_E \, \lambda t_{LOC} \, \lambda t_P. \; (t_E \genfrac{}{}{0pt}{}{\subseteq}{\supseteq} t_{LOC}) \prec t_S \subseteq t_P$

6.2 The attached *Imperfecto* as a test case for the PPC$_{SP}$'s cataphoric potential

In the corpus study reported in Chapter 5, we encountered examples suggesting that the PPC$_{SP}$ may cataphorically anchor a backgrounded *Imperfecto* that is interpreted as referentially picking up a time provided by the PPC$_{SP}$, as exemplified in (3).

(3) *¿Dónde <u>estaba</u> el Profesor cuando se <u>han escapado</u> 16 rehenes? ¿Dónde <u>estaba</u> cuando le <u>han abierto</u> la cabeza a Oslo?*[253]
'Where was the Professor when 16 hostages escaped? Where was he when Oslo's head was split open?'

Within a discourse-based approach to the PPC$_{SP}$'s grammaticalization, we assume that examples of the type illustrated in (3) may play a key role due to its innovative discursive potential. As discussed above, a purely quantificational account of the PPC$_{SP}$'s fails to account for (3). This point is further supported by the following three properties of the *Imperfecto*.

Contextual dependency and anaphoricity

The *Imperfecto* is a tense form that discursively seeks an anchor due to its "anaphoric character and strong contextual dependency" (Becker 2010a: 79). That is, it does not qualify to be autonomously introduced into the discourse but (mostly) presupposes an antecedent serving as a reference point (cf. Kamp and Rohrer 1983; cf. Leonetti 2018 though, who discusses exceptions to that rule for the Spanish *Imperfecto*'s continuous and progressive readings). The anchor that the *Imperfecto* refers to may be either provided by an adverbial time specification or by an event (cf. Becker 2010a: 87). Both of these are able to provide the needed discourse reference time t_R that is dynamically updated as discourse unfolds (cf. also Section 2.4). Typically, events that provide t_R for this operation are expressed by tense forms that dispose of a clearly perfective (not perfectal) viewpoint aspect and that direct their perspective time to the past time-sphere. In sum, the *Imperfecto* explicitly establishes a temporal relation with its cotext, which is, in particular, a typical property of the narrative discourse mode.

Perspective

The *Imperfecto* is typically described as perspectivizing an event's inside:

> The reference point for IMP is the time at which the observer perceives the situation as it takes place, from the inside. [...] IMP is a stativizer device that instructs the hearer to view a past situation from inside, cancelling possible limits or culmination points. (Leonetti 2018: 403, 405)

---

253. *La Casa de Papel*, 01/09.

Per default though, both quantificational and referential PPC$_{SP}$ perspectivize the present time-sphere, which is dissociated from the past time-sphere that, in turn, accommodates the eventuality. This assumption may be illustrated by the following perspectival clash that arises when trying to combine the PPC$_{SP}$ with a Past Perfect (*Pluscuamperfecto*):

(4) Perspectival clash (Carrasco Gutiérrez 2008: 26)[254]
    a. *Cuando <u>llegó</u> María, los invitados ya <u>se habían ido.</u>*
        'When Mary arrived, the guests had already left.'
    b. **Cuando <u>ha llegado</u> María, los invitados ya <u>se habían ido.</u>*
        'When Mary has arrived, the guests had already left.'

Given that the *Pluscuamperfecto* presupposes its perspective time to lie in the past time-sphere (cf. Becker 2020b), there is a perspectival clash in (4b) because of the PPC$_{SP}$'s perspectivizing of the present time-sphere. We would expect the same effect in sentences like (3).

Tempus relief

The *Imperfecto* has been characterized as a discursive device to establish a contrast between fore- and backgrounded past eventualities in the tradition of Weinrich's (1982) work on the *tempus relief* associated with the French *Imparfait*: "[t]he *tempus relief* management involves particularly tense forms, but also temporal connectors such as when or before/after" (Becker and Egetenmeyer 2018: 26). In this vein, the *Imperfecto* backgrounds a denoted eventuality e_2 (e.g. *estaba* in Example (3)) with respect to a foregrounded e_1 (*han escapado*). While a foregrounded eventuality answers a question like "What happened (next)?", a backgrounded one answers a question like "What was the situation like?" (cf. Becker and Egetenmeyer 2018: 26). Again, we assume that this elaborated fore- and background structuring establishing a hierarchy among e_1 and e_2 conflicts with the PPC$_{SP}$'s semantics of denoting an isolated (with respect to adjacent past eventualities), indefinite eventuality while perspectivizing its post-state in the present time-sphere.

In sum, attaching an *Imperfecto* to a PPC$_{SP}$ as attested in our corpus study and exemplified in (3) poses theoretical problems. We derive that the PPC$_{SP}$ may already feature updated discourse functions that account for the data. Furthermore, we assume that this innovation may function as the transitional bridge between the quantificational and the referential PPC$_{SP}$ and thus may fill the gap indicated by the question mark in Figure 6.2. In the next section, we propose a prominence-based account to solve the problems discussed above, that may explain the felicity of the PPC$_{SP}$'s cataphoric interaction with the *Imperfecto*.

---

254. English translations added.

6.3 Prominence and the PPC$_{SP}$

6.3.1 General remarks on prominence in discourse

In most general terms, the concept of prominence refers to a "basic underlying organizational principle of linguistic structuring" (Himmelmann and Primus 2015: 52). It aims at asymmetries established between elements of sets of equal type:

> [*Prominence*] is at times used interchangeably with the terms "salience", "accessibility", "attention" and "activation" in the literature on discourse pragmatics, "highlighting" in phonology, or "the higher rank of an element on a hierarchy of semantic or syntactic entities", such as the referentiality or animacy hierarchy (Aissen 2003).
> (von Heusinger and Schumacher 2019: 118)

The following examples provide a superficial glance into the profound interaction between prominence, phonology and semantics.

(5) a. Phonological Prominence and lexical meaning in German (bold=pitch accent)
   i. **um**fahren – '(to) run something over'
   ii. um**fah**ren – '(to) drive around something'
b. Semantic Prom. and pronoun resolution (Jasinskaja et al. 2015: 138f.)
   i. Sarah$_{GOAL}$ took the cat from Rebecca$_{SOURCE}$. She$_{SARAH}$ …
   ii. Sarah$_{SOURCE}$ passed the salt to Rebecca$_{GOAL}$. She$_{REBECCA}$ …

In (5a), the pitch accent (i.e. a prominent syllable) triggers one of the two indicated lexical meanings. In (5b), both sentences feature a set of individuals {Sarah, Rebecca} that are ranked such that the personal pronoun in the second sentence can retrieve its referent by picking the most prominent one at a given stage of discourse. In particular, the minimal pair illustrates the case where the semantic role of goal functions as a prominence-lending cue lending prominence to Sarah in (5-bi) and to Rebecca in (5-b-ii) respectively, by overriding syntactic prominence (i.e. word order). That is, the pronoun *she* in a continuation like "She really needed it" would be assigned to different discourse referents despite the identical syntactic structure in both examples.

Guided by the hypothesis of a diverse prominence-based structuring in language on multiple levels, Himmelmann and Primus (2015) provide the following three criteria for a general characterization:[255]

---

[255] These criteria mark the official working hypothesis of the Collaborative Research Center 1252 on Prominence in Language at the University of Cologne, cf. http://www.sfb1252.uni-koeln.de.

Prominence criterion 1: Prominence is a relational property that singles out one element from a set of elements of equal type and structure.
Prominence criterion 2: Prominent elements are structural attractors, i.e. they serve as anchors for the larger structures they are constituents of, and they may license more operations than their competitors.
Prominence criterion 3: Prominence status shifts in time (as discourse unfolds).

Criterion 1 emphasizes that prominence singles out an element out of a set of elements of equals by establishing an asymmetric scale between these. In (5a), the set is e.g. constituted by syllables. Criterion 2 adds explanatory power to the first criterion (which is descriptive). With regard to (5a), it motivates the link between the highlighting of a particular syllable and the licensing of a particular meaning of the underlying expression. Criterion 3 aims at the intrinsically dynamic nature of discourse: prominence relations are not stable over time, which means that asymmetries between sets of equals are permanently restructured and reevaluated as discourse unfolds.

6.3.2 Prominent event domain vs. prominent post-state domain

In this subsection, we propose that there is a prominence-based asymmetry established by the PPC_{SP} that is involved in uses as exemplified in (3). That is, we assume a prominence-based structuring to be of crucial relevance for the PPC_{SP}'s referential drift.

Singling out an element out of a set of equals
The cross-linguistic Present Perfect generally expresses a bipartite information. This has been captured to the point by Musan (2002), labelled as the principle of informative contrast (PIC):

> Principle of Informative Contrast (PIC):
> In a perfect construction, the situation time of the VP and the situation time of the post-state differ in some relevant way. (Musan 2002: 74)

Musan motivates the PIC based on the assumption that the two domains complementarily contribute different aspects of meaning:

> Because of the PIC, and using a perfect construction, a speaker always implicates that there is some contrast between the situation time of the VP and the situation time of the post-state. Its being a pragmatic principle accounts for some of its properties – i.e. that its force can be strengthened or weakened by contextual factors and that for pragmatic reasons it can attain different appearances.
> (Musan 2002: 74)

We assume the PIC to apply to the Spanish PPC$_{SP}$, as well, and that the set of equals required for prominence-structuring is composed of an event domain and a post-state domain.[256] Accordingly, the event domain and the post-state domain, both denoted by the PPC$_{SP}$, compete to become prominent. By default, the post-state domain is highlighted as prominent, which is in line with the PPC$_{SP}$'s strong orientation to the speech time, its non-narrative character, its lacking of a location time specifying the temporal location of the event, as well as its default discourse functions discussed in the Chapters 4 and 5. As part of an innovative reading though, we assume that there may be an attentional shift towards the event domain, that gets highlighted as prominent in this case. The two configurations are depicted in Figure 6.2.

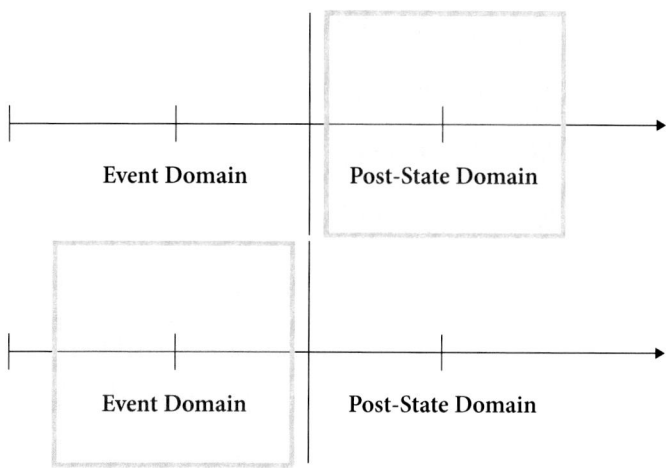

Figure 6.2 The PPC$_{SP}$ feat. prominent post-state domain vs. prominent event domain

In fact, Detges's (2000) figure-ground approach to the distinction of (i) the resultative PPC$_{SP}$ reading and (ii) the resultative *tener* construction (cf. discussion in Section 4.3) bears similarities to the distinction illustrated in Figure 6.2. Detges (2000: 349) assumes both (i) and (ii) to express an asymmetry between a past event and a present result. In this vein, the resultative PPC$_{SP}$ denotes a past event implying a present result (while the resultative *tener* construction denotes a present result implying a past event). Although this sketch does not aim at the quantificational

---

256. We opt for renaming Musan's components of situation time and post-state to event domain and poststate domain in order to emphasize the idea of competing domains. Furthermore, Musan's situation time complies with our framework's event time.

vs. referential distinction but at the *tener* vs. *haber* distinction on the level of the auxiliary, it shows that a similar approach, which also matches Musan's (2002) principle of informative contrast, has already been applied to the study of the PPC$_{SP}$. However, for the purpose of the study of the PPC$_{SP}$'s referential drift, the prominence-based account particularly adds a highly dynamic character of a permanent (re)shaping and (re)structuring of prominence-based asymmetries. That is, it does not only account for the illustration of semantic configurations of fixed readings of the PPC$_{SP}$ at a given evolutionary stage, but it may also account for the highly dynamic process of reinterpreting the ranking of the event domain and the post-state domain both from a diachronic and a synchronic perspective.

The prominent event domain as a structural attractor licensing discursive operations
Assuming that either the event or the post-state domain of the PPC$_{SP}$ may be highlighted as prominent, different linguistic operations can be accounted for by being licensed by the two configurations. In the case of being employed as a purely quantificational tense form featuring a prominent post-state domain, the PPC$_{SP}$ receives its typical interpretations and functions as discussed and investigated in the previous chapters. By contrast, highlighting the event domain as prominent, there is an attentional shift away from the post-state domain towards the event domain. Conspicuously, the perspective time still remains in the present time-sphere though. This causes a split between the perspectivized present time-sphere on the one hand, and the prominent event domain on the other hand (perspective time t$_P$ vs. prominent event time t$_E$).

With regard to examples as exemplified in (3), we assume that the promotion of the PPC$_{SP}$'s event domain as a prominent structural attractor licenses the discourse-semantic encoding of temporal relations of t$_E$ with adjacent eventualities, i.e. the attachment of an anaphoric *Imperfecto*. Figure 6.3 illustrates this idea. While the constellation of a prominent post-state in Figure 6.3a impedes the attachment of the *Imperfecto*, it is compatible with the prominent event domain configuration in Figure 6.3b.

The updated Table 6.3 summarizes our assumptions concerning the temporal discourse functions of the quantificational and referential PPC$_{SP}$. It now includes the intermediate stage of a PPC$_{SP}$ reading that builds on a prominent event domain functioning as a structural attractor on the micro-structural level of discourse. Apart from the updated prominence structure, i.e. apart from the attentional shift towards the event domain, we assume the semantic configuration of the transitional phase to remain the same. That is, there is still no location time included

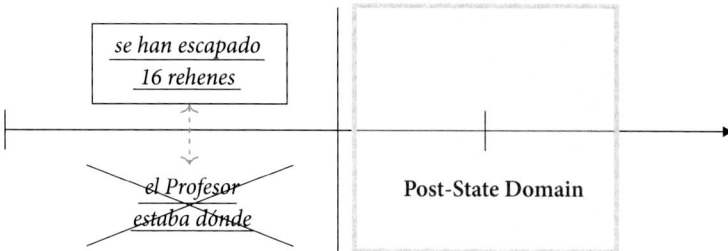

a. Prominent post-state domain: The event domain is not accessible for attaching an *Imperfecto* denoting an anaphoric, backgrounded past eventuality

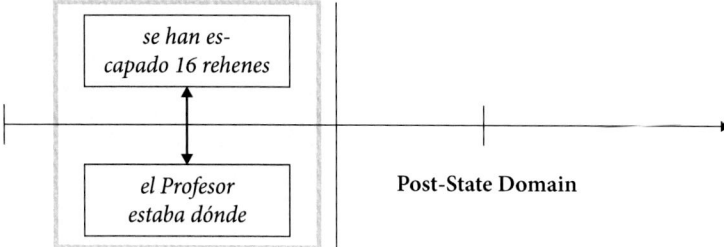

b. Prominent event domain: The event domain is accessible for attaching an *Imperfecto* denoting an anaphoric, backgrounded past eventuality

Figure 6.3 Prominence and the access to the PPC$_{SP}$'s event domain

in the PPC$_{SP}$'s temporal make-up before the PPC$_{SP}$ finally adopts referential semantics featuring a location time that finally turns t$_E$ definite. The promotion of t$_E$ as a prominent structural attractor licenses the explicit establishment of temporal relations with adjacent past eventualities, i.e. the attachment of an anaphoric *Imperfecto*. As discussed above, this operation is accompanied by the discursive effects of *tempus relief,* as well as the backgrounding of the *Imperfecto* with respect to the PPC$_{SP}$. As a consequence, a general extension of the PPC$_{SP}$'s discursive potential is initiated, which now starts to allow for narrative-like passages featuring discourse-semantically encoded temporal relations among eventualities within the past time-sphere. As suggested by relevant examples attested in our corpus study presented in Chapter 5, as well as Azpiazu Torres's (2019) synchronic, dialectal study, we assume that the Peninsular PPC$_{SP}$ is currently passing through this intermediate stage between quantification and reference. In the next section, we report an experimental study that we have conducted in order to test acceptability scores of the PPC$_{SP}$ featuring a prominent event domain to test this hypothesis.

Table 6.3 A discursive approach to the PPC$_{SP}$'s referential drift (box = prominent domain)

Discourse	Type	Temporal semantics
t_E denotes an indefinite, isolated event; temporal relations with adjacent eventualities are pragmatically inferred	Quantificational	$\lambda t_s \lambda t_E \lambda t_P.\ t_E \prec \boxed{t_s \subseteq t_P}$
⇓		⇓
t_E denotes an indefinite but prominent event enabling the establishment of temporal relations with adjacent eventualities	Prominent Event Domain:	$\lambda t_s \lambda t_E \lambda t_P.\ \boxed{t_e} \prec t_s \subseteq t_P$
⇓		⇓
t_E denotes a definite event featuring a location time; temporal relations with adjacent eventualities are semantically encoded	Referential	$\lambda t_s \lambda t_E \lambda t_{LOC} \lambda t_P.\ \boxed{(t_E \subseteq t_{LOC})} \prec t_s \subseteq t_P$

6.4 Experiment: Acceptability judgements of PPC$_{SP}$ + *Imperfecto*

In this section, we report an empirical study that we have conducted measuring acceptability judgments of sentences including a PPC$_{SP}$ featuring a prominent event domain (potentially) licensing the attachment of an anaphoric *Imperfecto*. Put differently, we tested those uses of the PPC$_{SP}$ that we assume to represent a transitional context in the PPC$_{SP}$'s path towards acquiring referential semantics, as illustrated in Table 6.3.

By performing the study, we intend to address the following research questions.

i. To what extent do participants accept the attachment of an anaphoric *Imperfecto* to a cataphoric PPC$_{SP}$?
ii. Does the testing of acceptability judgements based of micro-structural interactions with adjacent tense forms add fruitful linguistic evidence to the investigation of the PPC$_{SP}$'s referential drift such that it represents a promising methodological extension for future studies?

The first question aims at the general investigation of the status of the PPC$_{SP}$ in Peninsular Spanish with respect to the referential drift as illustrated in Table 6.3 (cf. below for a finer-grained diatopic graduation of the varieties under scrutiny). While the corpus study reported in the previous chapter did reveal examples suggesting that the PPC$_{SP}$ might already be productively employed as a cataphoric anchor in discourse, it remains unclear whether the small number of the attested examples is e.g. due to a highly controversial status of the construction among speakers, or if there are other factors that have had an impact on this finding. We thus assume that complementarily measuring acceptability scores helps determine the actual status of the PPC$_{SP}$'s cataphoric potential. Are the related items perfectly acceptable? Or are they rather unacceptable? Or are the constructions assigned intermediate scores located somewhere in between acceptable and unacceptable? Do participants score the items homogeneously? If not, does diatopic variation influence the scores? Or do even participants of the same variety judge the items heterogeneously? However, these questions are not approached by means of a fine-grained dialectal study, which, without a doubt, remains as a research desideratum for future studies if the applied methodology turns out to provide fruitful insights for the overall theory of the PPC$_{SP}$'s referential drift.

The second question aims at the methodological dimension. In particular, the question is whether approaching the referential drift based on an analysis of the PPC$_{SP}$'s microstructural discourse functions adds complementary linguistic evidence to the investigation of the PPC$_{SP}$'s referential drift. Intertwined with this methodological dimension, the question is furthermore whether acceptability judgement studies on the PPC$_{SP}$'s referential drift represent a promising (if not necessary) extension for future investigations by complementing existing corpus studies that measure frequencies of PPC$_{SP}$ vs. *Indefinido* or rely on forced choice tasks, where participants have to choose from PPC$_{SP}$ vs. *Indefinido* in particular contexts. As shown by Adli (2015), even individual speakers show differences in terms of their linguistic preferences and attitudes, as measured by means of acceptability judgements, and their actual linguistic performance, as measured by means of frequency analyses ("What you like is not what you do"). This might be due to that corpus data necessarily represent a particular register, while "acceptability data reflect the entire range of registers available to a speaker", still they are "tinted by norm"(Adli 2015: 194f.). Although it is not expected that the usage of the PPC$_{SP}$ is significantly influenced by restrictions imposed by the properties of a particular register, we still assume that acceptability judgements contribute complementary evidence to the study of the referential drift. While the measuring of frequencies of the PPC$_{SP}$ as opposed to the *Indefinido* in zones where the two compete, as well as forcing participants to choose from PPC$_{SP}$ vs. *Indefinido* in competing zones both rely on a categorical decision (PPC$_{SP}$ vs. *Indefinido*), acceptability scores may particularly help identify and study the gradual consolidation of the bridging context between quantification and reference based on a continuous scale. Put differently, measuring acceptability scores may help determine the status of innovative linguistic constructions that are not yet consolidated but already partially accepted among speakers.

6.4.1 Methodology

Participants were asked to rate sentences on a Likert scale ranging from 1 (bad) to 7 (good). Below, the task is described in more detail.

Participants
The participants were recruited via *Prolific*, a platform for the recruitment of scientific experiments.[257] Answers of 81 native speakers of Spanish were recorded (31 female, 50 male; 52x 18–30 years, 16x 31–40 years, 10x 41–50 years, 3x 51–60 years). 65 participants were included in the analysis (cf. discussion below).

Procedure
First, the participants were asked for their consent to participate voluntarily in the study. They were informed about the general flow of the experiment, that the protection of their data is guaranteed, that they might stop their participation at any time without running any potential disadvantage, that they agree that their anonymously recorded data may be shared with researchers involved in the project and that the data may be used for publication.[258] The participants agreed on being reimbursed with 2.28 Euros for 15 minutes (9.15 Euros per hour). The median of the processing time was 10.2 minutes per participant. There was no time constraint.

Next, the participants were asked for demographic data including age, sex, as well as provenance, current residence and the region that they consider their variety to belong to, choosing from *Andalucía, Aragón, Principado de Asturias, Islas Baleares, Canarias, Cantabria, Castilla-La Mancha, Castilla y León, Cataluña, Comunidad Valenciana, Extremadura, Galicia, La Rioja, Comunidad de Madrid, Region de Murcia, Comunidad Foral de Navarra, País Vasco, Ceuta, Melilla, Otro.*

---

257. www.prolific.co.

258. These guidelines are in line with the general approval of the Ethics Committee of the DGfS (Deutsche Gesellschaft für Sprachwissenschaft).

Then, the participants were instructed that they would be presented with sentences whose linguistic acceptability was to be judged based on a scale ranging from 1 (bad) to 7 (good). They were explicitly instructed to rate the linguistic acceptability by making use of their native intuition, not to reflect too much on each of the examples, and pointed out that they might consider reading the sentences out loud. After the evaluation of two test sentences, the participants started with the main study.

Design and materials
64 critical sentences were created and distributed over two lists.[259] The critical sentences consisted of a when-clause introducing a past eventuality followed by an *Imperfecto* combined with a progressive form establishing a temporal interpretation of simultaneity. The tense form in the when-clause was manipulated for PPC$_{SP}$ vs. *Indefinido*. Given that temporal remoteness is commonly identified as influencing the PPC$_{SP}$'s potential to denote past eventualities, we additionally manipulated the lexical condition of remoteness. Accordingly, we tested sentences disposing of eventualities that may be easily accommodated to the hodiernal time-sphere (present time-sphere), as well as sentences whose eventualities were very likely to receive an interpretation of having taken place prehodiernally, i.e. in the past time-sphere. That is, we explicitly avoided including tempo-aspectual adverbials to determine the affiliation to the present vs. past time-sphere. After all, in the corpus study reported in Chapter 5, approx. 90% of the instances of the PPC$_{SP}$ were not modified by tempo-aspectual adverbials at all. We derived that tempo-aspectual modification of the PPC$_{SP}$ represents the exception instead of the default. Since the study's goal is to investigate the PPC$_{SP}$'s discursive potential beyond the level of tempo-aspectual adverbials, we thus chose to omit them so as not to blur potential effects. Moreover, assuming that temporal remoteness is, in fact, fundamentally intertwined with the PPC$_{SP}$'s general functional load and referential drift, the implicitness of the temporal remoteness condition should not corrupt the results. Recall also that Schwenter and Cacoullos (2008) and Holmes and Balukas (2011) assume temporal indeterminacy to guide the PPC$_{SP}$'s grammaticalization which also suggests excluding (positional) temporal adverbials from the test sentences. The resulting 2x2 design, manipulating tense and temporal remoteness, is illustrated in (6). The full list of the items can be consulted in the Appendix.

---

[259]. Thanks to Nuria Martínez García (project A05, CRC 1252, University of Cologne) and Diego Romero Heredero (project B04, CRC 1252, University of Cologne) for checking the items. Cf. Appendix for an overview of the items included in the study.

(6) 2x2 conditions
    a. [−remote]: Hodiernal interpretation is possible and particularly likely in the PPC$_{SP}$ condition
        i. Indefinido
            Cuando la policía <u>entró</u>, el ladron estaba escapando del banco.
            'When the police entered, the thief was escaping from the bank.'
        ii. PPC
            Cuando la polícia <u>ha entrado</u>, el ladron estaba escapando del banco.
            'When the police has entered, the thief was escaping from the bank.'
    b. [+remote]: Hodiernal interpretation is unlikely if not impossible
        i. Indefinido
            Cuando el autor <u>escribió</u> su primer libro, la guerra estaba acabando.
            'When the author wrote his first book, the war was ending.'
        ii. PPC
            Cuando el autor <u>ha escrito</u> su primer libro, la guerra estaba acabando.
            'When the author has written his first book, the war was ending.'

Each list contained 16 [+remote] items and 16 [−remote] items. Each of these items was presented in either of the two tense conditions. Applied to (6), the distribution of the items thus obeyed the following structure: list A contained (6-a-i) and (6-b-ii) while list B contained (6-a-ii) and (6-b-i). That is, the participants were not directly confronted with the PPC$_{SP}$ vs. *Indefinido* contrast. Both lists consisted of 32 target items and 32 fillers (13 positive, 13 negative, 6 further test items not related to the study). The lists were created in *Qualtrics* and the order of the items was randomized by the built-in randomizer provided by *Qualtrics*.[260]

The tense condition
Expecting generally high acceptability scores for the *Indefinido* condition, we included this condition as a baseline for a relative interpretation of the judgements of the PPC$_{SP}$ conditions (cf. below for detailed description of hypotheses and expectations). We assumed that a comparison of the PPC$_{SP}$ with the *Indefinido* scores ensures an accurate evaluation of how speakers currently judge the PPC$_{SP}$'s cataphoric function featuring a prominent event domain. Additionally, the relative interpretation of the results allows for the detection of items that were lexically misconstructed. That is, items that consistently receive low ratings in the *Indefinido* condition might suggest effects other than the choice of the tense form.

---

260. https://www.qualtrics.com.

The remoteness condition
The temporal remoteness condition was included due to the widely shared assumption that the acceptability of PPC$_{SP}$ expressions depend on temporal remoteness effects. In most simplified terms, the temporal boundary dividing the timeline into a prehodiernal-(past) vs. a hodiernal (present) time-sphere is traditionally considered as corresponding to unacceptable vs. acceptable uses of the PPC$_{SP}$. We thus included the condition of temporal remoteness to investigate whether the prominence of the PPC$_{SP}$'s event domain and the associated cataphoric discourse function also underly a "gradual relaxation of the degree of recentness" (Comrie 1976: 61).

The attached Imperfecto
We chose to combine the *Imperfecto* with a progressive form in order to ensure that a temporal interpretation of simultaneity had to be derived while judging the sentences. This is inspired by Leonetti (2018) who argues that there are contexts in which the Spanish *Imperfecto* actually does not presuppose a temporal anchor, i.e. where the *Imperfecto* does not anaphorically retrieve a discursively provided or inferred reference time. This might be the case with continuous and habitual readings of the *Imperfecto* that "are acceptable in isolated sentences: they do not trigger the search for a temporal antecedent" (Leonetti 2018: 407). Accordingly, continuous and habitual contexts might fail to provide a test case for our study. By contrast, progressive interpretations of the *Imperfecto* are assumed to necessarily refer to a reference time. In our critical items, progressive readings were explicitly forced by combining the *Imperfecto* with a progressive.

Hypotheses and expectations
The following hypotheses were formulated.

H1: There is a main effect for tense reflected in better ratings for the *Indefinido* than for the PPC$_{SP}$, irrespectively of the remoteness condition.
H2: There is an effect of temporal remoteness in the PPC$_{SP}$ condition reflected in better ratings of hodiernal contexts than of prehodiernal contexts.

H1 expresses our expectation that the *Indefinido* represents the default tense form for the attachment of the *Imperfecto* establishing a complex temporal relationship between several eventualities in the past. This should be generally reflected in high acceptability scores for the *Indefinido*, as well as in the lack of an effect of temporal remoteness within the *Indefinido* condition. Regarding the PPC$_{SP}$ condition, we expect to obtain worse ratings. However, we expect the PPC$_{SP}$ to be rated better than the negative fillers. We expect such an intermediate position on the rating scale to be compatible with the assumption that the tested items fulfill a transitional function between the merely quantificational and the referential PPC$_{SP}$.

H2 expresses the assumption that the PPC_{SP}'s stepwise extension of its discursive potential – i.e. its overcoming of the mere denotation of indefinite, isolated past eventualities in favor of a promotion of its event domain enabling the establishment of temporal relations with adjacent past eventualities – also follows a "gradual relaxation of the degree of recentness", that is commonly assumed to escort the PPC_{SP}'s referential drift.

Diatopic variation

As discussed in Section 4.2, the use of the PPC_{SP} is affected by diatopic variation. Although the experiment does not aim to investigate fine-grained diatopic effects (cf. discussion above), the most important trends of the dialectal peculiarities associated with the use of the PPC_{SP} in the Spanish peninsula have to be taken into account for the selection of the participants and the analysis of their scores.

Concerning diatopic variation within Spain in general, Lipski (2012: 2) notes that "the most striking division – immediately noticeable by Spaniards and visitors alike – separates north and south." This distinction is, in fact, also reflected in the PPC_{SP}'s variation, as illustrated by Azpiazu Torres's (2019) sketch in Table 6.4 (cf. also Section 4.2). Accordingly, the northeastern dialects of Spain are generally classified as dispreferring the PPC_{SP}.

Table 6.4 The PPC_{SP}'s values in Peninsular Spanish according to Azpiazu Torres (2019: 204)

Value	Español peninsular	Noroeste peninsular	Canarias	Centro peninsular
P1	✓	✗	✓	✓
P2	✓	✗	✓	✓
P3	✓	✗	✗	✗/✓
P3b	✗	✗	✗	✗/✓

P1: Continuous or plural events, temporally indefinite; P2: Semelfactive anteriors with current relevance, temporally indefinite; P3: Temporally definite anteriors included in the XN interval; P3b: Aoristic event.

Azpiazu Torres's (2019) synchronic classification of the dialectal distribution of the meaning and functions of the PPC_{SP} within the Spanish peninsula suggests that *Español Peninsular* and *Centro Peninsular* represent the two macro varieties that give rise to the most innovative meanings and functions of the PPC_{SP}. This is expressed in that they (may) evoke P3 and P3b meanings. Ignoring, for now, which regions actually are included in *Español Peninsular* and *Centro Peninsular* (cf. below for a finer-grained classification of the regions included in our study), we want to focus on Azpiazu Torres' (2019) notion of P3. We assume that the potential to evoke P3 represents a minimal requirement that needs to be met such that the PPC_{SP}, in a given variety, may license the cataphoric discourse function featuring a prominent event domain anchoring an *Imperfecto*. This is in line with the assumption that the prominent event domain configuration of the PPC$_{SP}$ is an innovation operating at the interface between quantificational and referential temporal semantics by breaking down the purely quantificational character of the PPC$_{SP}$. In Azpiazu Torres's (2019) terminology, P3 is defined as allowing for "temporally definite anteriors included in the XN interval." It has to be stressed though that this notion of definiteness is not equivalent to our notion of temporal definiteness as associated with definite tense forms taking a location time as an argument (cf. e.g. discussion in Section 4.4 and the discussion of potential scope ambiguities of allegedly positional adverbials). Thus, in our framework, it remains unclear whether (i) P3 still denotes indefinite past eventualities that are restricted to the present time-sphere, creating an "illusion" of a temporally definite past eventuality, or whether (ii) P3 indeed denotes definite past eventualities that get assigned to a location time. In the second scenario, it would still remain unclear though where the temporal remoteness constraint of hodiernality actually stems from. By contrast, it may be motivated in the first scenario based on the assumption that it is the perspective time, which is included in the present time-sphere, that blocks prehodiernal contexts and adverbials (cf. also the discussion of the Present Perfect puzzle in Section 2.5 and the discussion of the scope of the tempo-aspectual adverbials in Section 2.3). In sum, and independently of the discussion of the exact theoretical status of Azpiazu Torres' (2019) P3, we assume that having reached P3 represents a necessary condition that needs to be met such that the PPC$_{SP}$'s may license the cataphoric discourse function (which is based on a prominent event domain configuration). Moreover, we assume the potential ambiguity of P3 between definiteness and indefiniteness to be intertwined with the referential drift.

With respect to our study, we derive to focus on participants from regions that Azpiazu Torres (2019) classifies as having reached the P3 value, or, at least, as having more or less reached the P3 value, as the [±] value in the *Centro Peninsular* variety indicates additional variation among the speakers. This suggests excluding participants of the northwestern regions of Galicia, Asturias and Castilla y León, as well as the Canary Islands from the analysis, as these these regions are expected to be too conservative with respect to the meanings and functions of the PPC$_{SP}$. This is also in line with Schwenter and Cacoullos (2008: 8), who also exclude these varieties from their analysis (with reference to Pato and Heap 2008). We furthermore extend the set of the northwestern regions adding Cantabria, País Vasco, Navarra and La Rioja. We thus included participants in the study if their variety belonged to the regions of Comunidad de Madrid, Extremadura, Castilla-La Mancha, Andalucía, Región de Murcia, Comunidad Valenciana, Aragón or Cataluña. This does not mean that we do not expect to find any diatopic variation between these regions. However, the referred regions are expected to represent *the* use of the PPC$_{SP}$ that might be conceived of as the peninsular standard use of the PPC$_{SP}$. We thus assume that these regions may most likely catalyze the referential drift by highlighting the PPC$_{SP}$'s event domain as prominent that, in turn, licenses the PPC$_{SP}$'s innovative cataphoric discourse function.

However, since variation is still expected to be found among these regions, they may be furthermore categorized into three macro varieties. Based on elicited data concerning the competing zones of PPC$_{SP}$ vs. *Indefinido*, Kempas (2008b: 401) determines a rather conservative character for Andalucía, which is expressed in higher frequencies of the *Indefinido* than the PPC$_{SP}$ in several temporal proximate contexts ("two minutes ago, two hours ago, this morning, today"). This classification of the Andalusian PPC$_{SP}$ as rather conservative is e.g. also discussed in Bertinetto and Squartini (2000: 416). By contrast, the PPC$_{SP}$ has advanced most in the east of the peninsula, including e.g. Valencia, followed by Cataluña. Furthermore, speakers from Madrid and Aragon seem to be located in between these two pillars of conservation vs. innovation. Inspired by Kempas's (2008b) findings, we classify those regions that are going to be included in the study (as identified above) into the three macro varieties of central (Comunidad de Madrid, Exteremadura, Castilla-La Mancha), south (Andaclucía) and eastern + Aragón (Region de Murcia, Comunidad Valenciana, Cataluña and Aragón). Although we do not expect to find significant differences between these three groups, there may be variation according to these clusters (cf. discussion in Section 6.4.3). Figure 6.4 illustrates how the discussed regions are distributed geographically.

6.4.2 Statistical analysis and results

The statistical analysis and plotting was performed in R Studio (R Core Team 2017).[261]

Participants included in the analysis
66 of the 81 participants specified their dialect as belonging to a region included in the three macro varieties specified above. After excluding one participant due to inconsistencies that suggested that the participant did not sufficiently pay attention to the task, the remaining 65 participants are listed in Figure 6.5.

We decided to treat the diatopic background of the participants as being specified by the region that they indicated as the one that their variety belongs to. 51 of the participants, i.e. the great majority, had identical answers for the three questions of place of birth, current residence and the region that they consider their variety to belong to. Only one participant indicated three different values for the three categories. Eleven participants indicated two different regions. These are illustrated in Table 6.5.

---

[261]. Thanks to Maximilian Hörl (project INF, CRC 1252, University of Cologne) for statistical consultancy.

Chapter 6. The PPC$_{SP}$'s referential drift **233**

Figure 6.4 Map of Spain (http://ontheworldmap.com/es/spain/ (01/11/21))

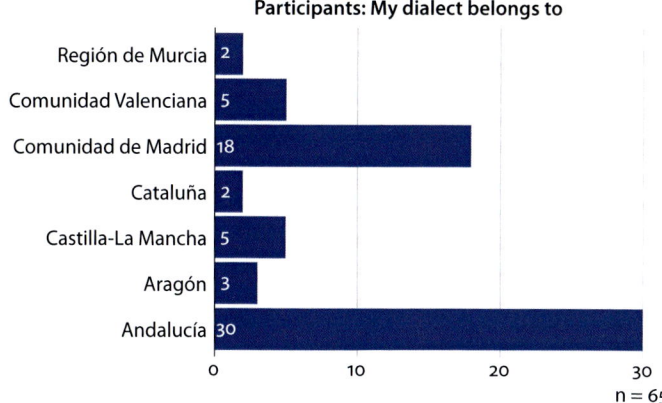

Figure 6.5 Participants' answers to "My dialect belongs to …"

Table 6.5 12/65 participants with non-uniform diatopic background

Home	Current residence	"My dialect"
Comunidad de Madrid	Cataluña	Comunidad Valenciana
Castilla-La Mancha	Aragón	Castilla-La Mancha
País Vasco	Comunidad Valenciana	Comunidad Valenciana
Andalucía	Castilla-La Mancha	Castilla-La Mancha
Comunidad de Madrid	Castilla-La Mancha	Castilla-La Mancha
NA	Comunidad Valenciana	Andalucía
Andalucía	Galicia	Andalucía
Comunidad de Madrid	Comunidad de Madrid	Comunidad Valenciana
Comunidad de Madrid	Castilla-La Mancha	Comunidad de Madrid
Aragón	Cataluña	Cataluña
Andalucía	Comunidad de Madrid	Comunidad de Madrid
Andalucía	Cataluña	Andalucía

Overview

First of all, it has to be mentioned that for 30 of the 65 participants, only 7 (instead of 8) ratings of the *Indefinido*-hodiernal condition were unintentionally recorded. However, since the *Indefinido* condition was included in the design as a baseline for a relative interpretation of the results of the PPC$_{SP}$ conditions, we expect this not to corrupt the analysis, particularly because of the highly consistent scores for the *Indefinido*-hodiernal condition (cf. below). The PPC$_{SP}$ conditions were not affected. In sum, the analysis includes 35 * 8 + 30 * 7 = 490 observations for the *Indefinido*-hodiernal condition, 65 * 8 = 520 observations for the *Indefinido*-prehodiernal-, PPC$_{SP}$-hodiernal- and PPC$_{SP}$-prehodiernal conditions each, 13 * 65 = 845 observations for the negative and positive fillers each, as well as 6 * 65 = 390 observations for items not related to the study, which makes a total of 4,130 judgments.

Figure 6.6 illustrates the general distribution of the acceptability scores per condition. The boxplot shows very high scores for the *Indefinido* condition in both remoteness conditions, as well as for the positive fillers (median = 7). The negative fillers received the lowest scores (median = 1). In between these two groups, the scores for the PPC$_{sp}$ condition show a median of 3 (hodiernal) and 2 (prehodiernal). The two PPC$_{sp}$ conditions show the greatest spread covering the entire scale (*PPC-HOD var* = 4.32; *PPC-PREHOD var* = 3.76). On the other hand, the two *Indefinido* conditions cover the scale only with outliers and show a generally smaller spread (*IND-HOD var* = 1.85; *IND-PREHOD var* = 1.73).

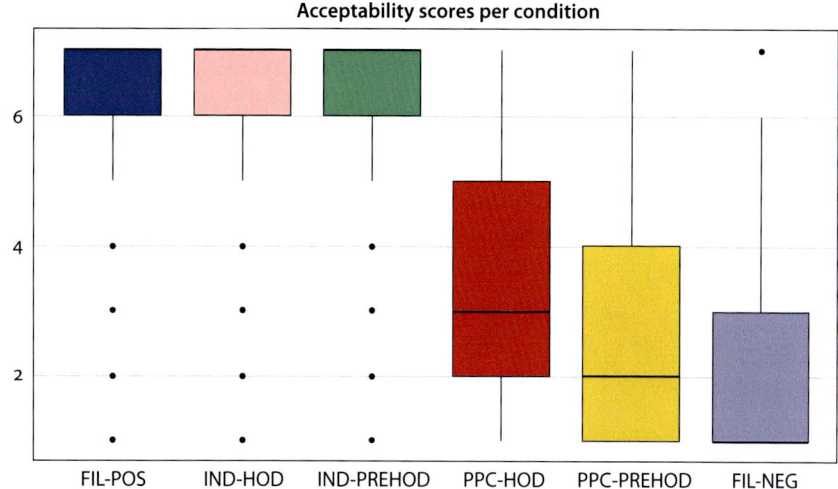

Figure 6.6 Acceptability scores per condition
FIL-POS: positive filler; IND-HOD: Indefinido hodiernal; IND-PREHOD: Indefinido prehodiernal; PPC-HOD: PPC$_{SP}$ hodiernal; PPC-PREHOD: PPC$_{SP}$ prehodiernal; FIL-NEG: negative filler.

Significant main effect of tense (H1)

We constructed a linear mixed effect model using the lme4 package (Bates et al. 2015). Tense was taken as a fixed effect. Aiming for a full set of random intercepts and random slopes for subjects and items (cf. Barr et al. 2013), we had to settle for random intercepts for subjects and items and random slopes for subjects, because the model with the maximal structure failed to converge.[262] The output of the model is presented in Table 6.6. The model showed a significant main effect for tense ($p < 0{,}001$) with a slope of 2.95. That is, the model predicts significantly better scores for the *Indefinido* with a mean difference between the *Indefinido* and the PPC$_{SP}$ condition that amounts to 2.95 points on the rating scale.

Table 6.6 Linear mixed effect model for the main effect of tense

Fixed effects	Estimate	SE	t-value	p
(Intercept)	4.68	0.11	40.72	< 0,001
Tense	2.95	0.23	12.76	< 0,001

---

[262]. The reported results are based on deviation contrasts (−0.5/+0.5) and a model with the following formula: `lmer(score ~ tense + (1 + tense | Subject) + (1 | item), data = df, REML = FALSE)`.

Significant interactional effect of PPC and remoteness (H2)
Next, we analyzed if there is an effect of remoteness within the PPC$_{SP}$ condition as hypothesized by H2. We conducted a pairwise test using the "emmeans" package (Lenth 2020) isolating the interactional effect of tense and remoteness for both tense conditions. This test revealed a significant effect ($p < 0,05$) with an estimate of 0.52 for remoteness within the PPC$_{SP}$ condition, as shown in Table 6.7. The test also revealed that with regard to the *Indefinido* condition, there was no such effect. That is, within the *Indefinido* condition, remoteness did not effect the scores. Although not explicitly formulated as a hypothesis, this is in line with the assumption that the *Indefinido*'s highly grammaticalized status causes that it does not depend on temporal remoteness.[263]

Table 6.7 Pairwise testing of tense interacting with remoteness

Tense	Contrast	Estimate	SE	t-value	p
Indefinido	HOD-PREHOD	0.00	0.21	0.01	> 0.05
PPC	HOD-PREHOD	0.52	0.20	2.57	< 0.05

Figure 6.7 illustrates the estimate for the PPC$_{SP}$ condition as opposed to the *Indefinido* conditions where remoteness does not seem to effect the scores, at all. The test thus suggests that the information of remoteness improves the modeling of the scores within the PPC$_{SP}$ condition.

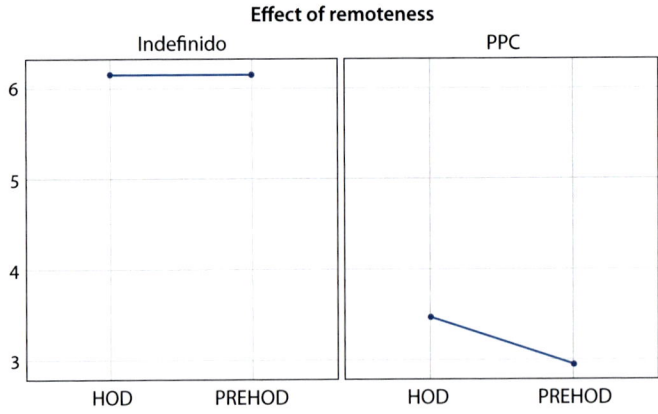

Figure 6.7 Remoteness per tense

---

263. We also checked for an interactional effect of tense and remoteness by adding remoteness as an interactional effect to the general model: score ~ tense * remoteness. This test did not reveal a significant interactional effect of tense and remoteness.

No significant effect for coarse-grained diatopic background as a fixed effect
We furthermore tested whether the diatopic background of the speakers shows an effect on the data. This was in order to test whether treating the participants as a (more or less) homogeneous group with respect to their judgments of the PPC_{sp} as a cataphoric anchor for an anaphoric *Imperfecto* would be justified by the data. The test was based on the tripartite classification of the participants' diatopic background as discussed above, i.e. based on the distinction of the three macro varieties of (i) central (23 participants, Comunidad de Madrid and Castilla La Mancha), (ii) south (30 participants, Andalucía) and (iii) eastern + Aragón (12 participants, Comunidad Valenciana, Región de Murcia, Cataluña and Aragón).

We first conducted a likelihood ratio test to see whether the model significantly improves when adding the participants' dialectal background as an additional interactional effect to the model. The test revealed no significant effect ($p > 0.05$).[264] In other words, the information of the speaker's dialectal background distinguishing center, south and eastern + Aragón as a fixed effect did not significantly improve the overall model.

Furthermore, we investigated whether being from different regions makes a difference for the ratings exclusively in the PPC_{SP} conditions. This was again based on a pairwise testing using the "emmeans" package.

Table 6.8 Contrasts between the PPC_{SP} scores across the three major dialectal groups

Condition	Group	Estimate	SE	t-value	p
HOD	Andalucía vs. Madrid	−0.30	0.41	−0.74	> 0.05
	Andalucía vs. Eastern + Aragón	−0.05	0.41	−0.13	> 0.05
	Madrid vs. Eastern + Aragón	0.24	0.46	0.54	> 0.05
PREHOD	Andalucía vs. Madrid	−0.65	0.41	−1.61	> 0.05
	Andalucía vs. Eastern + Aragón	−0.10	0.41	−0.23	> 0.05
	Madrid vs. Eastern + Aragón	0.56	0.46	1.22	> 0.05

As shown by the results in Table 6.8, the estimated mean differences between the regions amount to close to zero indeed, which suggests that there is no significant effect in any of the depicted contrasts. That means that neither in the prehodiernal, nor in the hodiernal PPC_{SP} condition, the information of the diatopic background of the participants (as based on the tripartite categorization discussed above) did significantly improve the model. All in all, the estimates are very small. The greatest contrast can be found between the scores of participants representing the group of Andalucía and Madrid in the prehodiernal condition amounting to −0.65 only. Put

---

264. Full model: lmer(score ~ tense * remoteness * dialect + (1+tense|Subject) + (1|question) ; null-model: lmer(score ~ tense * remoteness + (1+tense|Subject) + (1|question).

differently, the estimated mean for the prehodiernal PPC$_{SP}$ condition is 0.65 points higher for Andalucía than for Comunidad de Madrid and Castilla-La Mancha. On the other hand, the smallest contrast can be found in the hodiernal PPC$_{SP}$ condition, where the estimated mean for the group representing Andalucía is only 0.05 points higher than the estimated mean for the group representing eastern + Aragón.

However, it has to be taken into account that the experiment was not designed in order to test dialectal differences of the speakers, which is particularly reflected in the non-balanced numbers of participants per region. Still, we consider these results to be compatible with the approach of treating the participants included in the analysis as a (more or less) homogeneous group with respect to their judgements of the cataphoric potential of the PPC$_{SP}$ (cf. below for an exploration of finer-grained diatopic effects in the data).

6.4.3 Discussion

General observations
First of all, we interpret the boxplot shown in Figure 6.6 as suggesting that the participants whose answers were included in the analysis payed sufficient attention to the experimental stimuli such that we consider their answers to represent a reliable source for the testing of the hypotheses. We derive this assumption from the observation that the scores for the fillers occupy both extremes of the scale: while the positive fillers mainly obtained very high scores (median = 7), the negative fillers obtained very low scores (median = 1). Furthermore, the consistently high scores for the *Indefinido* conditions match our expectations that these were highly acceptable sentences. This furthermore suggests that the critical items did not contain serious disruptive factors like lexical obscurities that would corrupt the scores. Thus, the judgments of the PPC$_{SP}$ items should, indeed, trace back to the manipulation of the tense form.

Significant main effect of tense (H1)
The first hypothesis was confirmed by the significant effect of tense revealing the PPC$_{SP}$ to be rated 2.95 points worse than the *Indefinido*. Interestingly, this value indicates an intermediate status of the PPC$_{SP}$ between the highest and lowest scores on the scale. That is, the PPC$_{SP}$ received better scores than the negative fillers (cf. Figure 6.6): though not perfectly acceptable, the critical PPC items were rated better than unacceptable. We interpret this result as suggesting that the attachment of a progressive *Imperfecto* – which in our framework presupposes a prominent event domain – may, indeed, represent a transitional function between the merely quantificational and the innovative referential PPC$_{SP}$ which the PPC$_{SP}$ is currently passing through. This assumption is furthermore supported by the observation that

speakers judged the respective items quite heterogeneously (cf. the great spread of the whiskers in Figure 6.6 for the PPC$_{SP}$ condition). While speakers judged the *Indefinido* conditions (as well as the fillers) quite consistently, there is a greater variation in the data with respect to the PPC$_{SP}$. This suggests that the PPC$_{SP}$'s function of anchoring a progressive *Imperfecto* is not consolidated yet but highly controversial among speakers (cf. below for further explorations of that aspect). Most strikingly though, this result suggests that the PPC$_{SP}$ has not (yet) discourse-functionally replaced the *Indefinido* in hodiernal contexts. Despite the common view that "the Peninsular PP is well-established as a hodiernal perfective, because it is near categorical in hodiernal contexts" (Schwenter and Cacoullos 2008: 31), the results actually reveal that the PPC$_{SP}$ has not yet fully invaded – not even in hodiernal contexts – the functional domain of establishing complex temporal relationships with other past eventualities, which is typical for the discourse mode of narration, and which is typically assumed by the *Indefinido*. However, as suggested by the intermediate scores, the PPC$_{SP}$ might be on its way to assume this function as well. With regard to the discussion of whether hodiernal PPC$_{SP}$ uses actually do represent definite, perfective, referential readings – as e.g. stated in Schwenter and Cacoullos 2008: 31 ("hodiernal perfective"), Azpiazu Torres 2019: 139 ("perfective reading") and Kempas 2008b ("hodiernal aoristic/perfective use") – we interpret this result as empirically confirming our assumptions discussed on several occasions in our study (cf. e.g. Section 4.4). Accordingly, hodiernal uses do not unequivocally represent referential uses. Either they even still represent quantificational uses, or they ambiguously oscillate between a quantificational and a referential reading (which would explain the crucial role of hodiernal uses for the referential drift).[265] In sum, the significantly lower scores of the PPC$_{SP}$ as compared to the *Indefinido* support the assumption that the PPC$_{SP}$ has not yet acquired referential semantics. Instead, the prominence-based restructuring, that results in the highlighting of the PPC$_{SP}$'s event domain, has started to gradually license the micro-structural discourse operation of temporal cataphora, which we expect to accompany and catalyze the referential drift in the long run.

Significant effect of remoteness in the PPC$_{SP}$ condition (H2)
The second hypothesis turned out to be compatible with the data as well. As shown in Table 6.7, the effect of temporal remoteness turned out to be significant for the PPC$_{SP}$ items (as opposed to the *Indefinido* items). That is, the attachment of a progressive *Imperfecto* to the PPC$_{SP}$ received better scores for contexts accommodatable to the present time-sphere than for contexts accommodatable to the past

---

265. In our framework (cf. e.g. Chapter 2), perfective viewpoint aspect presupposes a location time provided by a referential tense form.

time-sphere, even though there were no explicit tempo-aspectual adverbials included in the items. Moreover, not only the scores for the hodiernal, but also for the prehodiernal PPC$_{SP}$ condition turned out to obtain higher scores than the negative fillers. That is, the prehodiernal PPC$_{SP}$ condition was generally perceived as quite unacceptable, however still slightly better than the ungrammatical, negative fillers.

As hypothesized – and in line with the common accounts of the PPC$_{SP}$'s grammaticalization – this finding suggests that the functional extension of the PPC$_{SP}$ in discourse does follow a "gradual relaxation of the degree of recentness" as well. Applying our terminology, that means that the highlighting of the PPC$_{SP}$'s event domain as a prominent structural attractor seems to be first acceptable with eventualities located in the present time-sphere – i.e. in contexts that are generally favored by the PPC$_{SP}$ due to its perspectivizing of the present time-sphere – before it might get further extended to the past time-sphere as well. The results furthermore reveal that temporal remoteness impacts the grammaticalization of the PPC$_{sp}$ as a discrete lexical-semantic factor, that is not necessarily tied to the inclusion of hodiernal adverbials as commonly assumed.

Further exploration: Fine-grained diatopic background of the participants
As shown in the analysis, a likelihood ratio test did not reveal significant differences between the three macro varieties of (i) Comunidad de Madrid, Castilla La Mancha, (ii) Andalucía and (iii) Región de Murcia, Comunidad Valenciana, Cataluña + Aragón. Again, it has to be stressed that our study was not designed as a fine-grained dialectal study, which is e.g. reflected in the unbalanced numbers of participants per region (cf. Table 6.5). This also impedes the derivation of statistically reliable results concerning fine-grained diatopic variation in the data. Nevertheless, an explorative overview of the scores for a fine-grained distinction between the regions is depicted in Figure 6.8. The two regions with the greatest number of observations – Comunidad de Madrid ($n = 18$) and Andalucía ($n = 30$) – show almost identical results with regard to the hodiernal PPC$_{SP}$ condition. These homogeneous scores slightly contradict the characterization of the Andalusian PPC$_{SP}$ as rather conservative as compared to the Madrilenian PPC$_{SP}$ in Kempas (2008b).

However, there is a difference in the prehodiernal PPC$_{SP}$ condition between the two regions, as the medians amount to 3 (Comunidad de Madrid) and 2 points Andalucía respectively, which, by contrast, is in line with the assumption of a more conservative character of the Andalusian PPC$_{SP}$. Interestingly, the scores of the Madrilenian speakers suggest that they do not perceive the temporal remoteness constraint as a very strict rule, as the median of the scores of the hodiernal and prehodiernal conditions equally amounts to 3 points on the scale. While temporal remoteness actually did turn out to show a significant effect in the overall data (cf. above), the distinction thus does not seem to be that clear-cut

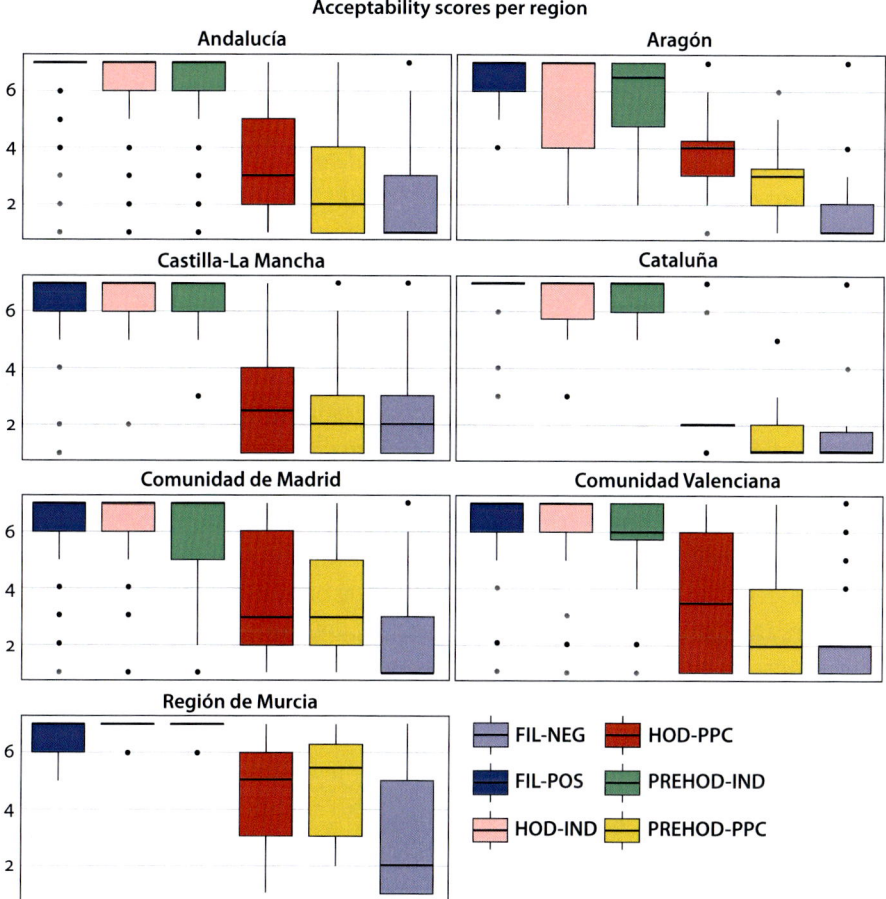

Figure 6.8 Acceptability scores per region

in for the data representing Comunidade de Madrid. Based on the observation that the Madrilenian speakers judged both PPC$_{SP}$ conditions as better than the negative fillers and as worse than the *Indefinido* conditions, the question arises if the PPC$_{SP}$'s cataphoric function in the Madrilenian variety might actually become more and more acceptable in the long run independently of the temporal remoteness constraint.

The eastern varieties, that Kempas (2008b) assigns the most innovative PPC$_{SP}$ uses and functions, indeed show the highest scores for the PPC$_{SP}$ conditions in the data. Accordingly, the participants of Comunidad Valenciana ($n = 5$) show higher scores in the hodiernal PPC$_{SP}$ condition than e.g. participants of Comunidad de Madrid. However, they equal in their scores for the prehodiernal condition. Assuming the eastern varieties to be most innovative is furthermore corroborated by the data for Región de Murcia ($n = 2$), that show the highest scores for both PPC$_{SP}$ conditions across the different regions. Even more strikingly, the median for the prehodiernal PPC$_{SP}$ condition slightly surpasses the hodiernal PPC$_{sp}$ condition, which was not predicted at all. In the Murcian data, the scores of PPC$_{SP}$ are thus almost approaching the scores of the *Indefinido*. Aragón ($n = 3$), whose PPC$_{SP}$ turns out to be similar to the Madrilenian PPC$_{SP}$ in Kempas's (2008b) data, shows slightly better scores as compared to Comunidad de Madrid in our data. This finding is compatible with the categorization of Aragón as not pertaining to the same macro variety as Madrid. However, Kempas's (2008b) general categorization of Aragón as disposing of a rather innovative PPC$_{SP}$ is, in fact, compatible with our data as well. As an exception to the generalization that the eastern varieties show the most innovative uses, participants representing Cataluña ($n = 2$) scored both PPC$_{SP}$ conditions very low. While the hodiernal condition received a median of 2 points, the prehodiernal condition received a median of 1 point, which is the same value as for the negative fillers. Nevertheless, it stands to reason that it is particularly Cataluña that would actually require a more detailed anaylsis and discussion. Due to the peculiar sociolinguistic situation of an intense language contact of Spanish and Catalan, the number of two participants is way too small for reliable conclusions. As already discussed, this also applies to some of the observations for the other regions whose data rely on a small number of participants. It is thus crucial to once again point out that the data presented in Figure 6.8 represent a merely descriptive and explorative overview. Yet, they might inspire future studies that aim for taking diatopic variation explicitly into account within an analysis of the PPC$_{SP}$'s micro-structural discourse potential. After all, the consistent scores of the positive and negative fillers in all of the regions suggest that the observations, though not statistically reliable, do represent valid findings. Furthermore, they are, to a great extent, in line with the PPC$_{SP}$'s intra-peninsular variation in the literature, as discussed above.

In sum, we derive from the exploration of the data representing the individual regions two crucial assumptions.

On the one hand, the PPC$_{SP}$'s cataphoric potential, as licensed by the highlighting of its event domain, seems to jointly progress with the general grammaticalization of the PPC$_{SP}$ as commonly discussed and studied in the literature. After all, the general diatopic trends of the PPC$_{SP}$ with respect to its grammaticalization as discussed e.g. in Kempas (2008b) and Azpiazu Torres (2019) most widely also appear in our data. This strikingly underpins the assumption that the extension of the micro-structural discourse functions of the PPC$_{SP}$ evolves in a parallel fashion as its truth conditions (cf. Table 6.3 in Section 6.3). We interpret this finding as confirming that the study the PPC$_{SP}$'s discursive potential indeed offers promising evidence for the general study of the PPC$_{SP}$'s referential drift.

On the other hand, the fine-grained diatopic exploration of the data might call into question that the temporal remoteness constraint is perceived as a ubiquitous and strict factor guiding the PPC$_{SP}$'s grammaticalization. This is suggested by the observation that the constraint did show a significant effect in the overall data, while e.g. the participants of Comunidad de Madrid did not seem to be influenced by the temporal remoteness. This assumption, that would require more systematic research, seems to be in line with Schwenter and Cacoullos's (2008), that call into question that the PPC$_{SP}$'s "road to perfective" is actually influenced by temporal remoteness, in favor of assuming its extension to occur in temporal indeterminate contexts. However since, in our items, temporal remoteness was encoded implicitly – that is, there were no tempo-aspectual adverbials included in the items – it would, again, require more systematic research to explicitly disentangle "temporal indeterminacy" (as discussed in Schwenter and Cacoullos 2008) and temporal remoteness.

Further exploration: innovative vs. conservative speakers?
Above, we mentioned the great spread of the scores for the PPC$_{SP}$ condition as compared to the other conditions. On the one hand, this might be explained based on the fact that the scores of the *Indefinido* and filler conditions are concentrated at the extremes of the scale, which necessarily causes a minor variance. Still, the data seem to suggest that the participants judged the PPC$_{SP}$ quite controversially. In particular, conceiving of the promotion of the PPC$_{SP}$'s event domain as a transitional bridge triggering the referential drift, the heterogeneity of the scores appears to be plausible. Accordingly, we might cluster the data into group A, featuring participants that judged the PPC$_{SP}$ conditions as rather acceptable, and group B, featuring participants that judged the PPC$_{SP}$ conditions as rather unacceptable. The two groups are illustrated in Figure 6.9.

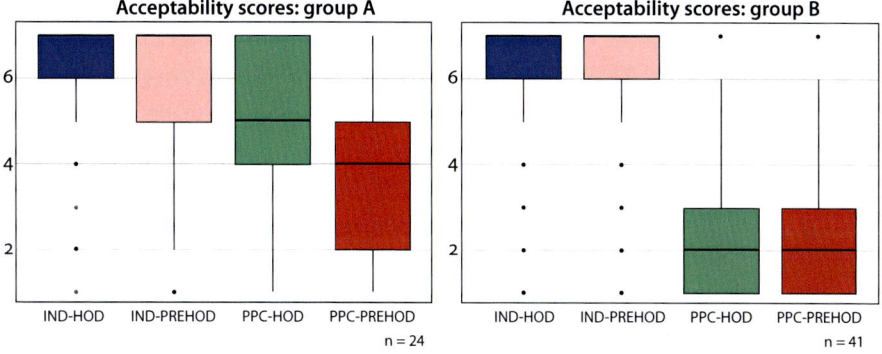

Figure 6.9 Acceptability scores of group A vs. group B

Concerning group A ($n = 24$), the medians for the PPC$_{SP}$ conditions amount to 5 and 4, respectively. In other words, the participants of group A seem to (already) consider the PPC$_{SP}$ anchoring an *Imperfecto* as quite acceptable. On the other hand, group B ($n = 41$) judged the PPC$_{SP}$ as quite unacceptable in both remoteness conditions. Although it may appear to be somewhat circular to divide the data into good scores vs. bad scores, the polarization may, in fact, hint at an ongoing change. In this vein, the scores of group A might be interpreted as representing the scores of rather innovative speakers, while the scores of group B might be interpreted as representing the scores of conservative speakers. In fact, grammaticalization theory has identified that linguistic change is accompanied by "a prior historical process of innovation and successful social diffusion" (Enfield 2008: 302) and that innovative speakers may further be distinguished "between innovators, early adopters, late adopters, and laggards" (Rogers 1995 apud Enfield 2008: 302). Distinguishing rather innovative and rather conservative participants suggests checking if age had an impact on the scores (as e.g. also mentioned in Bertinetto and Squartini 2000: 416). Accordingly, one might expect that younger participants tend to promote the innovative use of the PPC$_{PT}$ featuring a prominent event domain triggering the referential drift, while elderly participants might prefer to preserve the non-innovative, purely quantificational semantics of the PPC$_{SP}$. Thus, the PPC$_{SP}$ scores might decrease with an increasing age. The scores per age are illustrated in Figure 6.10.

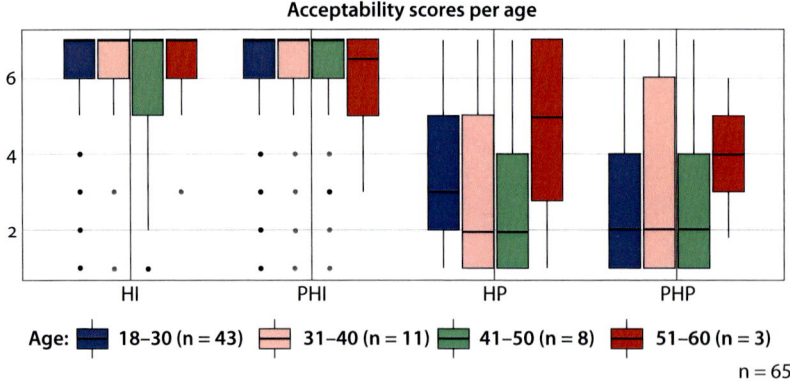

Figure 6.10 Acceptability scores per age

The distribution of the scores indicates, in fact, slightly higher scores for the hodiernal PPC$_{SP}$ condition in the 18–30 age group ($n = 44$) than in the 31–40 ($n = 11$) and 41–50 ($n = 8$) age groups. At the same time, the scores for the prehodiernal PPC$_{sp}$ condition are similar across these three groups. Most surprisingly though, the 51–60 age group of speakers ($n = 3$) show higher scores in both conditions.

This finding contradicts the assumption that the PPC$_{sp}$ featuring a prominent event domain might be more acceptable among younger participants. Thus, *either* the innovative vs. conservative scoring does not depend on the age, *or* the data for the elderly participants underly further factors that lie beyond the scope of the study. However, it is crucial to once again point out that the experiment was not designed for the testing of age, which is e.g. reflected in the small numbers of participants of the fourth group, such that the exploration depicted in Figure 6.10 does not indicate statistically reliable results. Though, it might again inspire future studies concerning the distinction of innovative vs. conservative speakers that tend to catalyze vs. inhibit the PPC$_{SP}$'s referential drift.

6.5 Conclusion

In this chapter, we have discussed the PPC$_{SP}$'s referential drift, i.e. the PPC$_{SP}$'s transition from a merely quantificational tense form denoting indefinite past eventualities to a referential tense form denoting definite past eventualities (with the peculiarity that the perspective time t$_P$ remains to be included in the present time-sphere).

We have proposed to investigate the referential drift by focussing on the PPC$_{SP}$'s micro-structural discourse potential. Based on examples revealed by the corpus study presented in the previous chapter, we have identified that the PPC$_{SP}$ may anchor a backgrounded *Imperfecto*, i.e. that it may function as a temporal cataphora, which would be predicted to be odd by a purely quantificational account of the PPC$_{SP}$. We argued that this micro-structural discourse function presupposes a reading that has already undergone a significant semantic update. Within a prominence-based account, we have argued that the PPC$_{SP}$ denotes an asymmetry established between the two competing domains of the event domain and the post-state domain. Either of these domains may be highlighted as prominent, whereas the highlighting of the event domain represents the innovative use. Accordingly, the reading featuring a prominent event domain, that at some point becomes available, licenses the innovative cataphoric function of attaching an adjacent past eventuality, such as a backgrounded *Imperfecto*. In the context of the referential drift, we thus hypothesized that this highly dynamic prominence-based promotion of the event domain does not only play a crucial role in synchrony but also a catalyzing role in diachrony for the PPC$_{SP}$'s general evolution. In this vein, we proposed that the attentional shift from the post-state towards the event domain triggers the referential drift. In the long run, we assume this development to be accompanied by a truth-conditional update of adding a location time, which finally turns the PPC$_{SP}$ into a definite, referential tense form.

Based on these assumptions and hypotheses, we have tested the PPC_{SP}'s cataphoric potential experimentally by means of an acceptability judgement study. Since several existing studies of the referential drift rely either on corpus data revealing frequencies of the PPC_{SP} in particular contexts or forced choice tasks where participants have to choose from PPC_{SP} vs. *Indefinido* in particular contexts, we assumed that measuring acceptability scores provides complementing evidence. In particular, we expected this method to provide fine-grained means to detect gradual trends in the evolution of the PPC_{SP}.

The study confirmed that the division between a past and a present time-sphere – which is traditionally considered as correlating with unacceptable vs. acceptable uses of the PPC_{SP} – also had an effect on the scores in the experiment: PPC_{SP} eventualities that could be accommodated to the present time-sphere while anchoring a backgrounded *Imperfecto* were judged as significantly better than PPC_{SP} eventualities highly likely to be accommodated to the past time-sphere while anchoring a backgrounded *Imperfecto*.

Furthermore, the results suggested a quite controversial status of the PPC_{SP}'s cataphoric discourse function among the participants, which was reflected in the intermediate location of the scores on the scale and their great spread. This finding is particularly compatible with the idea of a change currently going on in Peninsular Spanish. Moreover, this result suggested that the PPC_{SP} has not (yet) fully invaded the functional domain of the *Indefinido*, not even in hodiernal contexts, since the *Indefinido* was scored significantly better in each condition. This finding contradicts the characterization of the PPC_{SP} as a "hodiernal perfective" (Schwenter and Cacoullos 2008). Accordingly, the referential drift is not yet accomplished, which also holds for hodiernal contexts. Instead, we assume the PPC_{SP} to have reached a transitional stage between quantification and reference. This transitional stage is particularly characterized by the prominently highlighted event domain.

However, the data suggested that there might be a split between conservative speakers (rather rejecting the PPC_{SP}'s cataphoric function as licensed by a prominent event domain) vs. innovative speakers (rather accepting it), as younger participants partly showed better ratings than elderly participants (cf. the discussion concerning the group of the oldest participants though). In other words, the discussed intermediate status of the PPC_{SP} seems to be pronounced differently among speakers.

Concerning future studies, it seems to be fruitful applying a similar design to studies that aim at a systematic investigation of fine-grained diatopic effects and patterns, as well. Since the goal of the present study was to propose a general methodological shift towards investigating the PPC_{SP}'s micro-structural discourse potential by means of acceptability judgments, this enterprise thus remains as a research desideratum for future studies. However, the general diatopic trends attested in the literature with respect to the PPC$_{SP}$'s status in the context of the referential drift most widely matched the results of our investigation of the PPC$_{SP}$'s cataphoric potential. This finding strikingly underpins the assumption that the extension of the micro-structural discourse functions of the PPC$_{SP}$ evolves in a parallel fashion as its truth conditions. This, furthermore and once again, emphasizes the intrinsic intertwinement of the PPC$_{SP}$'s discourse functions and truth-conditional make-up, that may be conceived of as two sides of a coin.

In sum, the present chapter has empirically shown the currently intermediate position of the Peninsular PPC$_{SP}$ on the scale between quantification and reference by means of a discourse-based approach. From a theoretical perspective, we have argued that as soon as speakers tend to accept the establishment of complex temporal relationships (such as fore- and background, precedence and succession) between a past eventuality denoted by a PPC$_{SP}$ and adjacent past eventualities – e.g. expressed by an *Imperfecto* – the PPC$_{SP}$ must have already undergone a fundamental update expressed in a restructuring of the prominence-based asymmetry between the event and post-state domain. Accordingly, an attentional shift towards the event domain licenses the discourse-semantic attachment of adjacent eventualities. In the long run, we assume this interplay to catalyze the PPC$_{SP}$'s referential drift in a significant way.

CHAPTER 7

Conclusions

In this book, we have investigated the Portuguese *Pretérito Perfeito Composto* and the Spanish *Pretérito Perfecto Compuesto* within a synchronic perspective. This endeavour was guided by three main goals formulated in the introduction.

The first goal was to develop and apply a framework that allows the embedding of the study of the two tense forms in the context of a general semantic sketch of tense, aspect and the interplay of tense forms with tempo-aspectual adverbials. Most crucially, this sketch has been drawn based on the opposition of the semantics of quantification and reference, two global semantic concepts that are traditionally mainly studied in the nominal domain. This framework has offered a cross-linguistic view on the PPC_{PT} and PPC_{SP} that has contributed to the investigation of their meanings and readings within a comparative perspective.

The second goal was to explicitly shift the focus to the level of discourse. Particular emphasis has been put on the micro-structural level of discourse, conceived of as the study of the interactions that the PPC_{PT} and PPC_{SP} typically establish with co-textually present tense forms in given segments of discourse. Regarding the study of the PPC_{SP}'s referential drift, discourse prominence has been assigned a significant role in the PPC_{SP}'s transition from quantification to reference.

The third goal was to empirically substantiate the account by testing the generated hypotheses against new data. This has been approached by means of a qualitative corpus study on both the PPC_{PT} and PPC_{SP}, as well as a case study of the PPC_{SP}'s referential drift, which was designed as a quantitative acceptability judgement study.

Having worked through these goals, the main findings may be condensed into the results and conclusions presented in this final chapter. Section 7.1 summarizes the general semantic sketch of the PPC_{PT} and PPC_{SP}, highlighting their common quantificational core meaning and related implications. Section 7.2 summarizes the similarities and differences of the two tense forms on the level of discourse. In order to relate the results to previous studies, i.e. to integrate them into a general picture emphasizing their contribution to the general theory of the Romance Present Perfect, the main findings are furthermore reevaluated in the context of the seminal, diachronic stage model discussed in Harris (1982) and Bertinetto and Squartini (2000). Finally, Section 7.3 presents an outlook, including methodological considerations, still open questions and new questions that have been raised by the study.

7.1 PPC$_{PT}$ and PPC$_{SP}$ as quantificational tense forms

The framework developed in Chapter 2 has provided a cross-linguistic view on the PPC$_{PT}$ and PPC$_{SP}$, describing them as quantificational tense forms, i.e. as opposed to referential tense forms. Accordingly, both are grammaticalized forms taking an event time t_E, a perspective time t_P and the speech time t_S as arguments in order to systematically output these temporal meaning components in particular configurations (cf. Sections 3.3 and 4.3). Each of these configurations sets the event time to precede the speech time, the speech time to be included in the perspective time, whereas the perspective time is set to be included in the present time-sphere (which forms an opposition to the past time-sphere).

Crucially, the shared quantificational root has been shown to account for the PPC$_{PT}$'s and PPC$_{SP}$'s lacking of a location time argument (which referential tense forms, by contrast, dispose of). That means that the PPC denotes past eventualities that remain indefinite, since the event time t_E cannot be assigned to an adverbially provided (or morphosyntactically covert) location time t_{LOC}. Thus, t_E is quantified over, either existentially, when expressing the mere existence of an indefinite past eventuality, or universally, when expressing universal quantification. In other words, t_E is either denoted to be repeated/iterated or to be continuous/persistent, instead of being referentially assigned to a location time.

Due to this shared underlying temporal-semantic make-up, both tense forms furthermore show a similar behavior with respect to their interplay with tempo-aspectual adverbials (cf. Sections 3.4 and 4.5). They felicitously combine with those ones that aim for specifying one of their temporal meaning components. This holds for adverbials scoping over the event time t_E, i.e. quantificational or durative adverbials like "once, twice, often, sometimes, since, for", that answer implicit questions like "how many times?" or "how long?". Moreover, this holds for adverbials scoping over the perspective time t_P, i.e. XN-adverbials like "ever since" but also "today, this week", that answer an implicit question that might be paraphrased as "what is the perspectivized time?". Regarding the Portuguese PPC$_{PT}$, there are further restrictions on quantificational adverbials though, since definite quantification as in "once, twice" is ruled out in favor of indefinite pluractional existential (IPEX) quantification, as in "several times, a few times". As mentioned above, the lacking of a location time argument furthermore accounts for the PPC$_{PT}$'s and PPC$_{SP}$'s blocking of positional adverbials like "yesterday, last month" etc., since these aim for scoping over a location time t_{LOC}. In Section 2.5, we have argued that this assumption may also be suitable to generally account for the famous Present Perfect puzzle raised in Klein (1992). While the Portuguese PPC$_{PT}$ unexceptionally rules out positional adverbials, the Spanish PPC$_{SP}$ has been described in the literature as being combinable with those that denote a time which is included in the hodiernal time-sphere (i.e. the present time-sphere), like "today, this morning". However, we have argued that these allegedly positional adverbials bear potential scope ambiguities, since they may also be accounted for as being interpreted as XN-adverbials scoping over the perspective time t_P (cf. Section 4.5). In other words, we have argued that adverbials like "today, this morning" do not serve as a clear-cut test case to determine if the PPC$_{SP}$ may give rise to hodiernal perfective readings, i.e. referential readings. We have thus proposed to shift the investigation of the referential potential of the PPC$_{SP}$ to the level of discourse.

With regard to their readings, the PPC$_{PT}$ and PPC$_{SP}$ have been shown to spell out their temporal quantifier in a diverse fashion (cf. Sections 3.3 and 4.3). The Portuguese PPC$_{PT}$ has been defined as featuring a reading of indefinite pluractional existential quantification (IPEX), which denotes an indefinite but plural number of iterations of the underlying predicate. Besides, the PPC$_{PT}$ has been shown to give rise to a reading of universal quantification, which resembles the PPC$_{SP}$'s universal reading. However, the universal PPC$_{PT}$ reading may be affected by fine-grained variational restrictions which is e.g. reflected in the controversial discussion in the literature concerning the question of whether the PPC$_{PT}$ actually disposes of a strictly durative reading. Since fine-grained diatopic variation has not been explicitly addressed by our general account though, this question remains to be scrutinized in future studies (cf. also Section 7.3). Third, the PPC$_{PT}$ has been accounted for as disposing of a reading of characterizing quantification, a reading that expresses law-like regularities, i.e. abstractions based on episodic eventualities, which are temporally restricted to the present time-sphere.

By contrast, the widely "well-behaved" Spanish PPC$_{SP}$ has been accounted for as featuring the typical perfectal readings, based on universal quantification (universal reading), existential quantification (resultative, experiential and hot news readings), as well as the innovative existential reading featuring a prominent event domain (cf. below for details).

On several occasions, we have related the PPC$_{PT}$'s and PPC$_{SP}$'s quantificational semantics and the above summarized readings and meaning effects to the influential stage model of the diachronic development of the Romance Present Perfect in the tradition of Harris (1982) and Bertinetto and Squartini (2000). This provides an interpretation of our synchronic findings in the context of a general theory of the diachronic development of the PPC. Figure 7.1 presents an updated version of the preliminary one discussed in Section 5.4, illustrating how the results may be integrated into the model.

In line with the standard assumptions of the model, the universal and IPEX readings of the PPC$_{PT}$ are characterized as not having approached stage III but as having stagnated at stage II. Additionally, Figure 7.1 illustrates our assumption that the characterizing PPC$_{PT}$ has paved the way to an alternative grammaticalization

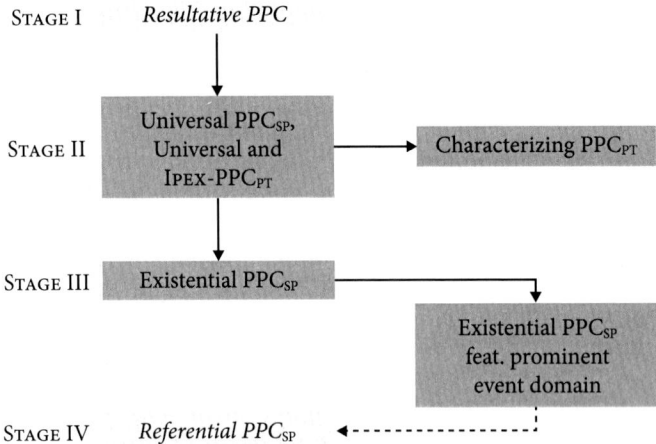

Figure 7.1 Integrating the account into the stage model

path. This is visualized by means of the horizontal extension, emphasizing the idea of an alternative development that escapes from the regular path along the vertical dimension towards stage III. We assume its peculiarity of expressing a temporally restricted genericity to justify its discrete role in the model. In this vein, its deviating position stresses its modal flavor: it ceases to denote episodic eventualities distributed along the virtual timeline, in favor of expressing law-like regularities, i.e. abstractions based on episodic eventualities that are temporally restricted to the present time-sphere. It remains to be investigated if it would be adequate to assume a characterizing/modal drift that the PPC$_{PT}$ might be affected by (cf. also Section 7.3).

On the other hand, the Spanish PPC$_{SP}$ is depicted as covering both stage II (universal reading) and stage III (existential readings). The occupation of these two stages particularly accounts for the widely known observation that the many Spanish varieties rank them differently, as e.g. the American varieties have been traditionally described as favoring stage II over stage III, whereas most of the the peninsular varieties invert that picture (cf. Section 4.2). The PPC$_{SP}$ is furthermore affected by the evolutionary dynamics of the referential drift, as discussed and investigated in detail in Chapter 6. At some point, the PPC$_{SP}$ is thus expected to undergo a fundamental semantic update of acquiring innovative referential semantics at stage IV. However, Figure 7.1 displays the PPC$_{SP}$, conceived of as a cross-dialectal abstraction, as not having reached stage IV yet. Instead, there is a reading located in between quantification and reference, that is supposed to occupy an intermediate stage. The discrete status of this stage particularly accounts for that the transition from quantification to reference marks a huge gap, requiring a transitional bridging context to trigger the innovative referential drift. Therefore, we have referred to the notion of prominence. As discussed in Section 6.3, the notion of prominence is defined as a "basic underlying organizational principle of linguistic structuring" (Himmelmann and Primus 2015: 52). Applied to the referential drift, it suggests a diachronic reshaping of a prominence-based asymmetry that is involved in the meaning of the PPC_{SP}. Accordingly, the PPC_{SP}'s event domain becomes, at some point, accessible for being highlighted as a prominent structural attractor. Due to the underlying attentional shift from the post-state domain towards the event domain, we have argued that this operation licenses the innovative micro-structural discourse function of temporal cataphora, i.e. of anchoring an anaphoric tense form. The existential reading featuring a prominent event domain has been experimentally investigated by means of an acceptability judgement study reported in Chapter 6. Consistently, the results have suggested that the PPC_{SP} has synchronically already entered the transitional phase between stages III and IV. Hence, the relative interpretation of the scores of the PPC_{SP} with regard to the scores of the *Indefinido* has shown that the PPC_{SP} has not yet fully invaded the functional domain of referential tense on the micro-structural level of discourse, as measured by means of the cataphoric potential, which means that it has not fully acquired referential semantics yet.

7.2 Similarities and differences on the level of discourse

Throughout the book, we have put emphasis on investigating the role that the PPC_{PT} and PPC_{SP} fulfill on the level of discourse. This was based on the assumption that this approach adds crucial insights to a semantic sketch of the two tense forms, as well as to the question of where the dividing lines between the two are exactly to be drawn. The hypotheses and expectations were generated based on the detailed accounts developed in Chapters 3 and 4. Both similar and diverging discourse functions were expected to be empirically attested in the corpus study reported in Chapter 5, reflecting both the PPC_{PT}'s and PPC_{SP}'s common quantificational core meaning, *and* their differences. Consistently, and against the backdrop of the common characterization of the two as evoking significantly diverging meanings and functions, the study has revealed a range of similarities and parallels on both the macro-structural and micro-structural discourse level. These are summarized first, and followed by a summary of the diverging discourse functions. Besides, the findings concerning the micro-structural discourse functions are, again, reevaluated in the context of the stage model in order to relate them to the general picture discussed above.

On the macro-structural level of discourse, conceived of as the modes of discourse in the sense of Smith (2003), the PPC$_{PT}$ and PPC$_{SP}$ show a similar potential as to the question of which modes they generally may be employed in. That means that despite the fact that the Spanish PPC$_{SP}$ represents the much more productive and versatile tense form as compared to the highly specialized PPC$_{PT}$, both satisfy the same tempo-aspectual requirements imposed by the modes of discourse (cf. Sections 3.5 and 4.6 for examples). This observation has once again stressed the semantic similarities between the PPC$_{PT}$ and PPC$_{SP}$ and shown how these are intertwined with their similar discursive performance.

On the one hand, both PPC$_{PT}$ and PPC$_{SP}$ block the modes of narration and description. Narration is defined as consisting of specific events and states that underly a dynamic temporal updating based on temporal relations established between them. Also, they typically perspectivize the past time-sphere. This conflicts with the quantificational PPC$_{PT}$'s and PPC$_{SP}$'s denotation of indefinite past eventualities, as well as their orientation towards the speech time as induced by the perspective time which is set to be included in the present time-sphere. Descriptions are defined as consisting of primarily atemporal statives such that there is no temporal progression at all. In its purest sense, the discourse mode of description is thus incompatible with the PPC$_{PT}$ and PPC$_{SP}$ since both denote past eventualities.

On the other hand, both PPC$_{PT}$ and PPC$_{SP}$ satisfy the tempo-aspectual demands of the modes of report, argument and information (cf. Sections 3.5 and 4.6 for examples). Reports are defined as denoting events, states and general statives that are anchored relatively to the speech time. This harmonizes with their perspectivizing of the present time-sphere, which opposes to the establishment of temporal relations among several past eventualities in the past time-sphere, which is typical for the mode of narration. The modes of argument and information share an atemporal character, which means that temporal progression is converted into a metaphorical motion through the text domain, which both PPC$_{PT}$ and PPC$_{SP}$ license.

On the micro-structural level, further similarities have been put forth by the study. These mainly pertain to the discursive management of the temporal perspective and the event-referential structure.

Regarding the temporal perspective, the study has shown that both PPC$_{PT}$ and PPC$_{SP}$ serve as means to establish perspectival shifts, as well as perspectival maintenance. In this vein, they contribute to the dynamic management of the perspectival structure which is permanently updated in light of the co-textual interplay of several tense forms (including also perspectivizing adverbials like e.g. "now"). As discourse unfolds, the perspective time may permanently oscillate between the present time-sphere and the past time-sphere, whereas both PPC$_{PT}$ and PPC$_{SP}$ assign t$_P$ to the present time-sphere. Obviously, this function is intertwined with the macro-structure of discourse. For example, while reporting several past eventualities, perspectival maintenance may serve to explicitly preserve the discourse mode of report, where past eventualities are anchored relatively to the speech time, from turning into a narration, where past eventualities are anchored relatively to each other.

Regarding the event-referential function, both PPC$_{PT}$ and PPC$_{SP}$ have been shown to contribute to the establishment of so-called actualization effects in the sense of Declerck et al. (2006). These are created in combination with co-textually present referential tense forms, most typically in combination with the Simple Past. Discursively exploiting the semantics of definiteness and indefiniteness, a quantificational PPC first introduces an indefinite past eventuality, which subsequently gets referentially picked up by a succeeding referential tense form that turns the past eventuality definite by actualizing it, e.g. by adding further information. In metaphorical terms, a preceding PPC sets the stage, whereas a succeeding referential Simple Past zooms in on the past eventuality that has just been introduced to the discourse universe. This dynamic referential management of temporal discourse entities bears parallels with the well-studied nominal domain. In the nominal domain, discourse entities are also assumed to be either indefinitely introduced to the discourse universe via quantificational forms, or, if already present in the discourse universe at a given stage, referred to via referential, definite forms.

In addition to these similarities, the study has also exposed different discourse functions associated with the PPC$_{PT}$ and PPC$_{SP}$. Crucially, these differences correlate with the diverging trends discussed above and depicted in Figure 7.1. In this vein, the characterizing PPC$_{PT}$ seems to have specialized in systematically contributing to quasi-logical reasoning in the sense of Perelman and Olbrechts-Tyteca (1971), i.e. to an argumentation technique that draws on the "prestige of logical thought". In particular, this rhetorical function concerns the exploiting of a co-textually established contrast between episodic propositions, e.g. expressed by a Simple Past, and generic propositions, expressed by the characterizing PPC$_{PT}$.

Regarding the PPC$_{SP}$, it is the existential PPC$_{SP}$ featuring a prominent event domain, which is situated between the stages III and IV, that may license – or at least has started to license (cf. also Section 7.1 and Chapter 6) – the micro-structural discourse function of cataphorically anchoring an anaphoric tense form, e.g. a progressive *Imperfecto*.

These findings concerning the micro-structural discourse functions typically assumed by the PPC$_{PT}$ and PPC$_{SP}$ may, again, be evaluated in the context of the stage model, as depicted in Figure 7.2.

As discussed, it shows that the functions correlate with certain readings. On the one hand, the stages II and III correlate with similar discourse functions. Thus, they might be conceived of as the core that gives rise to the central micro-structural discourse functions of the quantificational PPC. On the other hand, the deviating

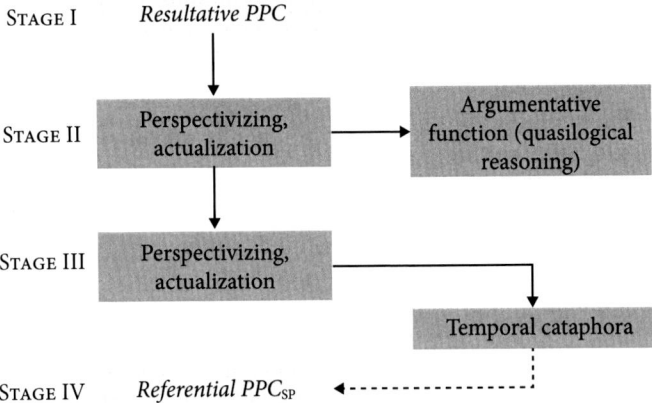

Figure 7.2 Micro-structural discourse functions and the stage model

readings, i.e. the characterizing PPC$_{PT}$ reading and the existential PPC$_{SP}$ reading featuring a prominent event domain, correlate with alternative micro-structural discourse functions.

7.3 Outlook

The study has raised a range of still open questions, as well as new questions, which remain to be investigated in the future. Most importantly, this concerns the level of variation. Regarding the Portuguese PPC$_{PT}$, the factor of diatopic variation requires more research. While it has been attested that the PPC$_{PT}$ is slightly more frequently used in European Portuguese than in Brazilian Portuguese (cf. Section 3.2), it particularly remains to be scrutinized whether diatopic variation has an affect on the readings. Accordingly, a given variety might exclude or prefer particular readings. As discussed in Section 3.2, it is particularly the status of the universal reading that requires further research, as it might be the reading that is affected most by diatopic variation. Moreover, the potential assumption of a characterizing/modal drift associated with the PPC$_{PT}$, conceived of as opposing with the PPC$_{SP}$'s referential drift, and which would mean that the characterizing reading becomes central to the PPC$_{PT}$ in the long run, would require further research. However, this would presuppose a linguistic test that might be able to distinguish the characterizing reading from the episodic PPC$_{PT}$ readings (i.e. from the universal and IPEX readings) to approach that question. That means that the associated rhetorical function of contributing to the argumentative structure based on micro-structural discourse mechanisms is not supposed to serve as a diagnostics precise enough for the identification of characterizing readings. Yet, the fact that many uses of the PPC_{PT} may remain ambiguous between two readings, i.e. that there might be cases in which they are hardly distinguishable based on clear cut linguistic tests, is not expected to contradict our account of treating them as discrete readings. Instead, reading ambiguities, especially those between IPEX and characterizing readings, may rather help approach the question of why the peculiar characterizing reading has emerged at all.

Since we have exposed that the characterizing PPC_{PT}'s micro-structural discourse function of contributing to quasi-logical reasoning seems to be dominantly exploited in communicative situations that favor this kind of prestigious rhetoric, it also remains to be determined in a systematic research design to what extent other factors of variation, such as diastratic, diaphasic and diamesic variation may interact with the diatopic dimension, by imposing further variational restrictions on the use of the PPC_{PT}. It would be especially of interest to investigate whether the PPC_{PT}'s use in competing zones, i.e. in contexts where it might compete with other tense forms, is rather affected by variation or actually by discourse-semantic strategies that speakers pursue. We assume that the concepts developed in our study of the PPC_{PT}'s micro-structural discourse functions may contribute to this research question.

As discussed in Section 4.2 and Chapter 6, diatopic variation certainly is of major importance to the Spanish PPC_{SP}. It thus remains to be tested if the developed framework helps account for the meanings and discourse functions of the PPC_{SP} in the manyfold varieties in the Spanish-speaking world. Particularly, this also holds for the study of the referential drift. As our study has shed light on the PPC_{SP}'s cataphoric potential based on the potential anchoring of a succeeding progressive *Imperfecto*, it would be useful to test whether one would obtain similar results when testing for the attachment of other anaphoric tense forms, such as the *Pluscuamperfecto*. After all, (more or less) similar results would be predicted by our prominence-based account.

Within a general semantic sketch, the study has proposed to reinterpret the well-known phenomenon of the aoristic drift as a referential drift, i.e. as the tendency of acquiring referential temporal semantics. As discussed on several occasions, this account is i.a. able to motivate the micro-structural discourse function of actualization, as it bears parallels to the well-studied semantics of definiteness in the nominal domain. In Section 2.4, we have furthermore touched on the notion of specific indefinites, as e.g. in "a student has cheated on the exam", where the indefinite "a student" actually stands for a referent known by the speaker. It remains to be studied in detail whether the concept of specific indefinites would also improve the account of the PPC_{PT} and PPC_{SP}. In this vein, it might be particularly worth exploring if assuming a specific indefinite event time t_E would fruitfully upgrade the prominence-based account of the PPC$_{SP}$'s referential drift, which draws on a highlighting of the event domain as prominent.

Another theoretical aspect pertains to the question of how the interplay of truth conditions and discourse functions of tense forms may be accounted for in a general formal semantic sketch. In Section 5.3.4, we have briefly illustrated the potential benefits of accounting for the discourse functions of a tense form based on the concept of use conditions, understood as a meaning component that principally complements the truth conditions of a linguistic expression. It seems to be promising to elaborate if a systematic use conditional approach would contribute a useful additional tool to the analysis.

In sum, we have shed new light on a range of problems and questions related to the study of the PPC$_{PT}$ and PPC$_{SP}$, based on new concepts, methodologies and new sources of data. In light of the poles of quantificational and referential tense, the particular focus on micro-structural discourse functions, as well as the explanatory potential of the dynamic notion of discourse prominence, the study has opened up fruitful research areas that demand to be deepened in the future. In this sense, we hope to have inspired further studies that also aim for getting closer to the research goal of an integral account of the *Pretérito Perfecto Compuesto* and the *Pretérito Perfeito Composto*.

Bibliography

Abraham, W. & Conradie, C. J. 2001. *Präteritumschwund und Diskursgrammatik. Areale Ausbreitung, heterogene Entstehung, Parsing sowie diskursgrammatische Grundlagen und Zusammenhänge*. Amsterdam: John Benjamins. https://doi.org/10.1075/z.103

Adli, A. 2015. What you like is not what you do: Acceptability and frequency in syntactic variation. In *Variation in Language: Usage-based vs. System-based Approaches*, A. Adli, M. García García & G. Kaufmann (eds), 173–200. Berlin: Mouton de Gruyter. https://doi.org/10.1515/9783110346855-008

Aissen, J. 2003. Differential object marking: Iconicity vs. economy. *Natural Language and Linguistic Theory* 21(3): 435–483. https://doi.org/10.1023/A:1024109008573

Altshuler, D. 2016. *Events, States and Times*. Warsaw: De Gruyter Open. https://doi.org/10.1515/9783110485912

Amaral, P. & Howe, C. 2012. Nominal and verbal plurality in the diachrony of the Portuguese Present Perfect. In *Verbal Plurality and Distributivity*, P. Cabredo Hofherr & B. Laca (eds), 25–54. Berlin: De Gruyter. https://doi.org/10.1515/9783110293500.25

Asher, N. & Lascarides, A. 2003. *Logics of conversation. Studies in Natural Language Processing*. Cambridge: CUP.

Azpiazu Torres, S. 2015. El antepresente de noticias recientes en la prensa digital Española. *Rilce. Revista de Filología Hispánica* 31(2): 341–364.

Azpiazu Torres, S. 2017. El sistema ps/pc en francés y español del s. xvii. estudio contrastivo a partir de la traducción del Quijote De César Oudin. *Orillas. Rivista d'Ispanistica* 6: 527–551.

Azpiazu Torres, S. 2019. *La composicionalidad temporal del perfecto compuesto en Español: Estudio sincrónico y dialectal*. Berlin: De Gruyter. https://doi.org/10.1515/9783110633658

Azpiazu Torres, S. 2021. The impact of the simultaneity vector on the temporal-aspectual development of the perfect tense in romance languages. In *The Perfect Volume. Papers on the Perfect* [Studies in Language Companion Series 217], K. Melum Eide & M. Fryd (eds), 213–240. Amsterdam: John Benjamins. https://doi.org/10.1075/slcs.217.09tor

Bach, E. 1981. On time, tense, and aspect: An essay in English metaphysics. In *Radical Pragmatics*, P. Cole (Ed.), 63–81. New York NY: Academic Press.

Barbosa Bertucci, J. 2008. Tenho feito/fiz a tese: Uma proposta de caracterização do pretérito perfeito no Português. PhD dissertation, Universidade Estadual Paulista (UNESP).

Barr, D. J., Levy, R., Scheepers, C. & Tily, H. J. 2013. Random effects structure for confirmatory hypothesis testing: Keep it maximal. *Journal of Memory and Language* 68(3): 255–278. https://doi.org/10.1016/j.jml.2012.11.001

Bartens, A. & Kempas, I. 2007. Sobre el valor aspectual del pretérito perfecto en el Español peninsular: Resultados de una prueba de reconocimiento realizada entre informantes universitarios. *Revista de Investigación Lingüística* 10: 151–171.

Bary, C. L. A. 2009. Aspect in Ancient Greek. A Semantic Analysis of the Aorist and Imperfective. PhD dissertation, Radboud Universiteit Nijmegen.

Bates, D., Maechler, M., Bolker, B. & Walker, S. 2015. Fitting linear mixed-effects models using lme4. *Journal of Statistical Software* 67(1): 1–48. https://doi.org/10.18637/jss.v067.i01

Becker, M. 2010a. Die ingredienzen des romanischen imperfekts. *Linguistische Berichte* 221: 79–108.

Becker, M. 2010b. Passé composé versus passé simple alles passé? *Romanische Forschungen* 122(1): 3–27. https://doi.org/10.3196/003581210790907477

Becker, M. 2016. O pretérito perfeito composto em diacronia – Uma evolução perfeita? *Estudos de Lingüística Galega* 8: 25–43. https://doi.org/10.15304/elg.8.3057

Becker, M. 2020a. Das pretérito perfeito composto – Ein Perfekt? Zur Semantik und Diachronie der ter + partizip-Konstruktion. In *Zwischen Sprechen und Sprache / Entre fala e língua* [Iberolinguistica. Studien zur Sprach- und Kulturwissenschaft 4], B. Meisnitzer & E. Pustka (eds), 83–110. Frankfurt: Peter Lang. (Cited version is a manuscript numbered 1–22).

Becker, M. 2020b. The pluperfect and its discourse potential in contrast: A comparison between Spanish, French and Italian. *Revue Romane* 56(2): 267–296. https://doi.org/10.1075/rro.20008.pro

Becker, M. 2022. More about the ppc – The ppc and its interaction with quantifiers in a diachronic perspective. In *Micro-variation and Complex Systems Theory in the Study of Portuguese Grammar*, D. Gerards, B. Meinsitzer & A. Wall (eds). *PhiN. Philologie im Netz: Beiheft* 28: 56–89.

Becker, M. & Egetenmeyer, J. 2018. A prominence-based account of temporal discourse structure. *Lingua* 214: 28–58. https://doi.org/10.1016/j.lingua.2018.08.002

Bertinetto, P. M. & Lenci, A. 2012. Habituality, pluractionality, and imperfectivity. In *The Oxford Handbook of Tense and Aspect*, R. I. Binnick (ed.), 852–880. Oxford: OUP.

Bertinetto, P. M. & Squartini, M. 2000. The simple and compound past in romance languages. In *Tense and Aspect in the Languages of Europe*, Ö. Dahl (ed.), 403–439. Berlin: Mouton de Gruyter.

Bonami, O., Godard, D. & Kampers-Manhe, B. 2004. Adverb classification. In *Handbook of French Semantics*, F. Corblin & H. de Swart (eds), 143–184. Stanford CA: CSLI.

Botne, R. & Kershner, T. L. 2008. Tense and cognitive space: On the organization of tense/aspect systems in Bantu languages and beyond. *Cognitive Linguistics* 19(2): 145–218. https://doi.org/10.1515/COG.2008.008

Brocher, A. & von Heusinger, K. 2018. A dual-process activation model: Processing definiteness and information status. *Glossa: A Journal of General Linguistics* 3(1: 108): 1–34. https://doi.org/10.5334/gjgl.457

Burgos, J. M. 2015. El pretérito perfecto compuesto en el ámbito hispánico. *Anuario de Letras. Lingüística y Filología* 3: 87–130. https://doi.org/10.19130/iifl.adel.3.1.2015.72

Bybee, J., Perkins, R. & Pagliuca, W. 1994. *The Evolution of Grammar: Tense, Aspect, and Modality in the Languages of the World*. Chicago IL: The University of Chicago Press.

Cabredo Hofherr, P., Carvalho, S. & Laca, B. 2010. When perfect means "plural": The present perfect in northeastern Brazilian Portuguese. In *Layers of Aspect*, P. Cabredo Hofherr & B. Laca (eds), 67–100. Chicago IL: The University of Chicago Press.

Campos, M. H. C. 1986. L'opposition du Portugais pretérito perfeito simples – Pretérito perfeito composto. In *Actes du XVII Congrès International de Linguistique et Philologie Romanes*, H. J. Verkuyl, H. de Swart & A. van Hout (eds), 409–422. Aix-Marseille: Publications Université de Provence.

Carrasco Gutiérrez, A. 2008. Los tiempos compuestos del Español: Formación, interpretación y sintaxis. In *Tiempos compuestos y formas verbales complejas*, A. Carrasco Gutiérrez (ed.), 13–64. Madrid: Iberoamericana Editorial. https://doi.org/10.31819/9783865278654-002

Carston, R. 1998. Informativeness, relevance and scalar implicature. In *Relevance Theory: Applications and Implications* [Pragmatics & Beyond New Series 37], R. Carston & S. Uchida (eds), 179–236. Amsterdam: John Benjamins. https://doi.org/10.1075/pbns.37.11car

Chamorro, M. D. P. 2012. Pluractionality and Aspectual Structure in the Galician Spanish Tener-Perfect. PhD dissertation, The Ohio State University.

Civardi, E. & Bertinetto, P. M. 2015. The semantics of degree verbs and the telicity issue. *Borealis: An International Journal of Hispanic Linguistics* 4(1): 57–77. https://doi.org/10.7557/1.4.1.3398

Comrie, B. 1976. *Aspect. An Introduction to the Study of Verbal Aspect and Related Problems*. Cambridge: CUP.

Dahl, Ö. 1985. *Tense and Aspect Systems*. Oxford: Basil Blackwell.

Dahl, Ö. 2013. How telicity creates time. *Journal of Slavic Linguistics* 21(1): 45–76. https://doi.org/10.1353/jsl.2013.0004

Dahl, Ö. & Hedin, E. 2000. Current relevance and event reference. In *Tense and Aspect in the Languages of Europe*, Ö. Dahl (ed.), 385–401. Berlin: Mouton de Gruyter. https://doi.org/10.1515/9783110197099.3.385

Davies, M. & Ferreira, M. 2006. Corpus do Português: 45 million words, 1300s-1900s. <https://www.corpusdoportugues.org/> (2 September 2022).

De Oliveira, L. C. 2010. Estágio da gramaticalização do pretérito perfeito composto no Espanhol escrito de sete capitais Hispano-Falantes. PhD dissertation, Federal University of Santa Catarina, Florianópolis.

Declerck, R., Reed, S. & Cappelle, B. 2006. *The Grammar of the English Verb Phrase*. Berlin: De Gruyter Mouton.

Depraetere, I. 1998. On the resultative character of present perfect sentences. *Journal of Pragmatics* 29(5): 597–613. https://doi.org/10.1016/S0378-2166(97)00084-2

Dery, J. E. 2012. Scene-salience-driven Effects in Discourse Processing. PhD dissertation, State University of New York at Buffalo.

Dessì Schmid, S. 2014. *Aspektualität: Ein onomasiologisches Modell am Beispiel der romanischen Sprachen*. Berlin: De Gruyter. https://doi.org/10.1515/9783110334449

Detges, U. 2000. Time and truth: The grammaticalization of resultatives and perfects within a theory of subjectification. *Studies in Language* 24(2): 345–377. https://doi.org/10.1075/sl.24.2.05det

Detges, U. 2006. Aspect and pragmatics. the passé composé in old French and the old Spanish perfecto compuesto. In *Change in Verbal Systems. Issues on Explanation*, K. Eksell & T. Vinther (eds), 47–72. Frankfurt: Peter Lang.

Detges, U. 2018. Te lo tengo dicho muchas veces. Resultatives between coercion, relevance and reanalysis. *Open Linguistics* 4: 260–279. https://doi.org/10.1515/opli-2018-0014

Dowty, D. R. 1979. *Word Meaning and Montague Grammar*. Dordrecht: Reidel. https://doi.org/10.1007/978-94-009-9473-7

Dowty, D. R. 1986. The effects of aspectual class on the temporal structure of discourse: Semantics or pragmatics? *Linguistics and Philosophy* 9(1): 37–61.

Enfield, N. 2008. Transmission biases in linguistic epidemiology. *Journal of Language Contact* 2(1): 299–310. https://doi.org/10.1163/000000008792525273

Enç, M. 1986. Towards a referential analysis of temporal expressions. *Linguistics and Philosophy* 9: 405–426. https://doi.org/10.1007/BF00603217

Fauconnier, G. 1997. *Mappings in Thought and Language*. Cambridge: CUP. https://doi.org/10.1017/CBO9781139174220

Fernández, L. G. 1999. Los complementos adverbiales temporales: La subordinación temporal. In *Gramática descriptiva de la lengua Española*, Vol. 2, I. Bosque & V. Demonte (eds), 3129–3208. Madrid: Espasa.

Ferreira, M. 2017. On the indexicality of portuguese past tenses. *Journal of Semantics* 34(4): 633–657. https://doi.org/10.1093/jos/ffx012

Filip, H. 2012. Lexical aspect. In *The Oxford Handbook of Tense and Aspect*, Robert I. Binnick (ed.), 721–751. Oxford: OUP.

Fleischman, S. 1983. From pragmatics to grammar: Diachronic reflections on complex pasts and futures in romance. *Lingua* 60: 183–214. https://doi.org/10.1016/0024-3841(83)90074-8

Fournier, N. 1998. *Grammaire du Français classique*. Paris: Belin Education.

García Fajardo, J. 2011. He esperado, he vuelto y he vivido: Su valor semántico en el Español de México. *Nueva Revista de Filología Hispánica* 2: 419–446. https://doi.org/10.24201/nrfh.v59i2.1012

García Fernández, L. 1999. El perfecto continuativo. *Verba: Anuario Galego de Filoloxia* 27: 343–358.

García Fernández, L. 2007. Características aspectuales de los predicados de estado. In *El tiempo y los eventos*, B. Camus Bergareche (ed.), 95–128. Castilla-La Mancha: Ediciones de La Universidade Castilla-La Mancha.

García Fernández, L. & Martínez-Atienza, M. 2003. La expresión de los eventos inconclusos en Español. *Revista Española de Lingüística* 33(1): 29–67.

Giorgi, A. & Pianesi, F. 1997. *Tense and Aspect: From Semantics to Morphosyntax* [Oxford Studies in Comparative Syntax]. Oxford: OUP.

Grice, H. P. 1975. Logic and conversation. In *Syntax and Semantics*, Vol. 3: *Speech Acts*, P. Cole & J. L. Morgan (eds), 41–58. New York NY: Academic Press.

Grønn, A. & von Stechow, A. 2016. Tense. In *The Cambridge Handbook of Formal Semantics*, M. Aloni & P. Dekker (eds), 313–341. Cambridge: CUP. https://doi.org/10.1017/CBO9781139236157.012

Grønn, A. and von Stechow, A. (2020). The Perfect. In *The Wiley Blackwell Companion to Semantics*, D. Gutzmann, L. Matthewson, C. Meier, H. Rullmann and T. Zimmermann (eds). https://doi.org/10.1002/9781118788516.sem046

Gutzmann, D. 2013. Expressives and beyond: An introduction to varieties of use-conditional meaning. In *Beyond Expressives: Explorations in Use-conditional Meaning*, D. Gutzmann & H.-M. Gärtner (eds), 1–58. Leiden: Brill. https://doi.org/10.1163/9789004183988_002

Gvozdanović, J. 2012. Perfective and imperfective aspect. In *The Oxford Handbook of Tense and Aspect*, R. I. Binnick & M.-E. Ritz (eds), 781–802. Oxford: OUP.

Hallman, P. 2009. Proportions in time: Interactions of quantification and aspect. *Natural Language Semantics* 17(1): 29–61. https://doi.org/10.1007/s11050-008-9038-y

Harris, M. 1982. The "past simple" and the "present perfect" in romance. In *Studies in the Romance Verb*, N. Vincent & M. Harris (eds), 42–70. London: Croom Helm.

Haßler, G. 2016. *Temporalität, Aspektualität und Modalität in romanischen Sprachen*. Berlin: De Gruyter. https://doi.org/10.1515/9783110312997

Heim, I. & Kratzer, A. 1998. *Semantics in Generative Grammar*. Oxford: Blackwell.

Heine, B. 2003. Grammaticalization. In *The Handbook of Historical Linguistics*, Brian D. Joseph & Richard D. Janda (eds), 575–601. Oxford: Blackwell. https://doi.org/10.1002/9780470756393.ch18

Henderson, C. 2005. *Aspectos semánticos pragmáticos y discursivos del pretérito perfecto compuesto.* XVI Congreso de Romanistas Escandinavos, Roskilde-Copenhague.

Henderson, C. 2010. El pretérito perfecto compuesto del español de Chile, Paraguay y Uruguay: Aspectos semánticos y discursivos. PhD dissertation, Stockholm University.

von Heusinger, K. 2002. Specificity and definiteness in sentence and discourse structure. *Journal of Semantics* 19(3): 245–274. https://doi.org/10.1093/jos/19.3.245

von Heusinger, K. & Schumacher, P. 2019. Discourse prominence: Definition and application. *Journal of Pragmatics* 154: 117–127. https://doi.org/10.1016/j.pragma.2019.07.025

Himmelmann, N. & Primus, B. 2015. Prominence beyond prosody – A first approximation. In *pS-prominenceS: Prominences in Linguistics. Proceedings of the International Conference*, A. De Dominicis (ed.), 38–58. Viterbo: Disucom Press.

Hinrichs, E. 1981. *Temporale Anaphora im Englischen*. Magisterarbeit, Universität Tübingen.

Holmes, B. C. & Balukas, C. 2011. Yesterday, all my troubles have seemed (pp) so far away: Variation in pre-hodiernal perfective expression in peninsular spanish. In *Selected Proceedings of the 5th Workshop on Spanish Sociolinguistics*, J. Michnowicz & R. Dodsworth (eds), 79–89. Somerville MA: Cascadilla Proceedings Project.

Howe, C. 2013. *The Spanish Perfects*. Houndmills: Palgrave Macmillan. https://doi.org/10.1057/9781137029812

Howe, C. & Schwenter, S. A. 2003. Present perfect for preterite across spanish dialects. *Penn Working Papers in Linguistics* 9(2): 61–75.

Hundertmark-Santos Martins, M. T. 2014. *Portugiesische Grammatik*, 3rd edn. Berlin: De Gruyter. https://doi.org/10.1515/9783110302363

Hurtado González, S. 1998. El perfecto simple y el perfecto compuesto en el Español actual: Estado de la cuestión. *Epos: Revista de Filología* 14: 51–67. https://doi.org/10.5944/epos.14.1998.10048

Iatridou, S., Anagnostopoulou, E. & Izvorski, R. 2003. Observations about the form and meaning of the perfect. In *Perfect Explorations*, A. Alexiadou, M. Rathert & A. von Stechow (eds), 153–205. Berlin: De Gruyter. https://doi.org/10.1515/9783110902358.153

Ilari, R. 2001. Notas sobre o passado composto em Português. Intuições compartilhadas. *Revista Letras* 55: 129–152. https://doi.org/10.5380/rel.v55i0.2822

Ilari, R. & Basso, R. M. 2008. O verbo. In *Gramática do Português culto falado no Brasil: Classes de palavras e processos de construção*, R. Ilari & M. H. de Moura Neves (eds), 163–365. Campinas SP: Editora da Unicamp.

Inoue, K. 1979. An analysis of the English present perfect. *Linguistics* 17: 561–590. https://doi.org/10.1515/ling.1979.17.7-8.561

Jara, M. 2009. El pretérito perfecto simple y el pretérito perfecto compuesto en las variedades del Español peninsular y americano. *Signo y Seña* 20: 263–291.

Jasinskaja, K., Chiriacescu, S., Donazzan, M., von Heusinger, K. & Hinterwimmer, S. 2015. Prominence in discourse. In *pS-prominenceS: Prominences in Linguistics. Proceedings of the International Conference*, A. De Dominicis (ed.), 134–153. Viterbo: Disucom Press.

Jasinskaja, K. and Karagjosova, E. (2020). Rhetorical Relations. In *The Wiley Blackwell Companion to Semantics*, D. Gutzmann, L. Matthewson, C. Meier, H. Rullmann and T. Zimmermann (eds). https://doi.org/10.1002/9781118788516.sem061

Kamp, H. 2013. Deixis in discourse. Reichenbach on temporal reference. In *Meaning and the Dynamics of Interpretation*, K. von Heusinger & A. ter Meulen (eds), 105–159. Leiden: Brill. https://doi.org/10.1163/9789004252882_006

Kamp, H. & Reyle, U. 1993. *From Discourse to Logic* [Studies in Linguistics and Philosophy 42]. Dordrecht: Kluwer.

Kamp, H. & Rohrer, C. 1983. Tense in texts. In *Meaning, Use, and Interpretation of Language*, R. Bäuerle, C. Schwarze & A. von Stechow (eds), 250–269. Berlin: De Gruyter. https://doi.org/10.1515/9783110852820.250

Kamp, H. & Rohrer, C. 1985. *Temporal reference in French*. Ms, University of Stuttgart.

Kamp, H., van Genabith, J. & Reyle, U. 2011. Discourse representation theory. In *Handbook of Philosophical Logic*, 2nd edn, D. M. Gabbay & F. Guenthner (eds), 125–394. Dordrecht: Springer. https://doi.org/10.1007/978-94-007-0485-5_3

Kaplan, D. 1999. *The meaning of ouch and oops: Explorations in the theory of meaning as use*. Ms, UCLA.

Kato, M. A. & Martins, A. M. 2016. European Portuguese and Brazilian Portuguese: An overview on word order. In *The Handbook of Portuguese Linguistics*, W. L. Wetzels, J. Costa, S. Menuzzi (eds), 15–40. Wiley Online Library. https://doi.org/10.1002/9781118791844.ch2

Kempas, I. 2002. Sobre las actitudes de estudiantes Españoles hacia el uso del pretérito perfecto prehodiernal en comparación con las de estudiantes santiagueños (Argentina). *Neuphilologische Mitteilungen* 103: 435–447.

Kempas, I. 2006a. Estudio sobre el uso del pretérito perfecto prehodiernal en el Español peninsular y en comparación con la variedad del Español Argentino hablada en Santiago del Estero. *Neuphilologische Mitteilungen* 107(3): 375–377.

Kempas, I. 2006b. "Me alegro de que por fin hayas visto a rafa ayer". Acerca del uso del pretérito perfecto en los contextos prehodiernales: Caso Santiago del Estero, Argentina. *Língua Americana* 18: 9–26.

Kempas, I. 2008a. El pretérito indefinido y el pretérito perfecto aorístico en combinación con el adverbio hoy. *Vox Romanica* 66: 182–204.

Kempas, I. 2008b. La elección de los tiempos verbales aorísticos en contextos hodiernales: Sinopsis de datos empeíticos recogidos en la España peninsular. In *Actas del XXXVII Simposio Internacional de la Sociedad España de Lingüística (SEL)*, 397–408. Pamplona: Servicio de Publicaciones de la Universidad de Navarra.

Kempas, I. 2009. El uso prehodiernal del pretírito perfecto desde el punto de vista de la deixis personal. *Neuphilologische Mitteilungen* 110: 177–196.

Kempas, I. 2017. ¿"pre-presente" o "pretérito perfecto compuesto aoristizado"? una mirada sobre dos planteamientos opuestos respecto a un cambio lingüístico en curso. *Moenia* 23: 239–256.

Klein, W. 1992. The present perfect puzzle. *Language* 68: 525–552. https://doi.org/10.2307/415793

Klein, W. 1994. *Time in Language*. London: Routledge.

Klein, W. 2000. An analysis of the german Perfekt. *Language* 76: 358–382. https://doi.org/10.1353/lan.2000.0140

Klein, W. 2009. How time is encoded. In *The Expression of Time*, W. Klein & P. Li (eds), 39–81. Berlin: Mouton de Gruyter. https://doi.org/10.1515/9783110199031.39

Koch, P. & Oesterreicher, W. 1985. Sprache der Nähe – Sprache der Distanz. *Romanistisches Jahrbuch* 36: 15–43. https://doi.org/10.1515/9783110244922.15

Krifka, M. 2008. Basic notions of information structure. *Acta Linguistica Hungarica* 55: 243–276. https://doi.org/10.1556/ALing.55.2008.3-4.2

Krifka, M., Pelletier, F. J., Carlson, G. N., Ter Meulen, A., Chierchia, G. & Link, G. 1995. Genericity: An introduction. In *The Generic Book*, G. N. Carlson & F. J. Pelletier (eds), 1–124. Chicago IL: The University of Chicago Press.

Laca, B. 2008. Perfect semantics: How universal are ibero-american present perfects? In *Selected proceedings of the 12th Hispanic Linguistics Symposion*, C. Borgonovo, M. Español-Echevarría, & P. Prévost (eds), 1–16. Somerville MA: Cascadilla Proceedings Project.

Laca, B. 2009. Acerca de los perfectos en las variedades ibero-americanas. In *Romanística sin complejos. Homenaje a Carmen Pensado*, F. Sánchez-Miret (ed.), 357–380. Bern: Peter Lang.

Leal, A., Oliveira, F. & Silva, F. 2014. Pretérito perfeito composto e quantificação em Português Europeu. In *Textos Selecionados, XXIX Encontro Nacional da Associação Portuguesa de Linguística*, A. Moreno, F. Silva, I. Falé, I. Pereira & J. Veloso (eds), 407–418. Porto: API.

Lenth, R. 2020. Emmeans: Estimated marginal means, aka least-squares means. R package version 1.5.1.

Leonetti, M. 2018. Temporal anaphora with spanish imperfecto. *Journal of Psycholinguistic Research* 47: 391–409. https://doi.org/10.1007/s10936-017-9539-2

Lindstedt, J. 2008. The perfect – aspectual, temporal and evidential. In *Tense and Aspect in the Languages of Europe 6*, Ö. Dahl (ed.), 365–384. Berlin: De Gruyter Mouton. https://doi.org/10.1515/9783110197099.3.365

Lipski, J. M. 2012. Geographical and social varieties of Spanish: An overview. In *The Handbook of Hispanic Linguistics*, J. I. Hualde, A. Olarrea & E. O'Rourke (eds), 1–26. Wiley Online Library. https://doi.org/10.1002/9781118228098.ch1

Lohnstein, H. 2011. *Formale Semantik und natürliche Sprache*. Berlin: De Gruyter. https://doi.org/10.1515/9783110223880

Lope Blanch, J. M. 1972. Sobre el uso del pretérito en el Español hablado de México. In *Estudios sobre el Español de México*, J. M. Lope Blanch (ed.), 130–143. México City: Universidad Nacional Autónoma de México.

Maienborn, C. 2003. Against a Davidsonian analysis of copula sentences. In *NELS 33 Proceedings*, M. Kadowaki & S. Kawahara (eds), 167–186. Amherst MA: GLSA.

Maienborn, C. & Schäfer, M. 2012. Adverbs and adverbials. In *Handbücher zur Sprach- und Kommunikationswissenschaft: Semantics*, C. Maienborn, K. von Heusinger & P. Portner (eds), 1390–1420. Berlin: De Gruyter Mouton. https://doi.org/10.1515/9783110253382

Mani, I., Pustejovsky, J. & Gaizauskas, R. 2005. *The Language of Time: A Reader*. Oxford: OUP.

Mann, W. C. & Thompson, S. A. 1988. Rhetorical structure theory: Toward a functional theory of text organization. *Text* 8(3): 243–281.

McCawley, J. D. 1971. Tense and time reference in English. In *Studies in Linguistic Semantics*, C. J. Fillmore & D. T. Langendoen (eds), 96–113. New York NY: Holt, Rinehart and Winston.

McCoard, R. W. 1978. *The English Perfect: Tense Choice and Pragmatic Inferences*. Amsterdam: North Holland.

Meisnitzer, B. 2015. Tempusgebrauch im spanisch-deutschen Sprachvergleich: Was leisten Tempora eigentlich? In *Aktuelle Perspektiven der kontrastiven Sprachwissenschaft. Deutsch-Spanisch-Portugiesisch: Zwischen Tradition und Innovation*, M. Meliss & B. Pöll (eds), 77–104. Tübingen: Narr.

Michaelis, L. A. 1994. The ambiguity of the English present perfect. *Journal of Linguistics* 30(1): 111–157. https://doi.org/10.1017/S0022226700016200

Mittwoch, A. 1988. Aspects of English aspect: On the interaction of perfect, progressive, and durational phrases. *Linguistics and Philosophy* 11, 203–254. https://doi.org/10.1007/BF00632461

Moens, M. 1987. Tense, Aspect and Temporal Reference. PhD dissertation, University of Edinburgh.

Móia, T. 2000. Identifying and Computing Temporal Locating Adverbials. PhD dissertation, University of Lisbon.

Molsing, K. V. 2006. The present perfect at the semantics/pragmatics interface: American English and Brazilian Portuguese. *Sinn und Bedeutung* 10: 239–250. https://doi.org/10.21248/zaspil.44.2006.313

Molsing, K. V. 2007. Universal and existential perfects in Brazilian Portuguese. *Revista Letras (Curitiba)* 73: 131–150.

Molsing, K. V. 2010. The Present Perfect: An Exercise in the Study of Events, Plurality and Aspect. PhD dissertation, Pontifícia Universidade Católica do Rio Grande do Sul.

Montague, R. 1973. The proper treatment of quantification in ordinary English. In *Approaches to Natural Language*, P. Suppes, J. Moravcsik & J. Hintikka (eds), 221–242. Dordrecht: Springer. https://doi.org/10.1007/978-94-010-2506-5_10

Montoro del Arco, E. T. 2017. El pretérito perfecto compuesto con valor aorístico en el habla urbana de granada. *Rivista d'Ispanistica* 6: 455–470.

Moreno de Alba, J. 1978. *Valores de las formas verbales en el Español de México*. México City: Universidad Nacional Autónoma de México.

Moreno-Torres Sánchez, I. 1999. Perfecto simple y perfecto compuesto: De la gramática al discurso. *ELUA. Estudios de Lingüística* 13: 229–250. https://doi.org/10.14198/ELUA1999.13.09

Müller, L. 2017. Die zentralen und peripheren Lesarten des portugiesischen Perfekts – Eine explorative Studie für ein integratives Modell. MA thesis, University of Cologne. https://doi.org/10.18716/kups/52009

Musan, R. 2002. *The German Perfect: Its Semantic Composition and its Interactions with Temporal Adverbials*. Dordrecht: Kluwer. https://doi.org/10.1007/978-94-010-0552-4

Nedjalkov, V. P. & Jaxontov, S. J. 1988. The typology of resultative constructions. In *Typology of Resultative Constructions. Translated from the Original Russian Edition (1983)* [Typological Studies in Language 12]. V. P. Nedjalkov (Ed.), tranlation edited by B. Comrie, 3–62. Amsterdam: John Benjamins. https://doi.org/10.1075/tsl.12.06ned

Newman, P. 1980. *The Classification of Chad within Afroasiatic*. Leiden: Universitaire Pers.

Nishiyama, A. & Koenig, J.-P. 2010. What is a perfect state? *Language* 86: 611–646. https://doi.org/10.1353/lan.2010.0014

Olbertz, H. 2018. The perfect in (Brazilian) Portuguese: A functional discourse grammar view. *Open Linguistics* 4: 478–508. https://doi.org/10.1515/opli-2018-0024

Oliveira, F. & Leal, A. 2012. Sobre a iteração do pretérito perfeito composto em Português Europeu. *Revista de Estudos Linguísticos da Univerdade do Porto* 7: 65–88.

Pakerys, J. 2018. On the development of past habitual from iterative in Lithuanian. *Baltistica* 52(2): 295–323. https://doi.org/10.15388/baltistica.52.2.2324

Parsons, T. 1990. *Events in the Semantics of English: A Study in Subatomic Semantics*. Cambridge: The MIT Press.

Partee, B. H. 1973. Some structural analogies between tenses and pronouns in English. *Journal of Philosophy* 70(18): 601–609. https://doi.org/10.2307/2025024

Partee, B. H. 1984. Nominal and temporal anaphora. *Linguistics and Philosophy* 7(3): 243–286. https://doi.org/10.1007/BF00627707

Pato, E. & Heap, D. 2008. La organización dialectal del Castellano: La distribución de las formas canté vs. he cantado en el Español peninsular. In *Actas del VII Congreso Internacional de Historia de la Lengua Española: Merida (Yucatán), 4–8 septiembre de 2006*, C. C. Company & J. G. M. de Alba (eds), 927–942. La Muralla: Arco Libros.

Perelman, C. & Olbrechts-Tyteca, L. 1971. *The New Rhetoric: A Treatise on Argumentation*. Notre Dame IN: University of Notre Dame Press.
Pinker, S. 2007. *The Stuff of Thought: Language as a Window into Human Nature*. London: Penguin.
Popper, K. 1935. *Logik der Forschung – Zur Erkenntnistheorie der modernen Naturwissenschaft*. Wien: Julius Springer.
Portner, P. 2003. The temporal semantics and modal pragmatics of the perfect. *Linguistics & Philosophy* 26: 459–510. https://doi.org/10.1023/A:1024697112760
Portner, P. 2012. Perfect and progressive. In *Handbücher zur Sprach- und Kommunikationswissenschaft: Semantics*, Vol. 2, C. Maienborn, K. von Heusinger & P. Portner (eds), 1217–1261. Berlin: De Gruyter Mouton.
Prior, A. 1967. *Past, Present and Future*. Oxford: Clarendon Press. https://doi.org/10.1093/acprof:oso/9780198243113.001.0001
R Core Team. 2017. *R: A Language and Environment for Statistical Computing*. Vienna: R Foundation for Statistical Computing.
Rathert, M. 2012. Adverbials. In *The Oxford Handbook of Tense and Aspect*, R. I. Binnick & M.-E. Ritz (eds), 237–268. Oxford: OUP.
Recanati, F. 2004. Pragmatics and semantics. In *The Handbook of Pragmatics*, L. R. Horn & G. Ward (eds), 442–462. Oxford: Blackwell.
Reichenbach, H. 1947. *Elements of Symbolic Logic*. New York NY: Macmillan.
Rocha, L. F. C. 2017. Uma análise dos aspectos semânticos de ter, tener e haber em construções com o particípio passado, no Português Brasileiro e no Espanhol. *Estudos Linguísticos* 46(1): 280–295. https://doi.org/10.21165/el.v46i1.1621
Rodrigues Parrinha, S. 2014. Valores pragmáticos y discursivos en el uso del pretérito perfecto compuesto en Buenos Aires. In *Formas simples y compuestas en el verbo Español*, S. Azpiazu Torres (ed.), 103–115. Lugo: Axac.
Rodrigues Parrinha, S. 2015. Sobre el uso del pretérito perfecto compuesto en el Español de Buenos Aires. In *Jóvenes aportaciones a la investigación lingüística*, C. J.Á. lvarez López, B. Garrido Martín & M. González Sanz (eds), 449–463. Sevilla: Ediciones Alfar.
Rogers, E. 1995. *Diffusion of Innovations*. New York NY: The Free Press.
Rojo, G. 1974. La temporalidad verbal en Español. *Verba. Anuario Galego de Filoloxía* 1: 68–149.
Rojo, G. & Veiga, A. 1999. El tiempo verbal. Los tiempos simples. In *Gramática descriptiva de la lengua Española*, Vol. II, I. Bosque & V. Demonte (eds), 2867–2934. Madrid: Espasa.
Rosemeyer, M. 2014. *Auxiliary Selection in Spanish: Gradience, Gradualness, and Conservation* [Studies in Language Companion Series 155]. Amsterdam: John Benjamins. https://doi.org/10.1075/slcs.155
Rothstein, B. 2008. *The Perfect Time Span: On the Present Perfect in German, Swedish and English* [Linguistik Aktuell/Linguistics Today 125]. Amsterdam: John Benjamins. https://doi.org/10.1075/la.125
Russell, B. 1905. On denoting. *Mind* 14(56): 479–493. https://doi.org/10.1093/mind/XIV.4.479
Schaden, G. 2009. Present perfects compete. *Linguistics and Philosophy* 32(2): 115–141. https://doi.org/10.1007/s10988-009-9056-3
Schmitt, C. 2001. Cross-linguistic variation and the present perfect: The case of Portuguese. *Natural Language & Linguistic Theory* 19(2): 403–453. https://doi.org/10.1023/A:1010759911058
Schwenter, S. A. 1994a. The grammaticalization of an anterior in progress: Evidence from a peninsular spanish dialect. *Rivista d'Ispanistica* 18(1): 71–111. https://doi.org/10.1075/sl.18.1.05sch

Schwenter, S. A. 1994b. "Hot news" and the grammaticalization of perfects. *Linguistics* 32(6): 995–1028. https://doi.org/10.1515/ling.1994.32.6.995

Schwenter, S. A. & Torres Cacoullos, R. 2008. Defaults and indeterminacy in temporal grammaticalization: The 'perfect' road to perfective. *Language Variation and Change* 20(1): 1–39. https://doi.org/10.1017/S0954394508000057

Serrano, M. 1995. Sobre el uso del pretérito perfecto y pretérito indefinido en el Español de Canarias: Pragmática y variación. *Boletín de Filología* 35(1): 533–566.

Silge, J. & Robinson, D. 2016. Tidytext: Text mining and analysis using tidy data principles in r. *JOSS* 1(3), 1–3. https://doi.org/10.21105/joss.00037

Smith, C. 1991. *The Parameter of Aspect*. Dordrecht: Kluwer. https://doi.org/10.1007/978-94-015-7911-7

Smith, C. 2003. *Modes of Discourse*. Cambridge: CUP. https://doi.org/10.1017/CBO9780511615108

Song, M.-Y. 2005. On the proper treatment of tense in English. *Language Research* 41: 829–854.

Spitzová, E. & Bayerová, M. 1987. Posición del perfecto compuesto en el sistema temporal del verbo en el Español de México. *Études Romanes de Brno* 18: 37–50.

Stalnaker, R. C. 1978. Assertion. In *Syntax and Semantics 9: Pragmatics*, P. Cole (ed.), 315–332. New York NY: Academic Press.

Suter, A. 1984. *Das portugiesische Pretérito Perfeito Composto*. Bern: Francke.

de Swart, H. 1991. *Adverbs of Quantification: A Generalized Quantifier Approach*. Groningen: Grodil.

de Swart, H. 1998. Aspect shift and coercion. *Natural Language & Linguistic Theory* 16(2): 347–385. https://doi.org/10.1023/A:1005916004600

de Swart, H. 2007. A cross-linguistic discourse analysis of the perfect. *Journal of Pragmatics* 39: 2273–2307. https://doi.org/10.1016/j.pragma.2006.11.006

de Swart, H. 2012. Verbal aspect. In *The Oxford Handbook of Tense and Aspect*, R. I. Binnick (ed.), 752–780. Oxford: OUP.

Tenny, C. 1994. *Aspectual Roles and the Syntax Semantics Interface* [Studies in Linguistics and Philosophy 52]. Dodrecht: Kluwer. https://doi.org/10.1007/978-94-011-1150-8

Veiga Rodríguez, A. 2014. Diacronía de "he cantado"/ "canté" en el sistema verbal Español. Subsistemas y variantes. In *Historia del Español hoy: Estudios y perspectivas*, J. L. R. Luengo & E. P. V. Upegui (eds), 151–179. Lugo: Axac.

Vendler, Z. 1957. Verbs and times. *The Philosophical Review* 66: 143–160. https://doi.org/10.2307/2182371

Verkuyl, H. J. 2005. Aspectual composition: Surveying the ingredients. In *Perspectives on Aspect*, H. J. Verkuyl, H. de Swart & A. van Hout (eds), 19–40. Dordrecht: Springer. https://doi.org/10.1007/1-4020-3232-3_2

Vlach, F. 1993. Temporal adverbials, tenses, and the perfect. *Linguistics and Philosophy* 19: 231–283. https://doi.org/10.1007/BF00985970

von Stechow, A. 1998. Eine erweiterte Extended-Now-Theorie für Perfekt und Futur. *Zeitschrift für Literaturwissenschaft und Linguistik* 29(1): 86–118. https://doi.org/10.1007/BF03379171

Weinrich, H. 1964. *Tempus: Besprochene und erzählte Welt*. Stuttgart: W. Kohlhammer.

Weinrich, H. 1982. *Textgrammatik der französischen Sprache*. Stuttgart: Klett.

Westmoreland, M. 1988. The distribution and the use of the present perfect and the past perfect forms in american Spanish. *Hispania* 71(2): 379–384. https://doi.org/10.2307/343085

Wickham, H., Averick, M., Bryan, J., Chang, W., McGowan, L. D., François, R., Grolemund, G., Hayes, A., Henry, L., Hester, J., Kuhn, M., Pedersen, T. L., Milller, E., Bache, S. M., Müller, K., Ooms, J., Robinson, D., Seidel, D. P., Spinu, V., Takahashi, K., Vaughan, D., Wilke, C., Woo, K. & Yutani, H.. 2019. Welcome to the tidyverse. *Journal of Open Source Software* 4(43), 1–6. https://doi.org/10.21105/joss.01686

Wigger, L.-G. 2005. Die Entwicklungsgeschichte der romanischen Vergangenheitstempora am Beispiel des Pretérito Perfeito Composto im Portugiesischen. PhD dissertation, University of Tübingen.

Wijffels, J. 2019. Udpipe: Tokenization, Parts of Speech Tagging, Lemmatization and Dependency Parsing with the 'UDPipe' 'NLP' Toolkit. R package version 0.8.3.

Wittgenstein, L. 1963[2016]. *Tractatus Logico-philosophicus – Logisch-philosophische Abhanlung*, 36th edn. Frankfurt: Suhrkamp.

Xiqués, T. M. 2015. Towards a Unified View of the Present Perfect. A Comparative Study on Catalan, English and Gĩkũyũ. PhD dissertation, Universitat Autónoma de Barcelona.

Xiqués, T. M. 2021. More on hodiernality. In *The Perfect Volume. Papers on the Perfect* [Studies in Language Companion Series 217], K. Melum Eide & M. Fryd (eds), 181–212. Amsterdam: John Benjamins. https://doi.org/10.1075/slcs.217.08xiq

Zwaan, R. A. 1996. Processing narrative time shifts. *Journal of Experimental Psychology: Learning, Memory, and Cognition* 22(5): 1196–1207.

List of items included in the experiment

Condition	Item
HOD-IND 1	*Cuando María llegó, los invitados se estaban yendo.*
HOD-IND 2	*Cuando la policía entró, el ladron estaba escapando del banco.*
HOD-IND 3	*Cuando el chico salió del bosque, estaba anocheciendo.*
HOD-IND 4	*Cuando el invitado canceló la reunion, el anfitrión estaba preparando la comida.*
HOD-IND 5	*Cuando el turista vio la cueva, el sol se estaba poniendo.*
HOD-IND 6	*Cuando la víctima llamó a la policía, el agresor estaba saliendo.*
HOD-IND 7	*Cuando la chica se levantó, su madre estaba preparando el desayuno.*
HOD-IND 8	*Cuando el anfitrión dio la bienvenida a sus amigos, su hijo estaba tocando el piano.*
HOD-IND 9	*Cuando la niña habló con su madre, su padre estaba viendo la tele.*
HOD-IND 10	*Cuando Pedro se fue de compras, su hermano estaba durmiendo.*
HOD-IND 11	*Cuando el empleado pasó por la oficina, su jefe lo estaba llamando.*
HOD-IND 12	*Cuando el doctor regresó a casa, su familia estaba cenando.*
HOD-IND 13	*Cuando el banquero se tomó un descanso, su colega estaba trabajando.*
HOD-IND 14	*Cuando el operador dio gritos de júbilo, la máquina estaba funcionando.*
HOD-IND 15	*Cuando la enfermera buscó ayuda, el enfermo estaba llorando.*
HOD-IND 16	*Cuando el cartero entregó la carta, el ama de casa estaba cocinando.*
HOD-PERF 1	*Cuando María ha llegado, los invitados se estaban yendo.*
HOD-PERF 2	*Cuando la policía ha entrado. el ladron estaba escapando del banco.*
HOD-PERF 3	*Cuando el chico ha salido del bosque, estaba anocheciendo.*
HOD-PERF 4	*Cuando el invitado ha cancelado la reunión, el anfitrión estaba preparando la comida.*
HOD-PERF 5	*Cuando el turista ha visto la cueva, el sol se estaba poniendo.*
HOD-PERF 6	*Cuando la víctima ha llamado a la policía, el agresor estaba saliendo.*
HOD-PERF 7	*Cuando la chica se ha levantado, su madre estaba preparando el desayuno.*
HOD-PERF 8	*Cuando el anfitrión ha dado la bienvenida a sus amigos, su hijo estaba tocando el piano.*
HOD-PERF 9	*Cuando la niña ha hablado con su madre, su padre estaba viendo la tele.*
HOD-PERF 10	*Cuando Pedro se ha ido de compras, su hermano estaba durmiendo.*
HOD-PERF 11	*Cuando el empleado ha pasado por la oficina, su jefe lo estaba llamando.*
HOD-PERF 12	*Cuando el doctor ha regresado a casa, su familia estaba cenando.*
HOD-PERF 13	*Cuando el banquero se he tomado un descanso, su colega estaba trabajando.*

Condition	Item
HOD-PERF 14	*Cuando el operador ha dado gritos de júbilo, la máquina estaba funcionando.*
HOD-PERF 15	*Cuando la enfermera ha buscado ayuda, el enfermo estaba llorando.*
HOD-PERF 16	*Cuando el cartero ha entregado la carta, el ama de casa estaba cocinando.*
PREHOD-IND 1	*Cuando el autor escribió su primer libro, la guerra estaba acabando.*
PREHOD-IND 2	*Cuando el atleta terminó su carrera, su esposa estaba trabajando como artista.*
PREHOD-IND 3	*Cuando el abogado se casó, su hijo estaba terminando la licenciatura.*
PREHOD-IND 4	*Cuando el médico compró sus gafas, las viejas se estaban rompiendo.*
PREHOD-IND 5	*Cuando el comerciante cerró su negocio, la crisis estaba alcanzando su momento álgido.*
PREHOD-IND 6	*Cuando la família vendió su casa, los precios estaban subiendo.*
PREHOD-IND 7	*Cuando el empresario fundó su empresa, la competencia estaba trazando un nuevo plan.*
PREHOD-IND 8	*Cuando la familia se mudó a Madrid, los problemas matrimoniales estaban empezando.*
PREHOD-IND 9	*Cuando la pandemia estalló, los científicos estaban trabajando en vacunas.*
PREHOD-IND 10	*Cuando el presidente asumió el poder, el mercado estaba prosperando.*
PREHOD-IND 11	*Cuando la actriz empezó a abrirse camino, los críticos la estaban encumbrando.*
PREHOD-IND 12	*Cuando el político se retiró, su sucesor estaba luchando por la democracia.*
PREHOD-IND 13	*Cuando la familia inmigró, la situación estaba mejorando significativamente.*
PREHOD-IND 14	*Cuando Pedro visitó París, su familia estaba viajando por toda Europa.*
PREHOD-IND 15	*Cuando Pedro aprendió a patinar, nuevos deportes estaban comenzando a hacerse populares.*
PREHOD-IND 16	*Cuando la guerra estalló, muchas familias estaban pasando hambre.*
PREHOD-PERF 1	*Cuando el autor ha escrito su primer libro, la guerra estaba acabando.*
PREHOD-PERF 2	*Cuando el atleta ha terminado su carrera, su esposa estaba trabajando como artista.*
PREHOD-PERF 3	*Cuando el abogado se ha casado su hijo estaba terminando la licenciatura.*
PREHOD-PERF 4	*Cuando el médico ha comprado sus gafas, las viejas se estaban rompiendo.*
PREHOD-PERF 5	*Cuando el comerciante ha cerrado su negocio, la crisis estaba alcanzando su momento álgido.*
PREHOD-PERF 6	*Cuando la família ha vendido su casa, los precios estaban subiendo.*
PREHOD-PERF 7	*Cuando el empresario ha fundado su empresa, la competencia estaba trazando un nuevo plan.*

Condition	Item
PREHOD-PERF 8	Cuando la familia se ha mudado a Madrid, los problemas matrimoniales estaban empezando.
PREHOD-PERF 9	Cuando la pandemia ha estallado los científicos estaban trabajando en vacunas.
PREHOD-PERF 10	Cuando el presidente ha asumido el poder, el mercado estaba prosperando.
PREHOD-PERF 11	Cuando la actriz ha empezado a abrirse camino, los críticos la estaban encumbrando.
PREHOD-PERF 12	Cuando el político se ha retirado, su sucesor estaba luchando por la democracia.
PREHOD-PERF 13	Cuando la familia ha inmigrado la situación estaba mejorando significativamente.
PREHOD-PERF 14	Cuando Pedro ha visitado París, su familia estaba viajando por toda Europa.
PREHOD-PERF 15	Cuando Pedro ha aprendido a patinar, nuevos deportes estaban comenzando a hacerse populares.
PREHOD-PERF 16	Cuando la guerra ha estallado, muchas familias estaban pasando hambre.
FILLER-POS 1	Salió de casa y volvió porque llovía.
FILLER-POS 2	La participación de Alemania en los Juegos Olímpicos ha sido una de las más destacadas desde que se realiza este evento.
FILLER-POS 3	Las aves habitan en todos los biomas terrestres y también en todos los océanos.
FILLER-POS 4	El águila imperial oriental es una especie de ave accipitriforme de la familia Accipitridae distribuida por Europa.
FILLER-POS 5	El águila está en peligro de extinción en Europa, donde ya ha desaparecido de muchas zonas.
FILLER-POS 6	El desayuno es la comida fundamental del día, ya que consumirlo o no, nos afecta de forma notable.
FILLER-POS 7	Las aves son animales vertebrados, de sangre caliente, que caminan, saltan o se mantienen solo sobre las extremidades posteriores.
FILLER-POS 8	John Bardeen es el único galardonado que ha ganado el Premio Nobel de Física en dos ocasiones.
FILLER-POS 9	La Real Academia Española (RAE) es una institución cultural con sede en Madrid (España).
FILLER-POS 10	Madrid es un influyente centro cultural y cuenta con museos de referencia internacional.
FILLER-POS 11	Érase una vez una niña que era muy querida por su abuelita.
FILLER-POS 12	Caperucita roja aprendió la lección y pidió perdón a su madre por desobedecerla.
FILLER-POS 13	Hansel y Gretel se quedaron tranquilos como su padre les había pedido.
FILLER-NEG 1	Fui al cine y compraba un ticket.
FILLER-NEG 2	Salí a la calle y vi que la bomba explota.

Condition	Item
FILLER-NEG 3	El pasajero llegó a Londres y salía del tren.
FILLER-NEG 4	El autor murió y escribió un libro.
FILLER-NEG 5	Las aves habitó en todos los biomas terrestres y también en todos los océanos.
FILLER-NEG 6	El piratería es una práctica de saqueo organizada.
FILLER-NEG 7	El águilas están en peligro de extinción en Europa, donde ya han desaparecido de muchas zonas.
FILLER-NEG 8	El profesor ya ha viajado a Londres cuando tendrá el dinero.
FILLER-NEG 9	A lo largo de su carrera profesional, Christano Ronaldo conseguido ha batir diversos récords.
FILLER-NEG 10	Cuando el acusado se fue, la víctima está sola.
FILLER-NEG 11	El desayuno es el comida fundamental del día, ya que consumirla o no, nos afectaron de forma notable.
FILLER-NEG 12	Juan ya ha escrito la carta a las tres.
FILLER-NEG 13	Cuando tomó pelota, esperaba lo taclearan.
OTHER 1	El año pasado he comprado un aire acondicionado y me da calor en vez de frío.
OTHER 2	Pedro ha hablado con su colega la semana pasada.
OTHER 3	Ayer he comprado un aire acondicionado y me da calor en vez de frío.
OTHER 4	La chica está triste porque ayer ha muerto su madre.
OTHER 5	Maria sabe la solución porque ha hablado con su colega la semana pasada.
OTHER 6	Ayer ha muerto el presidente.

Index

A
Absolute durativity 83
Actualization 49, 51–52, 144–146, 177–178, 187–188, 193–195
Adverbial
 durative 96, 138–139
 extended-now 37, 40, 66, 97–98, 137–139
 positional 37, 40, 66, 136–137, 139
 quantificational 37, 40
Ambiguity
 durative vs. XN 97, 168, 170
 existential vs. universal 62
 hodiernal/positional vs. XN 154, 156, 173–174
 quantificational vs. referential 134–135, 239
 resultative vs. experiential 123
Azpiazu Torres 116–119

B
Becker 73, 89
Bertinetto and Squartini *see* stage model
Bridging context 224–226
Besprochene vs. erzählte Welt 20, 41

C
Current relevance 60–61, 114–115

D
Declerck 19, 50–52
Deduction 179
Degree achievement 82
Diatopic variation 77–78, 116–118, 230–232

Direct resultant state 122–123
Drift
 aoristic 57–59, 61, 63
 modal 252, 256
 referential 131, 209

E
Event domain vs. post-state domain 220–223
Existential quantification 23–25, 62
Extended-now theory 73

F
French *see* Passé Composé

G
Generic quantification 91–92
Grammaticalization 52–58, 95, 135, 205–207, 212–214, 252, 256

H
Heine 135

I
Ilari 71–72
Imperfect 45–46, 94, 216–217
Imperfective 33–35
Incremental theme verb 82
Indefinido 115–116, 201
Induction 180–181

K
Krifka 90–92

M
Mexican Spanish 55–56, 59
Modality 91, 95, 101, 199–200, 252
Modes of discourse 41–44, 105–107, 152–154

P
Parsons 23–25
Partee 25–29
Passé Composé 56–58, 63, 143–144
Past- vs. present time-sphere 19–20, 39
Perfect time span 73
Perfective 33–35
Perspectival
 bridging 102–103, 148–149
 clash 133, 150–151, 156, 215–216, 218
 maintenance 190–193
 shift 147–148, 186, 189–190
Pluperfect *see* Pluscuamperfecto
Pluractionality 79–81
Pluscuamperfecto 149–151
PP puzzle 64–65
Present Tense 14–15
Pretérito Perfeito Simples 74, 77, 101
Prominence 219–224

Q
Quasi-logical reasoning 198–199

R
Reading
 characterizing/habitual 89–95, 100–101
 durative/universal 54, 62–63, 83, 127–129
 episodic 94
 existential 60, 62
 experiential 120–123
 gradual 81–82
 ipex 79–83
 iterative 79–83
 gradual 81–83

resultative 60, 122–123
referential *see* definite/
 referential tense
hodiernal/prehodiernal
 131–135, 212–214, 228–229
hot news 60, 62–63,
 126–127
Reichenbach 15
Recentness *see* remoteness
Remoteness 212–214, 239
Resultative conversational
 implicature 61
Rhetorical relation 140, 145

S
Scalar implicature 75–76
Scope ambiguity 134, 154
Schwenter 213
Simple Past 14–15, 22, 29, 35

Smith 41–44
Stage model 53–58, 252, 256

T
Telic 4, 56, 62, 71, 120–123, 166
Telicity 31–33, 71
Temporal
 anaphora 25, 42, 45–46,
  48–49, 196, 223
 cataphora 152, 196, 200, 217
 indeterminacy 214
Tempus relief 218
Tener-construction 123–125
Transitional context 134–135
Tense
 definite/referential 25–29,
  49–51, 131
 indefinite/quantificational
  23–25, 27–29, 49–51, 62

Time
 event 15–16
 location 16–18
 reference 20–21
 speech 15
 perspective 18–20
Truth condition 5–6, 22, 45,
 114, 200–203

U
Use condition 200–202

W
Weinrich *see* Besprochene vs.
 erzählte Welt